Behind the Scenes!!

01

STORY AND ART BY **BISCO HATORI**

Behind the Scenes !! 01

CONTENTS

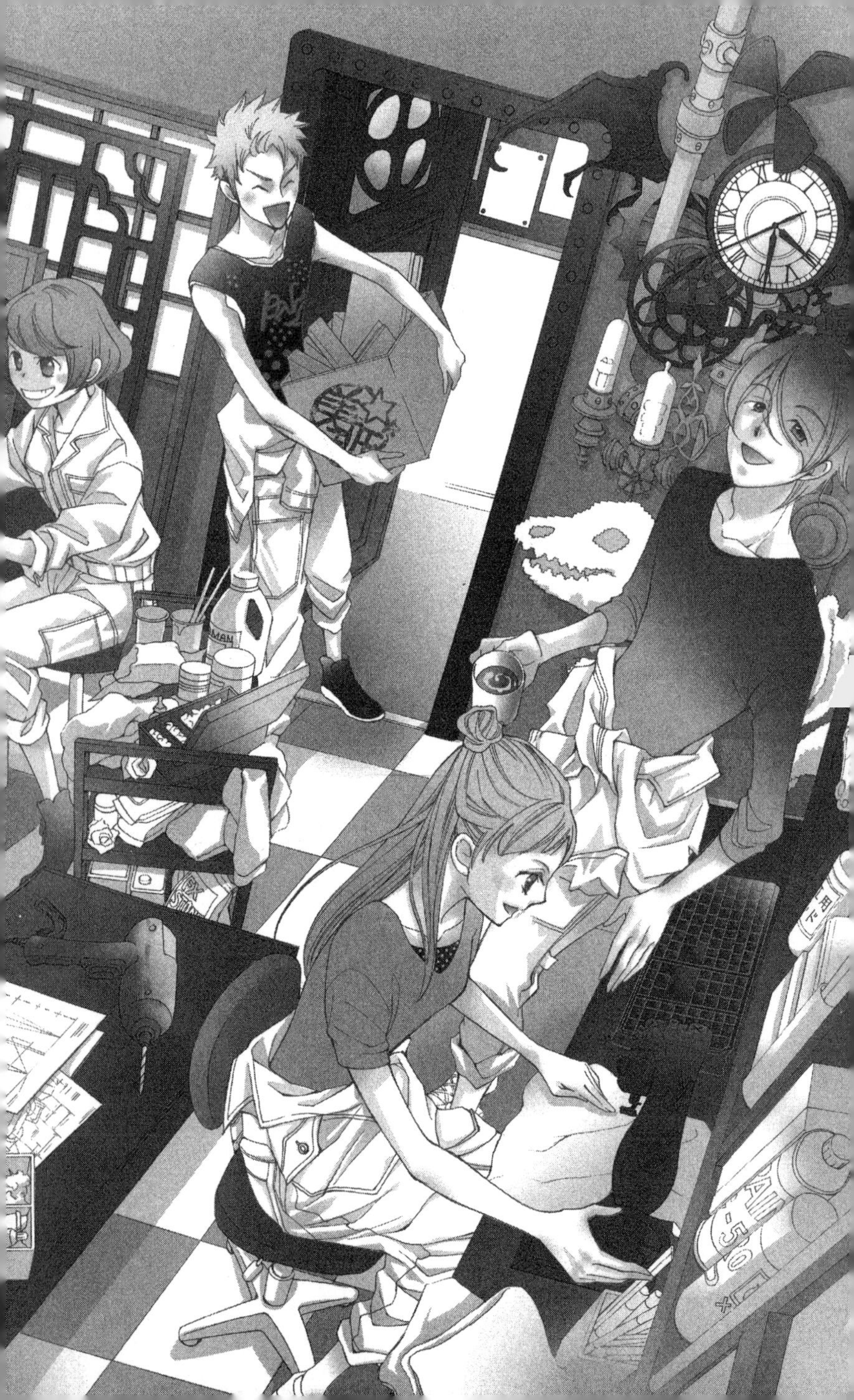

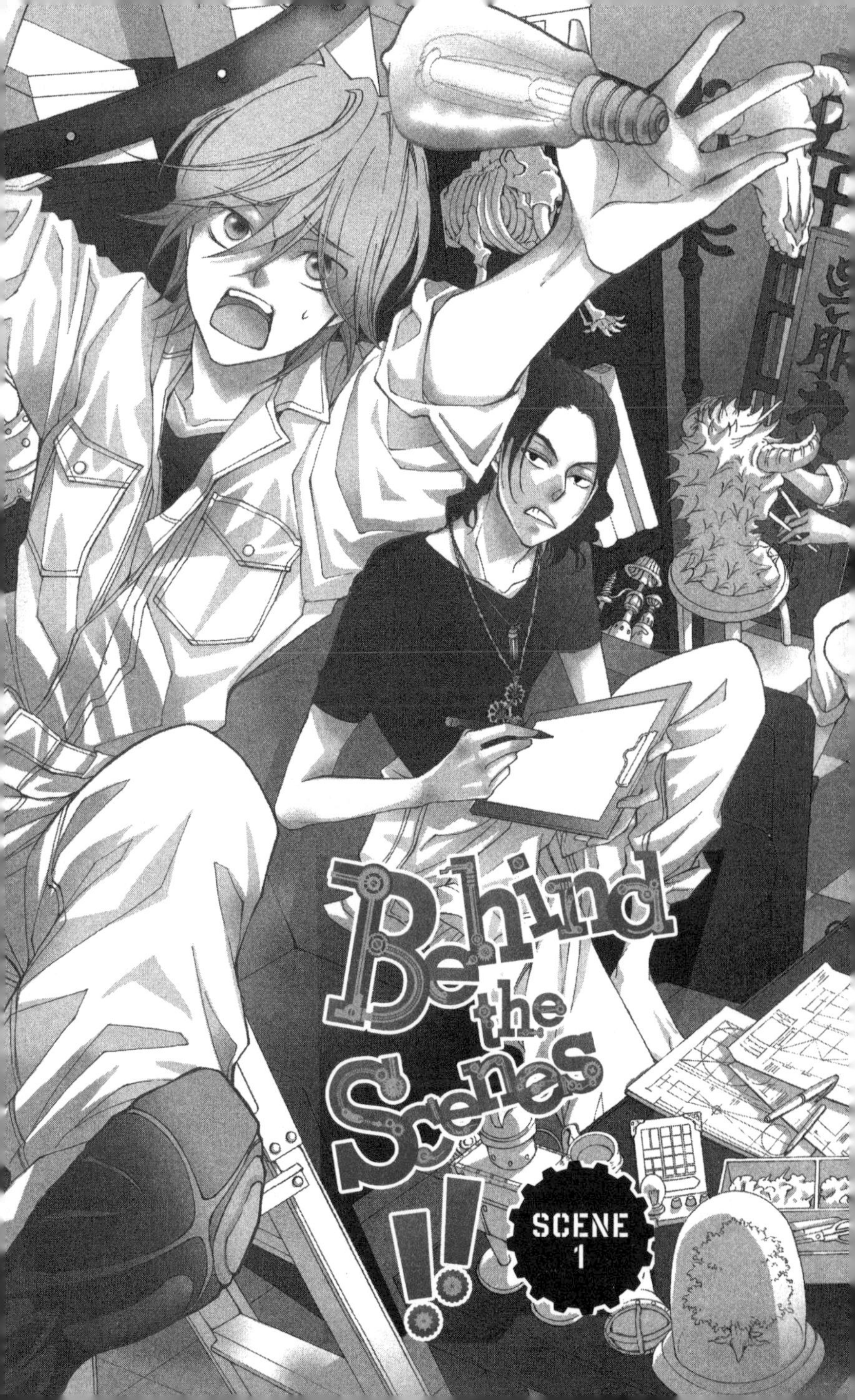
Behind the Scenes!!
SCENE 1

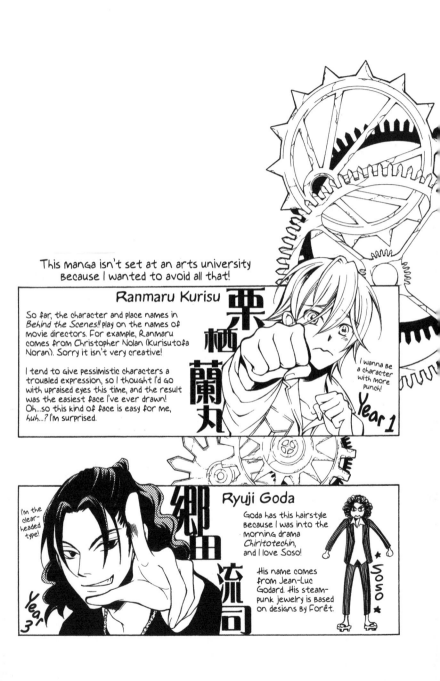

This manga isn't set at an arts university because I wanted to avoid all that!

Ranmaru Kurisu

So far, the character and place names in *Behind the Scenes!!* play on the names of movie directors. For example, Ranmaru comes from Christopher Nolan (Kurisutofa Noran). Sorry it isn't very creative!

I tend to give pessimistic characters a troubled expression, so I thought I'd go with upraised eyes this time, and the result was the easiest face I've ever drawn! Oh...so this kind of face is easy for me, *huh...?* I'm surprised.

栗栖蘭丸
I wanna be a character with more punch!
Year 1

Ryuji Goda

郷田流司
I'm the clear-headed type!
Year 3

Goda has this hairstyle because I was into the morning drama *Chiritotechin*, and I love Soso!

★ Soso ★

His name comes from Jean-Luc Godard. His steampunk jewelry is based on designs by Forêt.

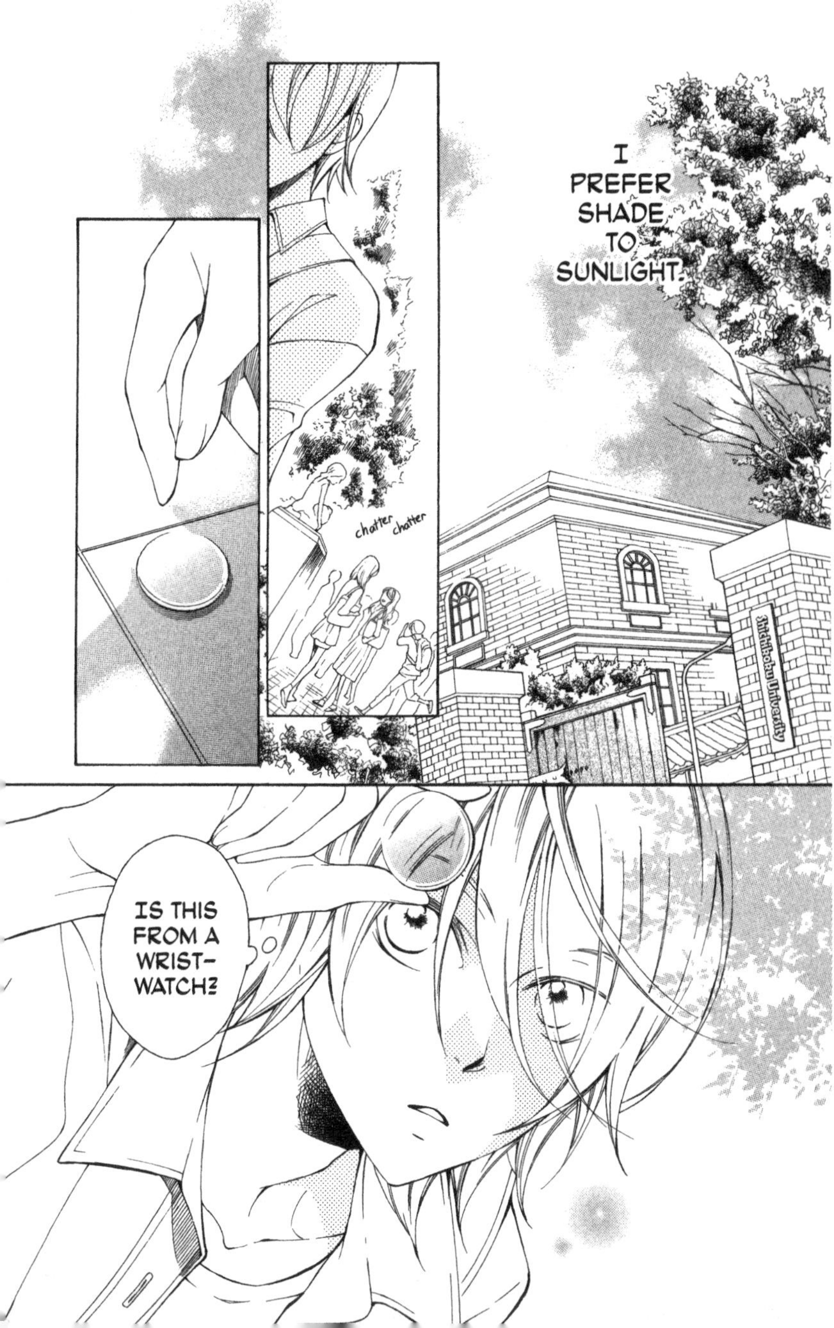
I PREFER SHADE TO SUNLIGHT.
Shichikoku University
chatter chatter
IS THIS FROM A WRIST-WATCH?

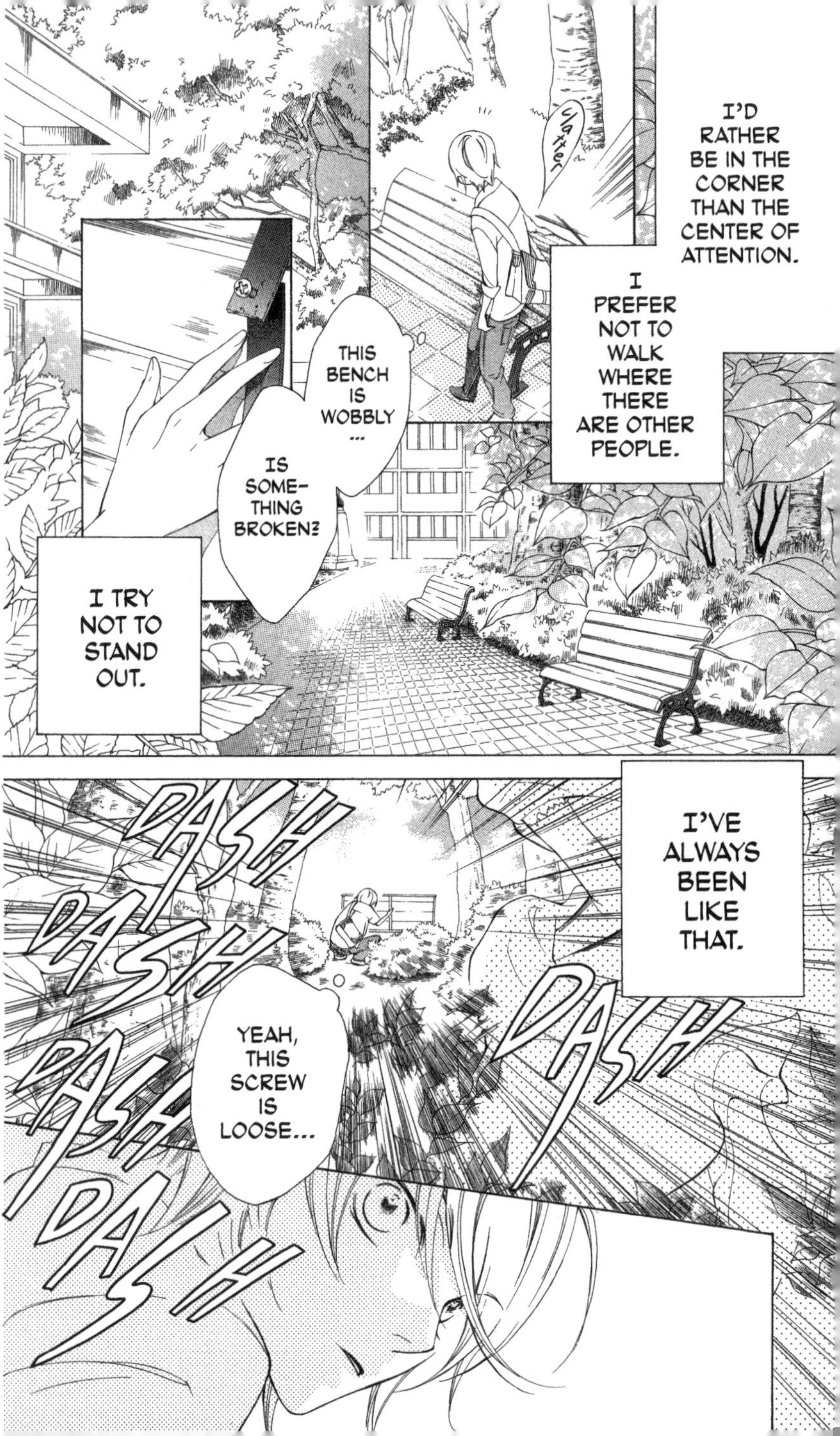
I'D RATHER BE IN THE CORNER THAN THE CENTER OF ATTENTION.
clatter
I PREFER NOT TO WALK WHERE THERE ARE OTHER PEOPLE.
THIS BENCH IS WOBBLY...
IS SOMETHING BROKEN?
I TRY NOT TO STAND OUT.
I'VE ALWAYS BEEN LIKE THAT.
DASH
YEAH, THIS SCREW IS LOOSE...
DASH
DASH
DASH
DASH

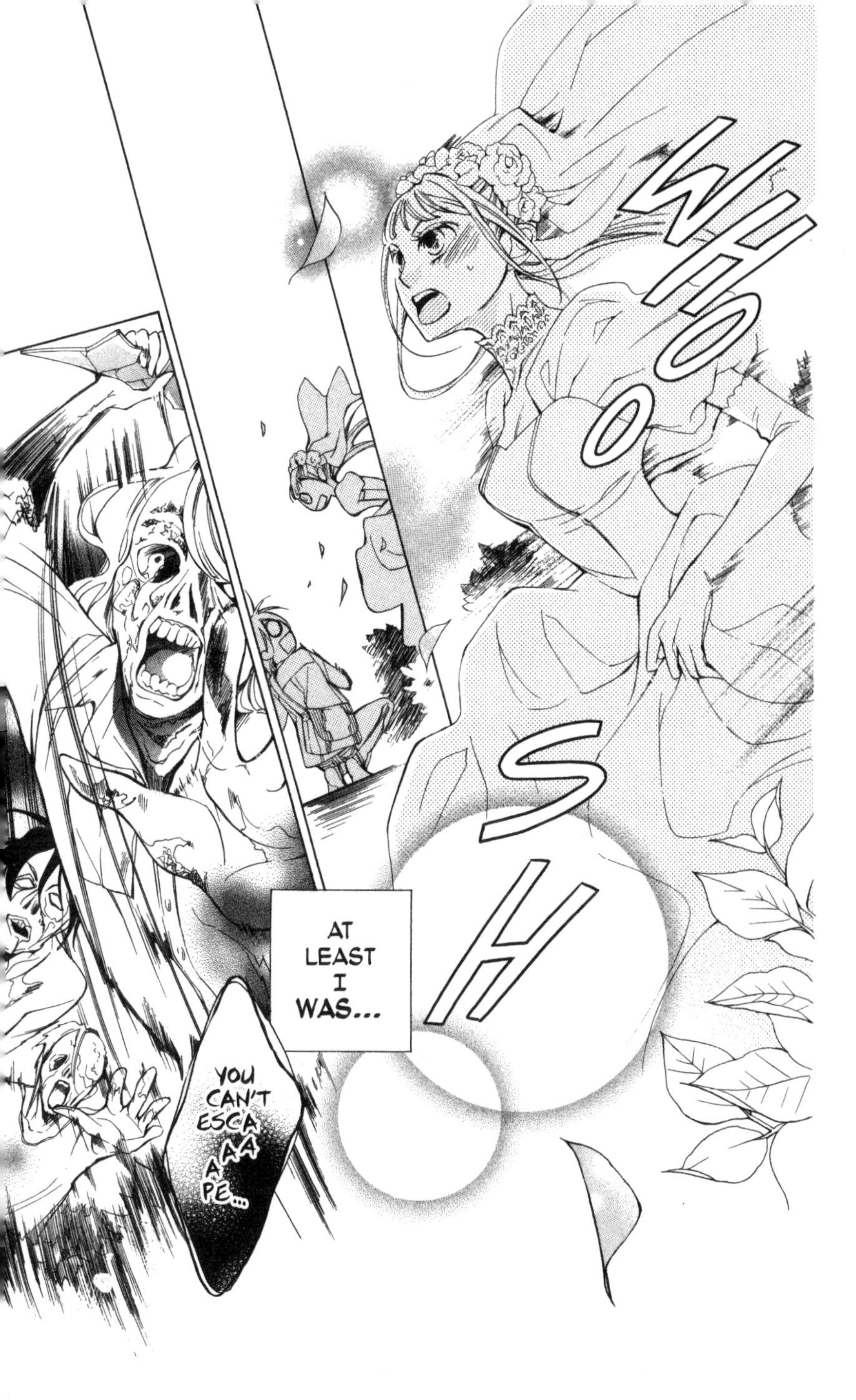
WHOOOSH
AT LEAST I WAS...
YOU CAN'T ESCAAAAPE...

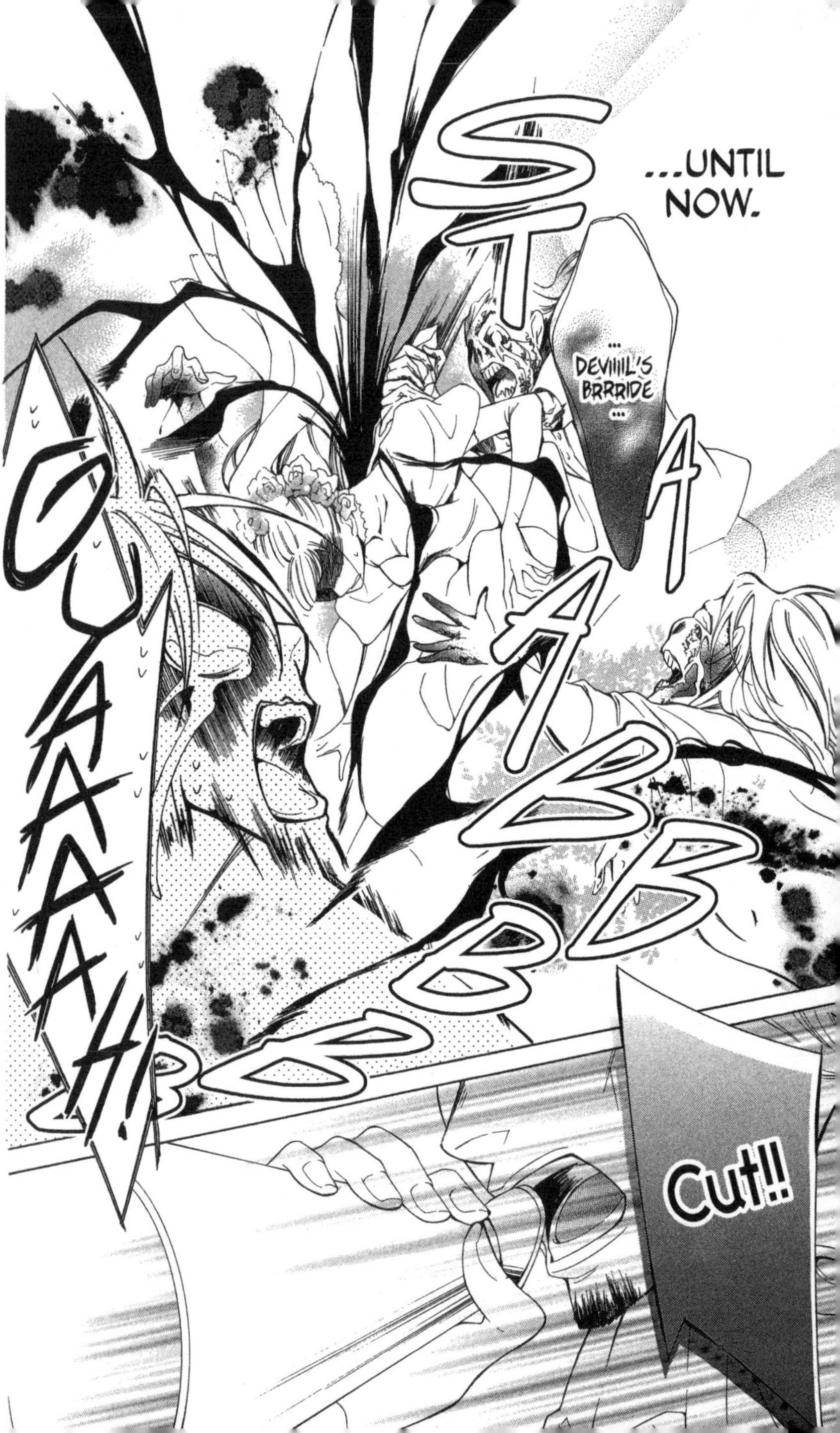
...UNTIL NOW.
...DEVIIIIL'S BRRRIDE...
STAABBBBB
UUAAAAH!!
Cut!!

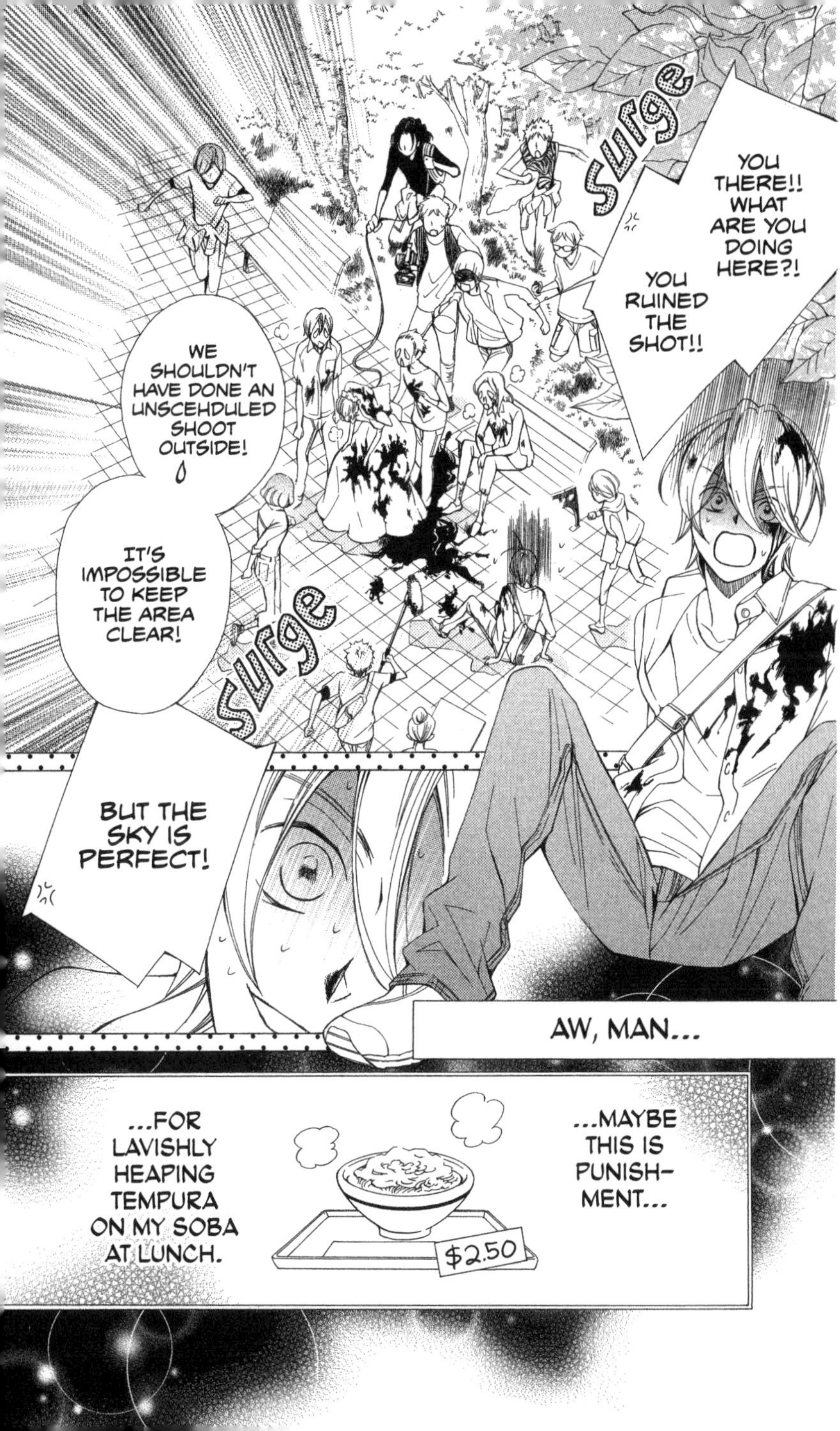
YOU THERE!! WHAT ARE YOU DOING HERE?!
YOU RUINED THE SHOT!!
Surge
WE SHOULDN'T HAVE DONE AN UNSCEHDULED SHOOT OUTSIDE!
IT'S IMPOSSIBLE TO KEEP THE AREA CLEAR!
Surge
BUT THE SKY IS PERFECT!
AW, MAN...
...MAYBE THIS IS PUNISH-MENT...
$2.50
...FOR LAVISHLY HEAPING TEMPURA ON MY SOBA AT LUNCH.

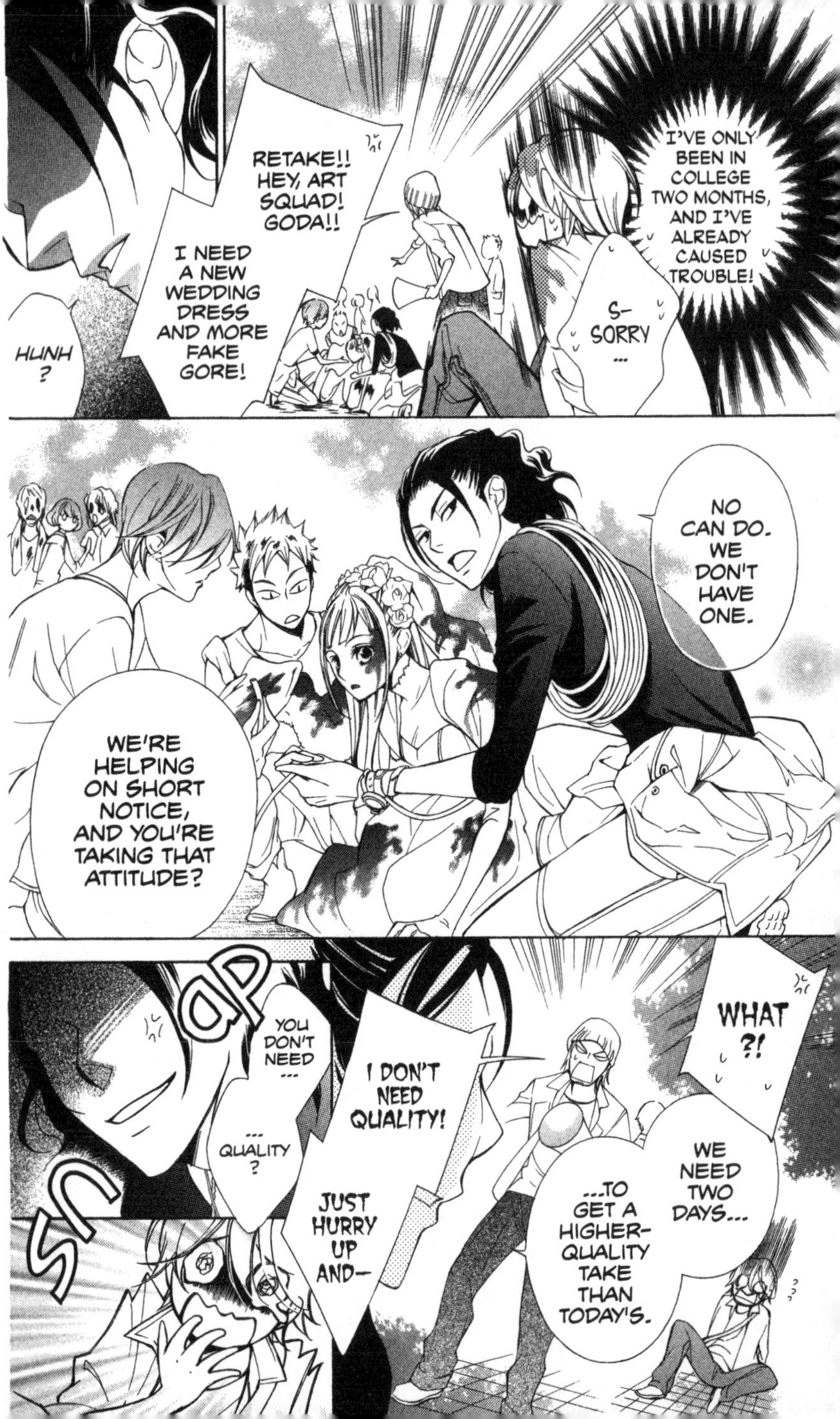
I'VE ONLY BEEN IN COLLEGE TWO MONTHS, AND I'VE ALREADY CAUSED TROUBLE!
S-SORRY...
RETAKE!! HEY, ART SQUAD! GODA!!
I NEED A NEW WEDDING DRESS AND MORE FAKE GORE!
HUNH?
NO CAN DO. WE DON'T HAVE ONE.
WE'RE HELPING ON SHORT NOTICE, AND YOU'RE TAKING THAT ATTITUDE?
WHAT?!
WE NEED TWO DAYS...
...TO GET A HIGHER-QUALITY TAKE THAN TODAY'S.
I DON'T NEED QUALITY!
JUST HURRY UP AND—
SNAP
YOU DON'T NEED...
...QUALITY?

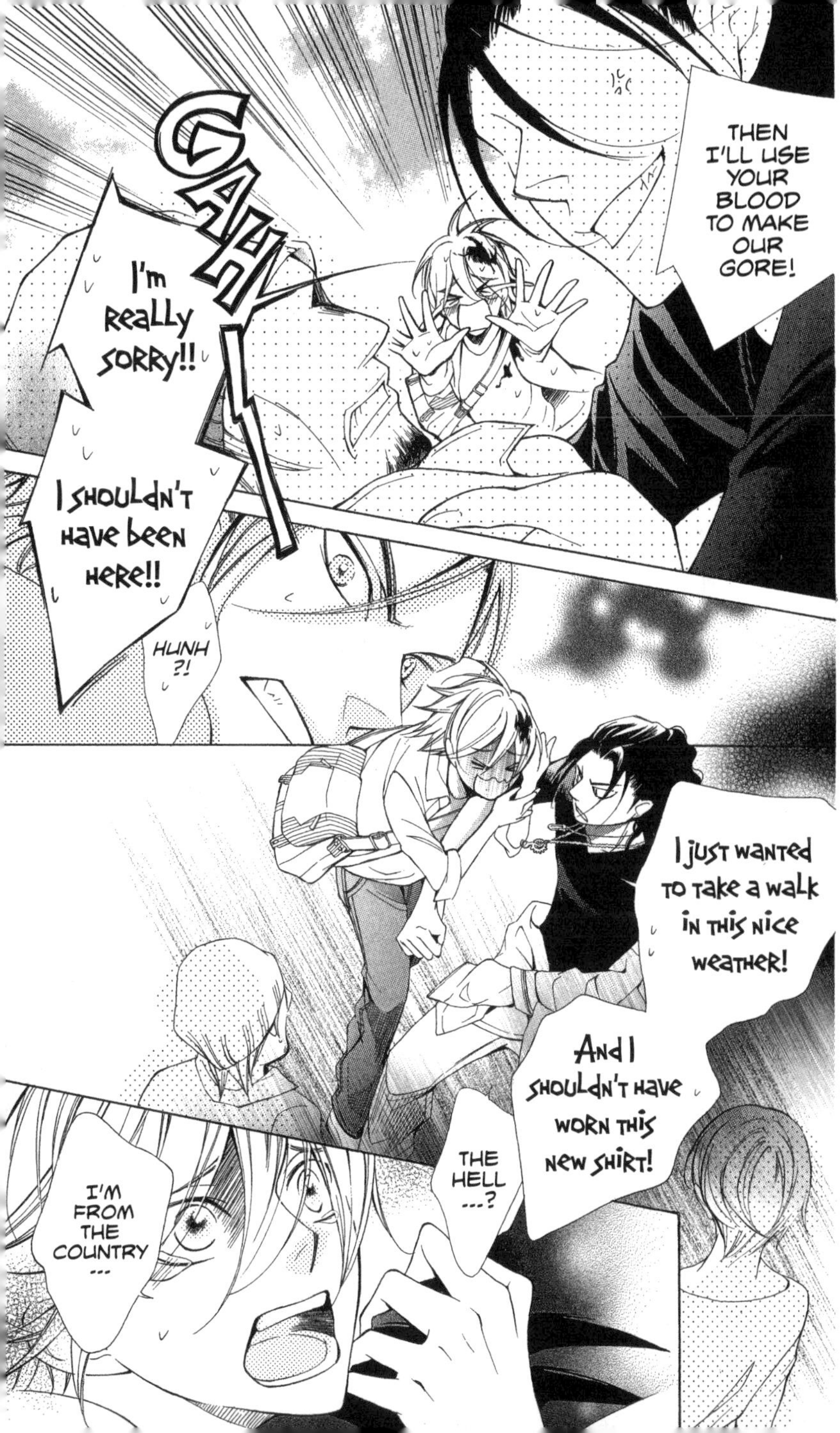
THEN I'LL USE YOUR BLOOD TO MAKE OUR GORE!
I'm really sorry!!
I shouldn't have been here!!
HUNH ?!
I just wanted to take a walk in this nice weather!
And I shouldn't have worn this new shirt!
THE HELL ...?
I'M FROM THE COUNTRY ...

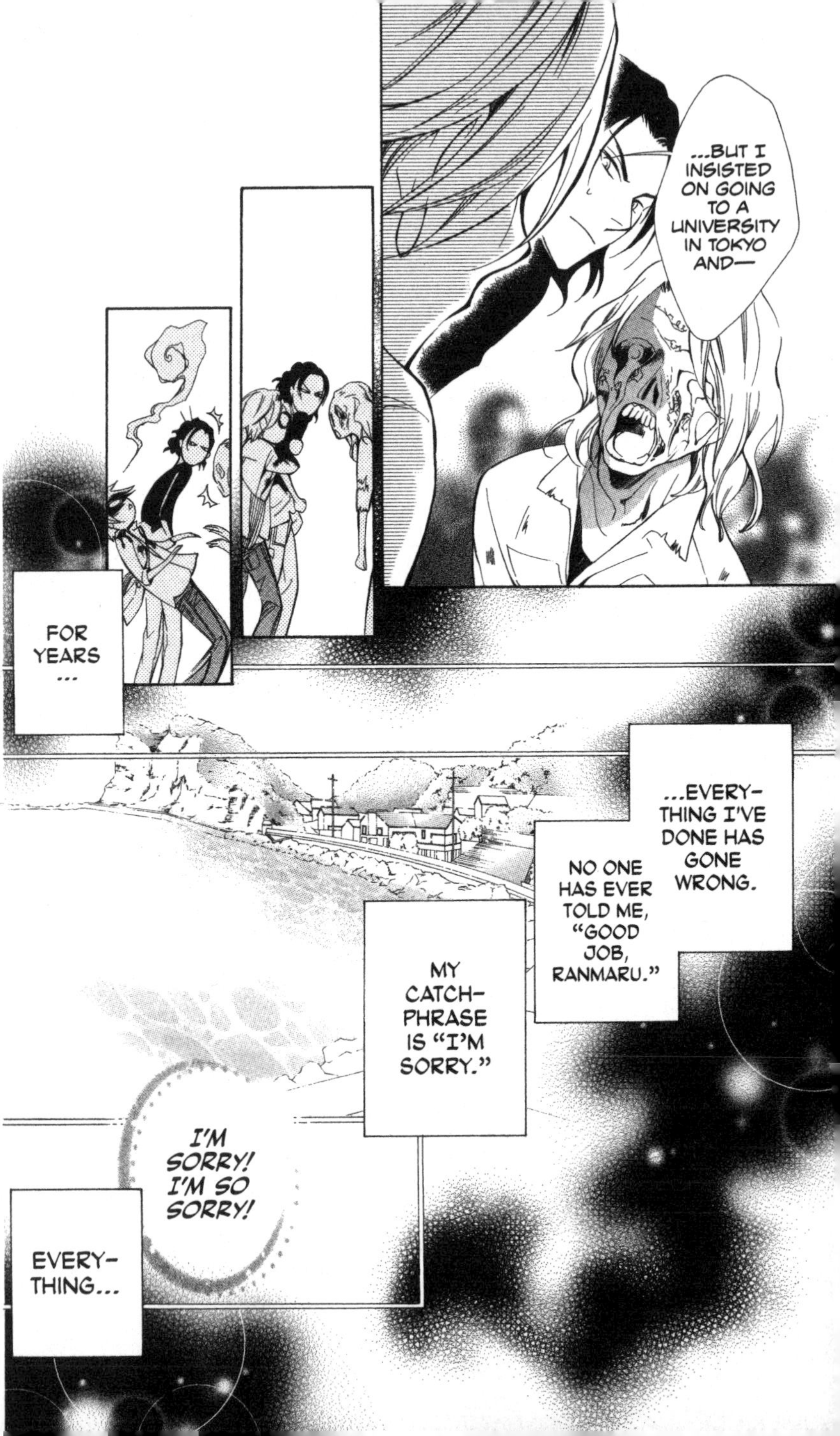
...BUT I INSISTED ON GOING TO A UNIVERSITY IN TOKYO AND—
FOR YEARS...
...EVERYTHING I'VE DONE HAS GONE WRONG.
NO ONE HAS EVER TOLD ME, "GOOD JOB, RANMARU."
MY CATCHPHRASE IS "I'M SORRY."
I'M SORRY! I'M SO SORRY!
EVERYTHING...

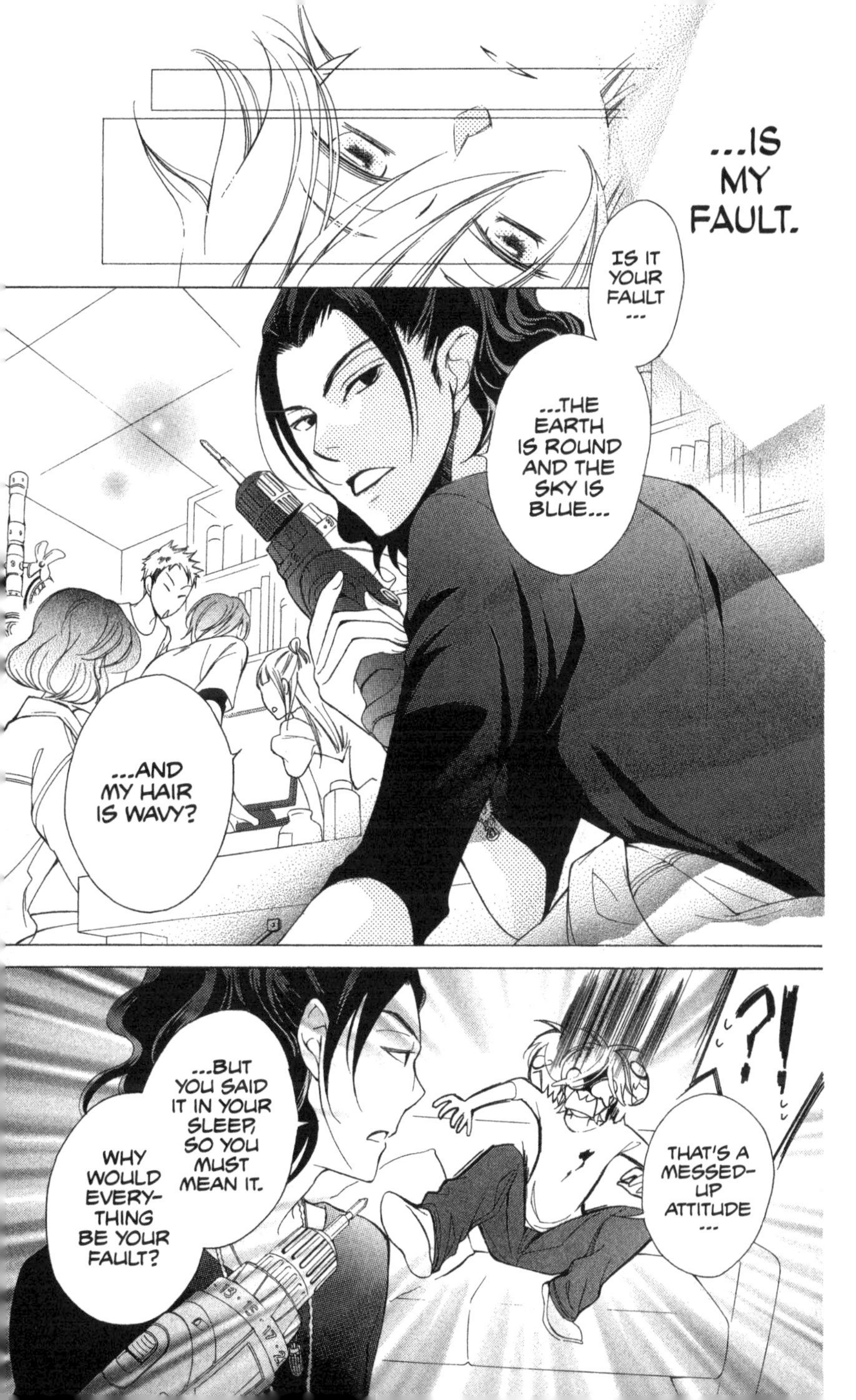
...IS MY FAULT.
IS IT YOUR FAULT...
...THE EARTH IS ROUND AND THE SKY IS BLUE...
...AND MY HAIR IS WAVY?
?!
THAT'S A MESSED-UP ATTITUDE...
...BUT YOU SAID IT IN YOUR SLEEP, SO YOU MUST MEAN IT.
WHY WOULD EVERY-THING BE YOUR FAULT?

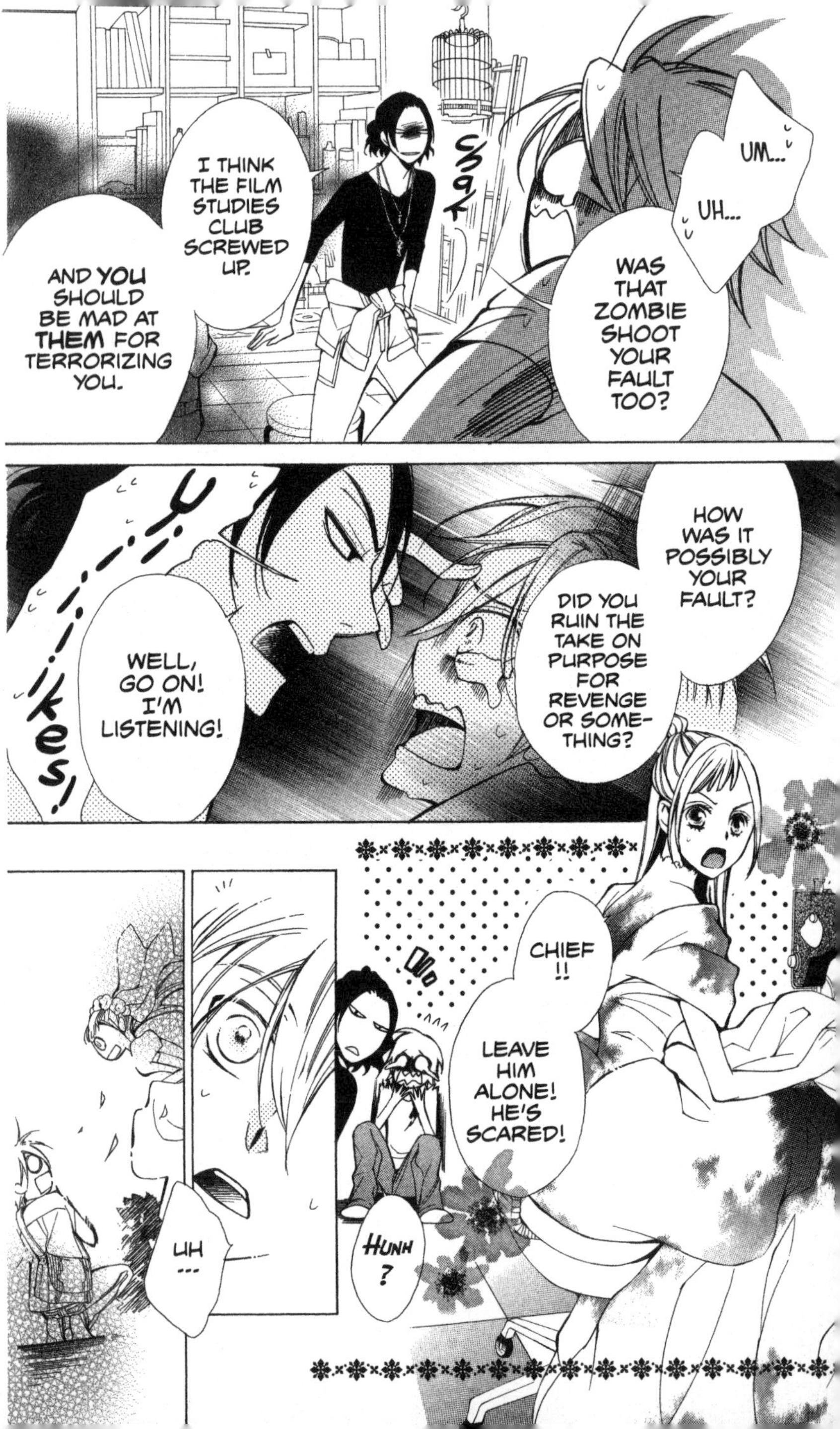
UM...
UH...
WAS THAT ZOMBIE SHOOT YOUR FAULT TOO?
I THINK THE FILM STUDIES CLUB SCREWED UP.
AND YOU SHOULD BE MAD AT THEM FOR TERRORIZING YOU.
HOW WAS IT POSSIBLY YOUR FAULT?
DID YOU RUIN THE TAKE ON PURPOSE FOR REVENGE OR SOME-THING?
WELL, GO ON! I'M LISTENING!
Y...i...kes!
CHIEF!!
LEAVE HIM ALONE! HE'S SCARED!
HUNH?
UH...

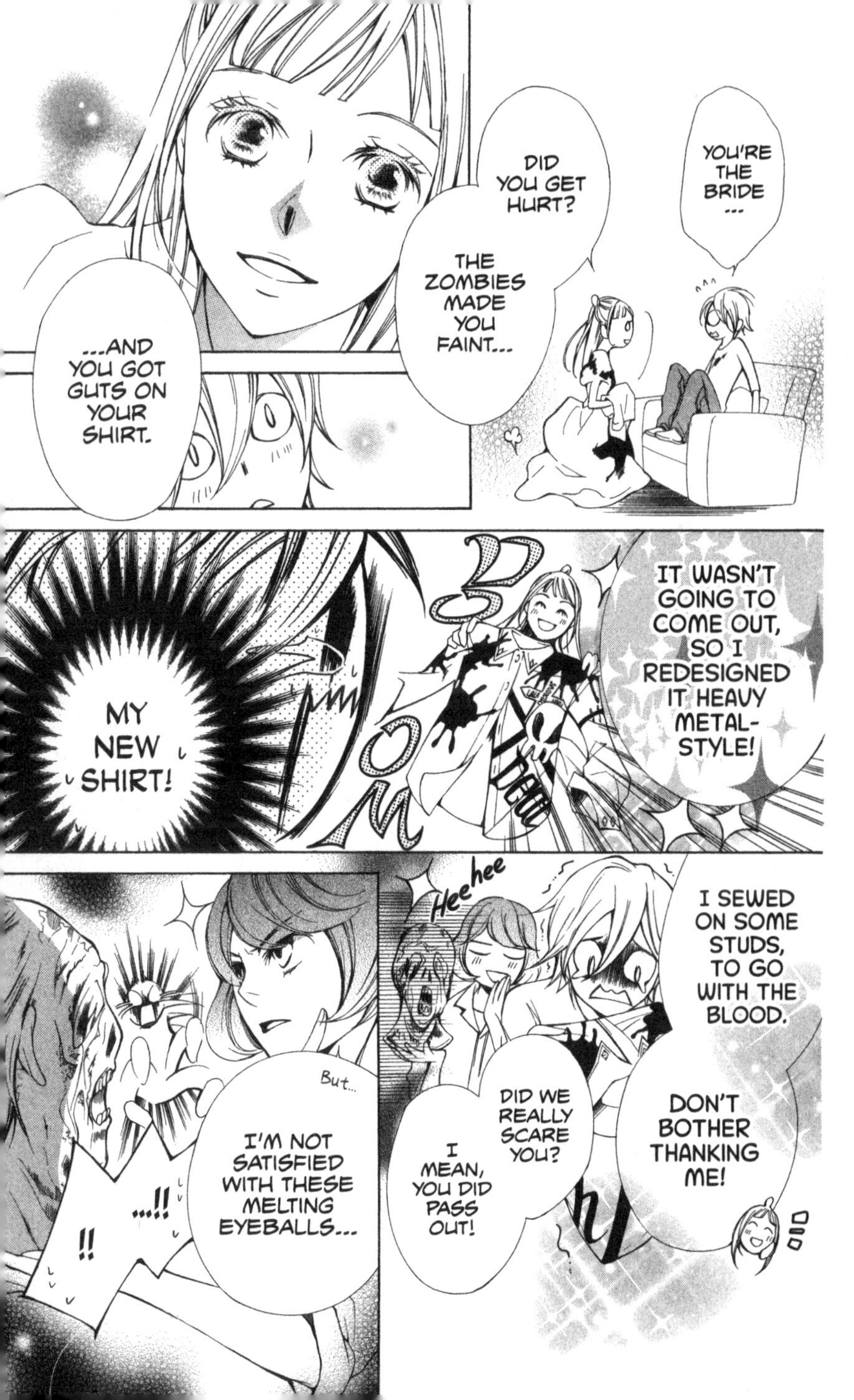
YOU'RE THE BRIDE...
DID YOU GET HURT?
THE ZOMBIES MADE YOU FAINT...
...AND YOU GOT GUTS ON YOUR SHIRT.
IT WASN'T GOING TO COME OUT, SO I REDESIGNED IT HEAVY METAL-STYLE!
MY NEW SHIRT!
I SEWED ON SOME STUDS, TO GO WITH THE BLOOD.
DON'T BOTHER THANKING ME!
Heehee
DID WE REALLY SCARE YOU?
I MEAN, YOU DID PASS OUT!
But...
I'M NOT SATISFIED WITH THESE MELTING EYEBALLS...
...!!
!!

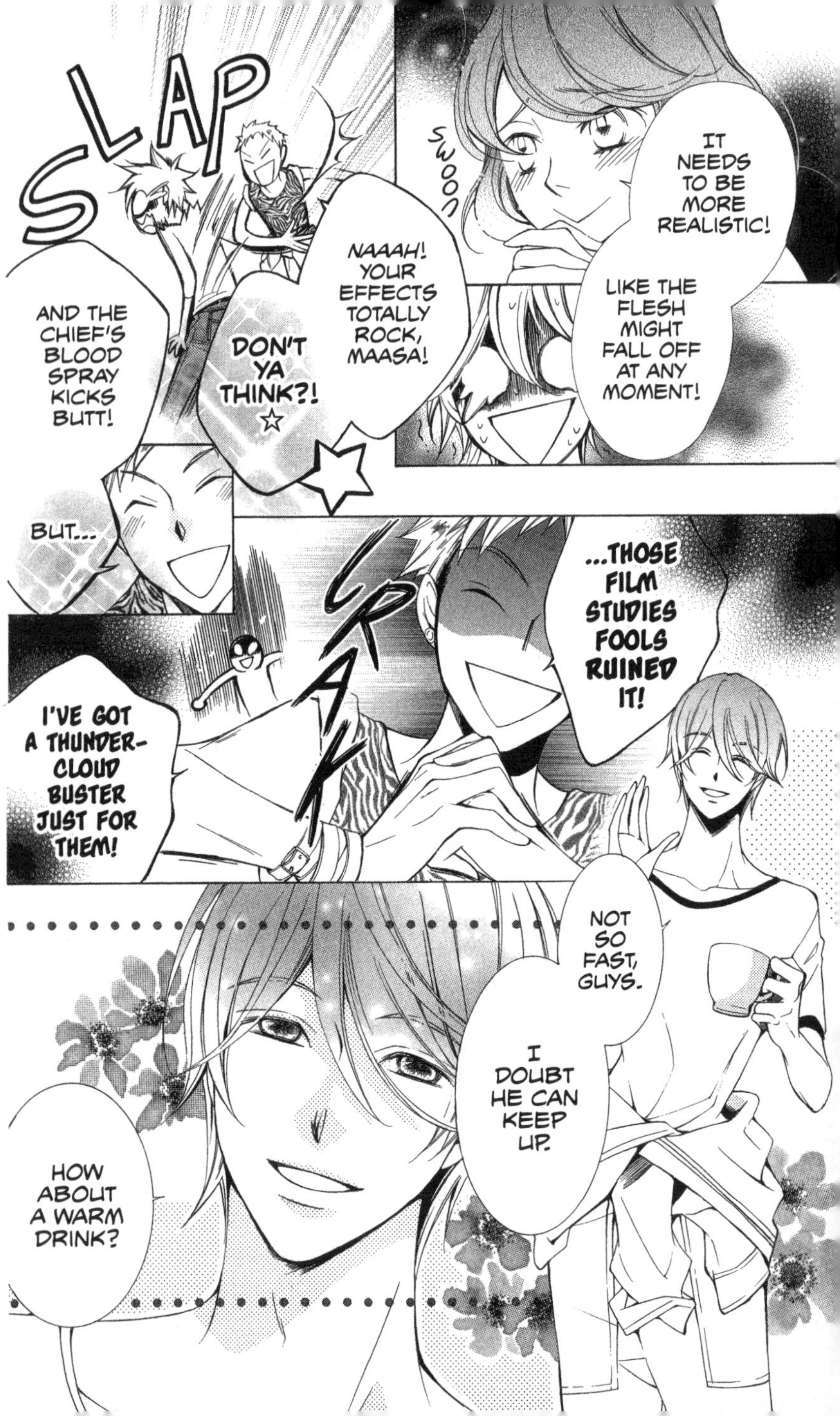
SWOOON
IT NEEDS TO BE MORE REALISTIC!
LIKE THE FLESH MIGHT FALL OFF AT ANY MOMENT!
SLAP
NAAAH! YOUR EFFECTS TOTALLY ROCK, MAASA!
AND THE CHIEF'S BLOOD SPRAY KICKS BUTT!
DON'T YA THINK?! ☆
BUT...
...THOSE FILM STUDIES FOOLS RUINED IT!
CRAAK
I'VE GOT A THUNDER-CLOUD BUSTER JUST FOR THEM!
NOT SO FAST, GUYS.
I DOUBT HE CAN KEEP UP.
HOW ABOUT A WARM DRINK?

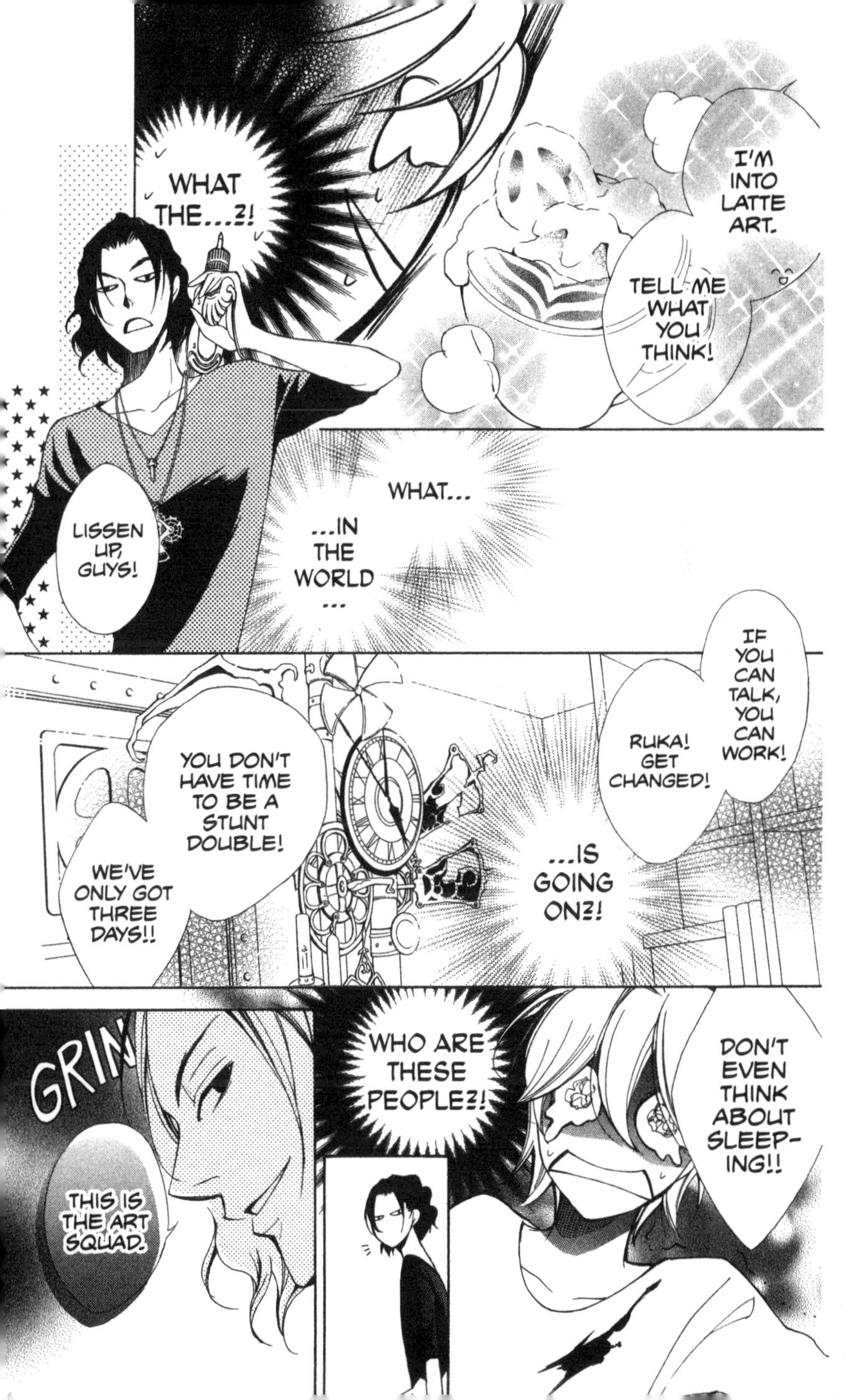
I'M INTO LATTE ART.
TELL ME WHAT YOU THINK!
WHAT...
...IN THE WORLD ...
WHAT THE...?!
LISSEN UP, GUYS!
IF YOU CAN TALK, YOU CAN WORK!
RUKA! GET CHANGED!
...IS GOING ON?!
YOU DON'T HAVE TIME TO BE A STUNT DOUBLE!
WE'VE ONLY GOT THREE DAYS!!
DON'T EVEN THINK ABOUT SLEEPING!!
WHO ARE THESE PEOPLE?!
GRIN
THIS IS THE ART SQUAD.

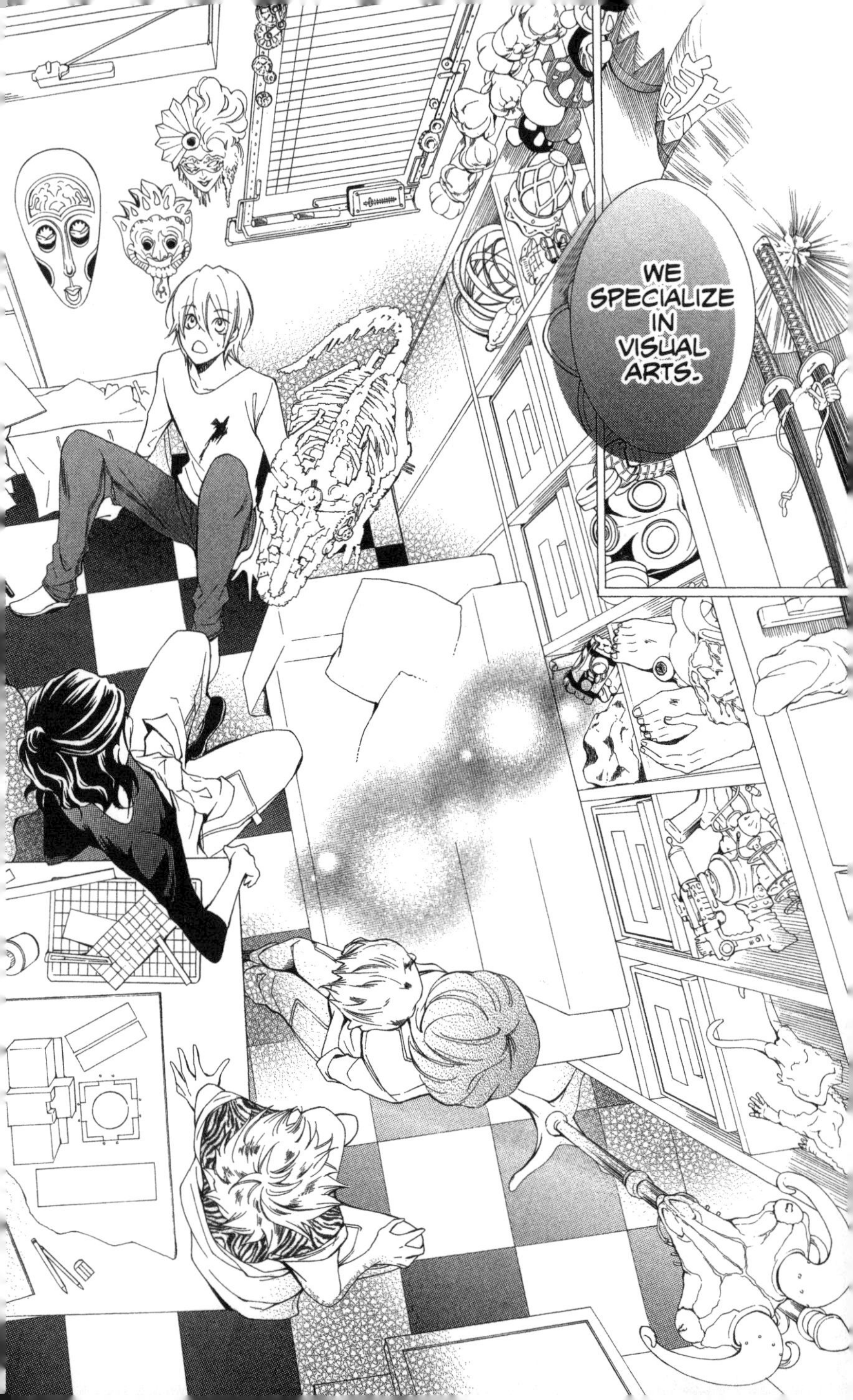
WE SPECIALIZE IN VISUAL ARTS.

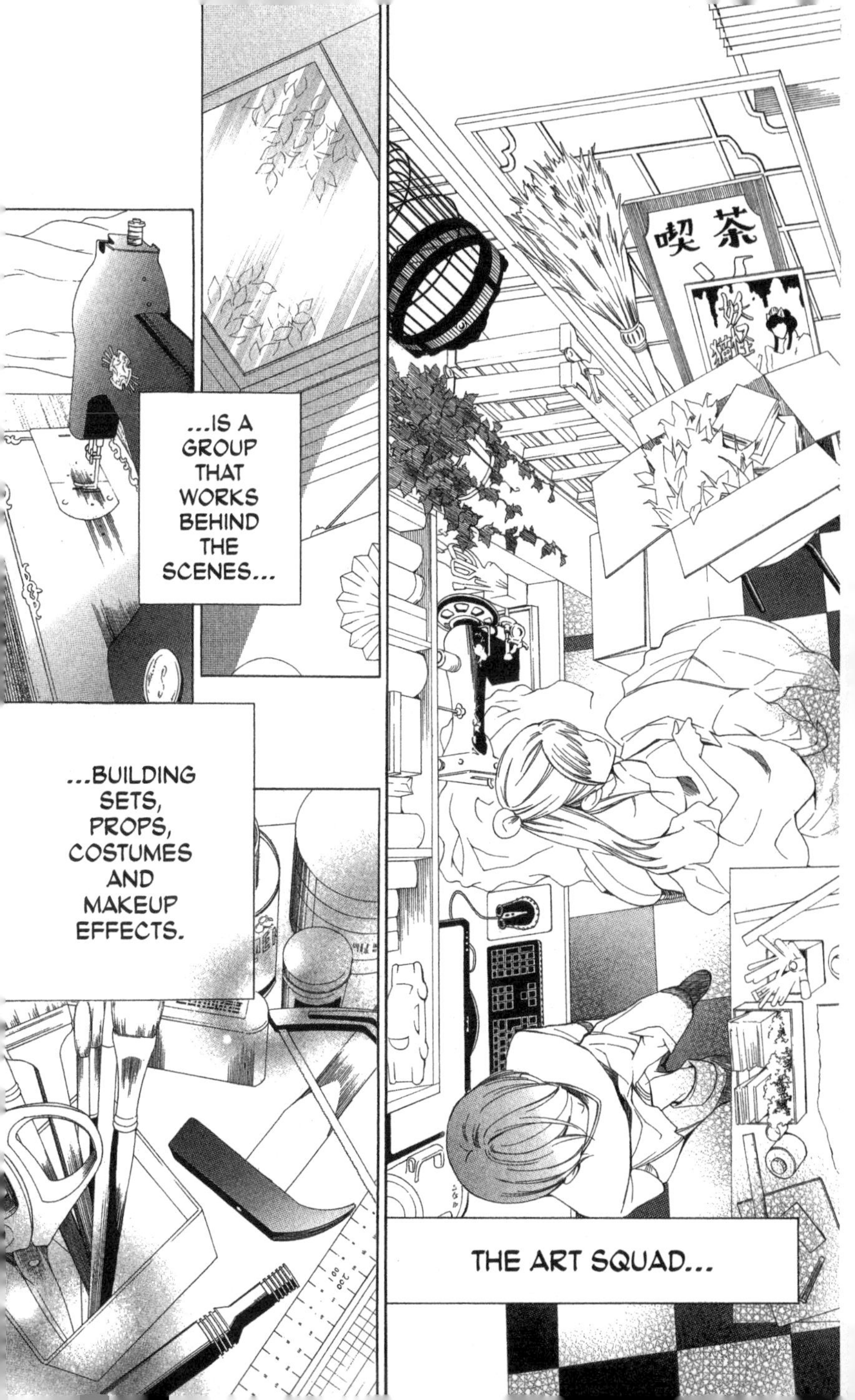
喫茶
THE ART SQUAD...
...IS A GROUP THAT WORKS BEHIND THE SCENES...
...BUILDING SETS, PROPS, COSTUMES AND MAKEUP EFFECTS.

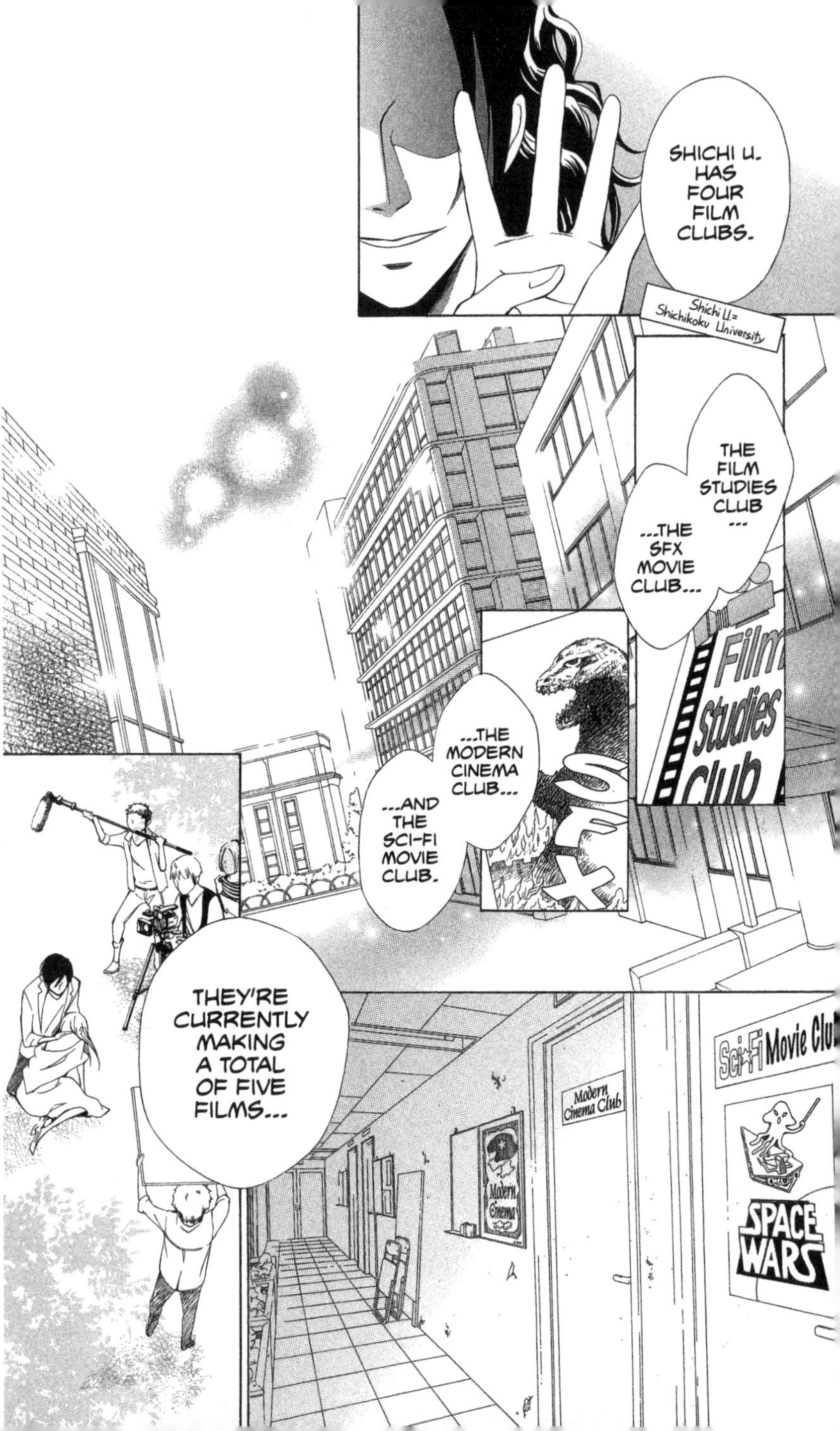
SHICHI U. HAS FOUR FILM CLUBS.
Shichi U.= Shichikoku University
THE FILM STUDIES CLUB...
...THE SFX MOVIE CLUB...
Film Studies Club
SFX
...THE MODERN CINEMA CLUB...
...AND THE SCI-FI MOVIE CLUB.
THEY'RE CURRENTLY MAKING A TOTAL OF FIVE FILMS...
Sci-Fi Movie Club
SPACE WARS
Modern Cinema Club
Modern Cinema

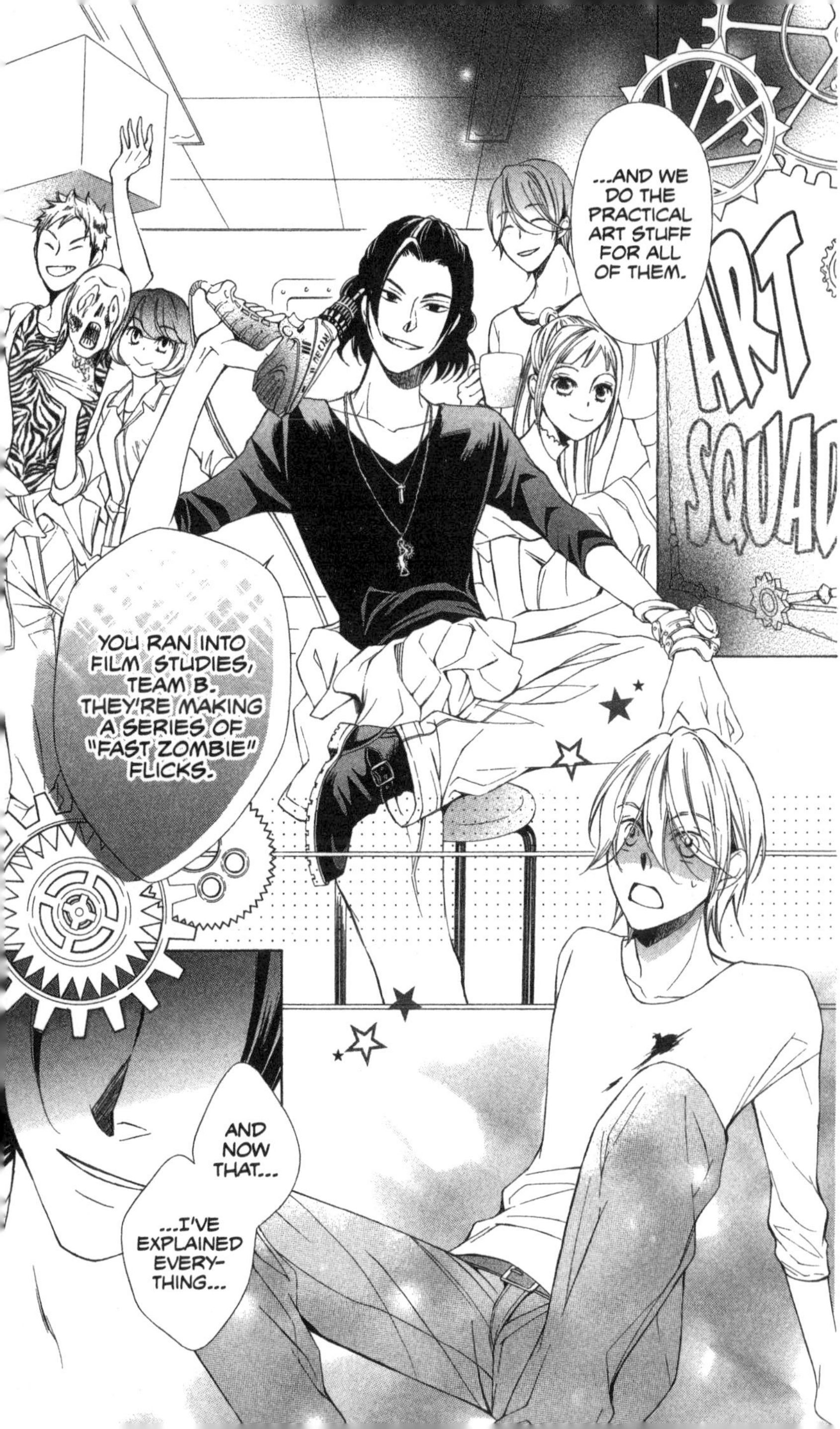
...AND WE DO THE PRACTICAL ART STUFF FOR ALL OF THEM.
ART SQUA
YOU RAN INTO FILM STUDIES, TEAM B. THEY'RE MAKING A SERIES OF "FAST ZOMBIE" FLICKS.
AND NOW THAT...
...I'VE EXPLAINED EVERY-THING...

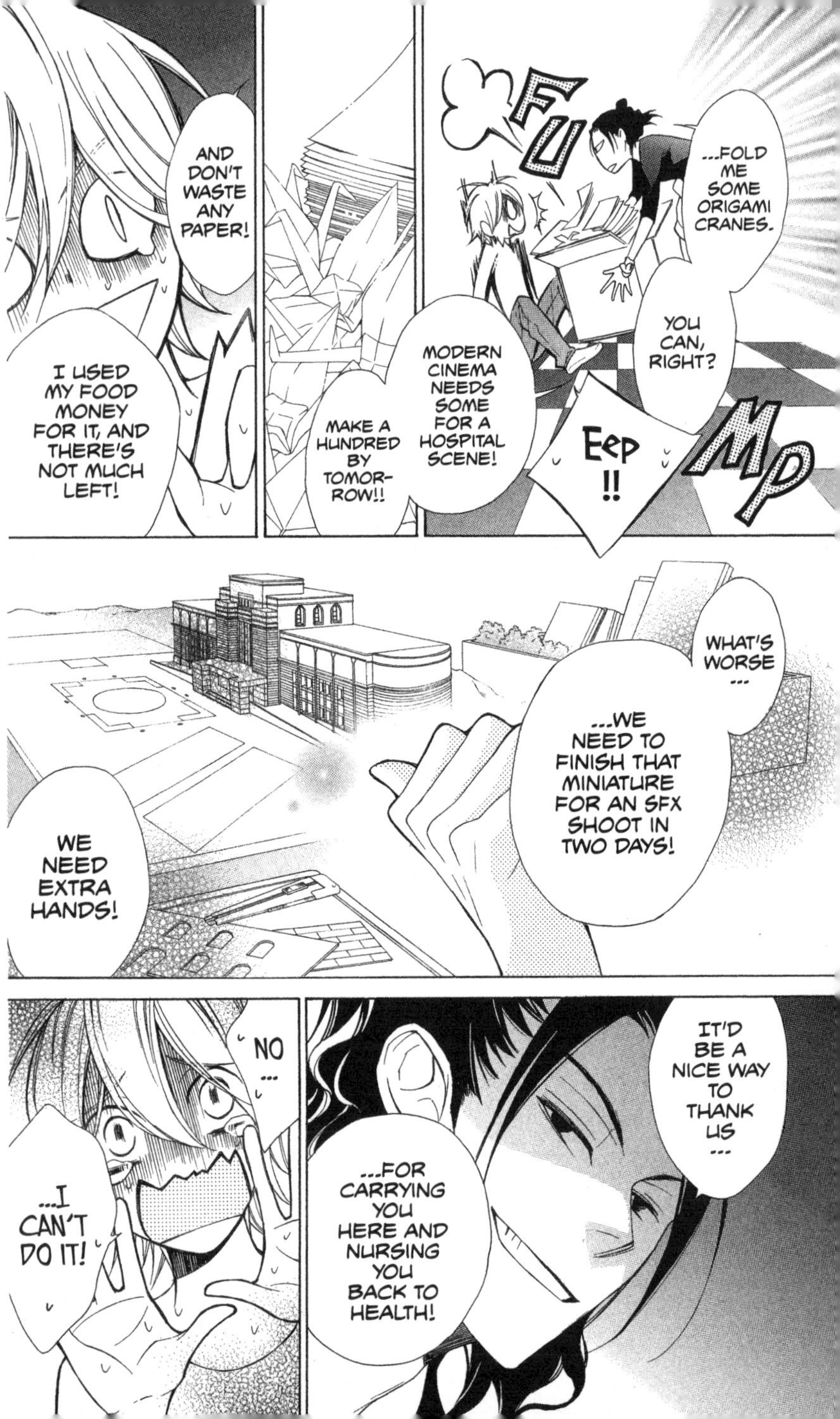

...FOLD ME SOME ORIGAMI CRANES.
FU
YOU CAN, RIGHT?
MP
Eep!!
MODERN CINEMA NEEDS SOME FOR A HOSPITAL SCENE!
MAKE A HUNDRED BY TOMORROW!!
AND DON'T WASTE ANY PAPER!
I USED MY FOOD MONEY FOR IT, AND THERE'S NOT MUCH LEFT!
WHAT'S WORSE...
...WE NEED TO FINISH THAT MINIATURE FOR AN SFX SHOOT IN TWO DAYS!
WE NEED EXTRA HANDS!
IT'D BE A NICE WAY TO THANK US...
...FOR CARRYING YOU HERE AND NURSING YOU BACK TO HEALTH!
NO...
...I CAN'T DO IT!

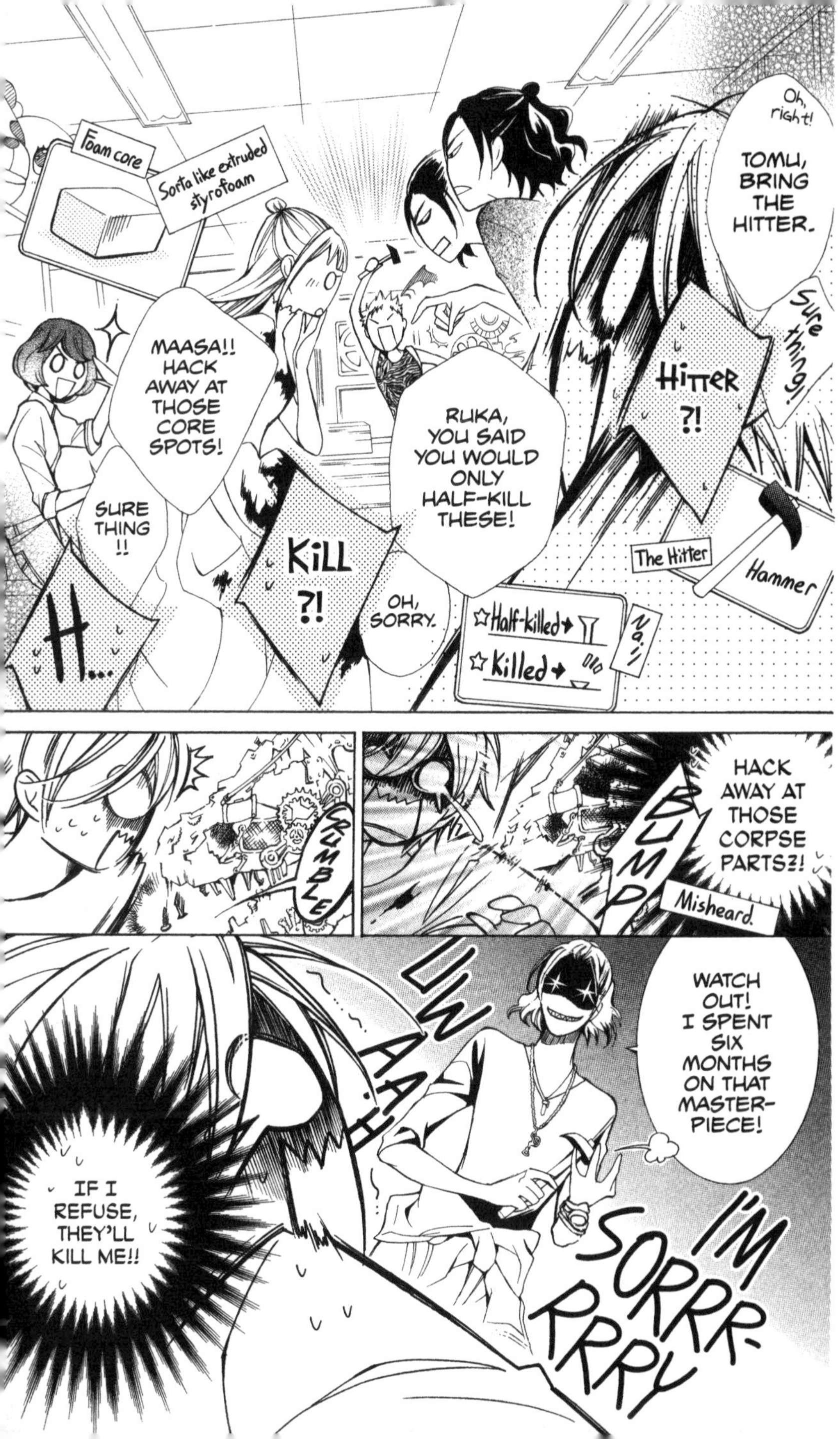

Oh, right!
TOMU, BRING THE HITTER.
Sure thing!
HITTER ?!
The Hitter
Hammer
RUKA, YOU SAID YOU WOULD ONLY HALF-KILL THESE!
OH, SORRY.
Nail
☆Half-killed →
☆Killed →
KILL ?!
MAASA!! HACK AWAY AT THOSE CORE SPOTS!
Sorta like extruded styrofoam
Foam core
SURE THING !!
H...
HACK AWAY AT THOSE CORPSE PARTS?!
BUMP
Misheard.
CRUMBLE
WATCH OUT! I SPENT SIX MONTHS ON THAT MASTER-PIECE!
I'M SORRRRRRY
UWAAAH
IF I REFUSE, THEY'LL KILL ME!!

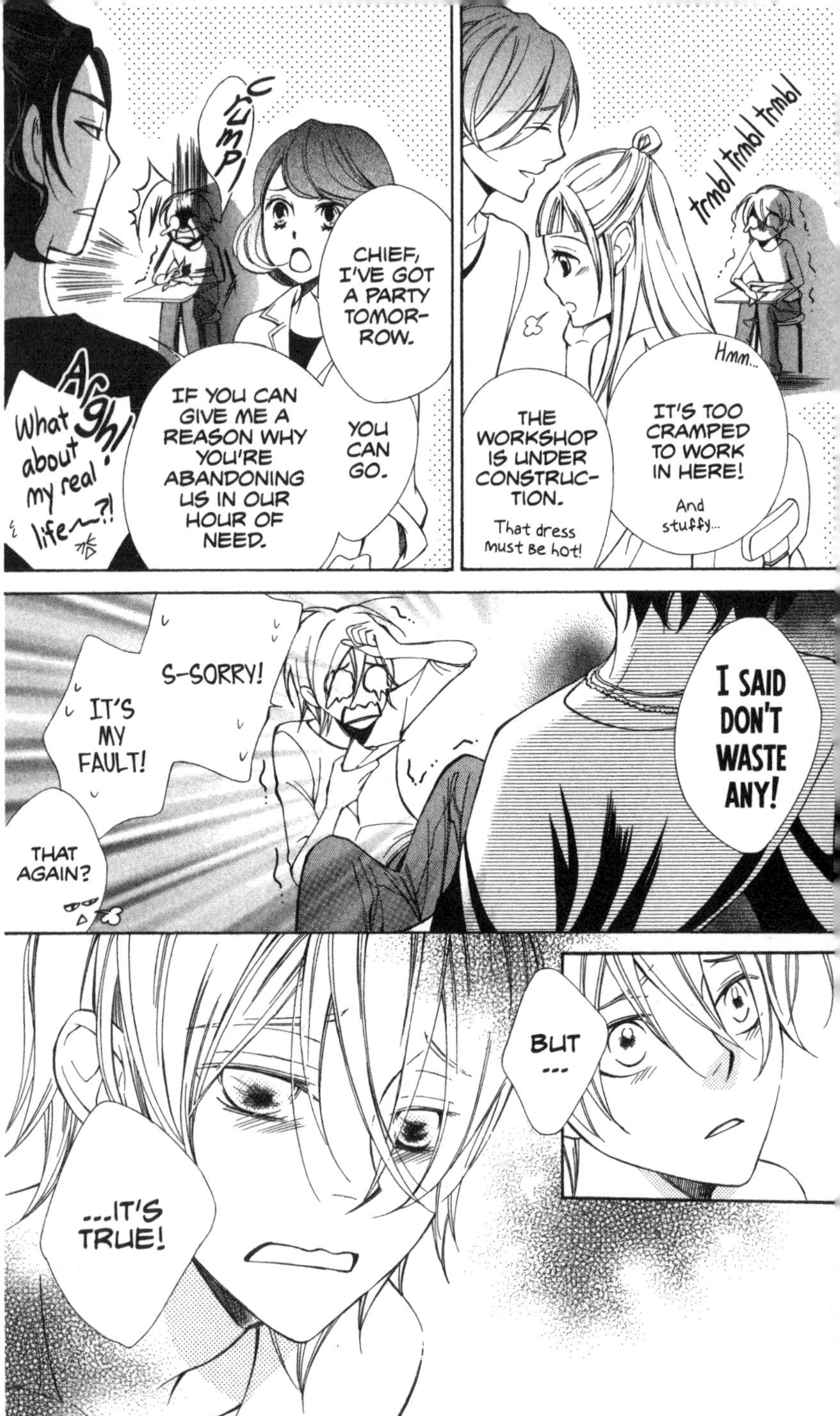
trmbl trmbl trmbl
Hmm...
IT'S TOO CRAMPED TO WORK IN HERE!
And stuffy...
THE WORKSHOP IS UNDER CONSTRUCTION.
That dress must be hot!
CRUMP!
CHIEF, I'VE GOT A PARTY TOMORROW.
YOU CAN GO.
IF YOU CAN GIVE ME A REASON WHY YOU'RE ABANDONING US IN OUR HOUR OF NEED.
Argh!
What about my real life~?!
I SAID DON'T WASTE ANY!
S-SORRY!
IT'S MY FAULT!
THAT AGAIN?
BUT ...
...IT'S TRUE!

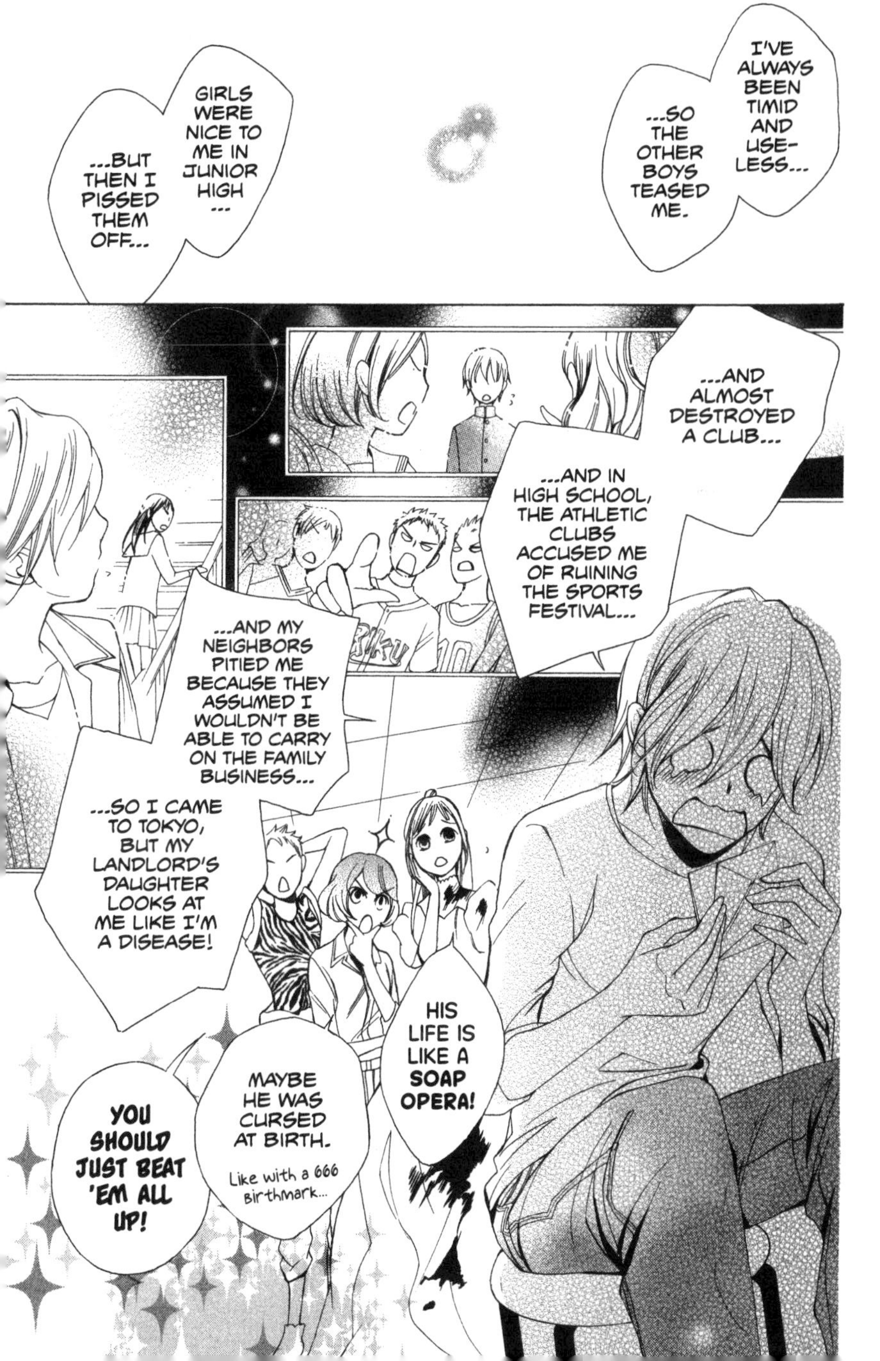

I'VE ALWAYS BEEN TIMID AND USE-LESS...
...SO THE OTHER BOYS TEASED ME.
GIRLS WERE NICE TO ME IN JUNIOR HIGH...
...BUT THEN I PISSED THEM OFF...
...AND ALMOST DESTROYED A CLUB...
...AND IN HIGH SCHOOL, THE ATHLETIC CLUBS ACCUSED ME OF RUINING THE SPORTS FESTIVAL...
...AND MY NEIGHBORS PITIED ME BECAUSE THEY ASSUMED I WOULDN'T BE ABLE TO CARRY ON THE FAMILY BUSINESS...
...SO I CAME TO TOKYO, BUT MY LANDLORD'S DAUGHTER LOOKS AT ME LIKE I'M A DISEASE!
HIS LIFE IS LIKE A SOAP OPERA!
MAYBE HE WAS CURSED AT BIRTH.
Like with a 666 Birthmark...
YOU SHOULD JUST BEAT 'EM ALL UP!

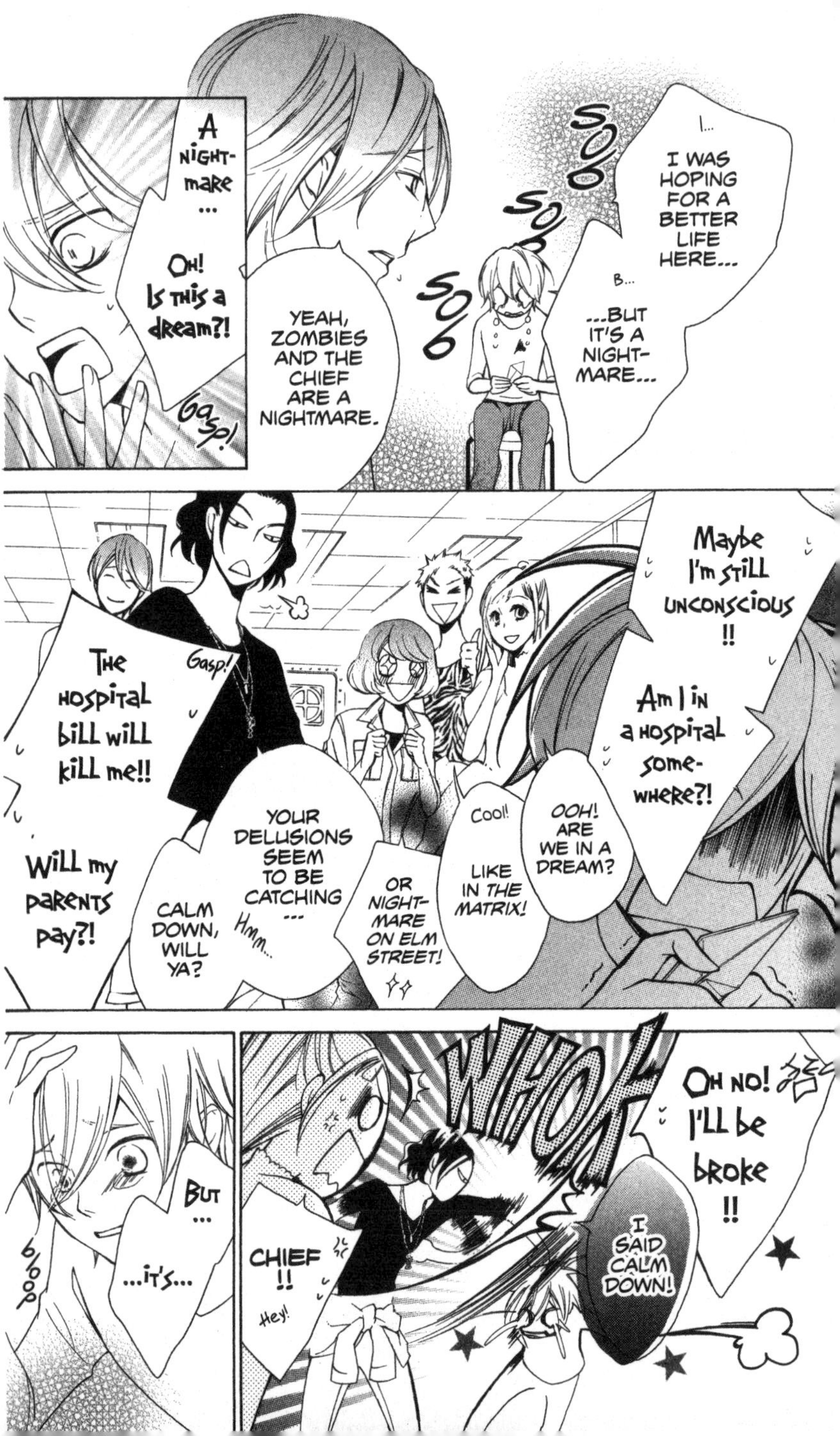
SOB SOB SOB
I...
I WAS HOPING FOR A BETTER LIFE HERE...
B...
...BUT IT'S A NIGHTMARE...
YEAH, ZOMBIES AND THE CHIEF ARE A NIGHTMARE.
A nightmare...
Oh! Is this a dream?!
Gasp!
Maybe I'm still unconscious!!
Am I in a hospital somewhere?!
OOH! ARE WE IN A DREAM?
Cool!
LIKE IN THE MATRIX!
OR NIGHTMARE ON ELM STREET!
YOUR DELUSIONS SEEM TO BE CATCHING...
Hmm...
CALM DOWN, WILL YA?
The hospital bill will kill me!!
Gasp!
Will my parents pay?!
Oh no! I'll be broke!!
WHOK
I SAID CALM DOWN!
CHIEF!!
Hey!
But...
...it's...
bloop

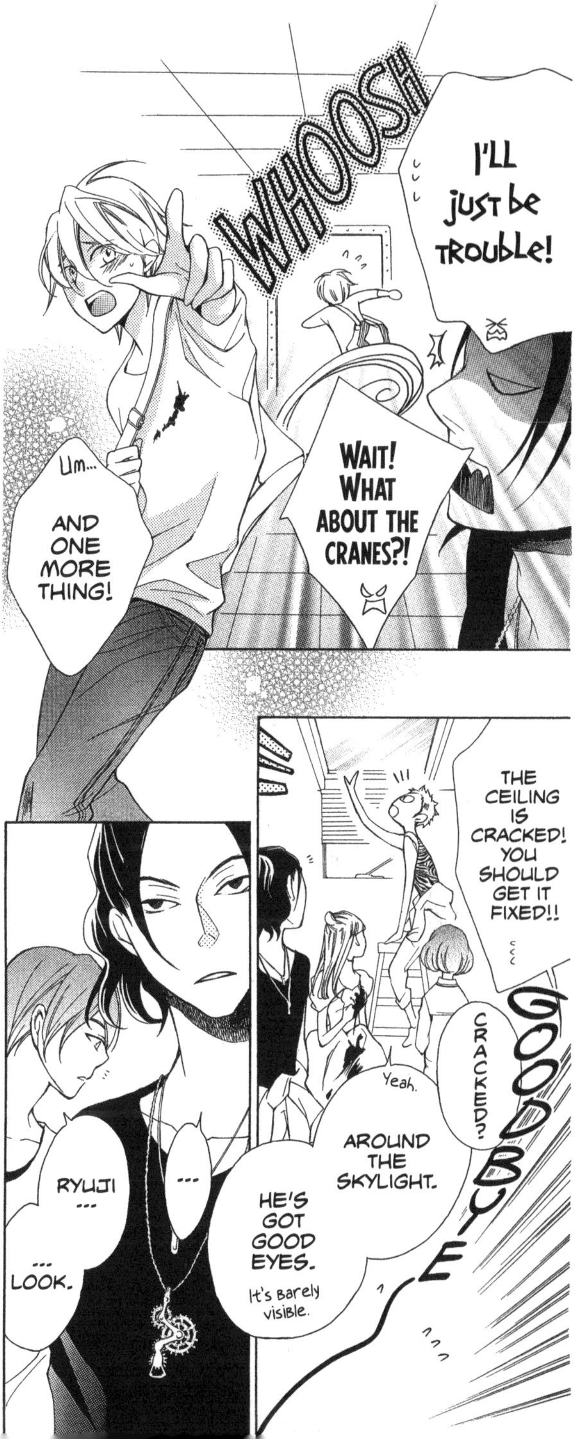
WHOOSH
I'LL just be TROUBLE!
WAIT! WHAT ABOUT THE CRANES?!
Um...
AND ONE MORE THING!
THE CEILING IS CRACKED! YOU SHOULD GET IT FIXED!!
GOODBYE
CRACKED?
Yeah.
AROUND THE SKYLIGHT.
HE'S GOT GOOD EYES.
It's barely visible.
...
RYUJI...
...LOOK.

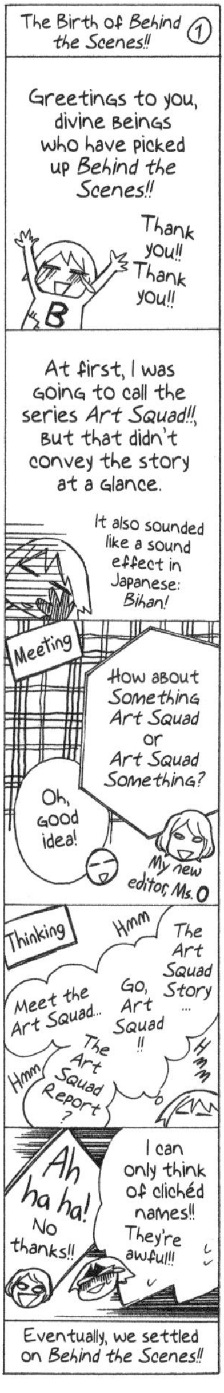
The Birth of Behind the Scenes!! 1
Greetings to you, divine beings who have picked up Behind the Scenes!!
Thank you!! Thank you!!
B
At first, I was going to call the series Art Squad!!, but that didn't convey the story at a glance.
It also sounded like a sound effect in Japanese: Bihan!
Meeting
How about Something Art Squad or Art Squad Something?
Oh, good idea!
My new editor, Ms. O
Thinking
Hmm
The Art Squad Story...
Go, Art Squad!!
Meet the Art Squad...
The Art Squad Report?
Hmm
Hmm
Ah ha ha! No thanks!!
I can only think of clichéd names!! They're awful!!
Eventually, we settled on Behind the Scenes!!

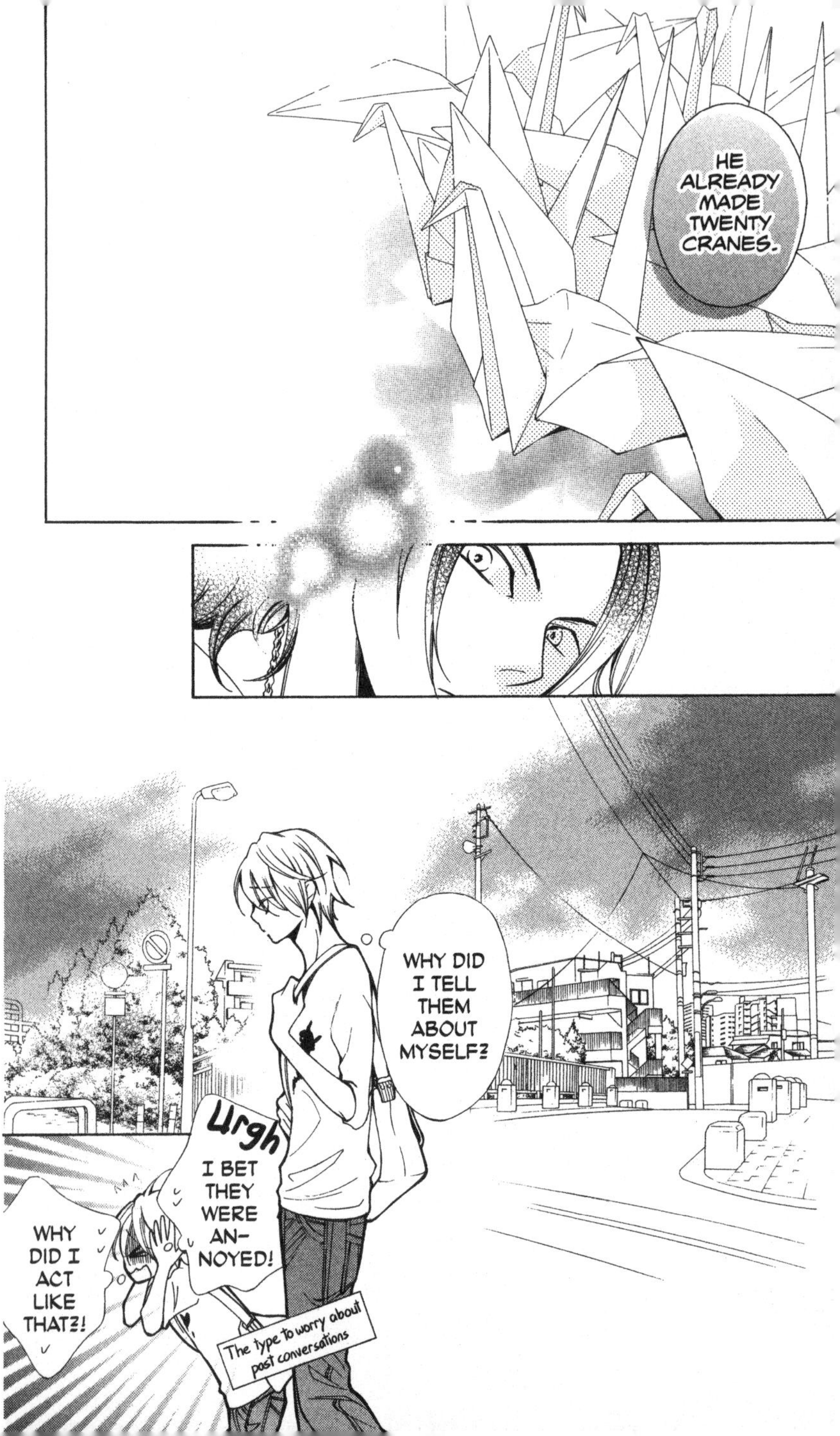
HE ALREADY MADE TWENTY CRANES.
WHY DID I TELL THEM ABOUT MYSELF?
Urgh
I BET THEY WERE AN-NOYED!
WHY DID I ACT LIKE THAT?!
The type to worry about past conversations

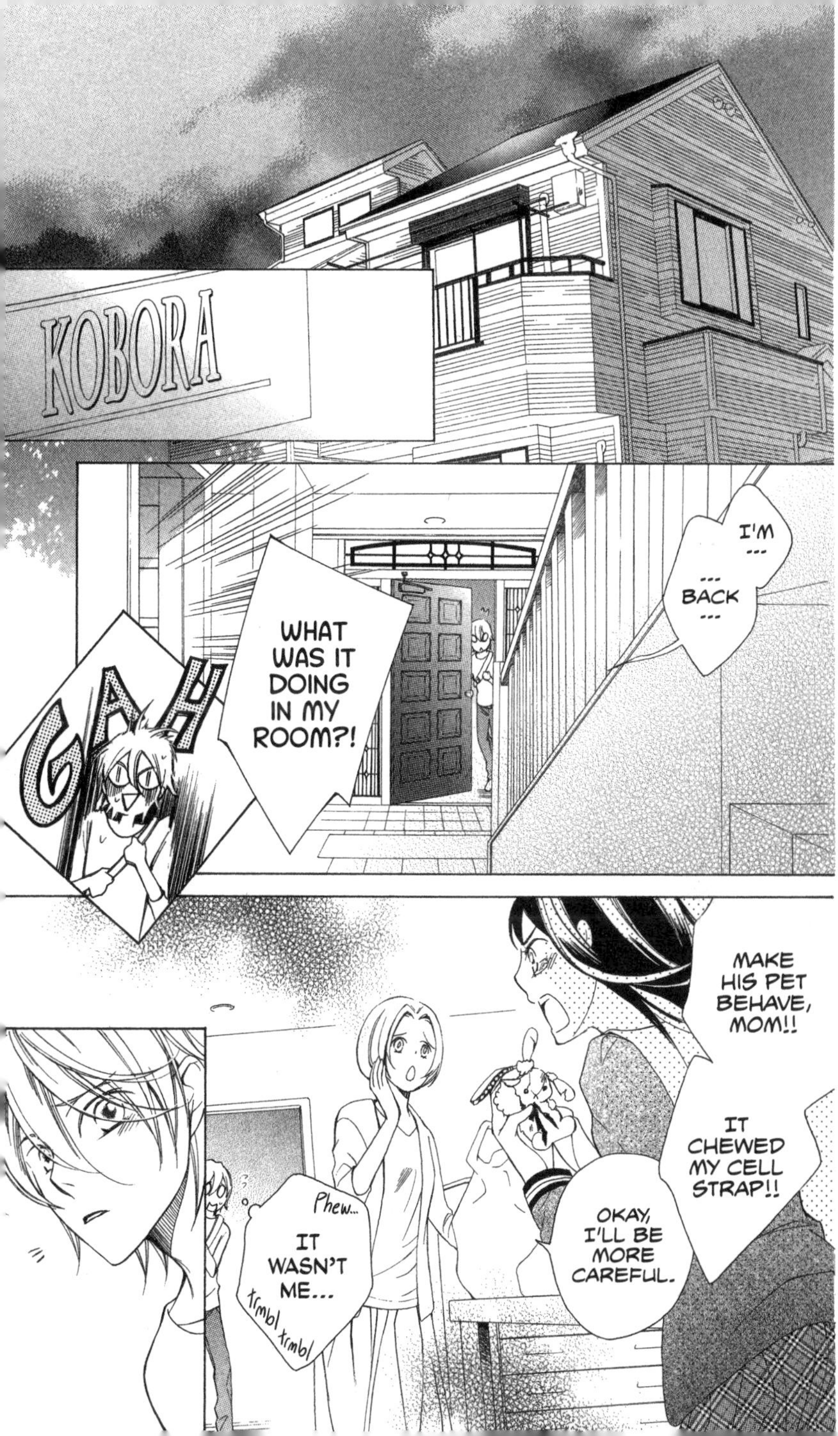
KOBORA
I'M ... ... BACK ...
WHAT WAS IT DOING IN MY ROOM?!
GAH
MAKE HIS PET BEHAVE, MOM!!
IT CHEWED MY CELL STRAP!!
OKAY, I'LL BE MORE CAREFUL.
Phew...
IT WASN'T ME...
trmbl trmbl

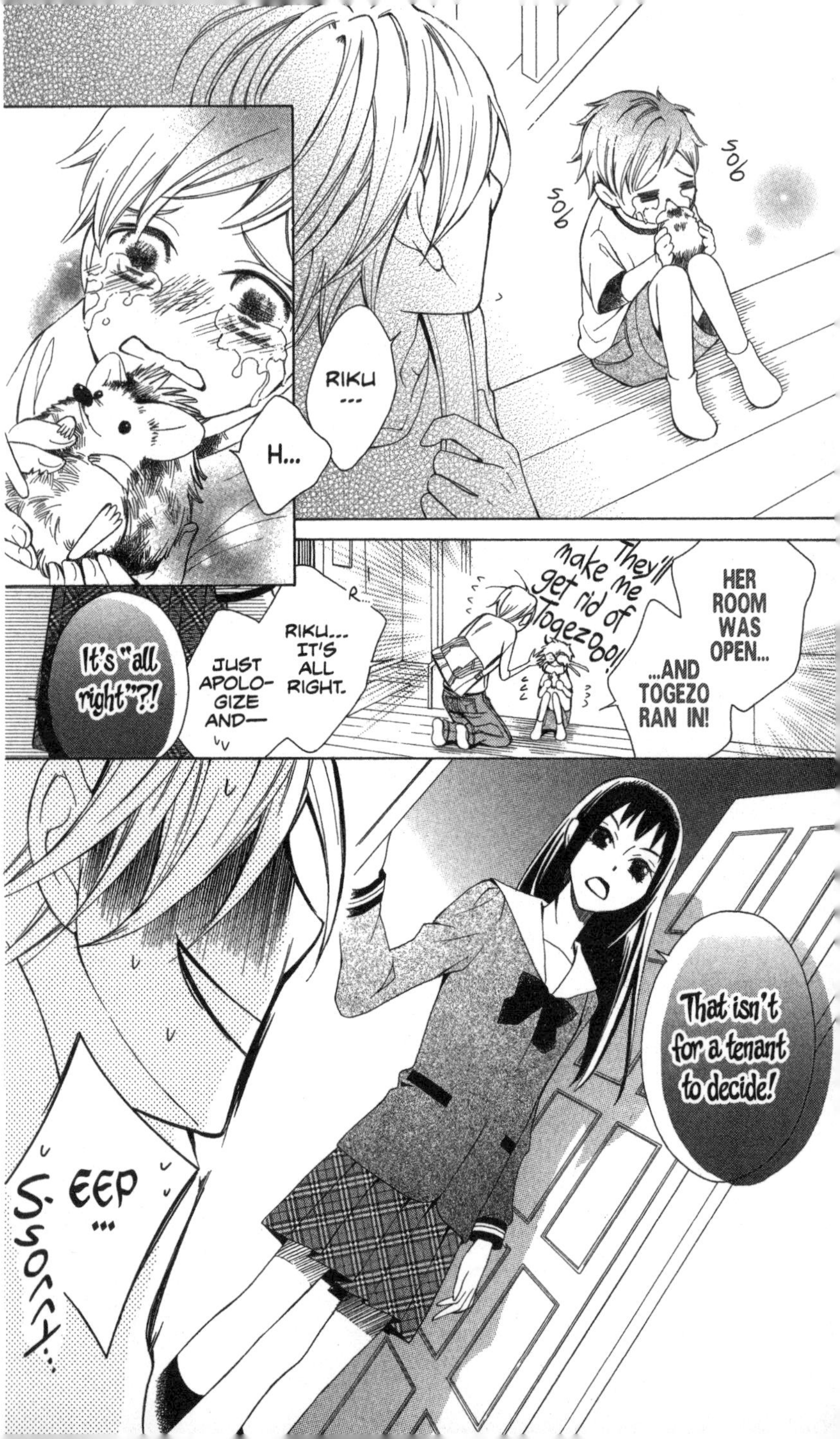
sob
sob
RIKU...
H...
HER ROOM WAS OPEN...
...AND TOGEZO RAN IN!
They'll make me get rid of Togezo!
R...
RIKU... IT'S ALL RIGHT.
JUST APOLOGIZE AND—
It's "all right"?!
That isn't for a tenant to decide!
EEP...
S-sorry...

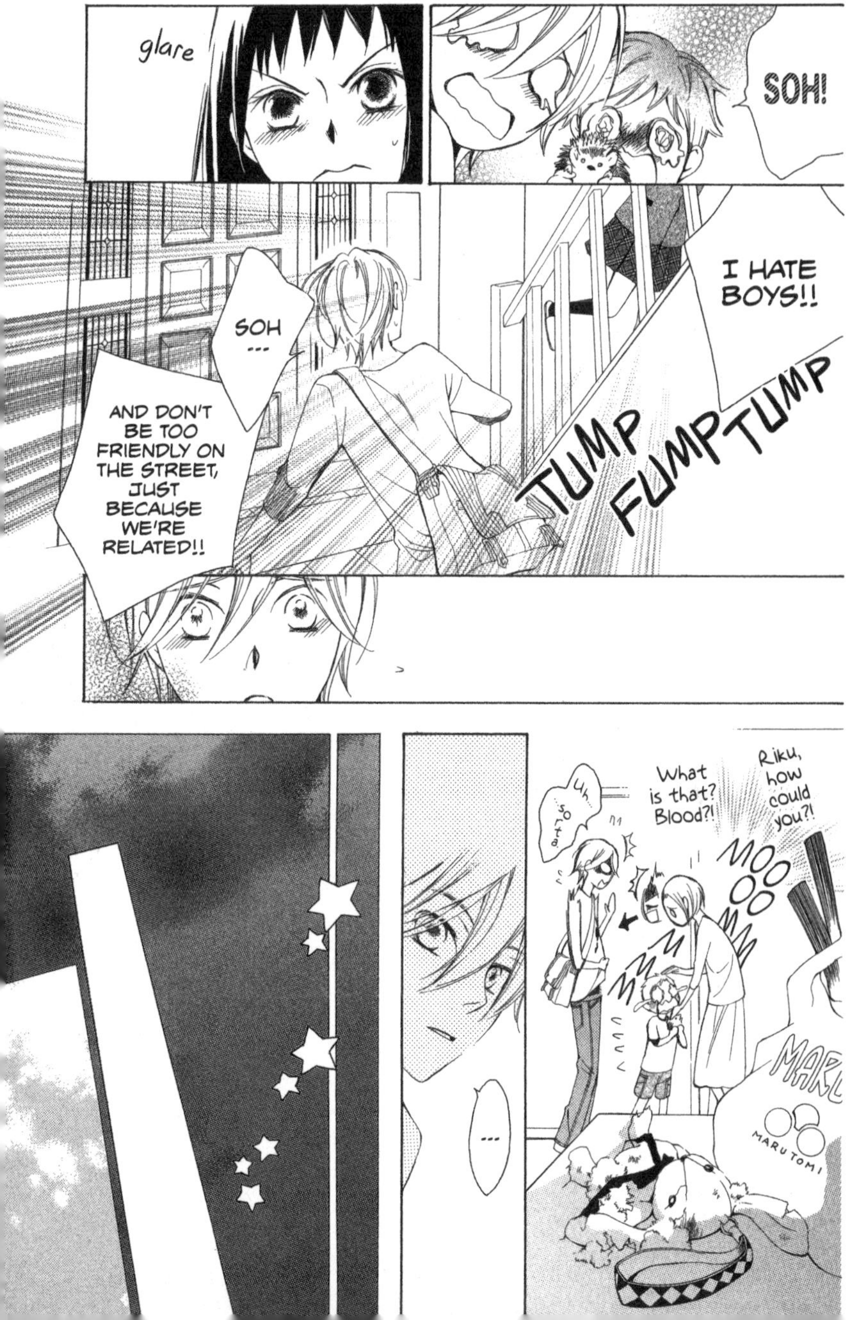
SOH!
glare
I HATE BOYS!!
TUMP FUMP TUMP
SOH ...
AND DON'T BE TOO FRIENDLY ON THE STREET, JUST BECAUSE WE'RE RELATED!!
Riku, how could you?!
What is that? Blood?!
Uh... sorta.
MOOOOM
MARU
MARUTOMI
...

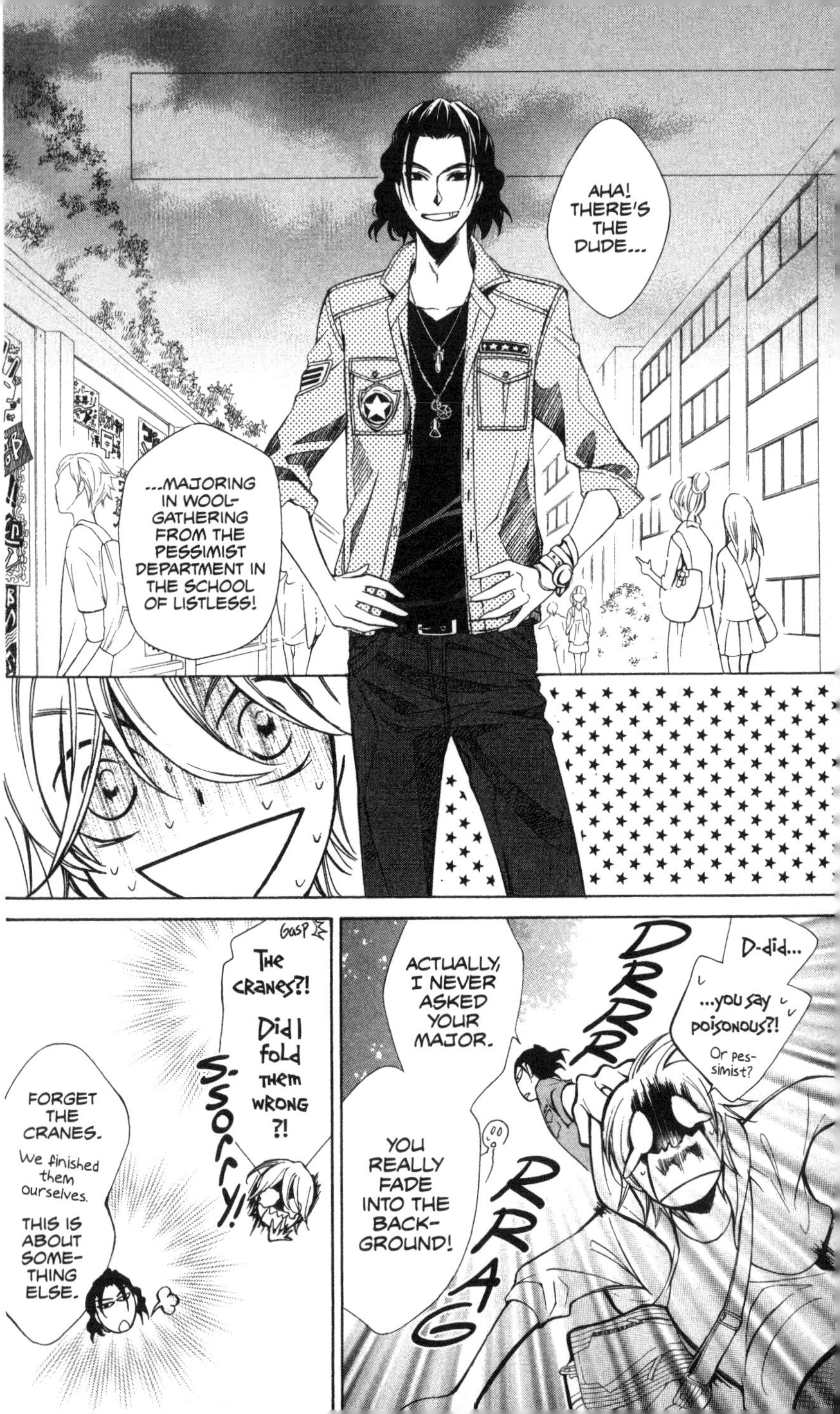
AHA! THERE'S THE DUDE...
...MAJORING IN WOOL-GATHERING FROM THE PESSIMIST DEPARTMENT IN THE SCHOOL OF LISTLESS!
D-did...
...you say poisonous?!
Or pes-simist?
DRRRRRAG
ACTUALLY, I NEVER ASKED YOUR MAJOR.
YOU REALLY FADE INTO THE BACK-GROUND!
Gasp
The cranes?!
Did I fold them wrong?!
S-sorry!
FORGET THE CRANES.
We finished them ourselves.
THIS IS ABOUT SOMETHING ELSE.

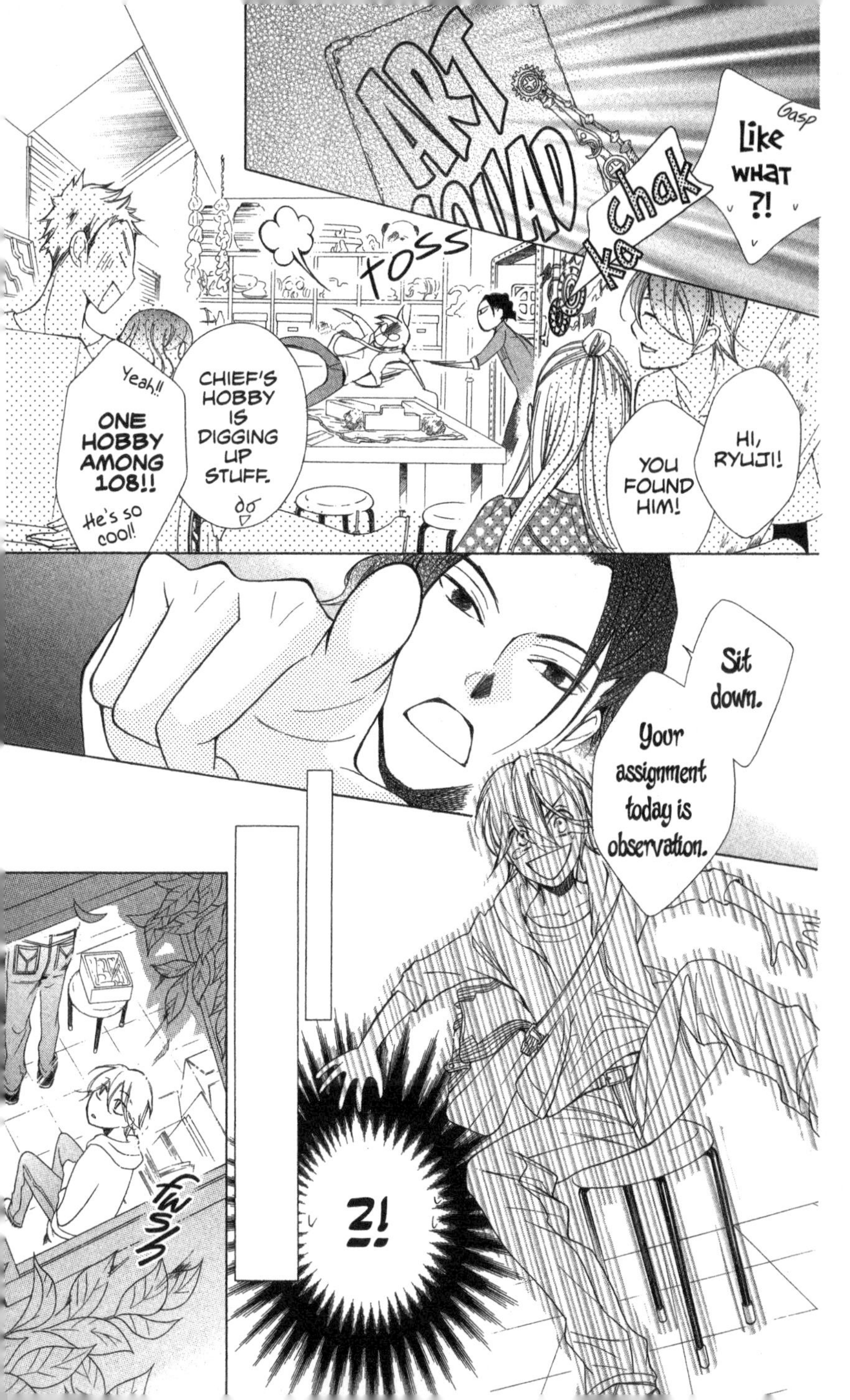
Gasp
Like what?!
ka chak
ART
Hi, Ryuji!
You found him!
TOSS
Chief's hobby is digging up stuff.
Yeah!!
One hobby among 108!!
He's so cool!
Sit down.
Your assignment today is observation.
?!
FWSH

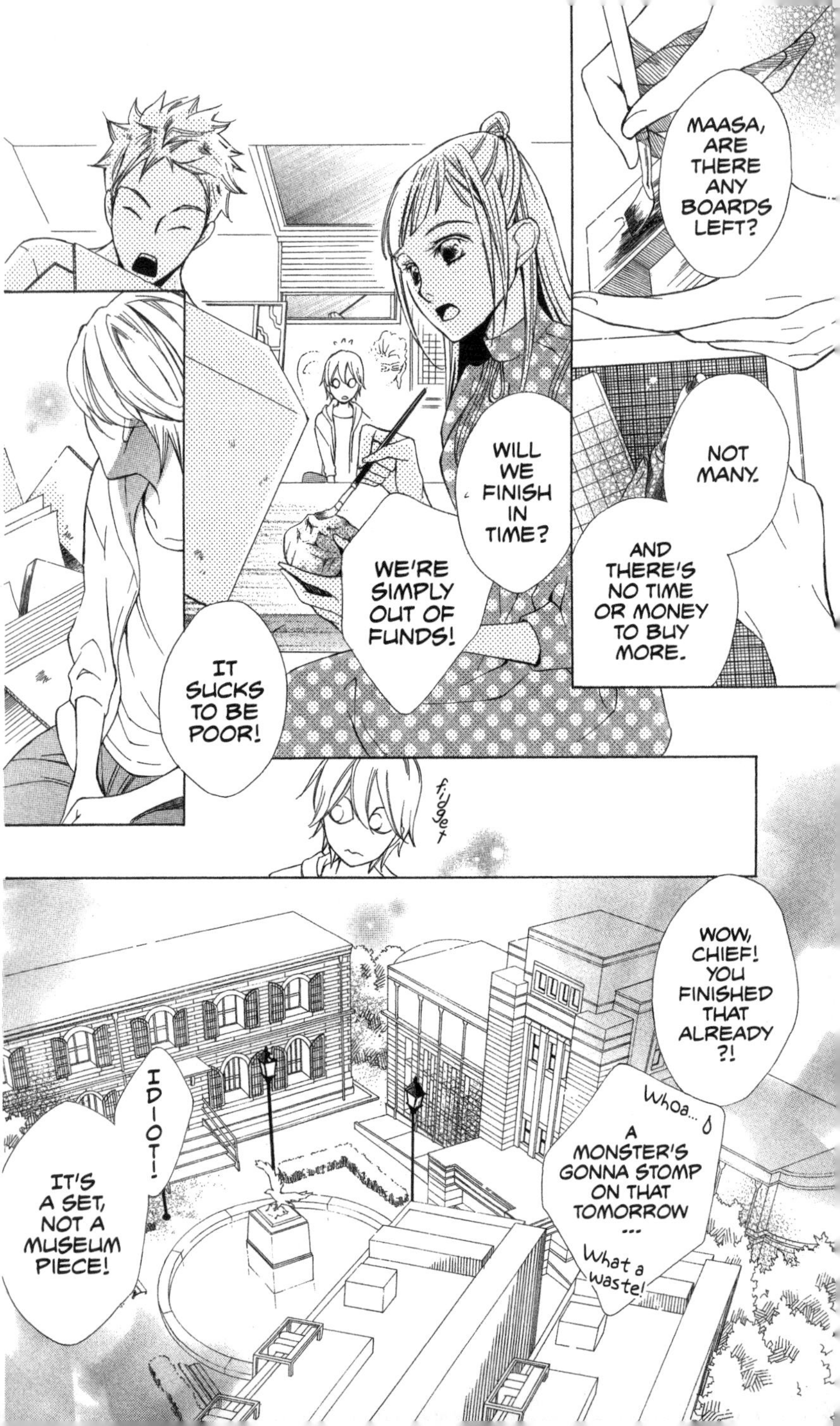
MAASA, ARE THERE ANY BOARDS LEFT?
NOT MANY.
AND THERE'S NO TIME OR MONEY TO BUY MORE.
WILL WE FINISH IN TIME?
WE'RE SIMPLY OUT OF FUNDS!
IT SUCKS TO BE POOR!
fidget
WOW, CHIEF! YOU FINISHED THAT ALREADY?!
Whoa...
A MONSTER'S GONNA STOMP ON THAT TOMORROW...
What a waste!
IDIOT!
IT'S A SET, NOT A MUSEUM PIECE!

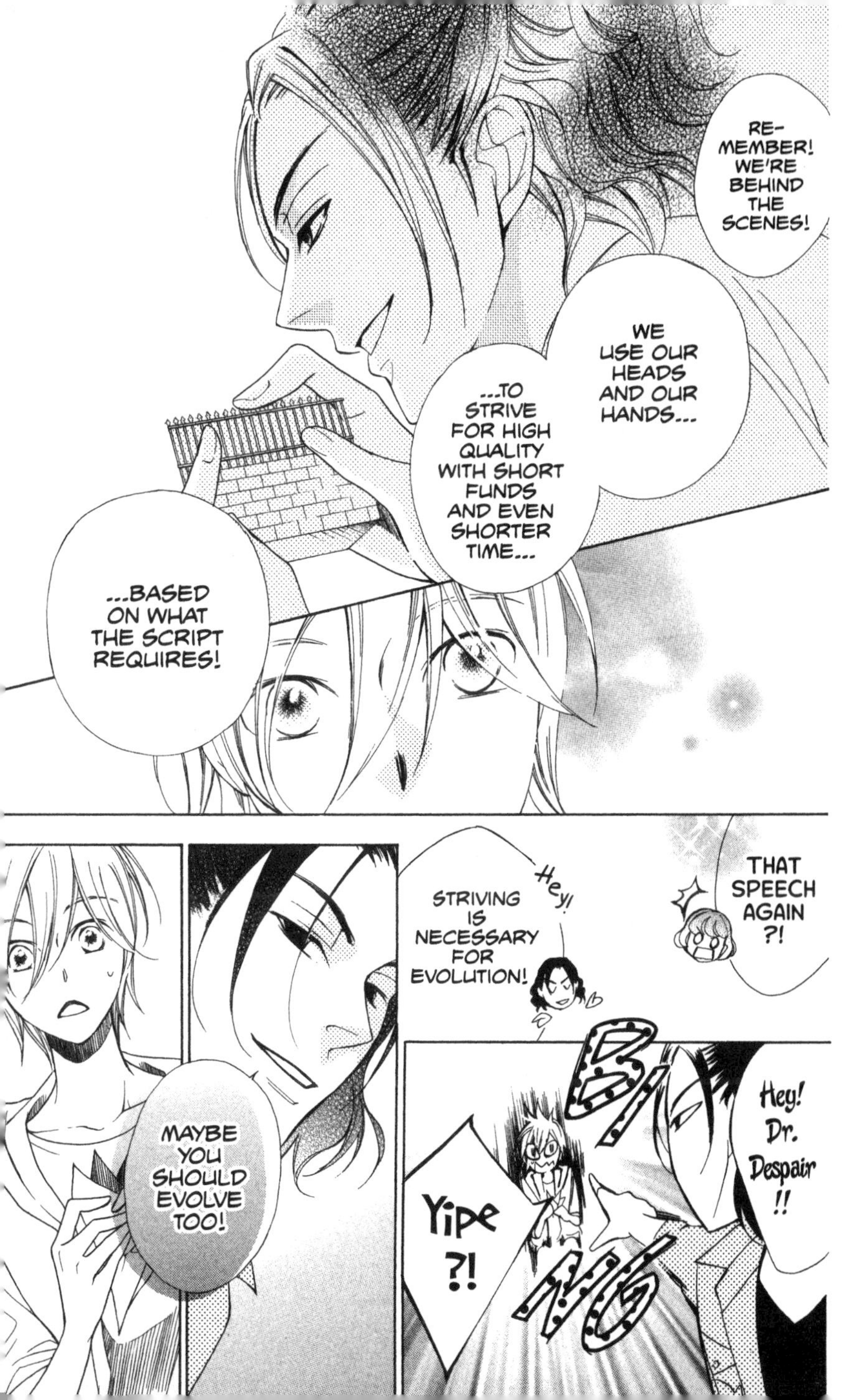

RE-MEMBER! WE'RE BEHIND THE SCENES!
WE USE OUR HEADS AND OUR HANDS...
...TO STRIVE FOR HIGH QUALITY WITH SHORT FUNDS AND EVEN SHORTER TIME...
...BASED ON WHAT THE SCRIPT REQUIRES!
THAT SPEECH AGAIN?!
Hey!
STRIVING IS NECESSARY FOR EVOLUTION!
Hey! Dr. Despair!!
BING
Yipe?!
MAYBE YOU SHOULD EVOLVE TOO!

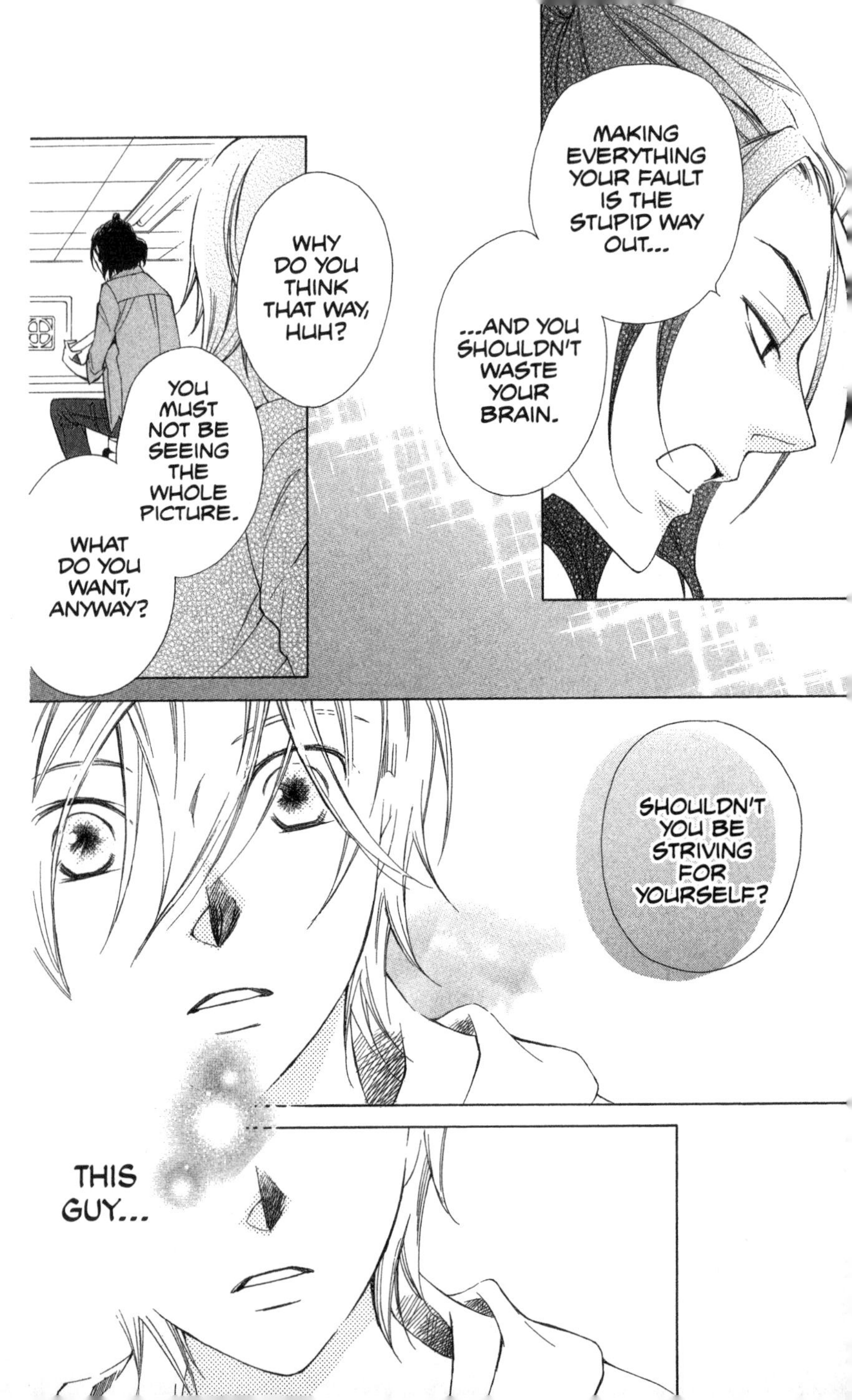
MAKING EVERYTHING YOUR FAULT IS THE STUPID WAY OUT...
...AND YOU SHOULDN'T WASTE YOUR BRAIN.
WHY DO YOU THINK THAT WAY, HUH?
YOU MUST NOT BE SEEING THE WHOLE PICTURE.
WHAT DO YOU WANT, ANYWAY?
SHOULDN'T YOU BE STRIVING FOR YOURSELF?
THIS GUY...

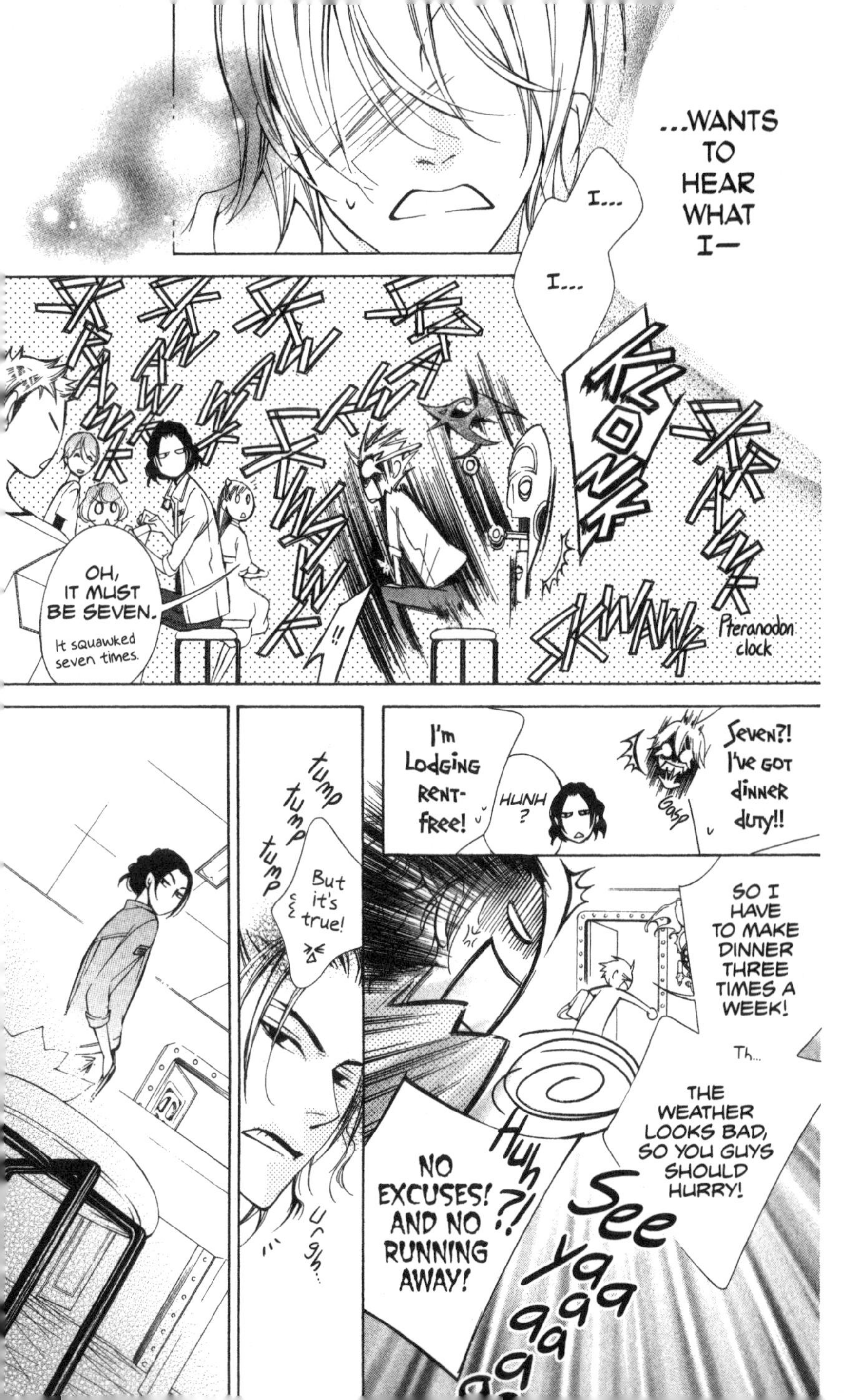
...WANTS TO HEAR WHAT I—
I...
I...
KLONK
SKRAWK
Pteranodon clock
SKWAWK
SKWAWK
SKWAWK
SKWAWK
SKRAWK
OH, IT MUST BE SEVEN.
It squawked seven times.
Seven?! I've got dinner duty!!
Gasp
HUNH?
I'm lodging rent-free!
SO I HAVE TO MAKE DINNER THREE TIMES A WEEK!
Th...
THE WEATHER LOOKS BAD, SO YOU GUYS SHOULD HURRY!
See yaaaaa
Huh?!
NO EXCUSES! AND NO RUNNING AWAY!
tump tump tump
But it's true!
Urgh...

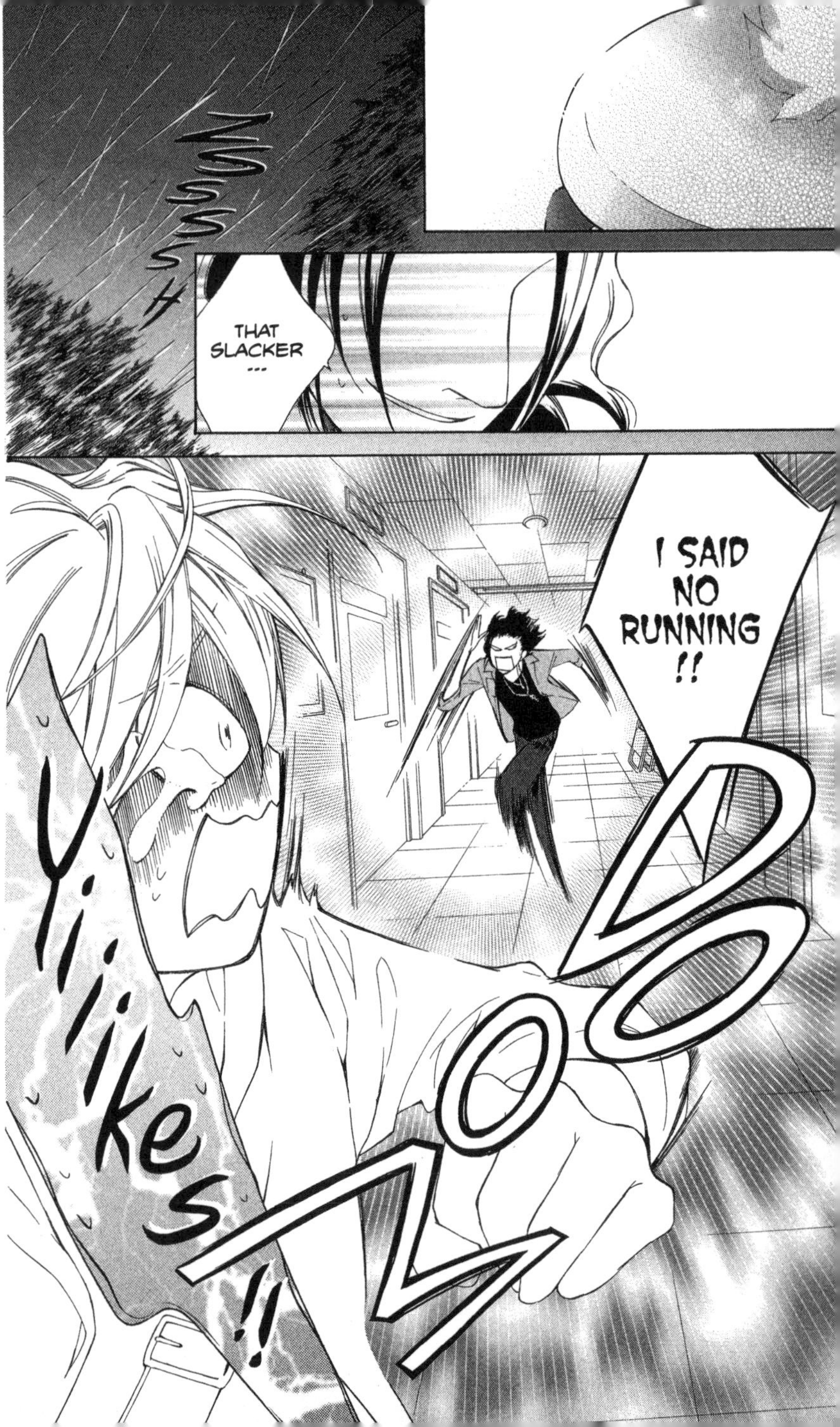
WHOOSH
THAT SLACKER ...
I SAID NO RUNNING !!
ZOOM
Yiiikes !!

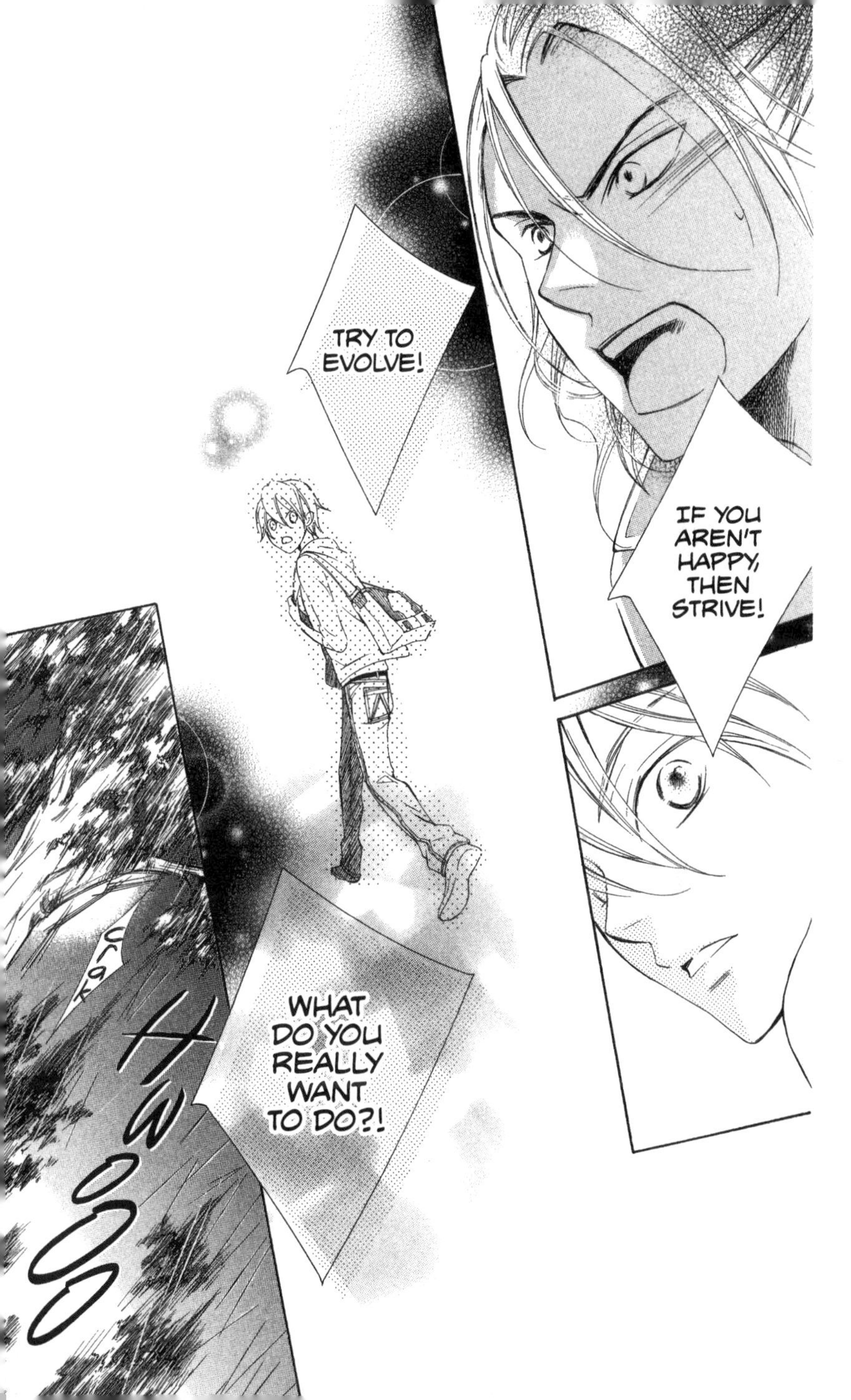
IF YOU AREN'T HAPPY, THEN STRIVE!
TRY TO EVOLVE!
WHAT DO YOU REALLY WANT TO DO?!
crak

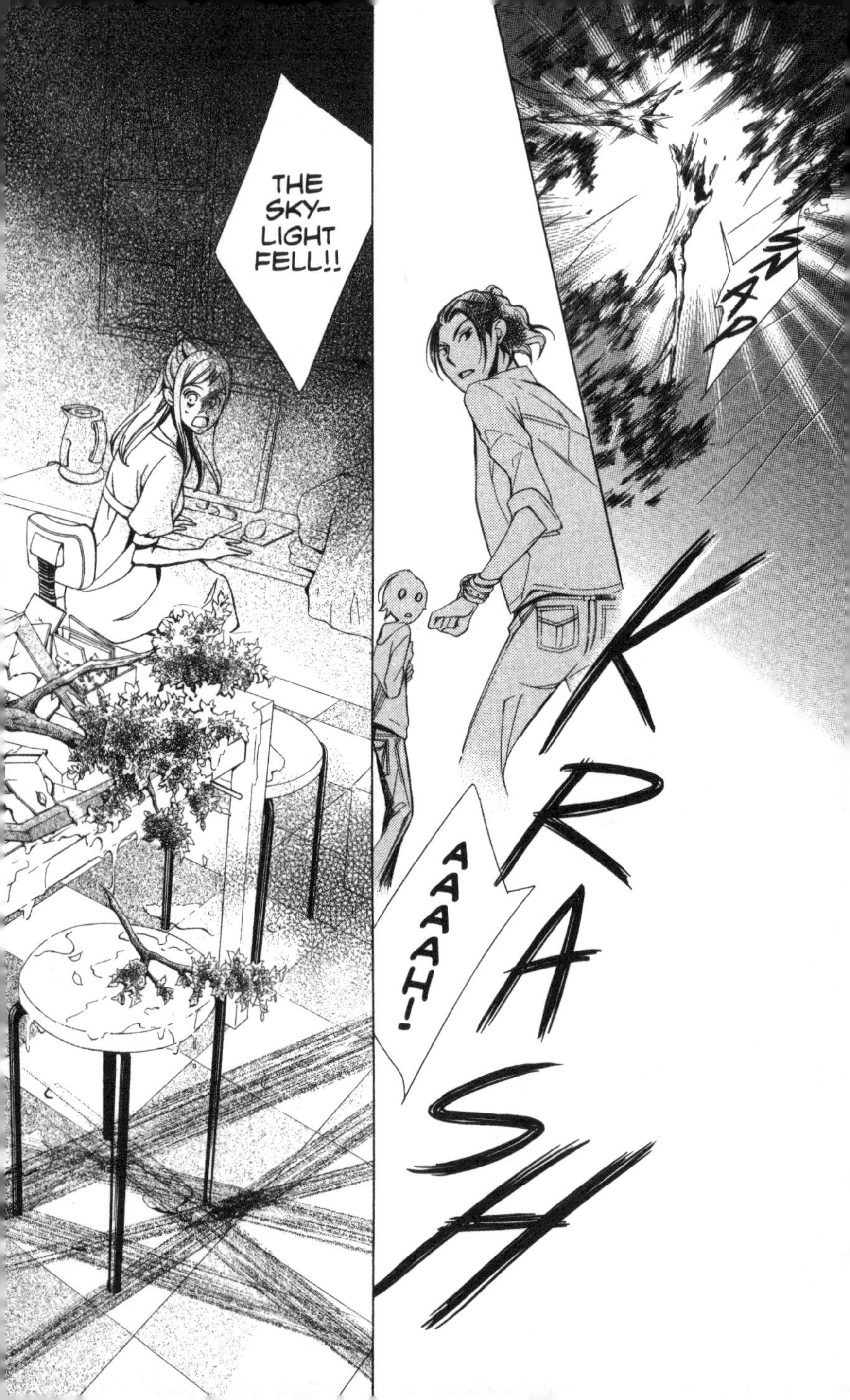
SNAP
KRASH
AAAAH!
THE SKY-LIGHT FELL!!

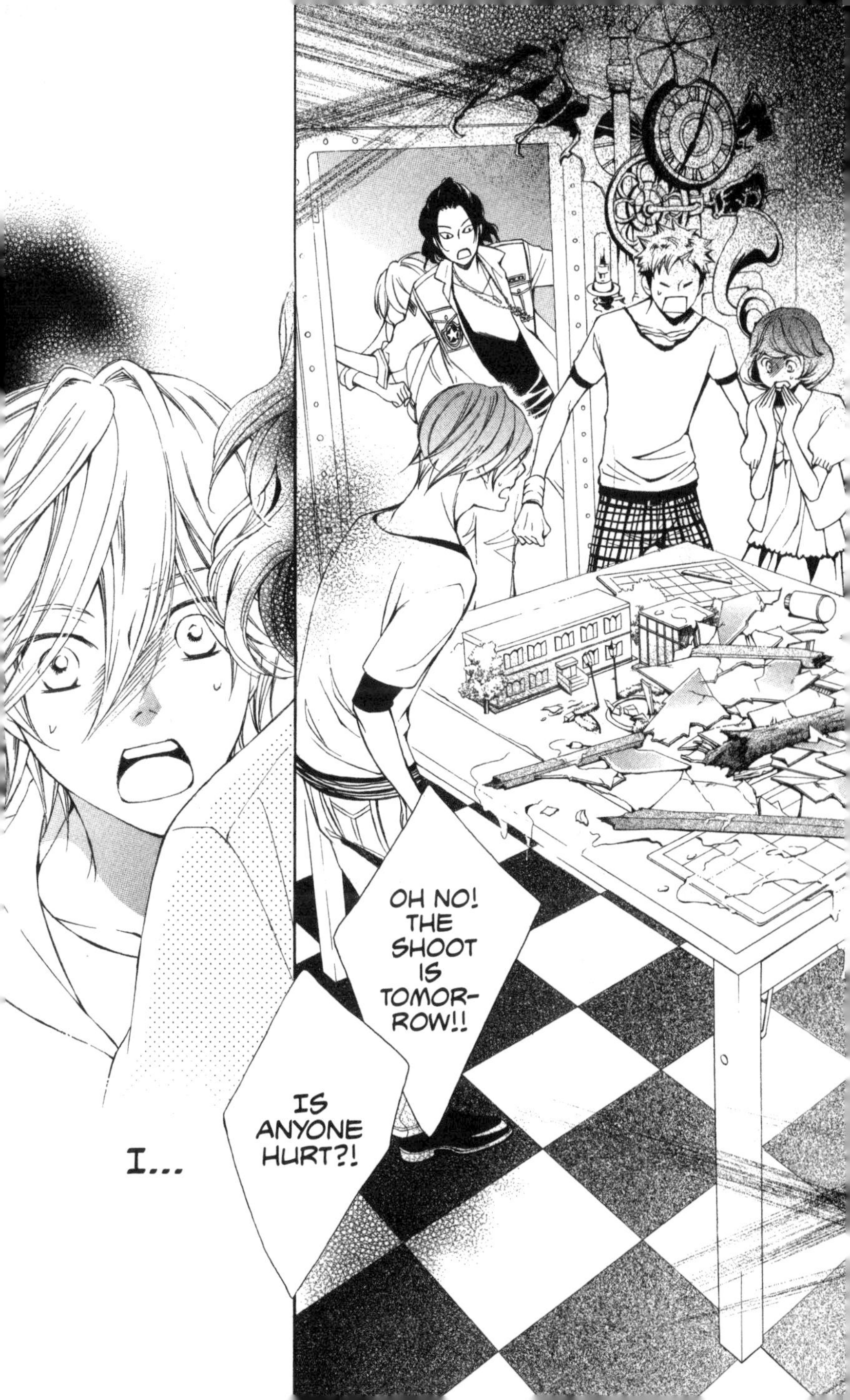
OH NO! THE SHOOT IS TOMORROW!!
IS ANYONE HURT?!
I...

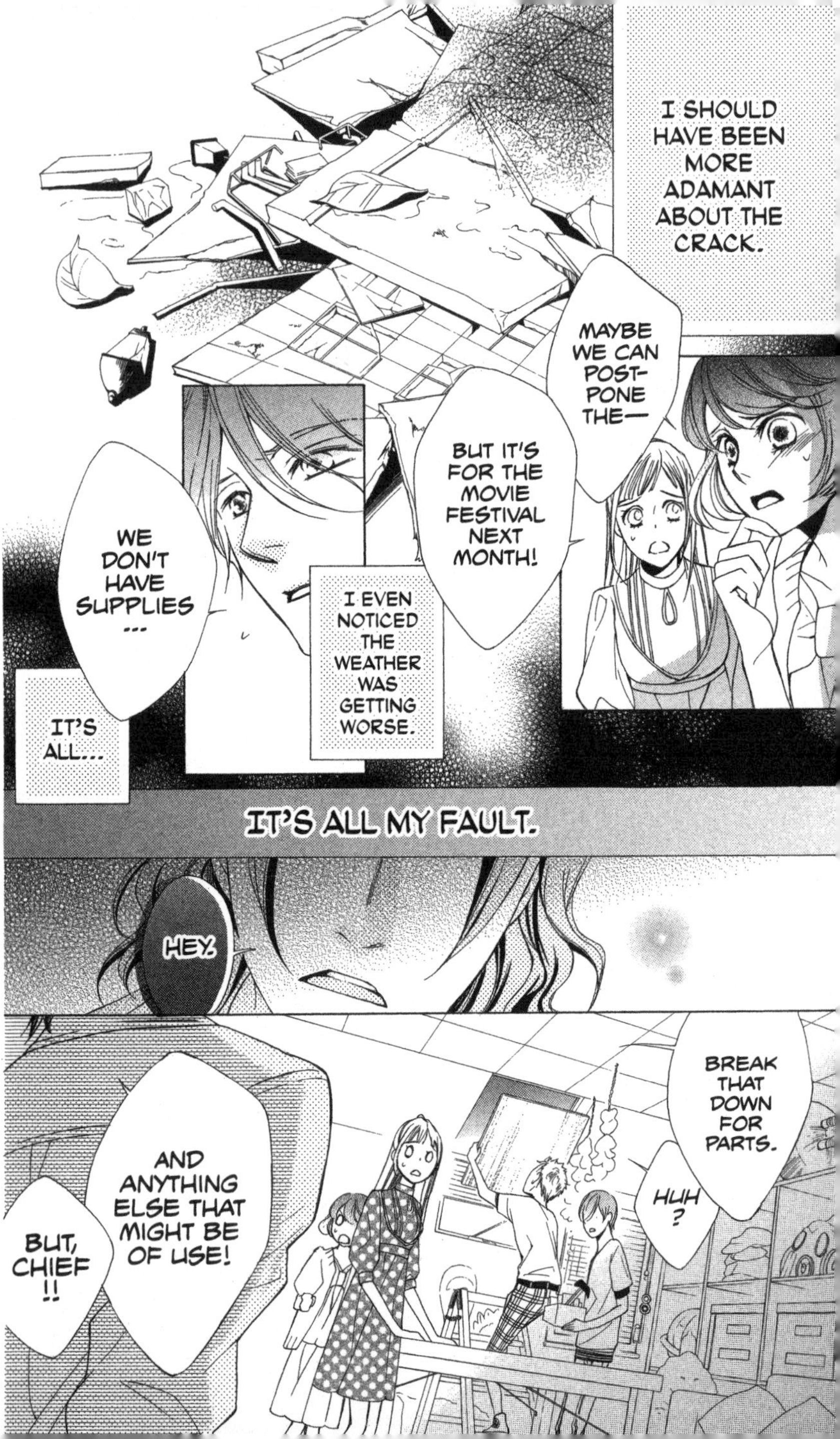
I SHOULD HAVE BEEN MORE ADAMANT ABOUT THE CRACK.
MAYBE WE CAN POST-PONE THE—
BUT IT'S FOR THE MOVIE FESTIVAL NEXT MONTH!
I EVEN NOTICED THE WEATHER WAS GETTING WORSE.
WE DON'T HAVE SUPPLIES...
IT'S ALL...
IT'S ALL MY FAULT.
HEY.
BREAK THAT DOWN FOR PARTS.
HUH?
AND ANYTHING ELSE THAT MIGHT BE OF USE!
BUT, CHIEF!!

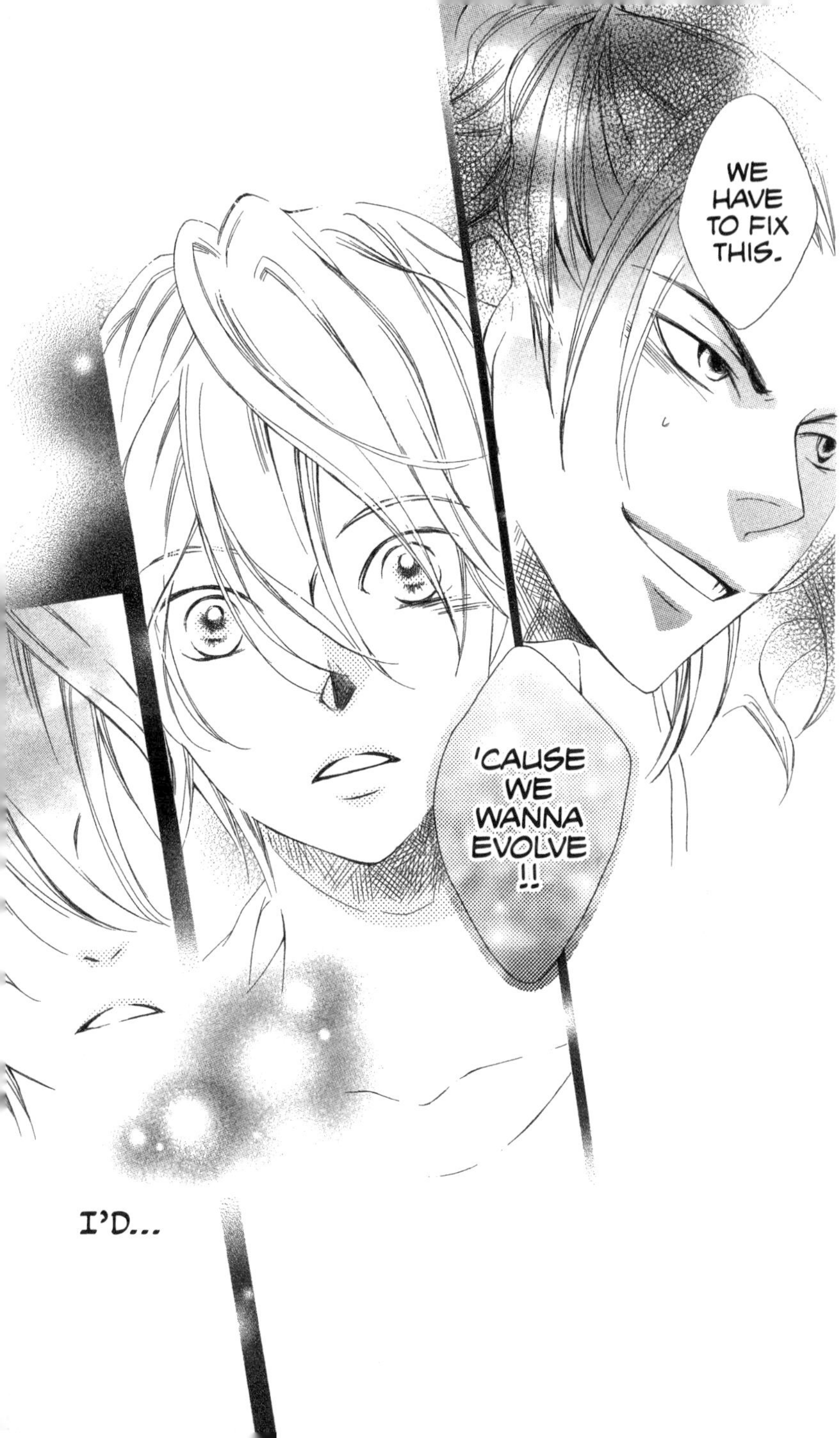
WE HAVE TO FIX THIS.
'CAUSE WE WANNA EVOLVE!!
I'D...

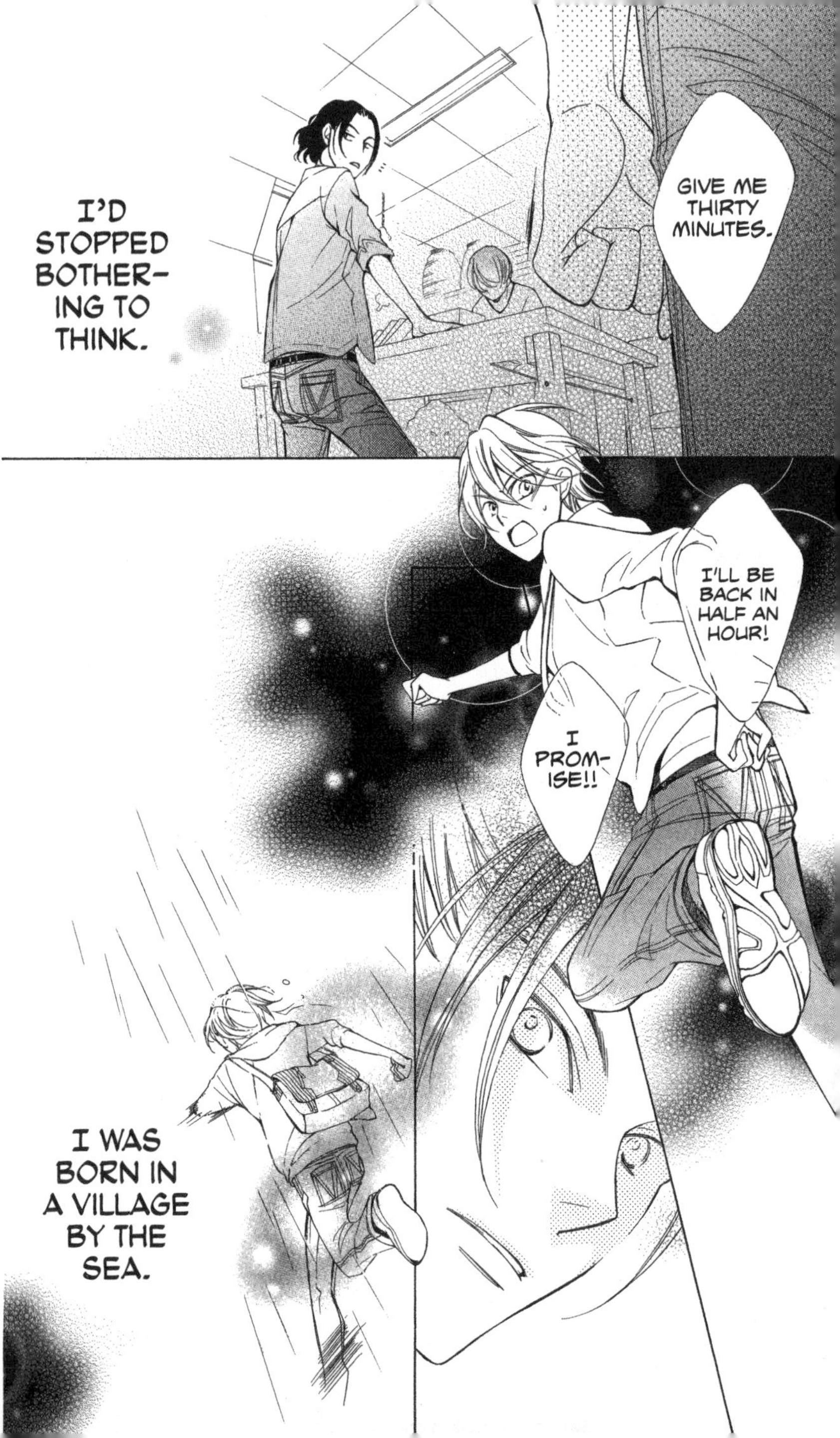
GIVE ME THIRTY MINUTES.
I'D STOPPED BOTHERING TO THINK.
I'LL BE BACK IN HALF AN HOUR!
I PROMISE!!
I WAS BORN IN A VILLAGE BY THE SEA.

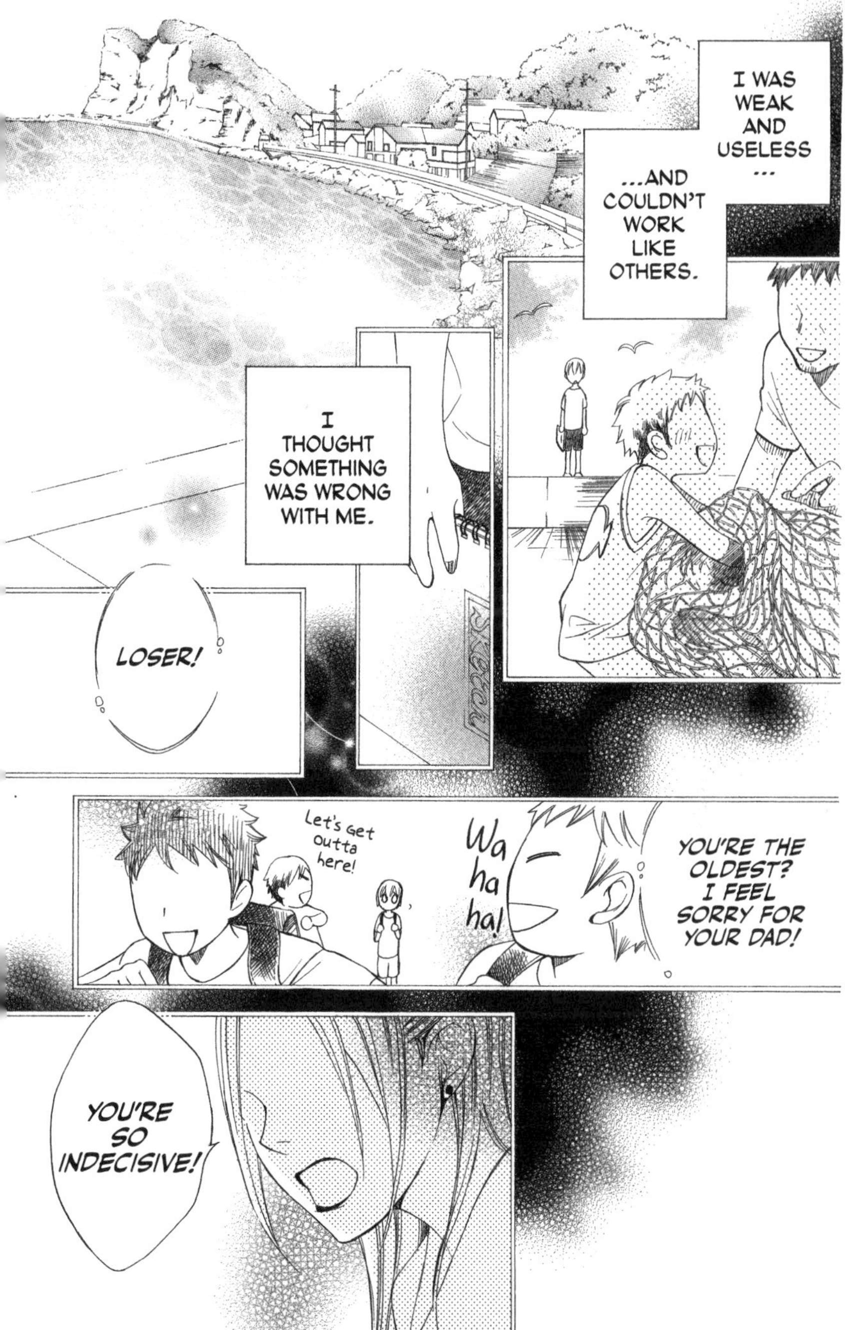
I WAS WEAK AND USELESS...
...AND COULDN'T WORK LIKE OTHERS.
I THOUGHT SOMETHING WAS WRONG WITH ME.
LOSER!
YOU'RE THE OLDEST? I FEEL SORRY FOR YOUR DAD!
Wa ha ha!
Let's get outta here!
YOU'RE SO INDECISIVE!

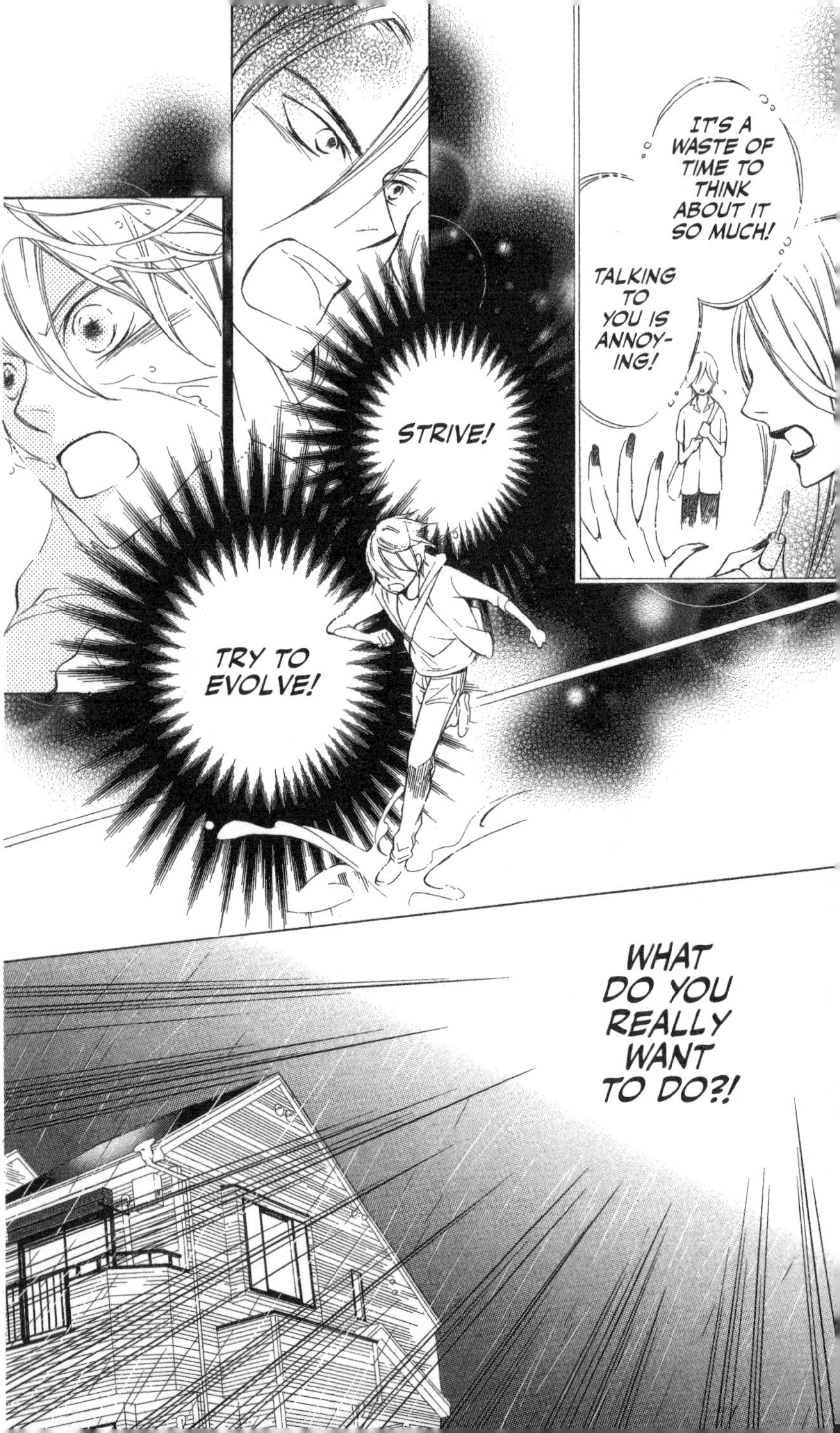
IT'S A WASTE OF TIME TO THINK ABOUT IT SO MUCH!
TALKING TO YOU IS ANNOY-ING!
STRIVE!
TRY TO EVOLVE!
WHAT DO YOU REALLY WANT TO DO?!

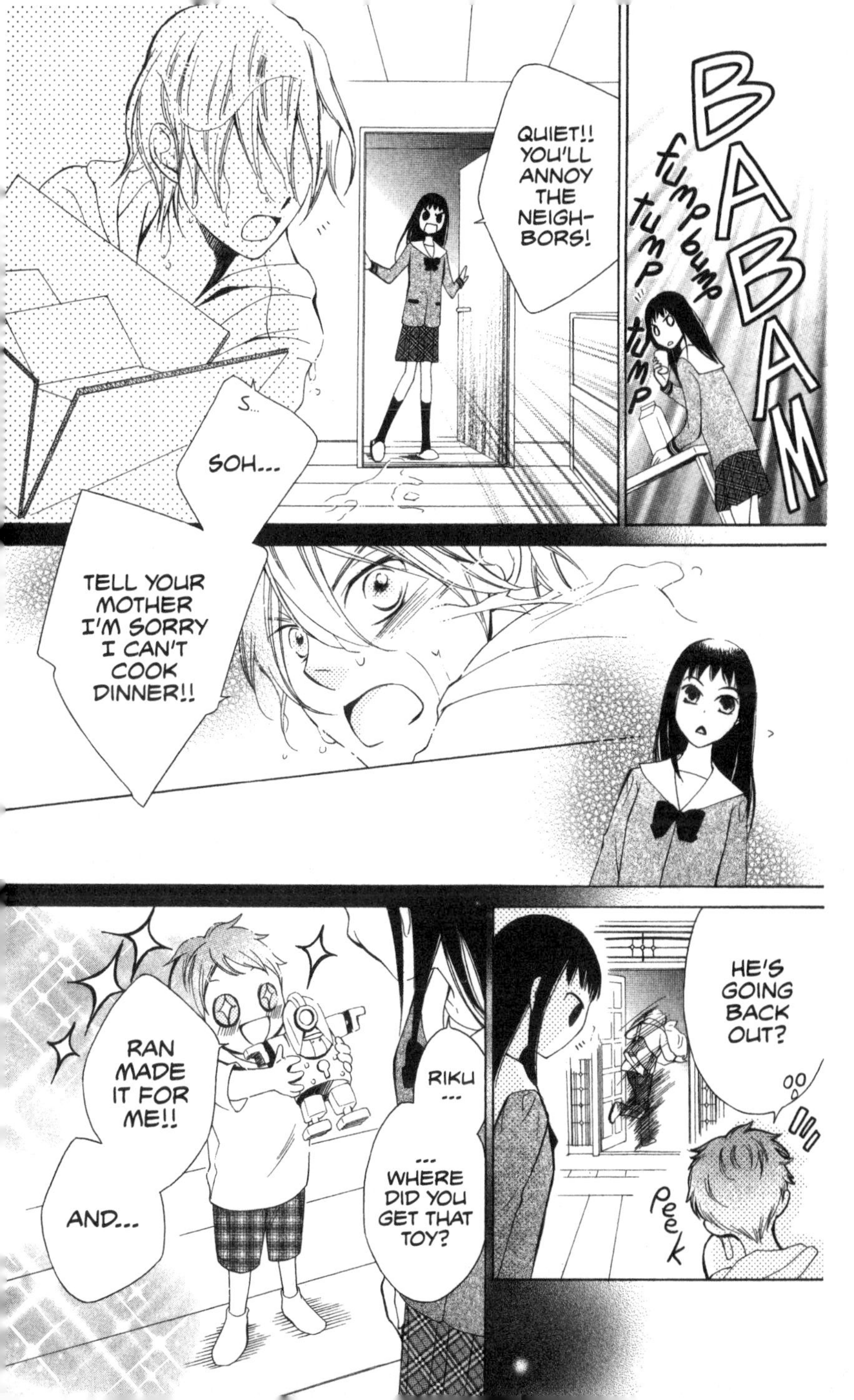
BABAM
fump bump
tump
tump
QUIET!! YOU'LL ANNOY THE NEIGHBORS!
S...
SOH...
TELL YOUR MOTHER I'M SORRY I CAN'T COOK DINNER!!
HE'S GOING BACK OUT?
Peek
RIKU ...
... WHERE DID YOU GET THAT TOY?
RAN MADE IT FOR ME!!
AND...

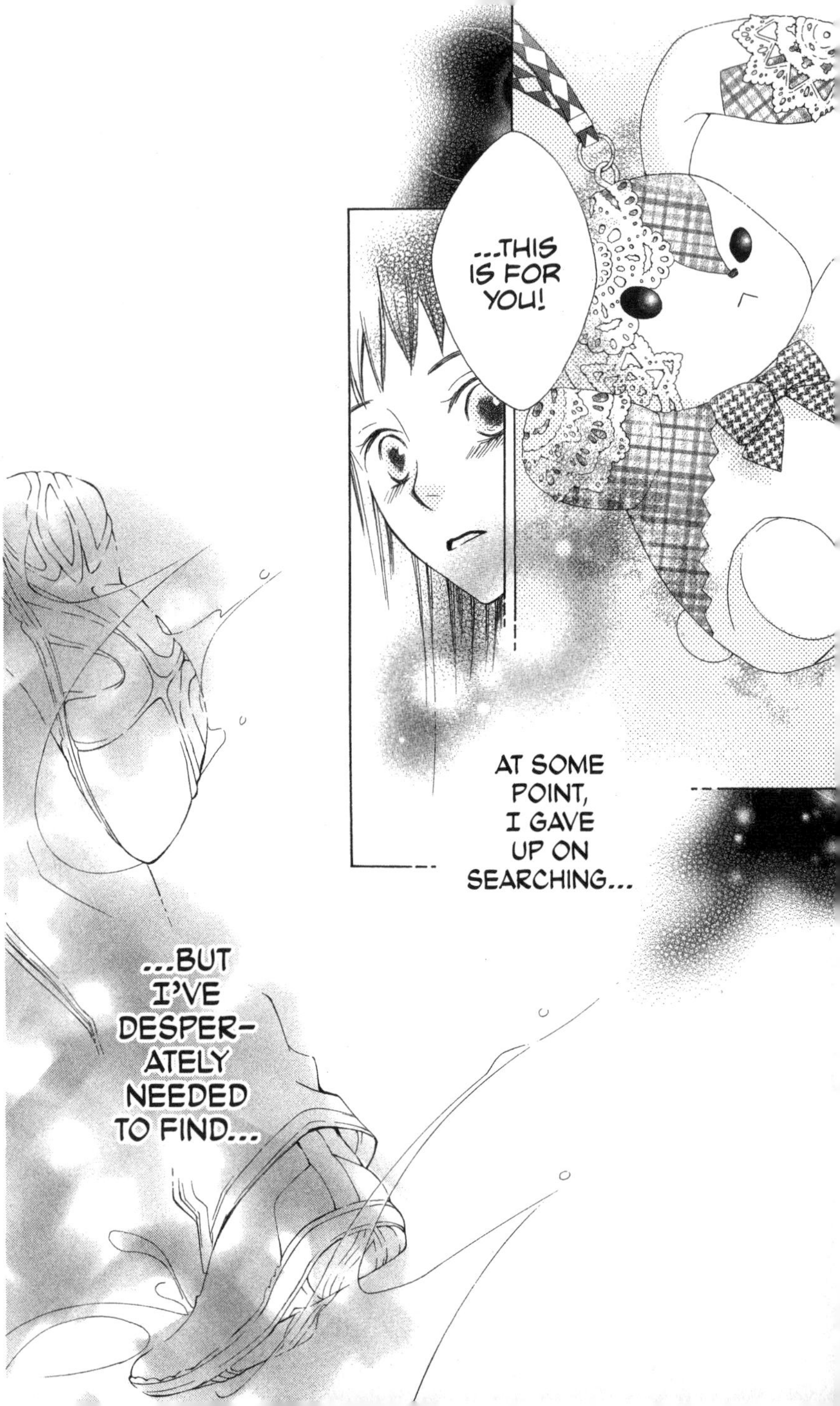
...THIS IS FOR YOU!
AT SOME POINT, I GAVE UP ON SEARCHING...
...BUT I'VE DESPER-ATELY NEEDED TO FIND...

...A
PLACE
TO
BELONG.

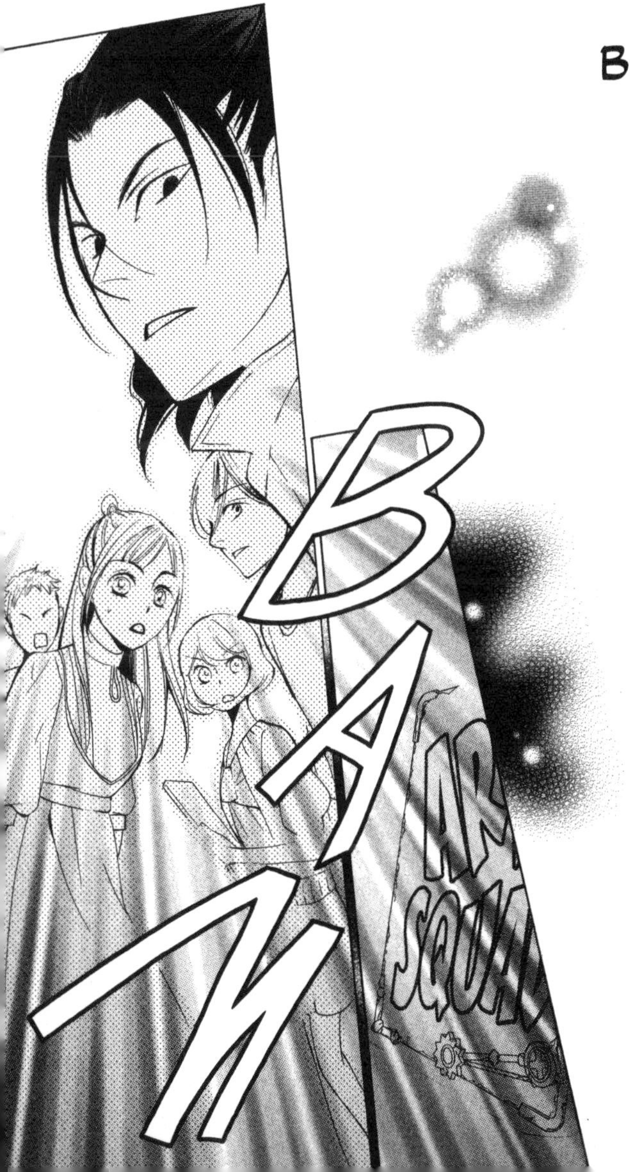
BAM

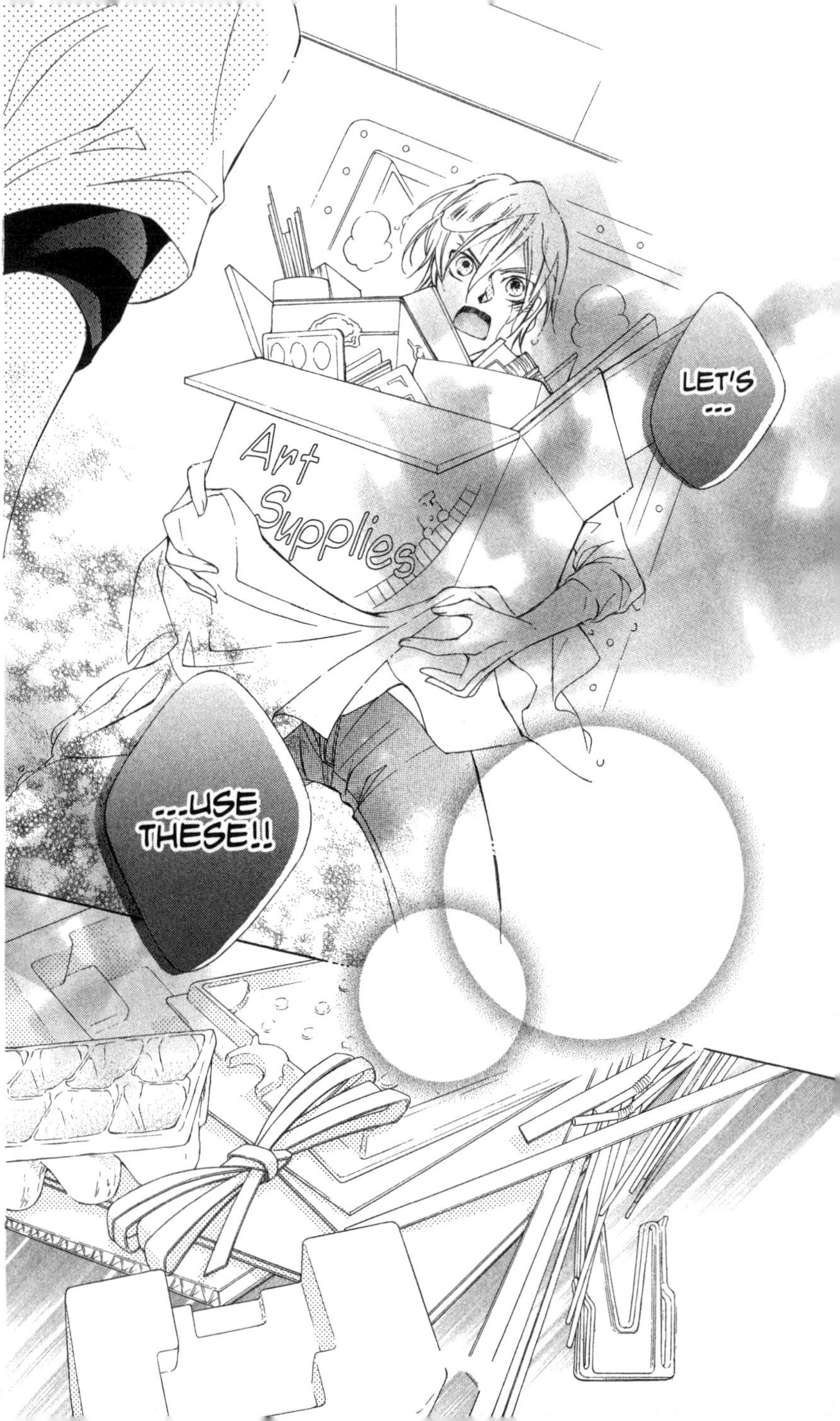
LET'S...
Art Supplies
...USE THESE!!

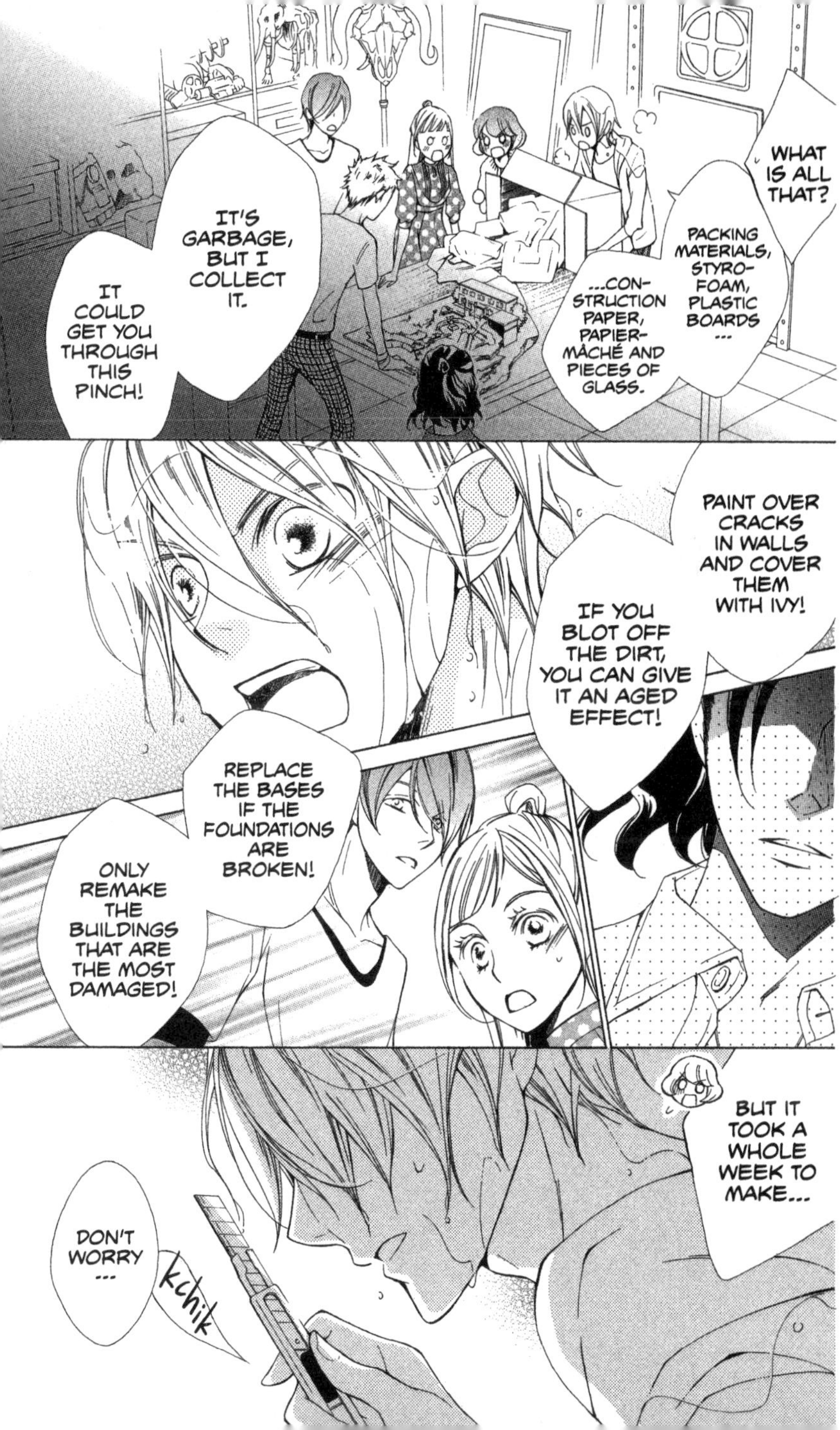
WHAT IS ALL THAT?
PACKING MATERIALS, STYRO-FOAM, PLASTIC BOARDS...
...CON-STRUCTION PAPER, PAPIER-MÂCHÉ AND PIECES OF GLASS.
IT'S GARBAGE, BUT I COLLECT IT.
IT COULD GET YOU THROUGH THIS PINCH!
PAINT OVER CRACKS IN WALLS AND COVER THEM WITH IVY!
IF YOU BLOT OFF THE DIRT, YOU CAN GIVE IT AN AGED EFFECT!
REPLACE THE BASES IF THE FOUNDATIONS ARE BROKEN!
ONLY REMAKE THE BUILDINGS THAT ARE THE MOST DAMAGED!
BUT IT TOOK A WHOLE WEEK TO MAKE...
kchik
DON'T WORRY...

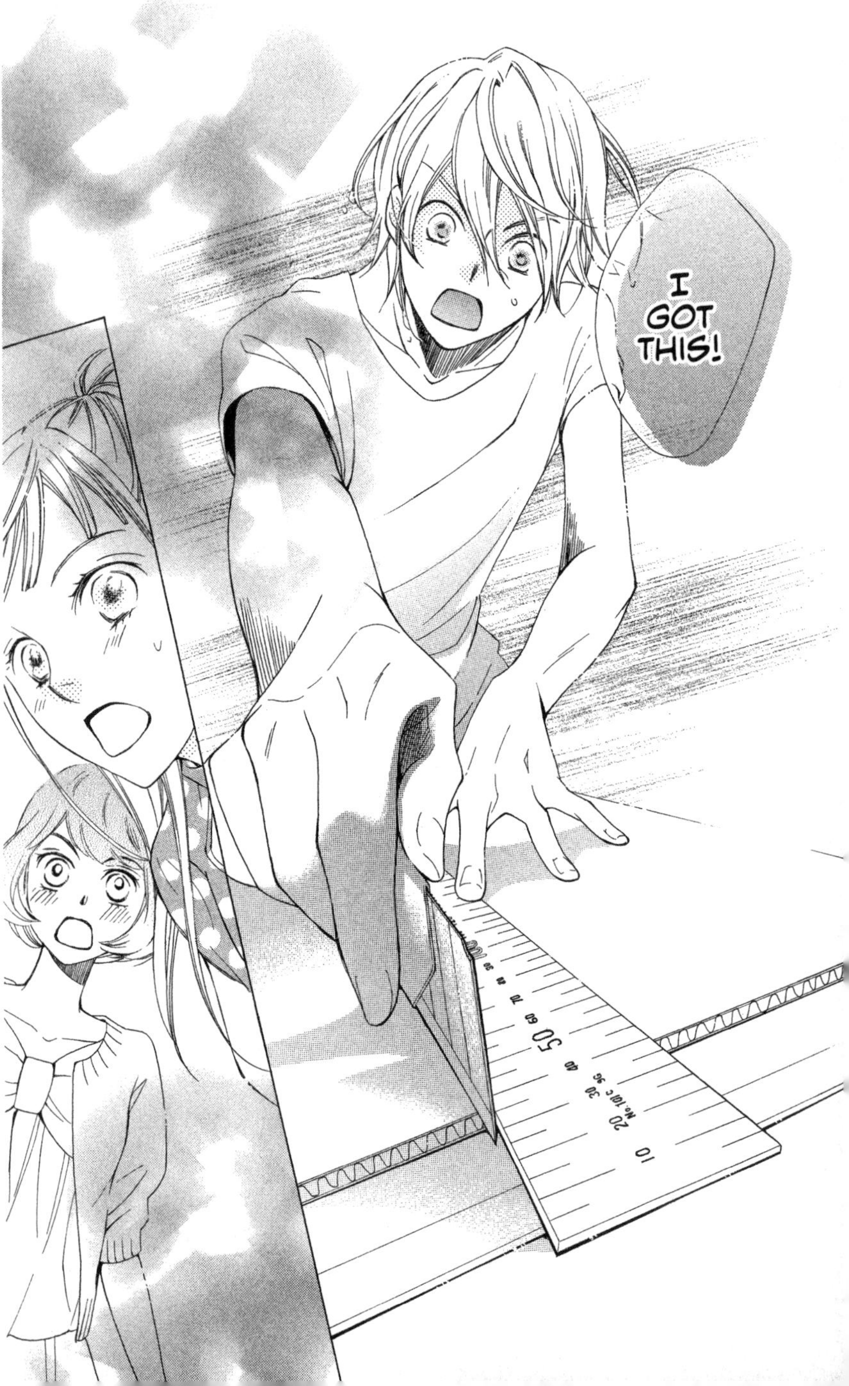
I GOT THIS!

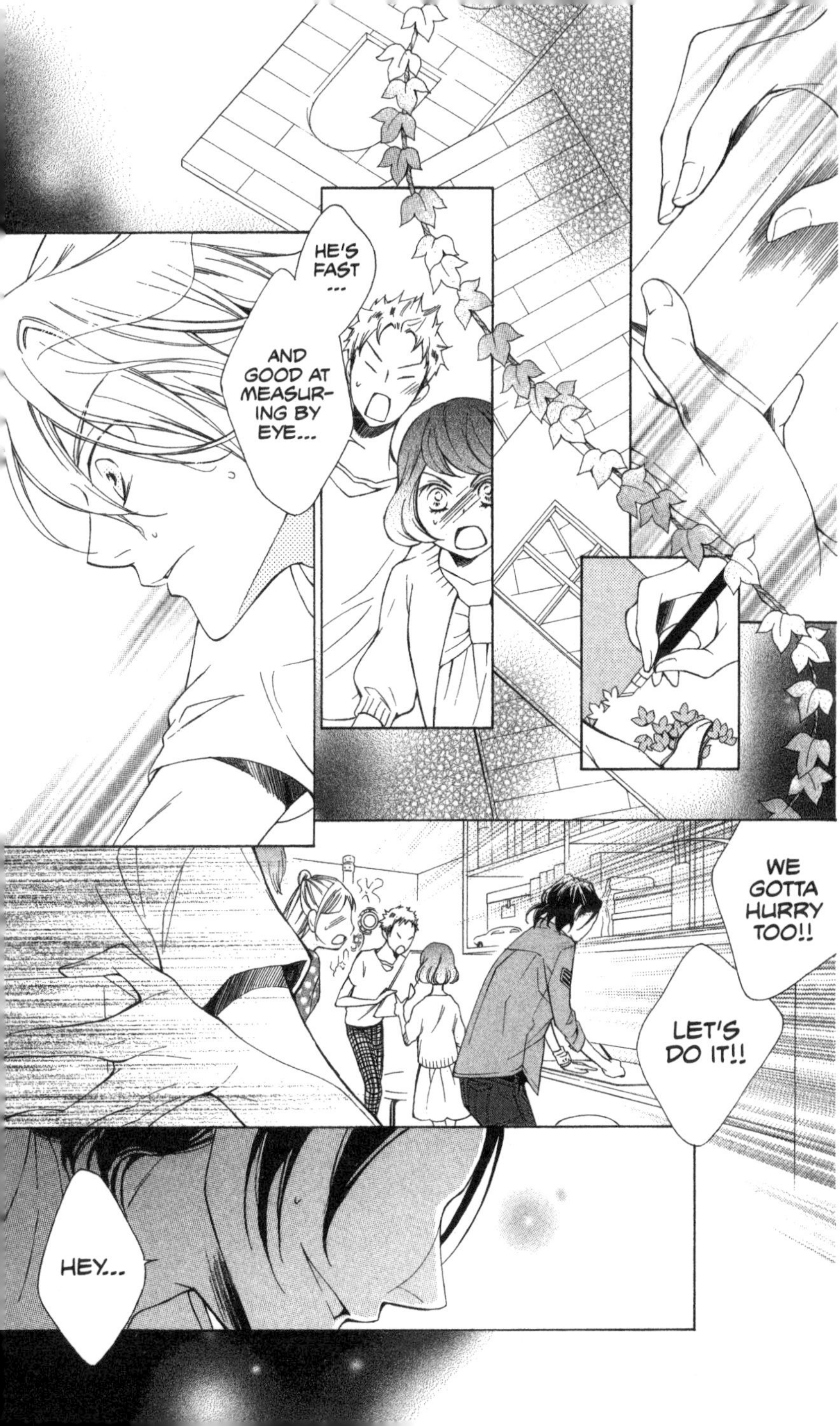
HE'S FAST...
AND GOOD AT MEASURING BY EYE...
WE GOTTA HURRY TOO!!
LET'S DO IT!!
HEY...

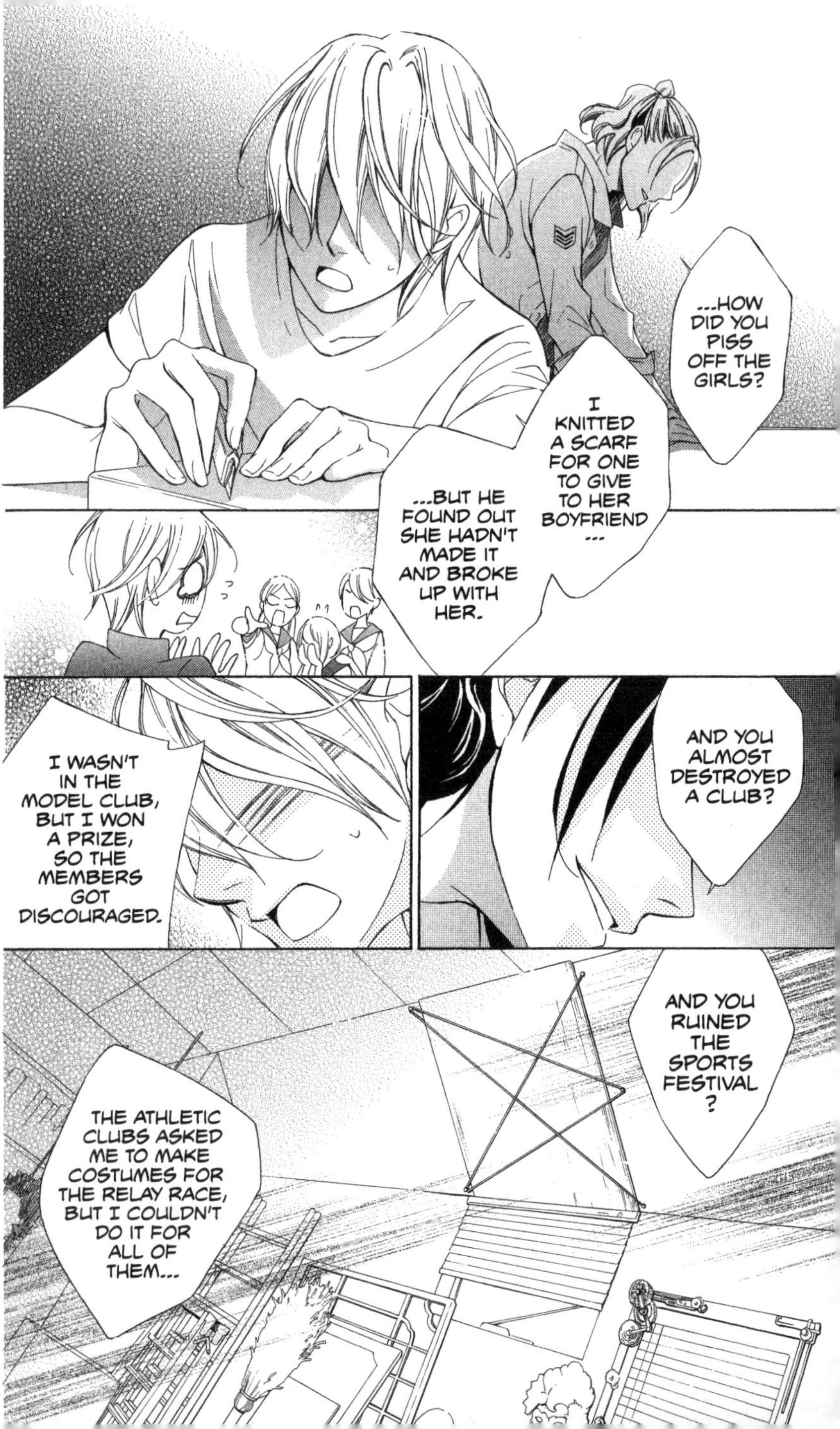
...HOW DID YOU PISS OFF THE GIRLS?
I KNITTED A SCARF FOR ONE TO GIVE TO HER BOYFRIEND...
...BUT HE FOUND OUT SHE HADN'T MADE IT AND BROKE UP WITH HER.
AND YOU ALMOST DESTROYED A CLUB?
I WASN'T IN THE MODEL CLUB, BUT I WON A PRIZE, SO THE MEMBERS GOT DISCOURAGED.
AND YOU RUINED THE SPORTS FESTIVAL?
THE ATHLETIC CLUBS ASKED ME TO MAKE COSTUMES FOR THE RELAY RACE, BUT I COULDN'T DO IT FOR ALL OF THEM...

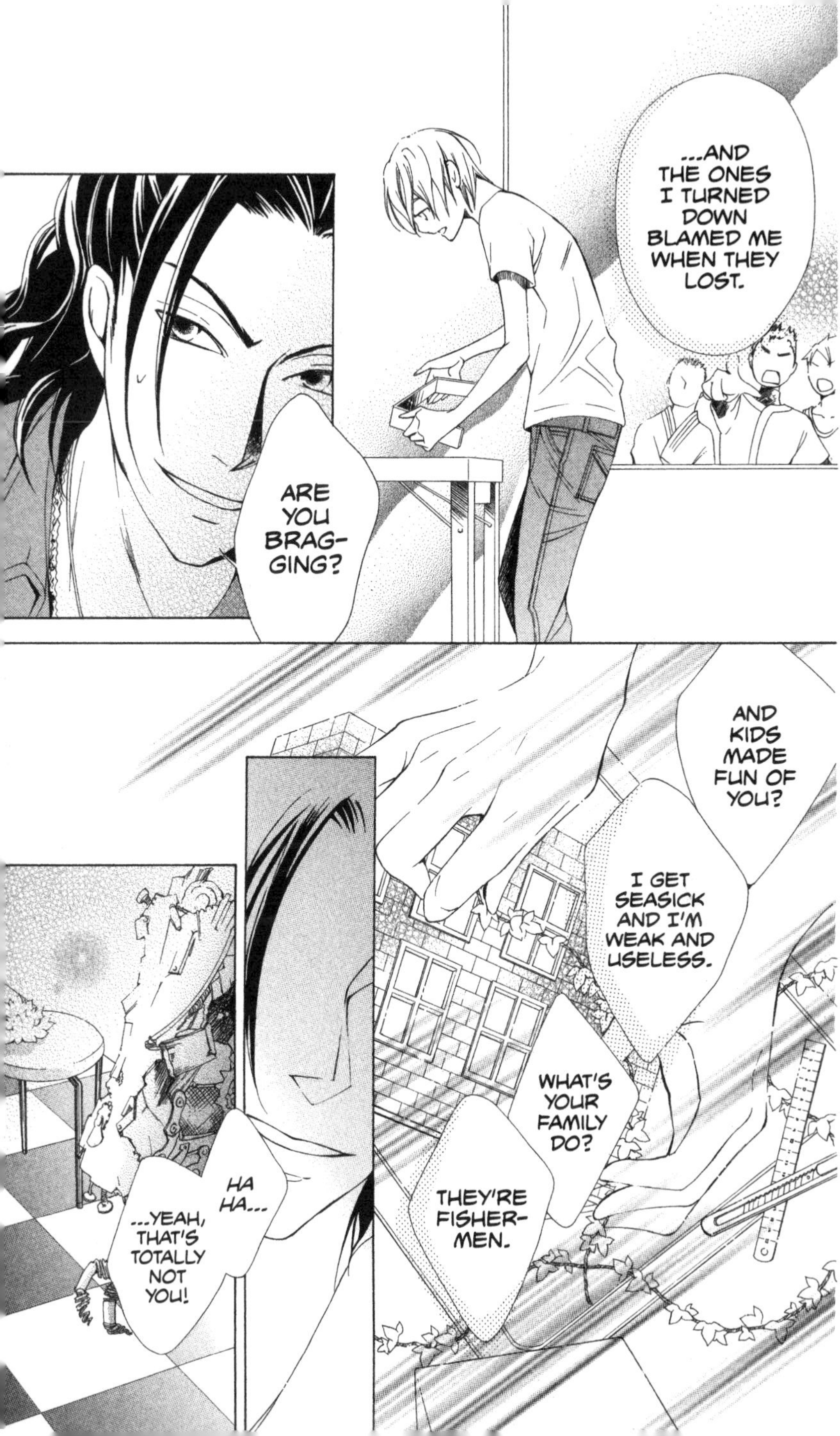
...AND THE ONES I TURNED DOWN BLAMED ME WHEN THEY LOST.
ARE YOU BRAG-GING?
AND KIDS MADE FUN OF YOU?
I GET SEASICK AND I'M WEAK AND USELESS.
WHAT'S YOUR FAMILY DO?
THEY'RE FISHER-MEN.
HA HA...
...YEAH, THAT'S TOTALLY NOT YOU!

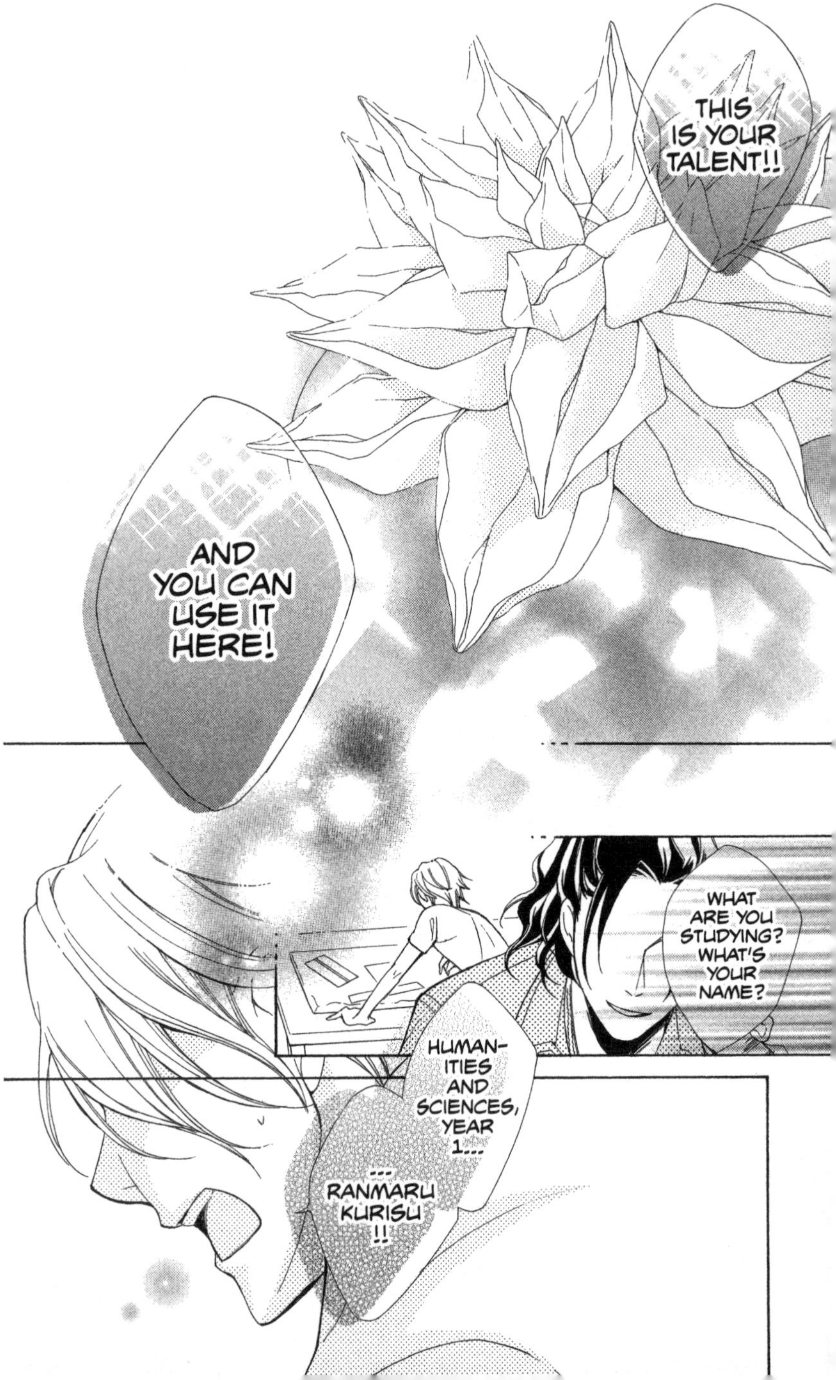
THIS IS YOUR TALENT!!
AND YOU CAN USE IT HERE!
WHAT ARE YOU STUDYING? WHAT'S YOUR NAME?
HUMAN-ITIES AND SCIENCES, YEAR 1...
...RANMARU KURISU!!

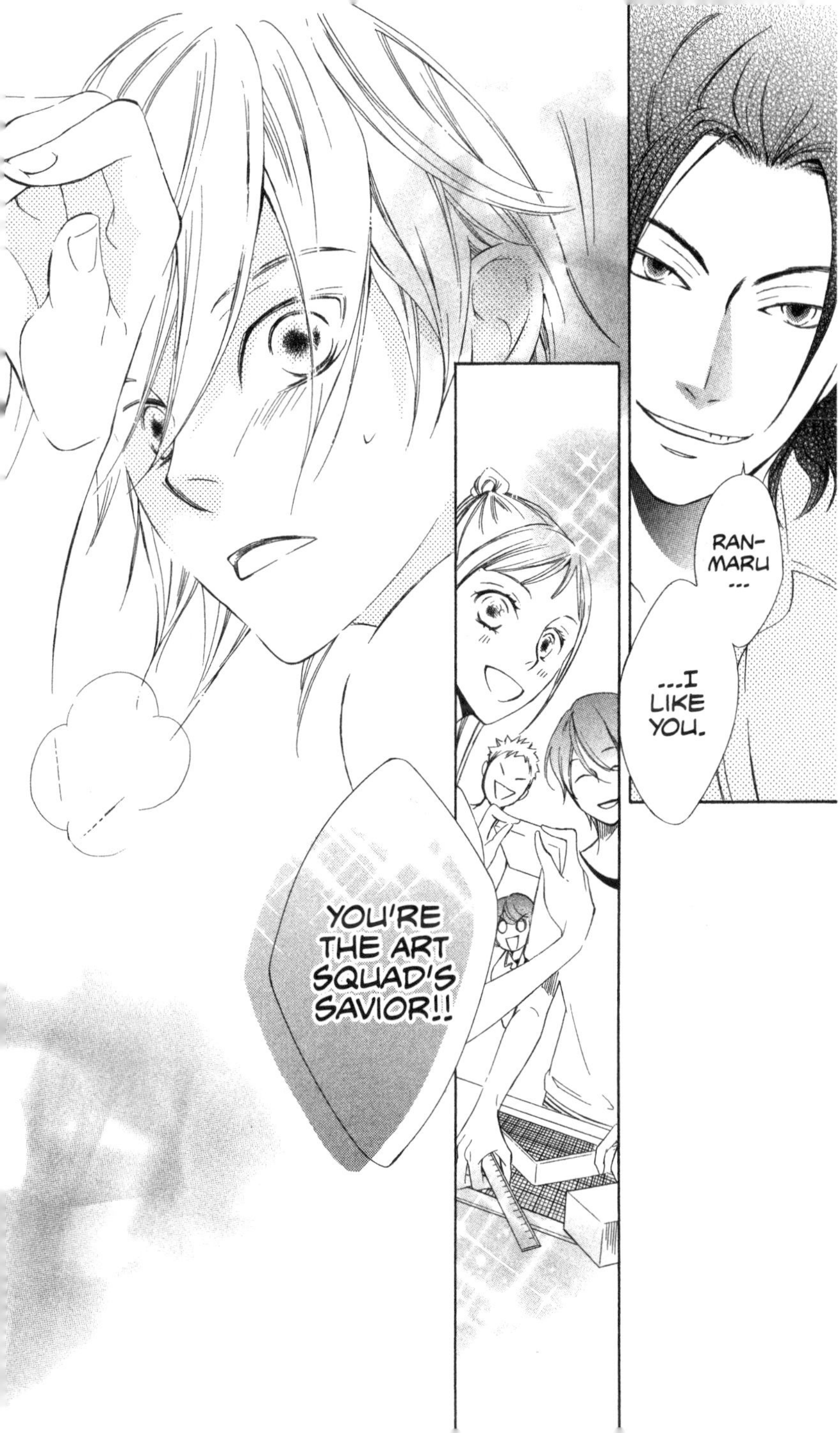
RAN-MARU...
...I LIKE YOU.
YOU'RE THE ART SQUAD'S SAVIOR!!

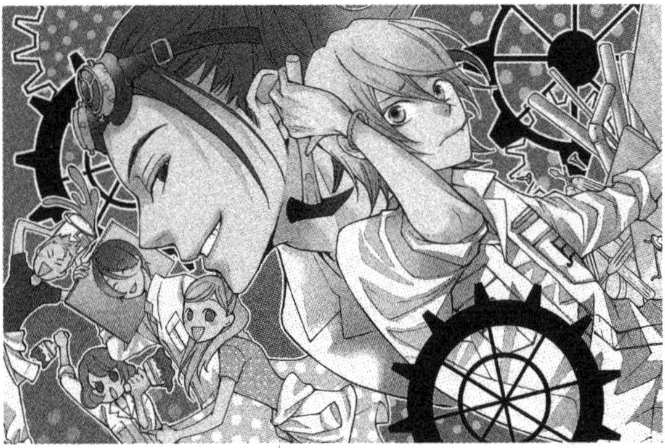

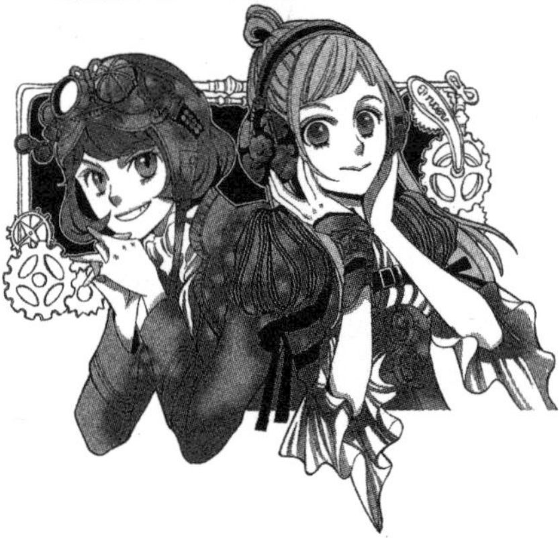

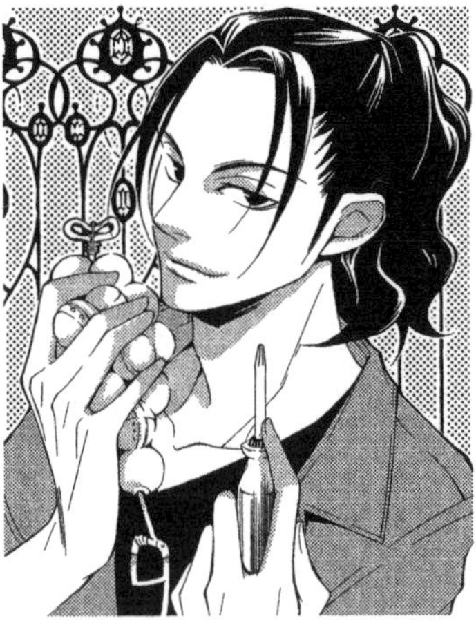

Ads, Illustrations, Etc.

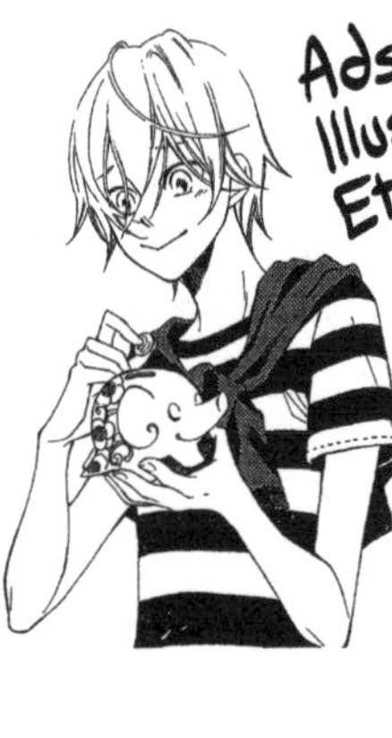

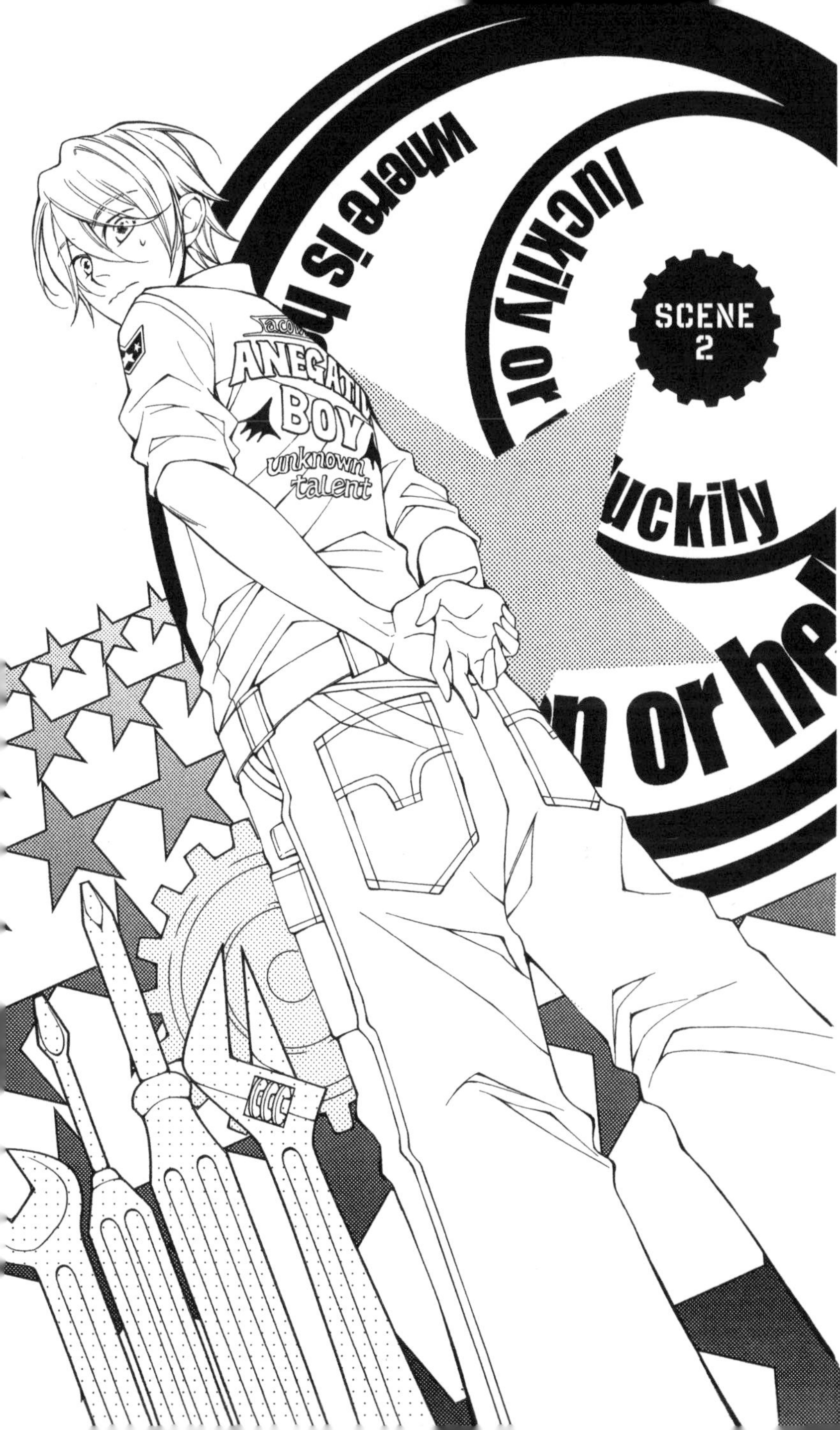
SCENE
2
luckily or
uckily
BOY
unknown
talent

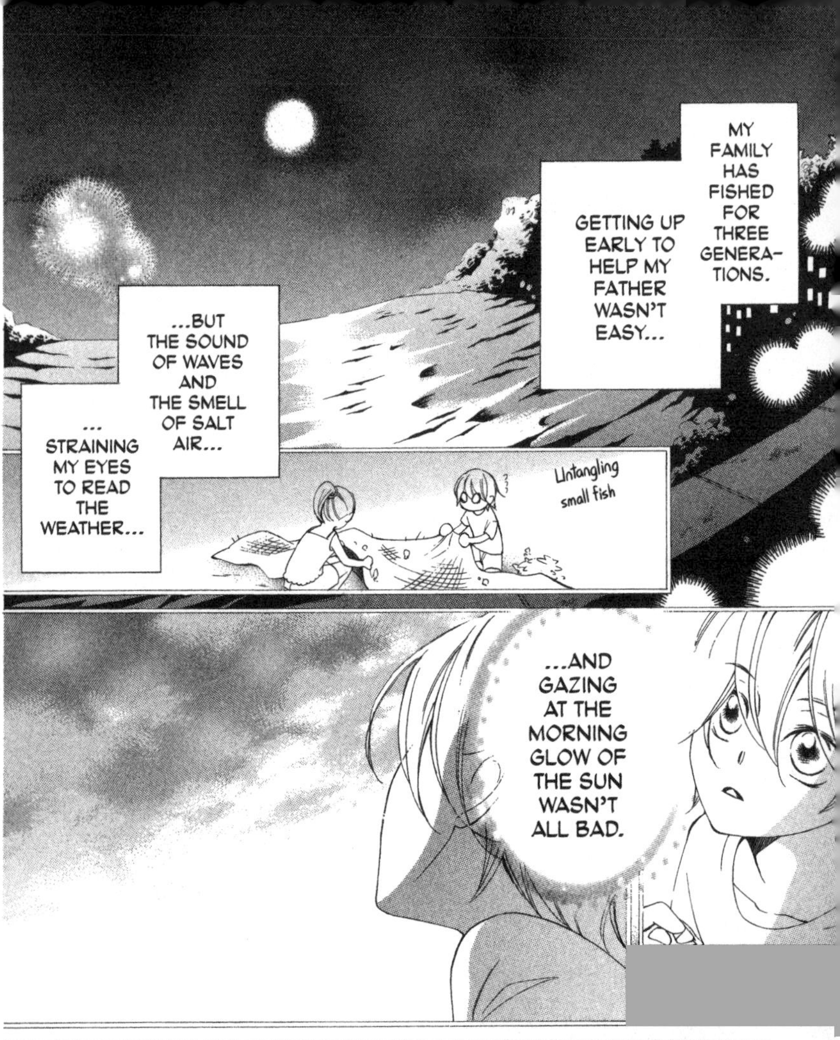
MY FAMILY HAS FISHED FOR THREE GENERATIONS.
GETTING UP EARLY TO HELP MY FATHER WASN'T EASY...
...BUT THE SOUND OF WAVES AND THE SMELL OF SALT AIR...
...STRAINING MY EYES TO READ THE WEATHER...
Untangling small fish
...AND GAZING AT THE MORNING GLOW OF THE SUN WASN'T ALL BAD.

Ruka Enjoji

She often re-creates the costumes she sees in movies to wear herself. In scene 2, her outfit is from *Roman Holiday*. In scene 4, it's from *The Great Gatsby*.

Her name comes from director George Lucas. I love the three original *Star Wars* movies, especially the relationship between Han Solo and Princess Leia as seen from a shojo manga perspective!

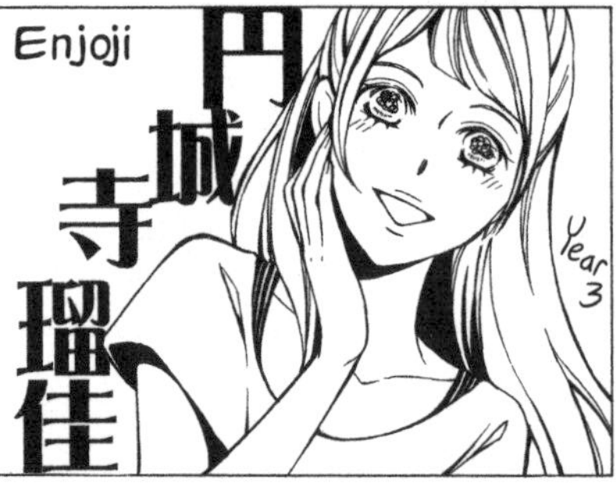
円城寺瑠佳
Year 3

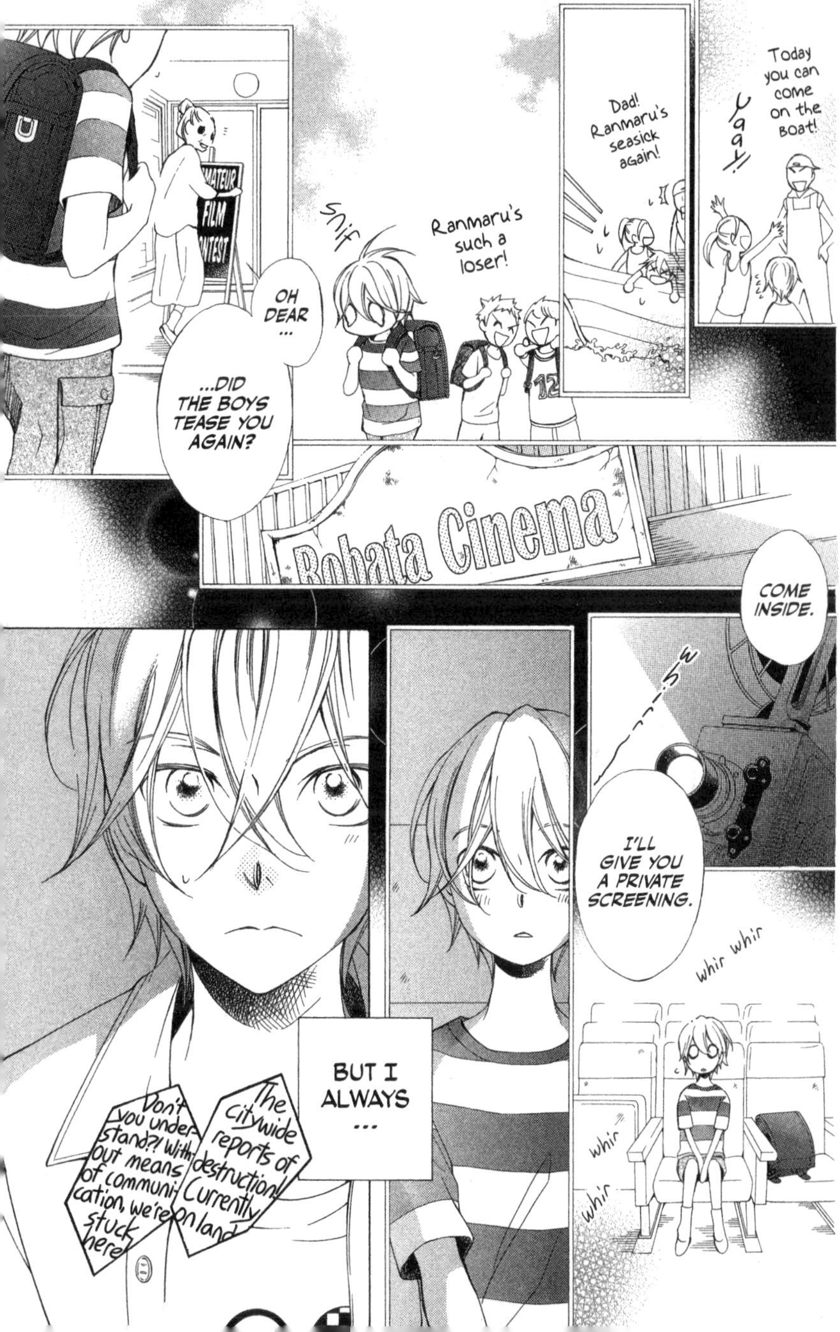
Today you can come on the boat!
Yaay!
Dad! Ranmaru's seasick again!
Ranmaru's such a loser!
Sniff
OH DEAR...
...DID THE BOYS TEASE YOU AGAIN?
AMATEUR FILM CONTEST
Bohata Cinema
COME INSIDE.
Whir...
I'LL GIVE YOU A PRIVATE SCREENING.
whir whir
whir
whir
BUT I ALWAYS...
The citywide reports of destruction! Currently on land
Don't you understand?! Without means of communication, we're stuck here!

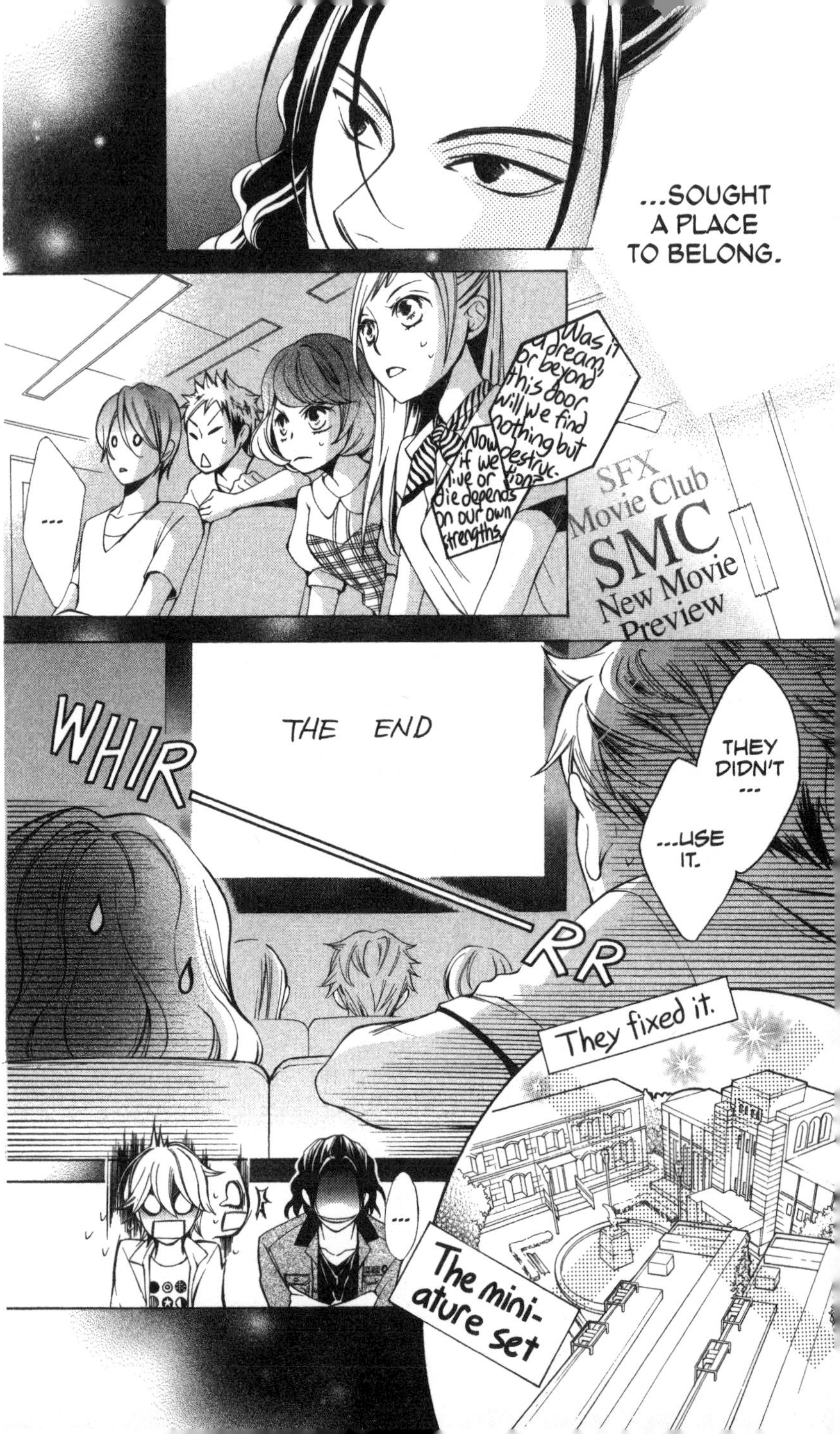
...SOUGHT A PLACE TO BELONG.
Was it a dream, or beyond this door will we find nothing but destruction?
Now if we live or die depends on our own strengths.
SFX Movie Club SMC New Movie Preview
...
THEY DIDN'T ...
...USE IT.
THE END
WHIRRR
They fixed it.
The miniature set
...

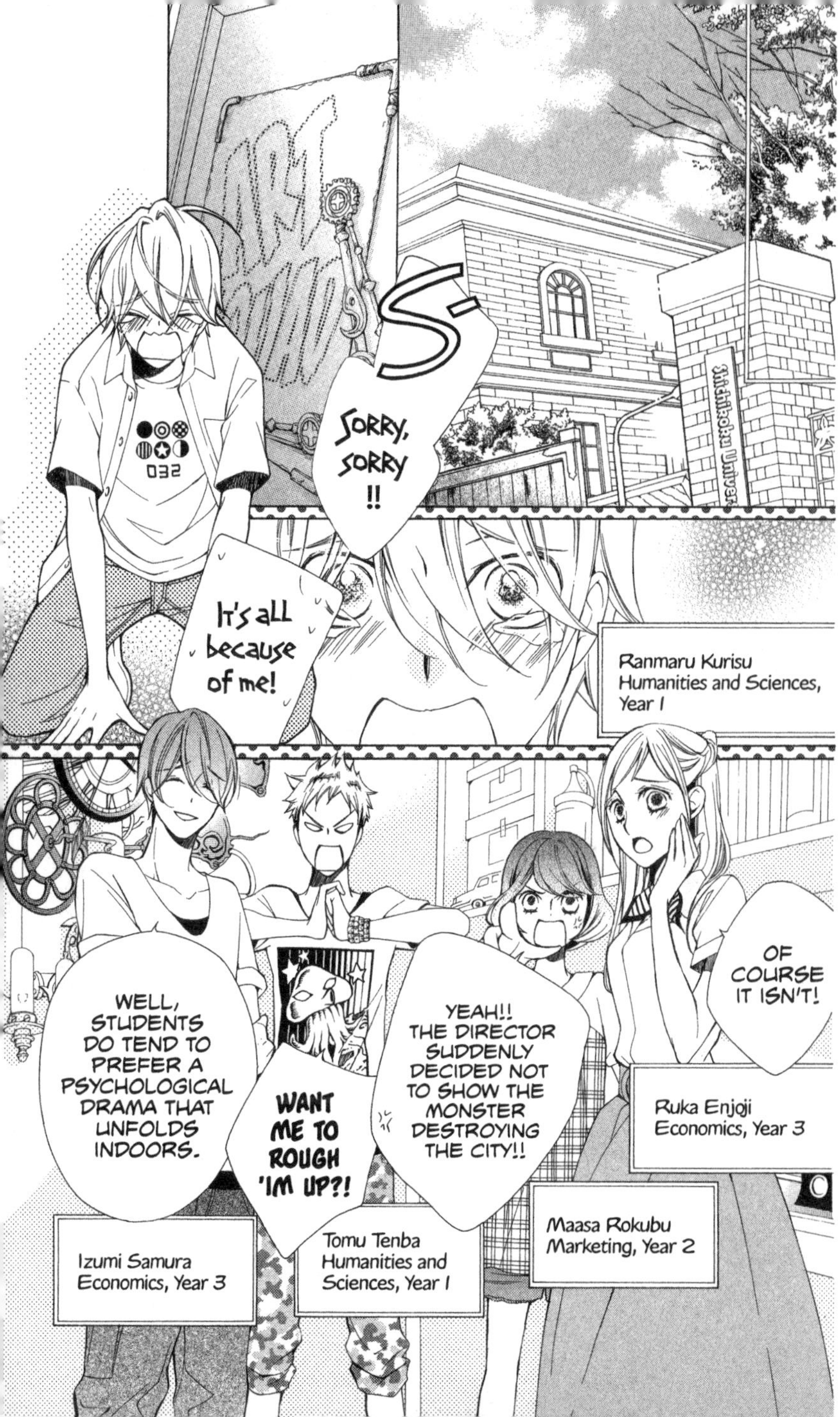
S-
SORRY, SORRY !!
Ranmaru Kurisu Humanities and Sciences, Year 1
It's all because of me!
OF COURSE IT ISN'T!
Ruka Enjoji Economics, Year 3
Maasa Rokubu Marketing, Year 2
YEAH!! THE DIRECTOR SUDDENLY DECIDED NOT TO SHOW THE MONSTER DESTROYING THE CITY!!
Tomu Tenba Humanities and Sciences, Year 1
WANT ME TO ROUGH 'IM UP?!
WELL, STUDENTS DO TEND TO PREFER A PSYCHOLOGICAL DRAMA THAT UNFOLDS INDOORS.
Izumi Samura Economics, Year 3

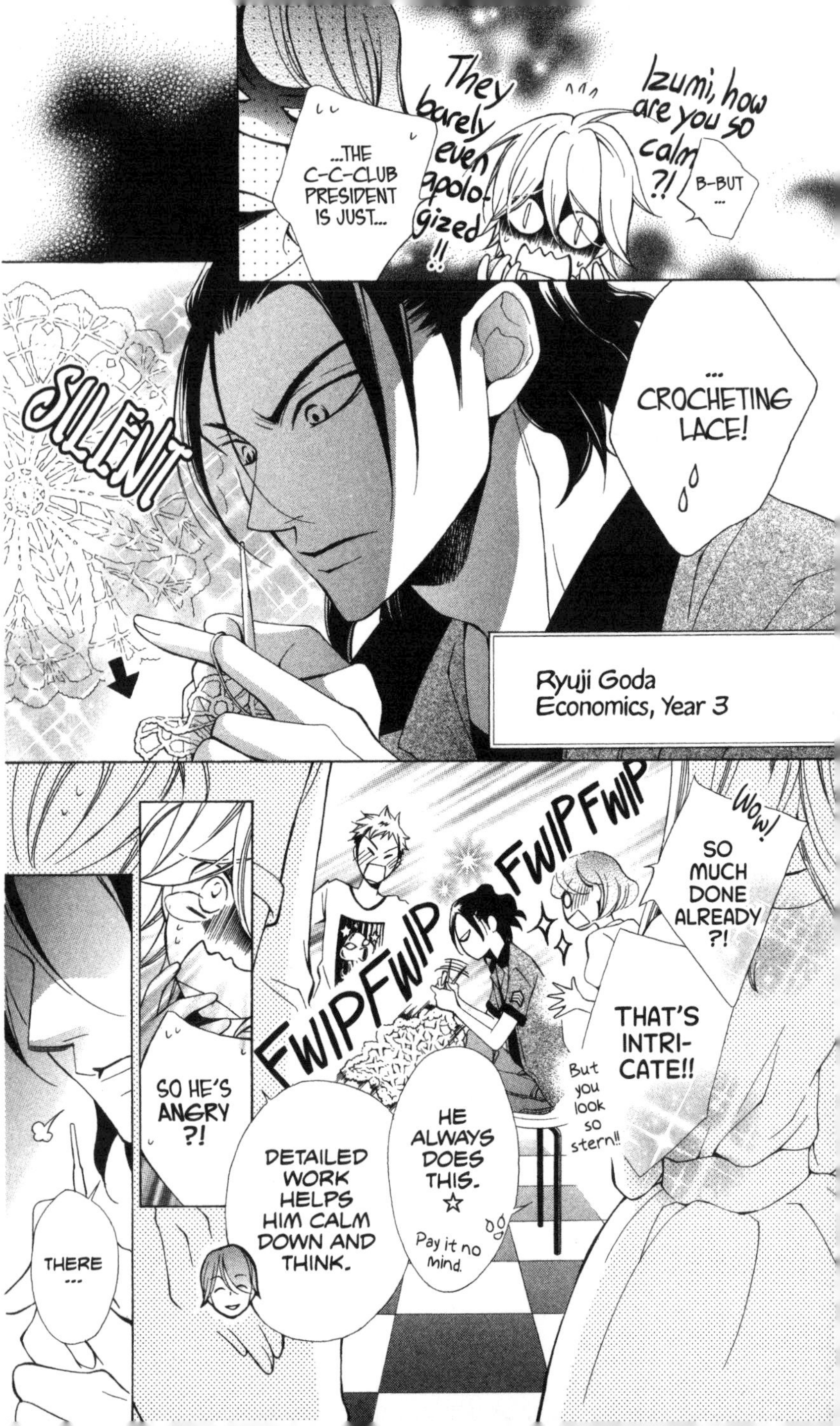

Izumi, how are you so calm?!
B-BUT ...
They barely even apologized!!
...THE C-C-CLUB PRESIDENT IS JUST...
... CROCHETING LACE!
SILENT
Ryuji Goda
Economics, Year 3
Wow!
SO MUCH DONE ALREADY?!
FWIP FWIP
FWIP FWIP
THAT'S INTRI-CATE!!
But you look so stern!!
HE ALWAYS DOES THIS. ☆
Pay it no mind.
DETAILED WORK HELPS HIM CALM DOWN AND THINK.
SO HE'S ANGRY?!
THERE ...

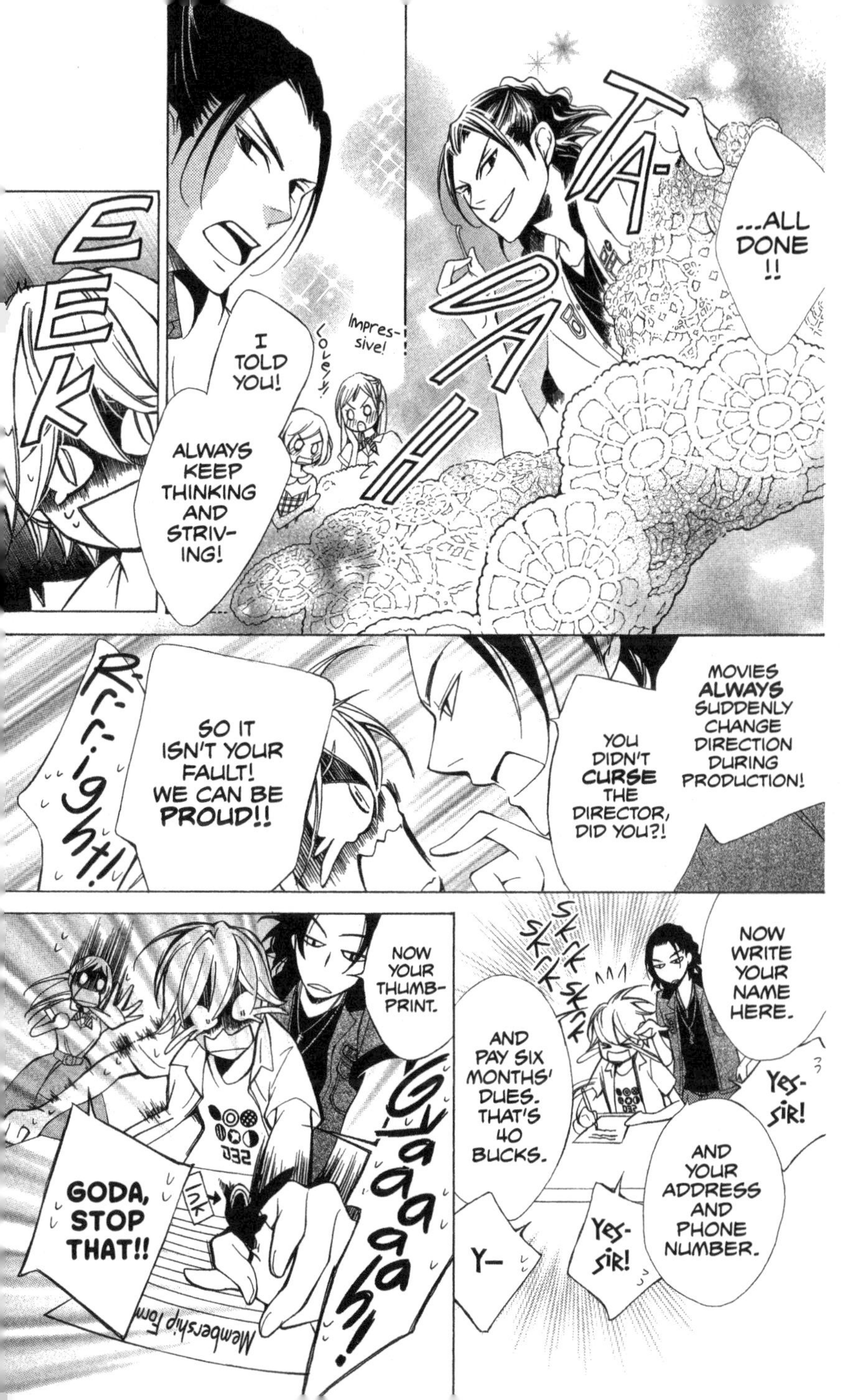
...ALL DONE!!
TA-DAAH
Impres-sive!
Lovely!
I TOLD YOU!
ALWAYS KEEP THINKING AND STRIV-ING!
EEEK
MOVIES ALWAYS SUDDENLY CHANGE DIRECTION DURING PRODUCTION!
YOU DIDN'T CURSE THE DIRECTOR, DID YOU?!
SO IT ISN'T YOUR FAULT! WE CAN BE PROUD!!
R-r-r-right!!
NOW WRITE YOUR NAME HERE.
Skrik skrik skrik skrik
Yes-sir!
AND YOUR ADDRESS AND PHONE NUMBER.
Yes-sir!
AND PAY SIX MONTHS' DUES. THAT'S 40 BUCKS.
Y—
NOW YOUR THUMB-PRINT.
Gyaaaaaah!!
GODA, STOP THAT!!
Ink
Membership Form

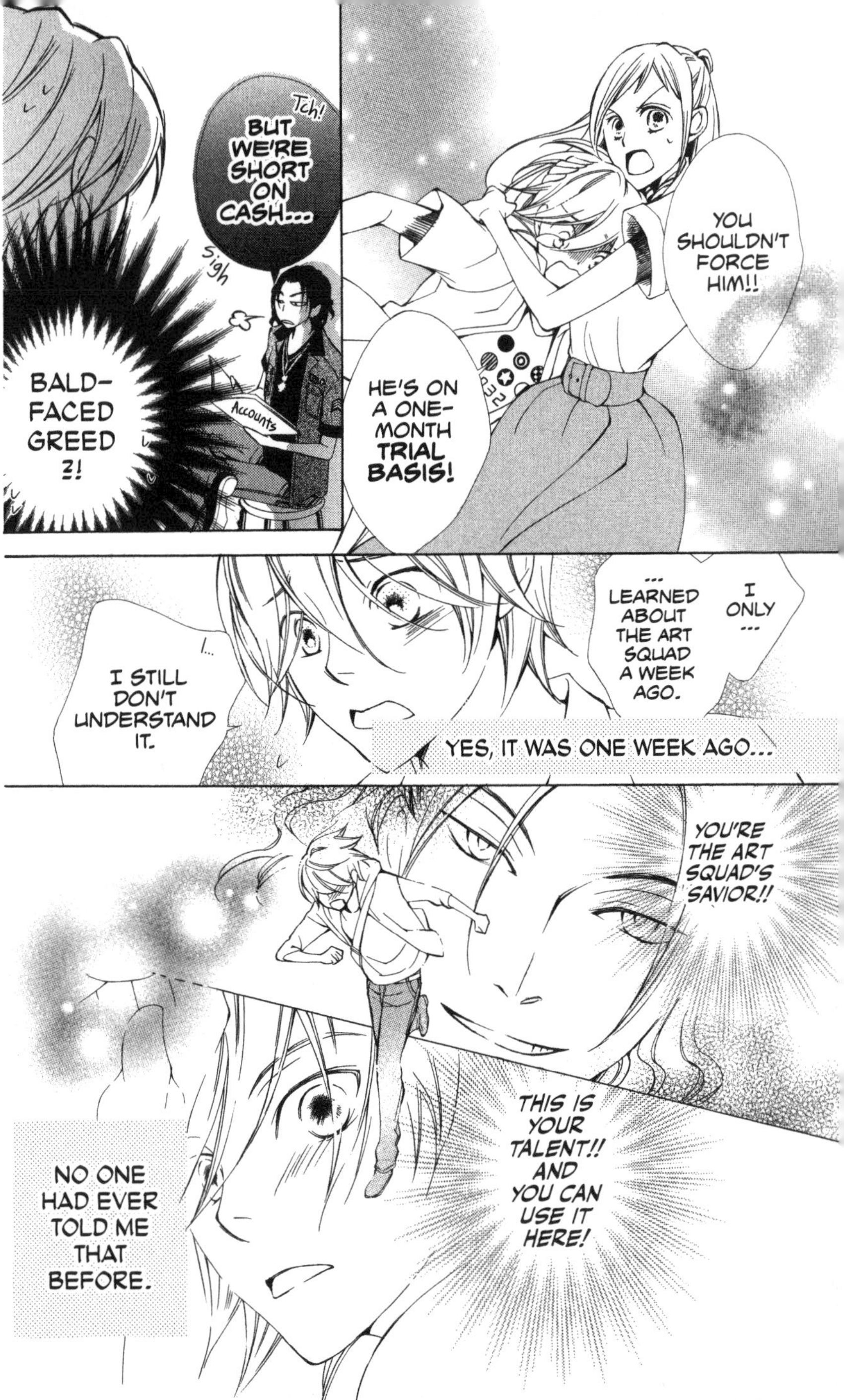
YOU SHOULDN'T FORCE HIM!!
HE'S ON A ONE-MONTH TRIAL BASIS!
Tch!
BUT WE'RE SHORT ON CASH...
Sigh
Accounts
BALD-FACED GREED?!
I ONLY ...
...LEARNED ABOUT THE ART SQUAD A WEEK AGO.
I...
I STILL DON'T UNDERSTAND IT.
YES, IT WAS ONE WEEK AGO...
YOU'RE THE ART SQUAD'S SAVIOR!!
THIS IS YOUR TALENT!! AND YOU CAN USE IT HERE!
NO ONE HAD EVER TOLD ME THAT BEFORE.

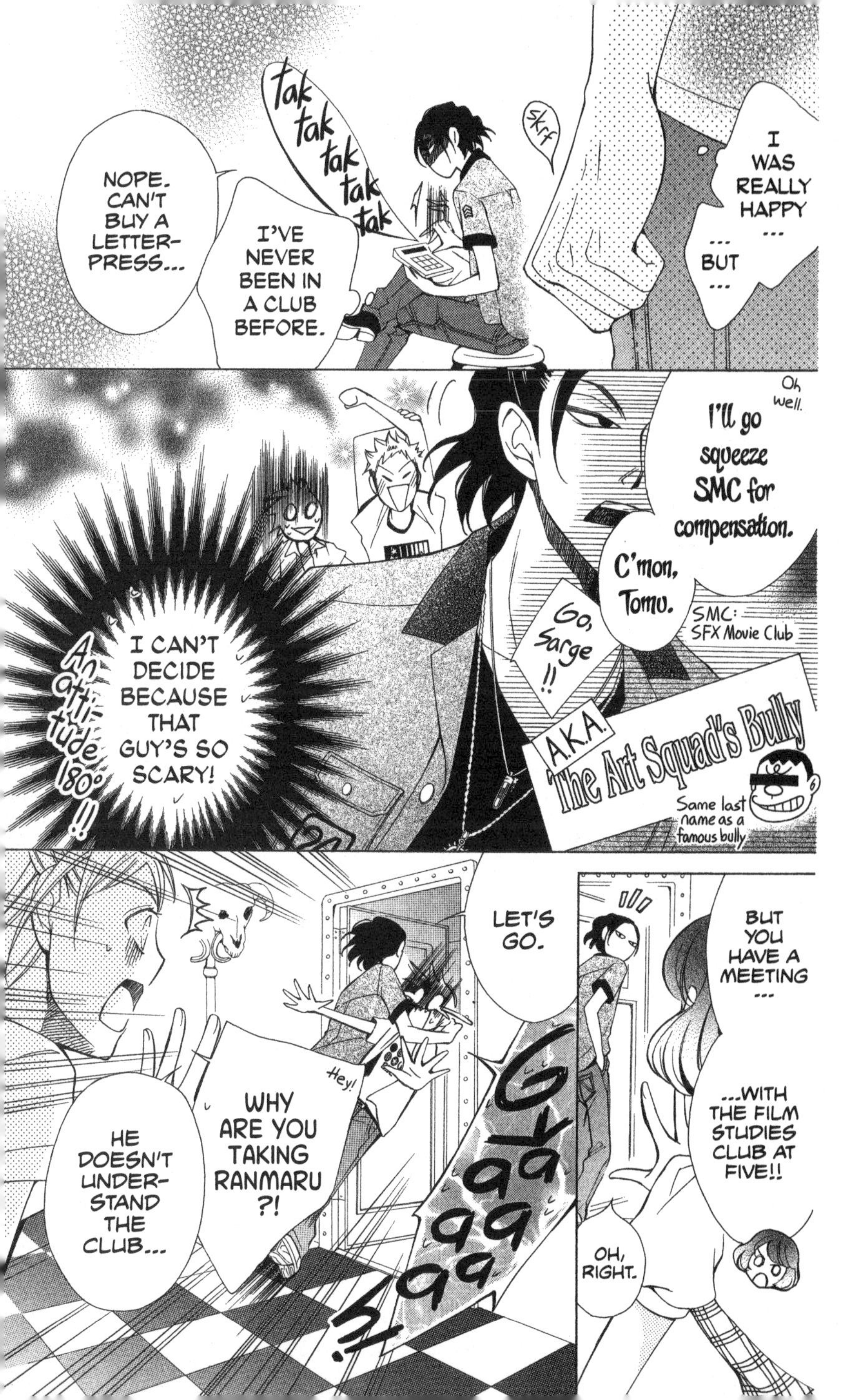
I WAS REALLY HAPPY... BUT...
skrf
tak tak tak tak tak
I'VE NEVER BEEN IN A CLUB BEFORE.
NOPE. CAN'T BUY A LETTER-PRESS...
Oh well.
I'll go squeeze SMC for compensation.
C'mon, Tomu.
SMC: SFX Movie Club
Go, Sarge!!
A.K.A. The Art Squad's Bully
Same last name as a famous bully
I CAN'T DECIDE BECAUSE THAT GUY'S SO SCARY!
An atti-tude 180°!!
BUT YOU HAVE A MEETING...
...WITH THE FILM STUDIES CLUB AT FIVE!!
OH, RIGHT.
LET'S GO.
Gaaaaaa?!
Hey!
WHY ARE YOU TAKING RANMARU?!
HE DOESN'T UNDER-STAND THE CLUB...

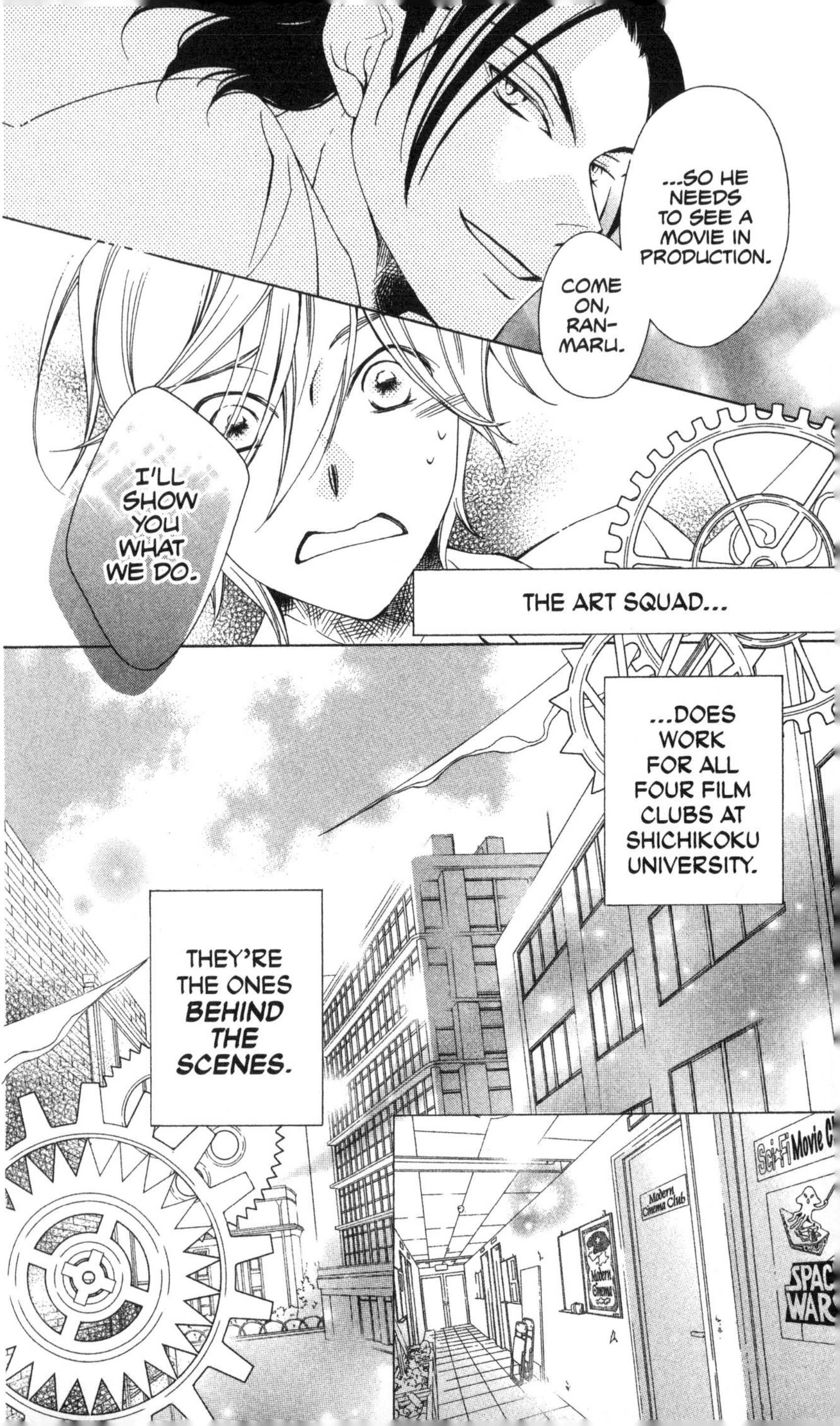
...SO HE NEEDS TO SEE A MOVIE IN PRODUCTION.
COME ON, RAN-MARU.
I'LL SHOW YOU WHAT WE DO.
THE ART SQUAD...
...DOES WORK FOR ALL FOUR FILM CLUBS AT SHICHIKOKU UNIVERSITY.
THEY'RE THE ONES *BEHIND THE SCENES.*
Modern Cinema Club

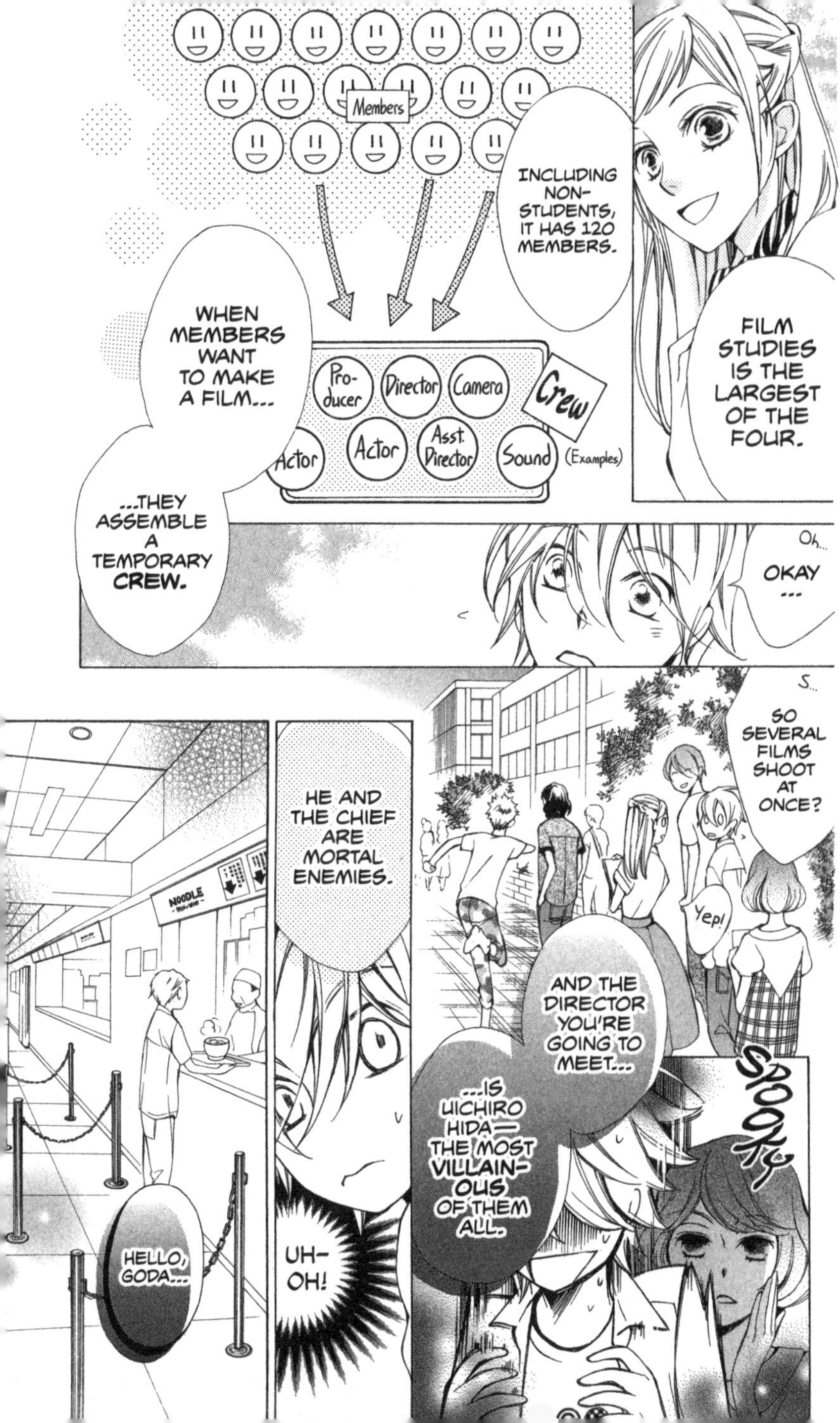
FILM STUDIES IS THE LARGEST OF THE FOUR.
INCLUDING NON-STUDENTS, IT HAS 120 MEMBERS.
Members
WHEN MEMBERS WANT TO MAKE A FILM...
Producer
Director
Camera
Crew
Actor
Actor
Asst. Director
Sound
(Examples)
...THEY ASSEMBLE A TEMPORARY CREW.
Oh...
OKAY...
S...
SO SEVERAL FILMS SHOOT AT ONCE?
Yep!
AND THE DIRECTOR YOU'RE GOING TO MEET...
...IS UICHIRO HIDA—THE MOST VILLAINOUS OF THEM ALL.
SPOOKY
HE AND THE CHIEF ARE MORTAL ENEMIES.
UH-OH!
NOODLE
HELLO, GODA...

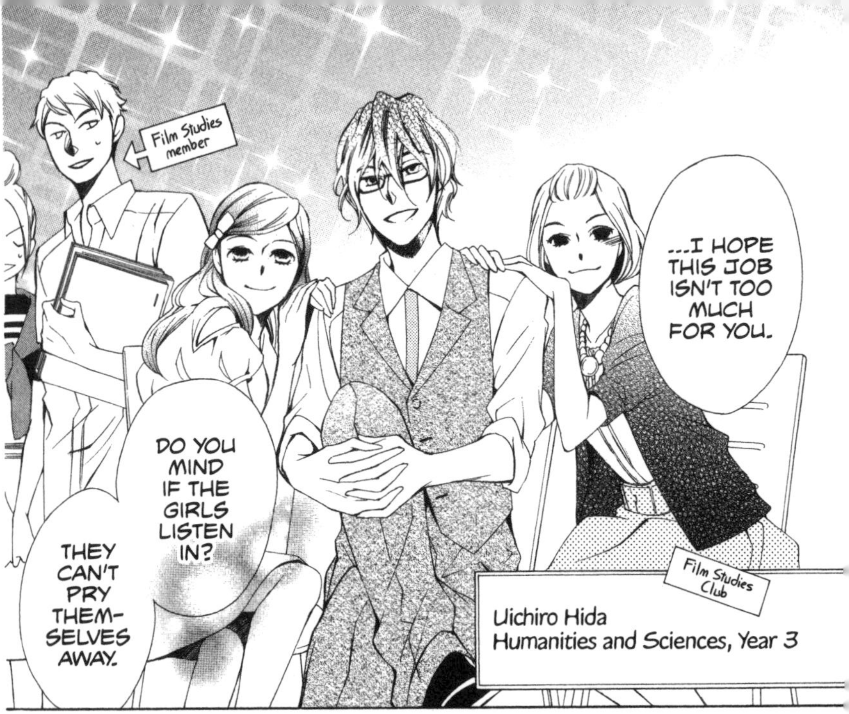
...I HOPE THIS JOB ISN'T TOO MUCH FOR YOU.
Film Studies member
DO YOU MIND IF THE GIRLS LISTEN IN?
THEY CAN'T PRY THEM-SELVES AWAY.
Film Studies Club
Uichiro Hida
Humanities and Sciences, Year 3

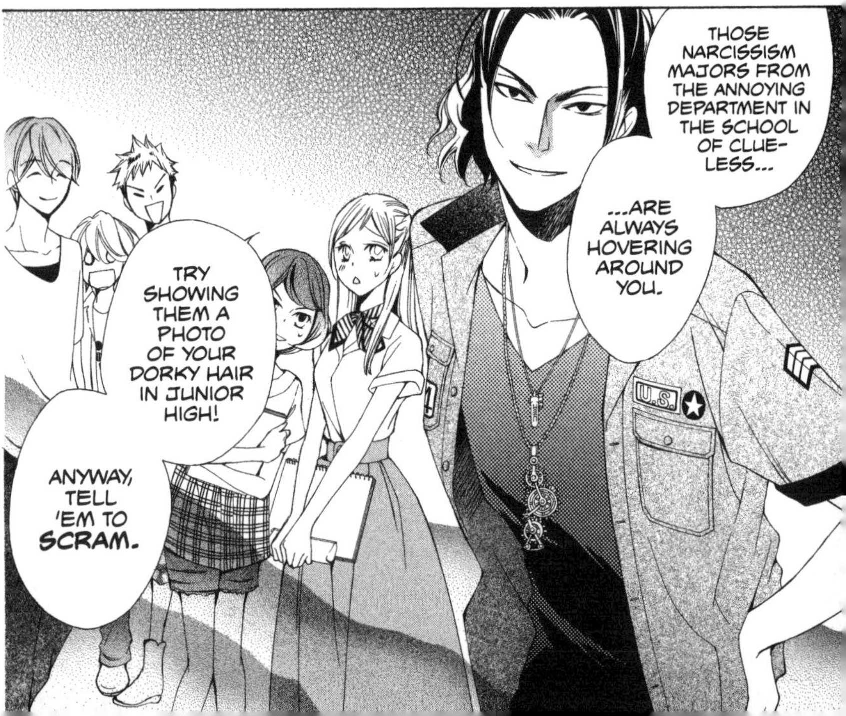
THOSE NARCISSISM MAJORS FROM THE ANNOYING DEPARTMENT IN THE SCHOOL OF CLUE-LESS...
...ARE ALWAYS HOVERING AROUND YOU.
TRY SHOWING THEM A PHOTO OF YOUR DORKY HAIR IN JUNIOR HIGH!
ANYWAY, TELL 'EM TO SCRAM.

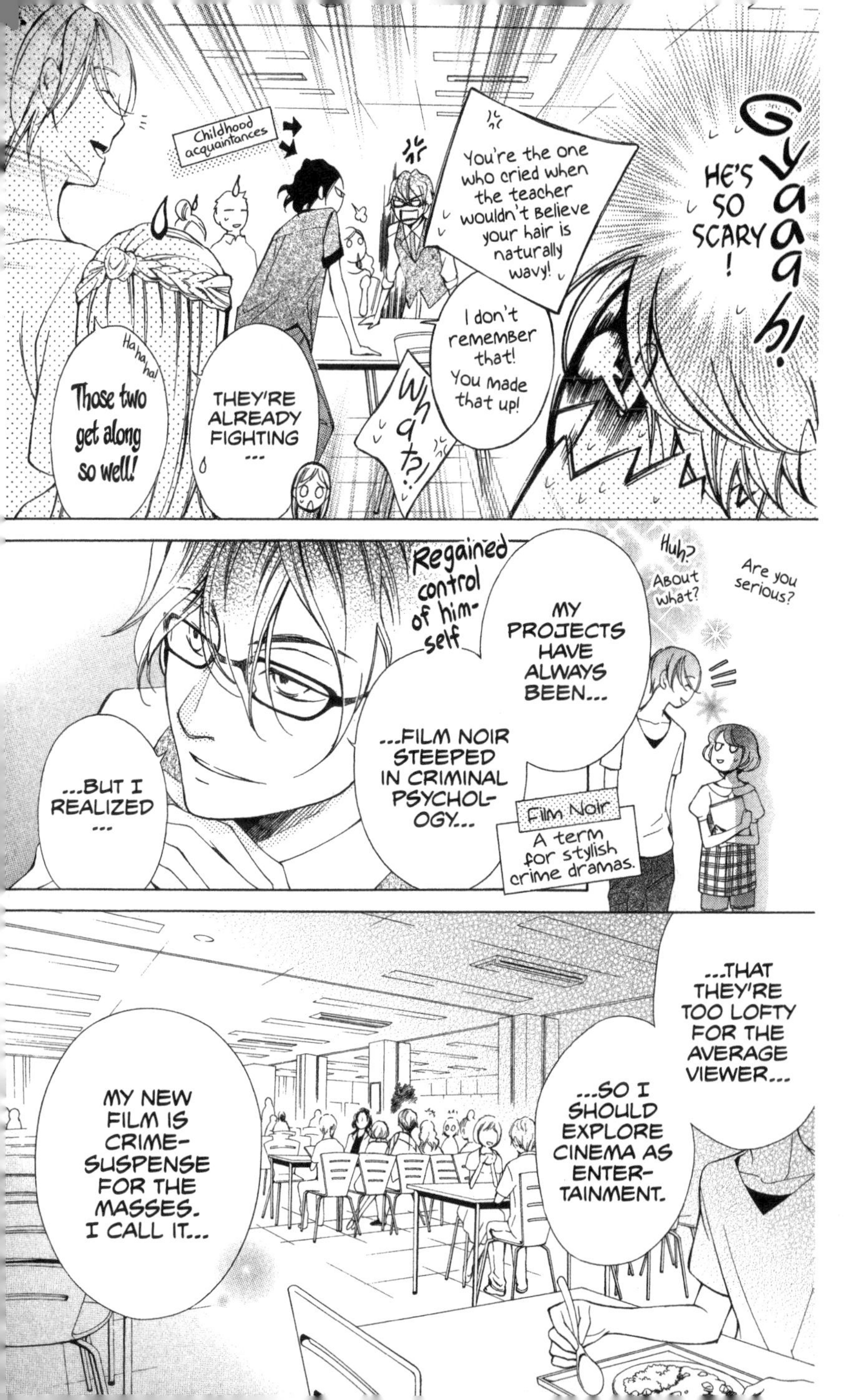

Gyaaah!
HE'S SO SCARY!
You're the one who cried when the teacher wouldn't believe your hair is naturally wavy!
I don't remember that! You made that up!
What?!
Childhood acquaintances
THEY'RE ALREADY FIGHTING...
Ha ha ha!
Those two get along so well!
Are you serious?
Huh? About what?
Regained control of him-self
MY PROJECTS HAVE ALWAYS BEEN...
...FILM NOIR STEEPED IN CRIMINAL PSYCHOL-OGY...
Film Noir
A term for stylish crime dramas.
...BUT I REALIZED...
...THAT THEY'RE TOO LOFTY FOR THE AVERAGE VIEWER...
...SO I SHOULD EXPLORE CINEMA AS ENTER-TAINMENT.
MY NEW FILM IS CRIME-SUSPENSE FOR THE MASSES. I CALL IT...

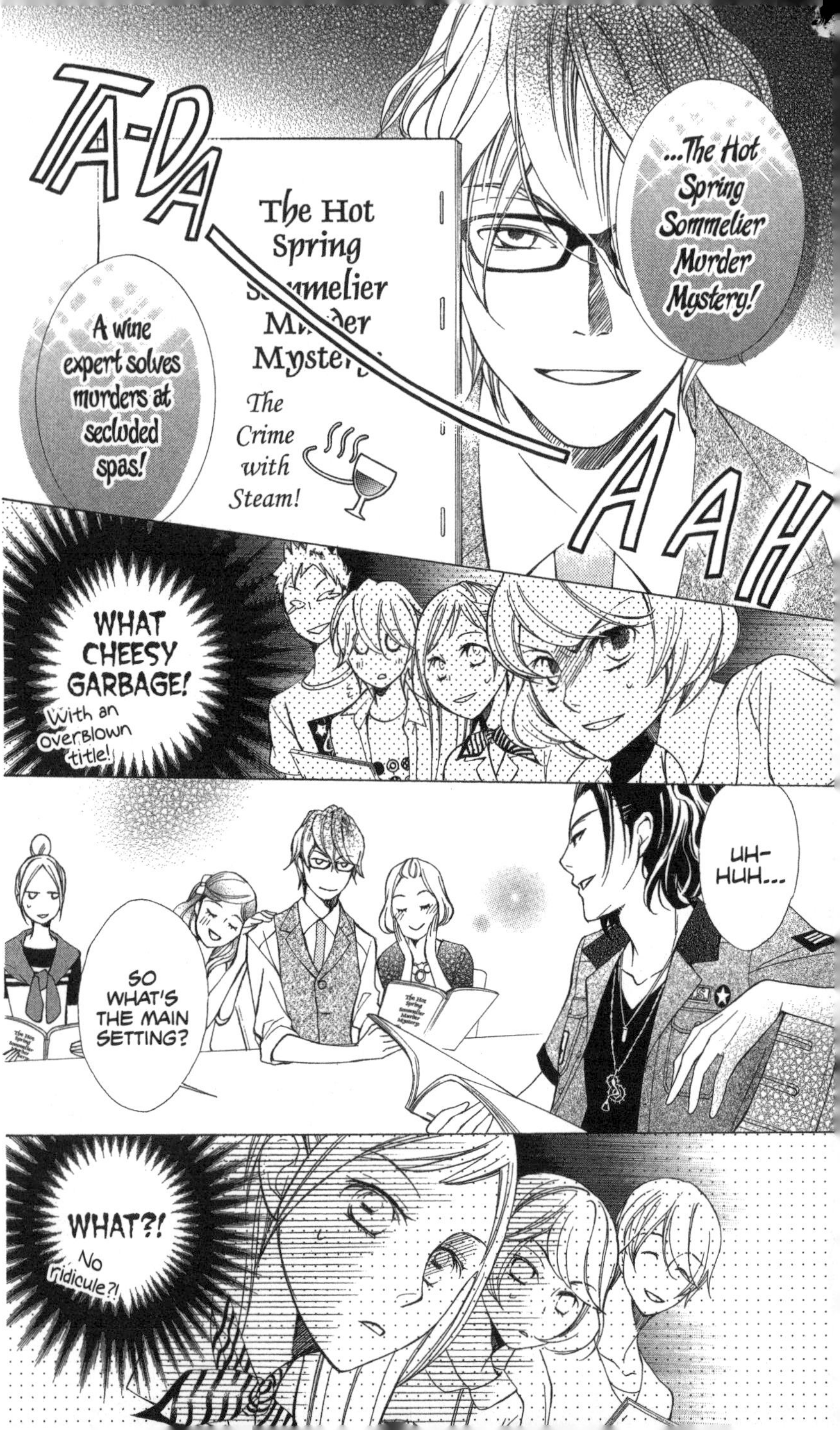

...The Hot Spring Sommelier Murder Mystery!
TA-DAAAH
The Hot Spring
The Crime with Steam!
A wine expert solves murders at secluded spas!
WHAT CHEESY GARBAGE!
With an overblown title!
UH-HUH...
SO WHAT'S THE MAIN SETTING?
WHAT?!
No ridicule?!

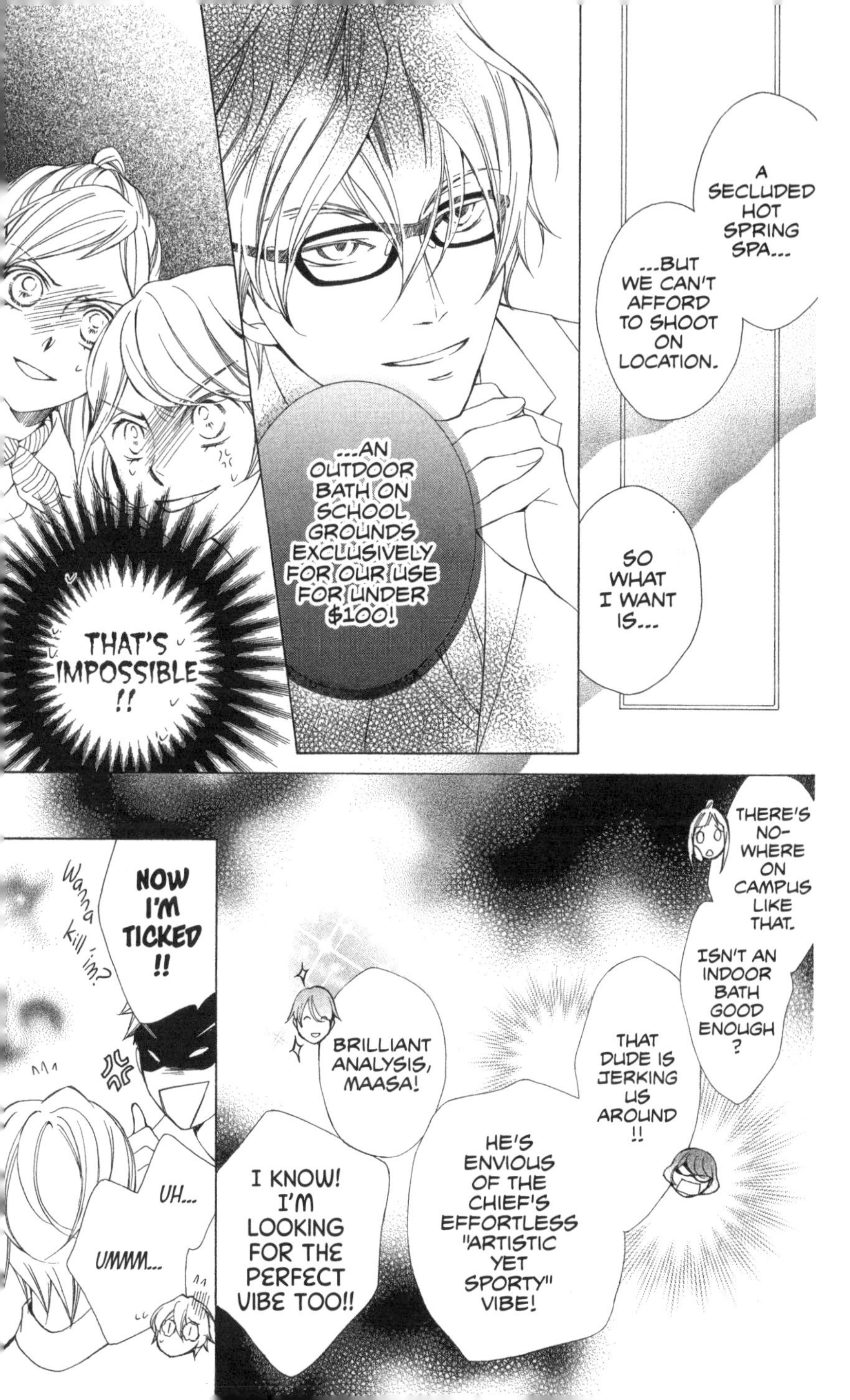

A SECLUDED HOT SPRING SPA...
...BUT WE CAN'T AFFORD TO SHOOT ON LOCATION.
SO WHAT I WANT IS...
...AN OUTDOOR BATH ON SCHOOL GROUNDS EXCLUSIVELY FOR OUR USE FOR UNDER $100!
THAT'S IMPOSSIBLE!!
THERE'S NO-WHERE ON CAMPUS LIKE THAT.
ISN'T AN INDOOR BATH GOOD ENOUGH?
THAT DUDE IS JERKING US AROUND!!
BRILLIANT ANALYSIS, MAASA!
HE'S ENVIOUS OF THE CHIEF'S EFFORTLESS "ARTISTIC YET SPORTY" VIBE!
I KNOW! I'M LOOKING FOR THE PERFECT VIBE TOO!!
NOW I'M TICKED!!
Wanna kill 'im?
UH...
UMMM...

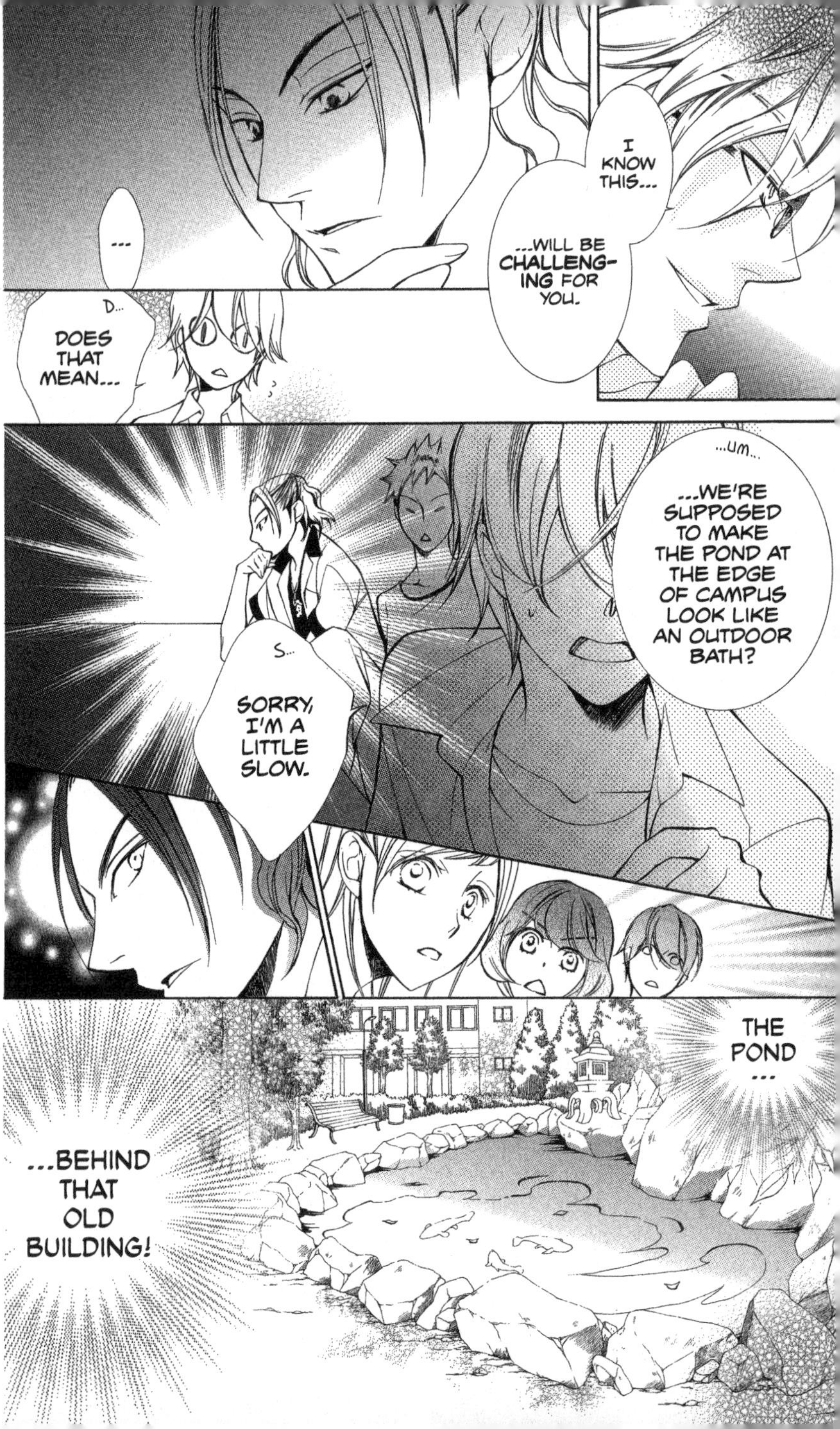
I KNOW THIS...
...WILL BE CHALLENGING FOR YOU.
...
D... DOES THAT MEAN...
...UM... ...WE'RE SUPPOSED TO MAKE THE POND AT THE EDGE OF CAMPUS LOOK LIKE AN OUTDOOR BATH?
S... SORRY, I'M A LITTLE SLOW.
THE POND...
...BEHIND THAT OLD BUILDING!

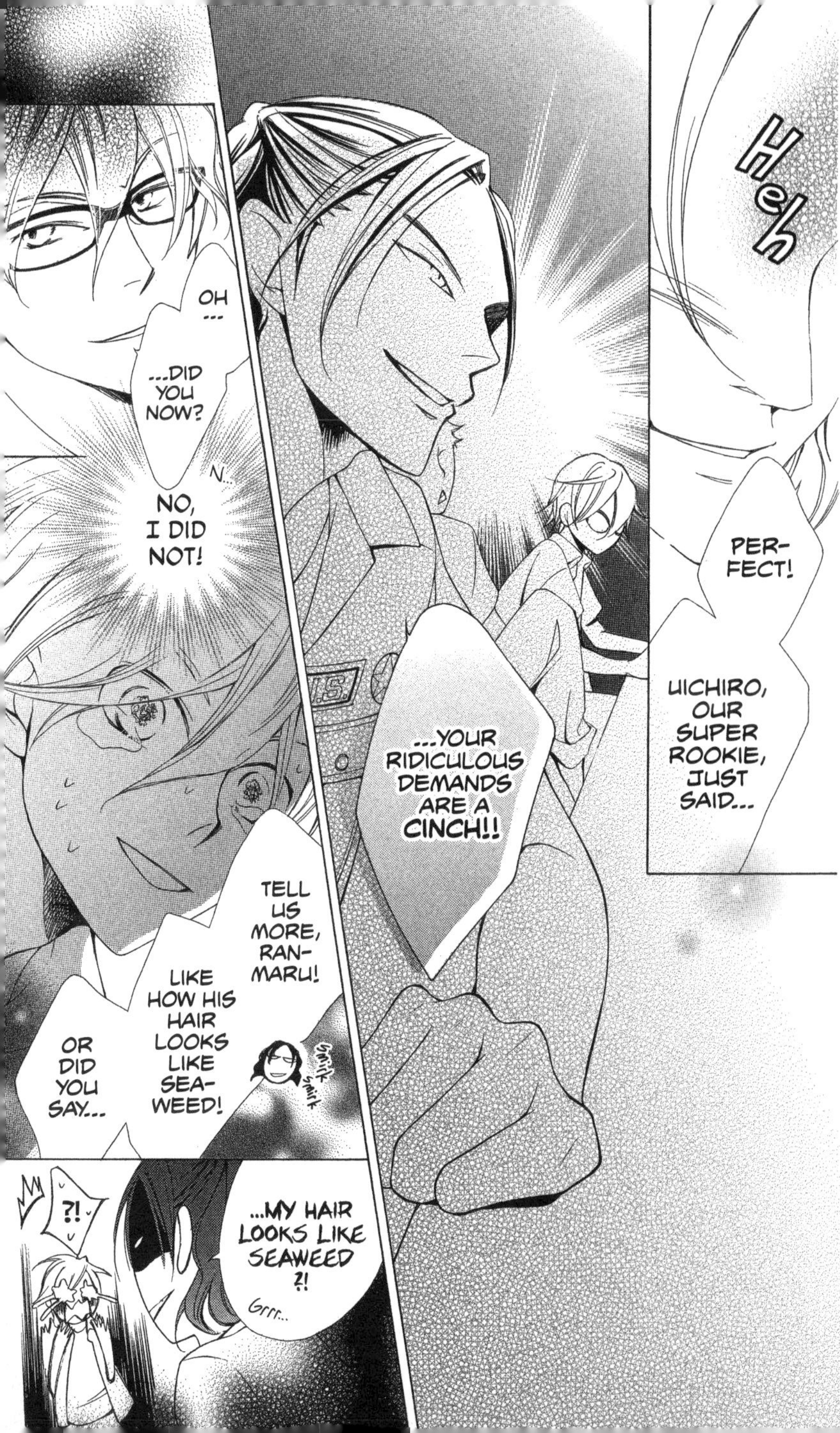
Heh
PER-FECT!
UICHIRO, OUR SUPER ROOKIE, JUST SAID...
...YOUR RIDICULOUS DEMANDS ARE A CINCH!!
OH ---
...DID YOU NOW?
N...
NO, I DID NOT!
TELL US MORE, RAN-MARU!
LIKE HOW HIS HAIR LOOKS LIKE SEA-WEED!
OR DID YOU SAY...
Smirk smirk
...MY HAIR LOOKS LIKE SEAWEED ?!
Grrr...
?!

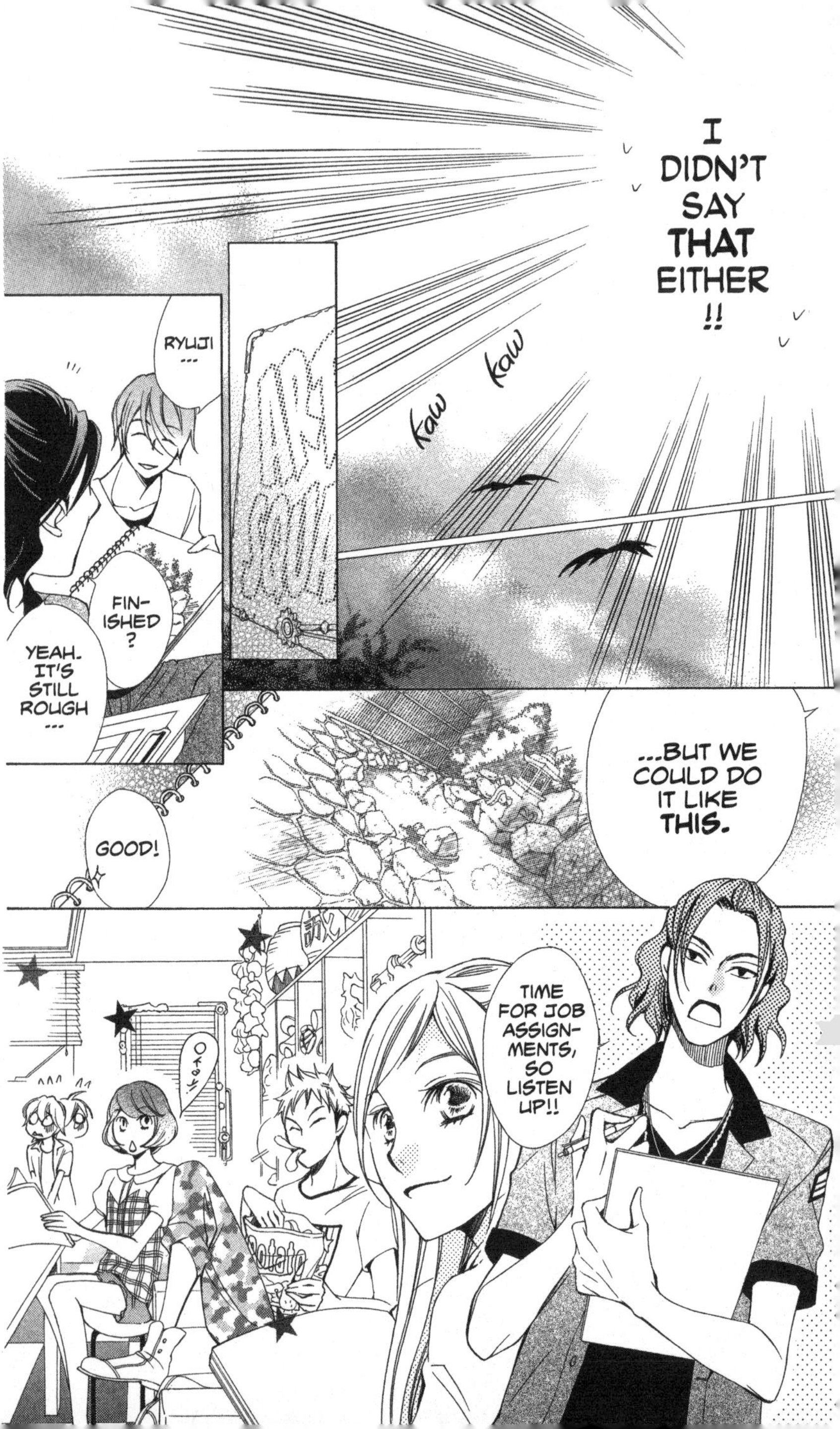
I DIDN'T SAY THAT EITHER!!
kaw kaw
RYUJI...
FIN-ISHED?
YEAH. IT'S STILL ROUGH...
...BUT WE COULD DO IT LIKE THIS.
GOOD!
TIME FOR JOB ASSIGN-MENTS, SO LISTEN UP!!

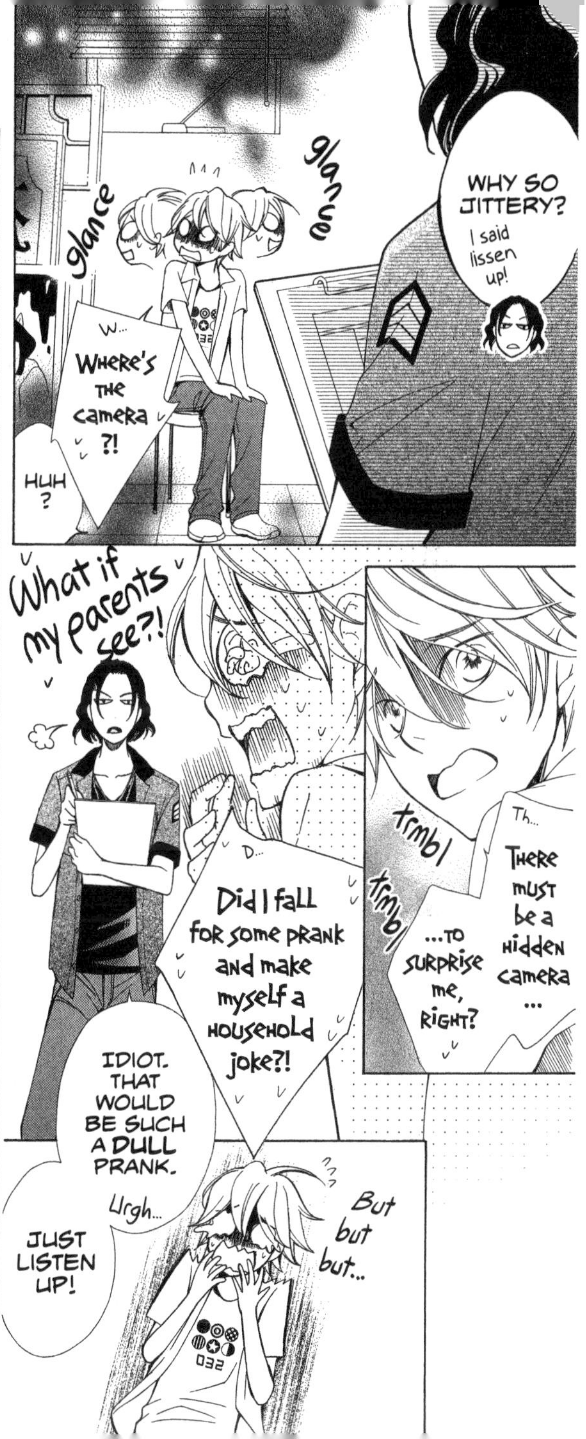
WHY SO JITTERY?
I said lissen up!
glance
glance
W... WHERE'S THE CAMERA?!
HUH?
Th... THERE MUST BE A HIDDEN CAMERA...
...TO SURPRISE ME, RIGHT?
trmbl
trmbl
D... Did I fall for some prank and make myself a household joke?!
What if my parents see?!
IDIOT. THAT WOULD BE SUCH A DULL PRANK.
But but but...
Urgh...
JUST LISTEN UP!

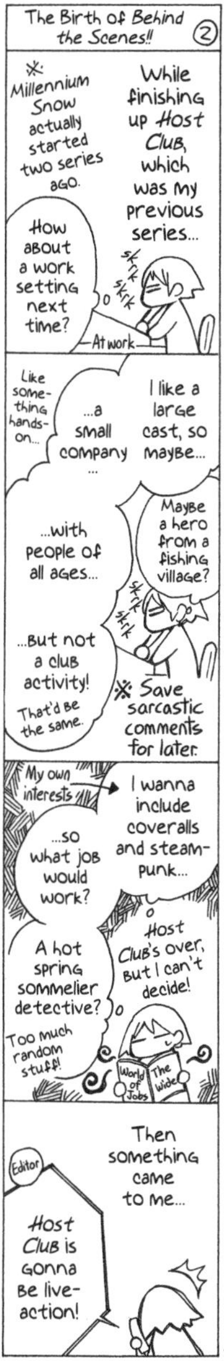
The Birth of Behind the Scenes!! ②
While finishing up Host Club, which was my previous series...
※ Millennium Snow actually started two series ago.
How about a work setting next time?
skrik skrik
At work
I like a large cast, so maybe...
...a small company...
Like something hands-on...
Maybe a hero from a fishing village?
...with people of all ages...
skrik skrik
...But not a club activity!
That'd be the same.
※ Save sarcastic comments for later.
I wanna include coveralls and steampunk...
My own interests
...so what job would work?
Host Club's over, but I can't decide!
A hot spring sommelier detective?
Too much random stuff!
World of Jobs
The Wide
Then something came to me...
Editor
Host Club is gonna be live-action!

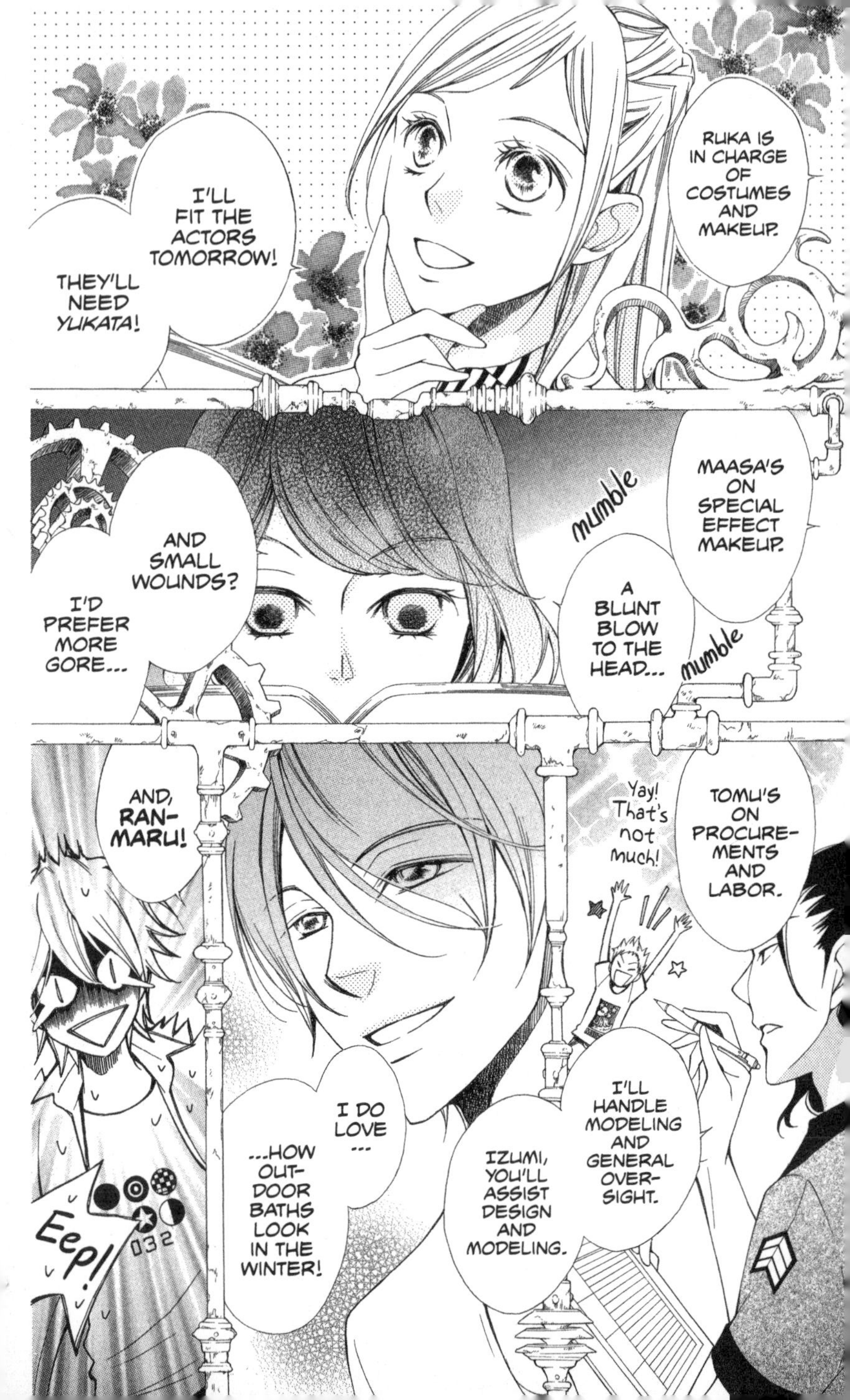
RUKA IS IN CHARGE OF COSTUMES AND MAKEUP.
I'LL FIT THE ACTORS TOMORROW!
THEY'LL NEED *YUKATA*!
MAASA'S ON SPECIAL EFFECT MAKEUP.
mumble
A BLUNT BLOW TO THE HEAD...
mumble
AND SMALL WOUNDS?
I'D PREFER MORE GORE...
TOMU'S ON PROCUREMENTS AND LABOR.
Yay! That's not much!
AND, **RANMARU**!
I'LL HANDLE MODELING AND GENERAL OVERSIGHT.
IZUMI, YOU'LL ASSIST DESIGN AND MODELING.
I DO LOVE...
...HOW OUTDOOR BATHS LOOK IN THE WINTER!
Eep!

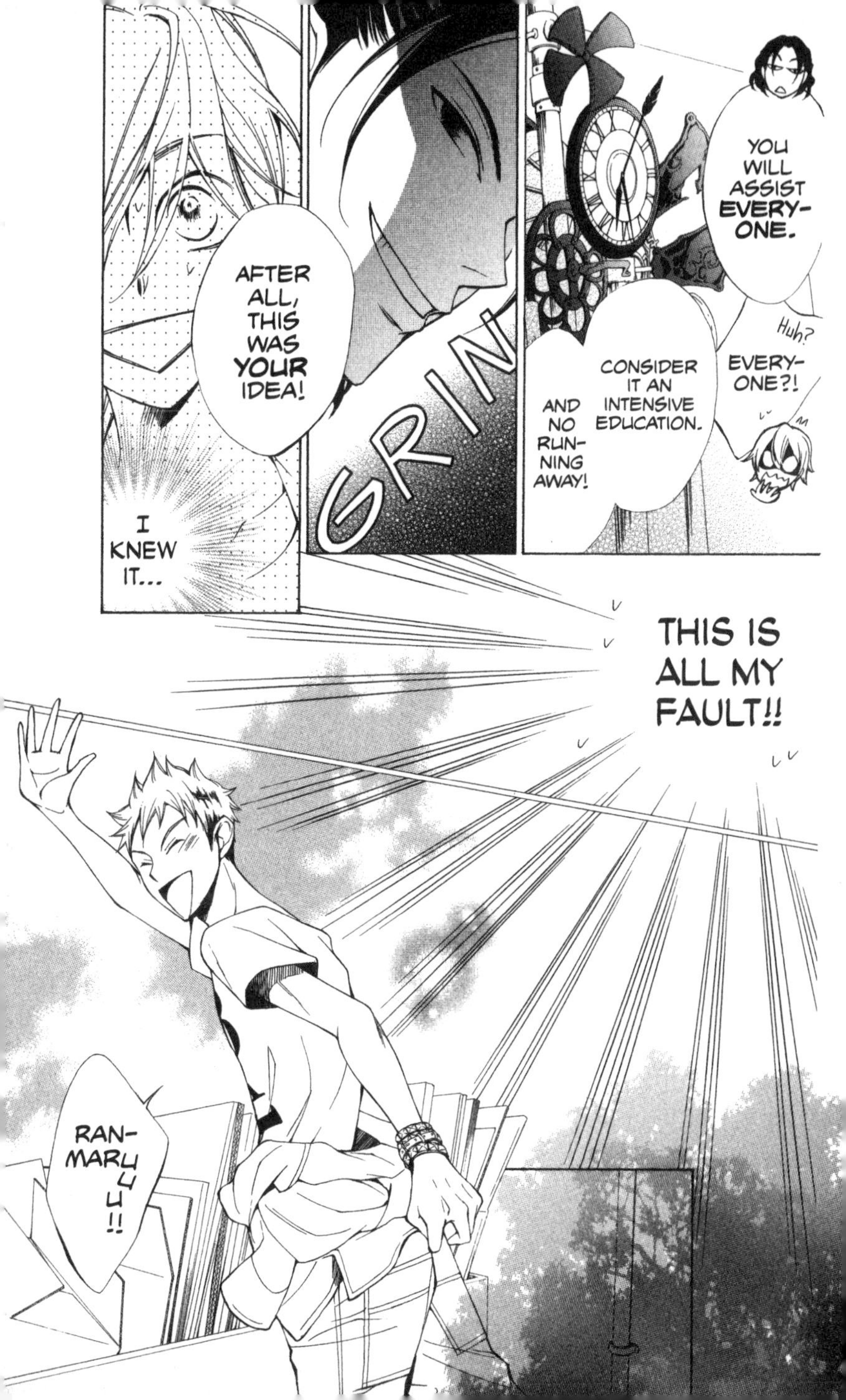
YOU WILL ASSIST EVERYONE.
Huh?
EVERY-ONE?!
CONSIDER IT AN INTENSIVE EDUCATION.
AND NO RUN-NING AWAY!
GRIN
AFTER ALL, THIS WAS YOUR IDEA!
I KNEW IT...
THIS IS ALL MY FAULT!!
RAN-MARUUU!!

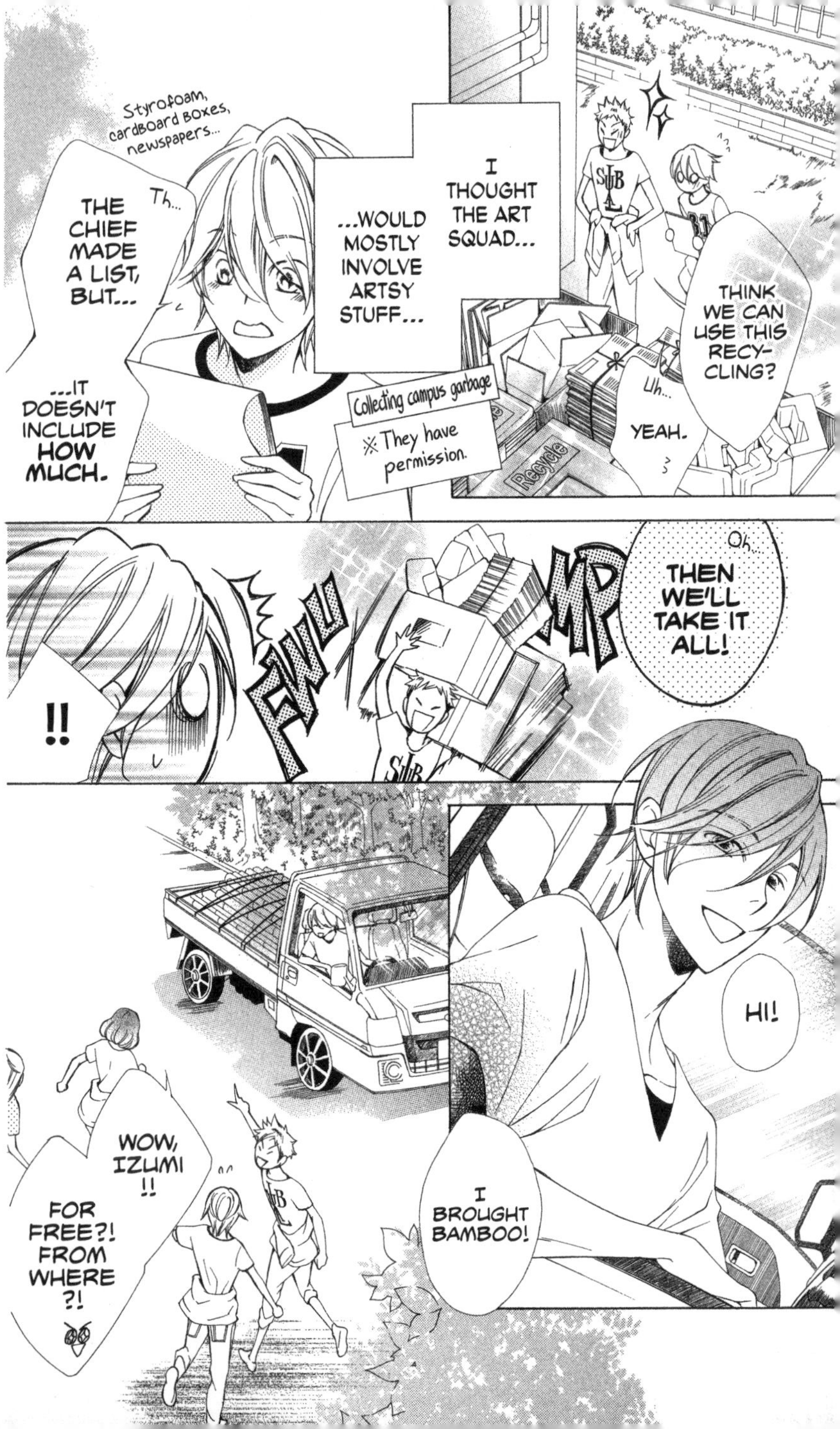

I THOUGHT THE ART SQUAD...
...WOULD MOSTLY INVOLVE ARTSY STUFF...
THINK WE CAN USE THIS RECY- CLING?
Uh... YEAH.
Collecting campus garbage
※They have permission.
Recycle
Styrofoam, cardboard boxes, newspapers...
Th...
THE CHIEF MADE A LIST, BUT...
...IT DOESN'T INCLUDE HOW MUCH.
Oh...
THEN WE'LL TAKE IT ALL!
FWU
MP
!!
HI!
I BROUGHT BAMBOO!
WOW, IZUMI !!
FOR FREE?! FROM WHERE ?!

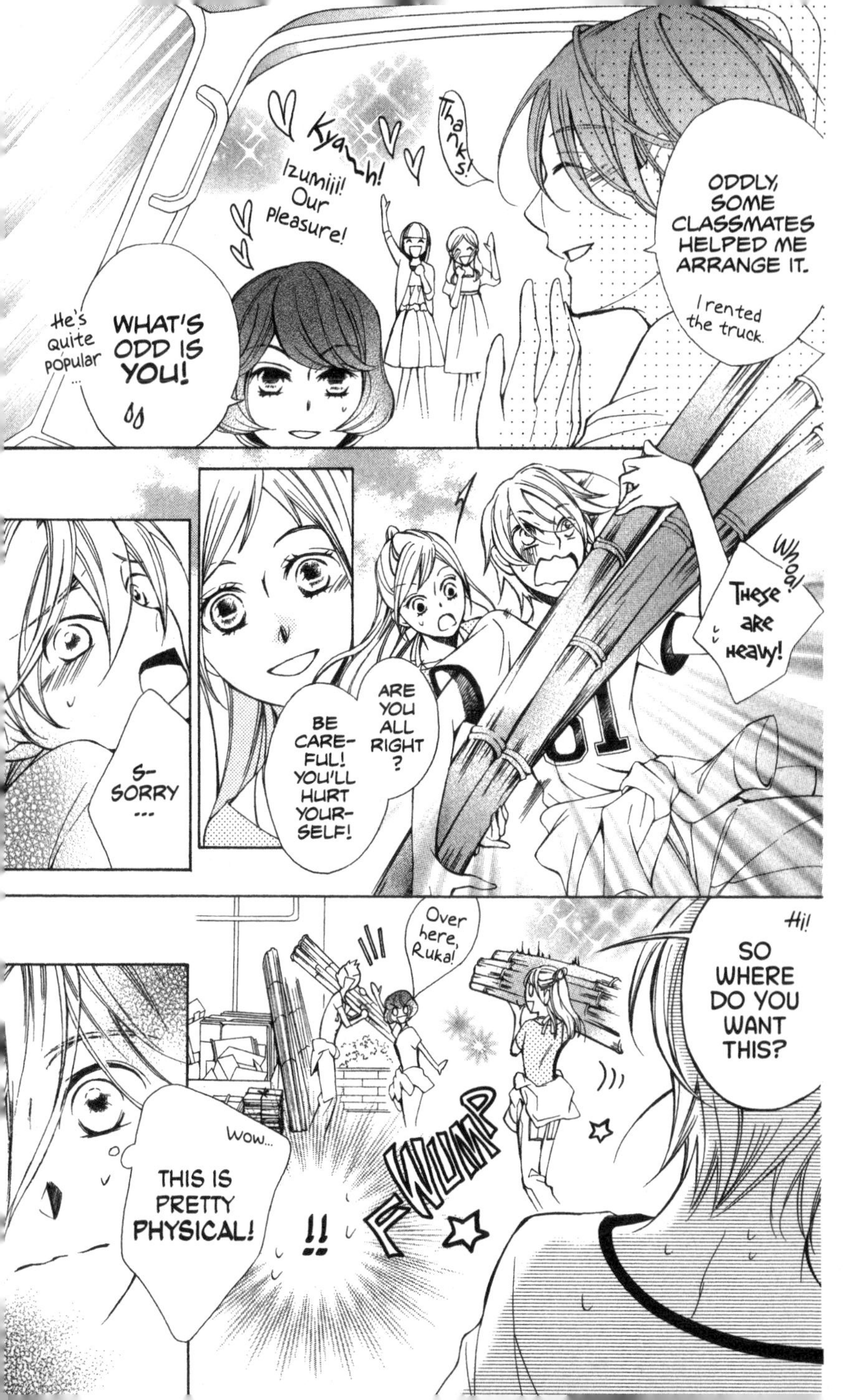
ODDLY, SOME CLASSMATES HELPED ME ARRANGE IT.
I rented the truck.
Thanks!
Kyaah!
Izumiii! Our pleasure!
WHAT'S ODD IS YOU!
He's quite popular...
Whoa! These are heavy!
ARE YOU ALL RIGHT?
BE CAREFUL! YOU'LL HURT YOURSELF!
S-SORRY...
Hi!
SO WHERE DO YOU WANT THIS?
Over here, Ruka!
FWUMP
!!
Wow...
THIS IS PRETTY PHYSICAL!

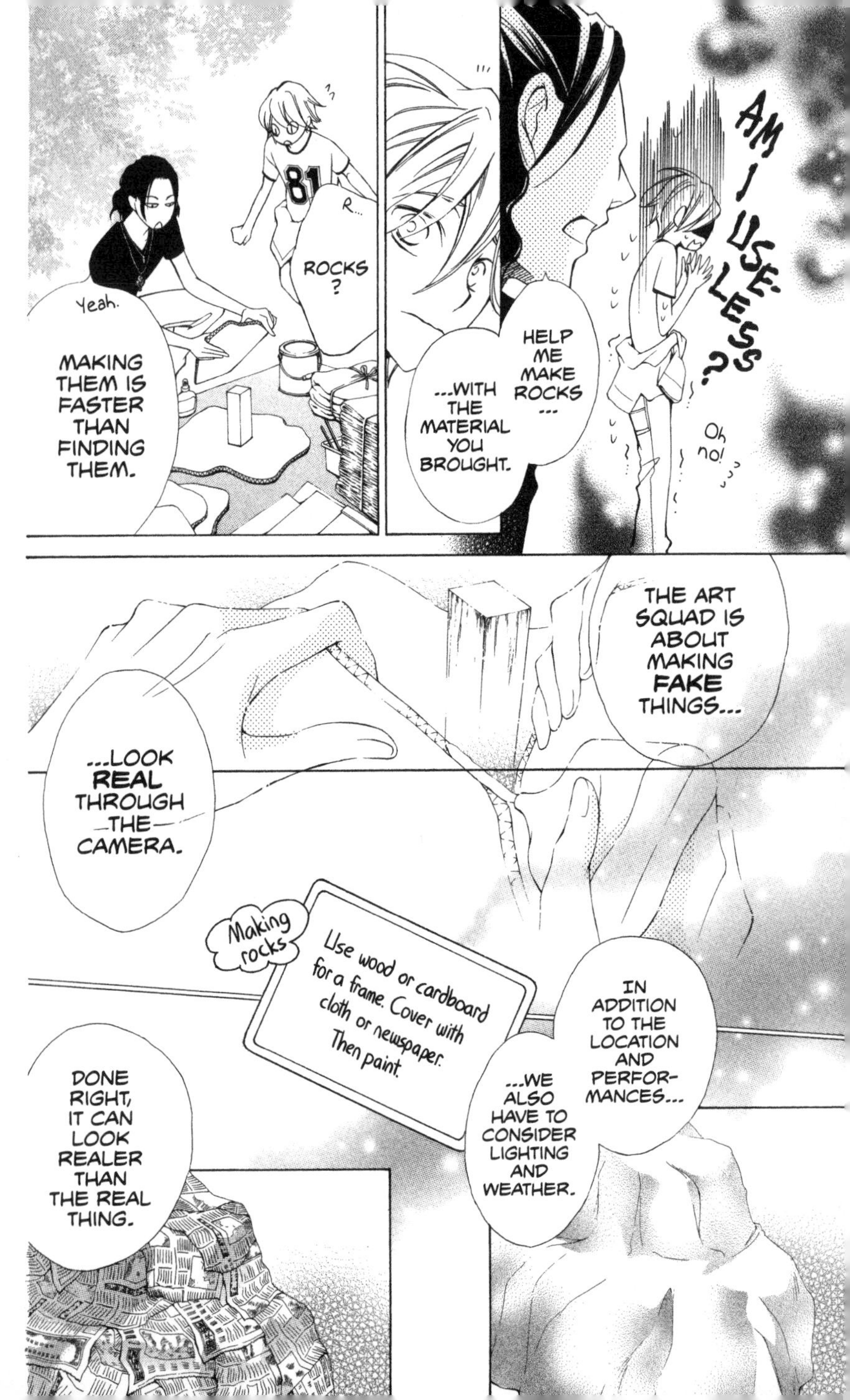
AM I USELESS?
Oh no!
HELP ME MAKE ROCKS...
...WITH THE MATERIAL YOU BROUGHT.
R...
ROCKS?
Yeah.
MAKING THEM IS FASTER THAN FINDING THEM.
THE ART SQUAD IS ABOUT MAKING FAKE THINGS...
...LOOK REAL THROUGH THE CAMERA.
IN ADDITION TO THE LOCATION AND PERFORMANCES...
...WE ALSO HAVE TO CONSIDER LIGHTING AND WEATHER.
Making rocks
Use wood or cardboard for a frame. Cover with cloth or newspaper. Then paint.
DONE RIGHT, IT CAN LOOK REALER THAN THE REAL THING.

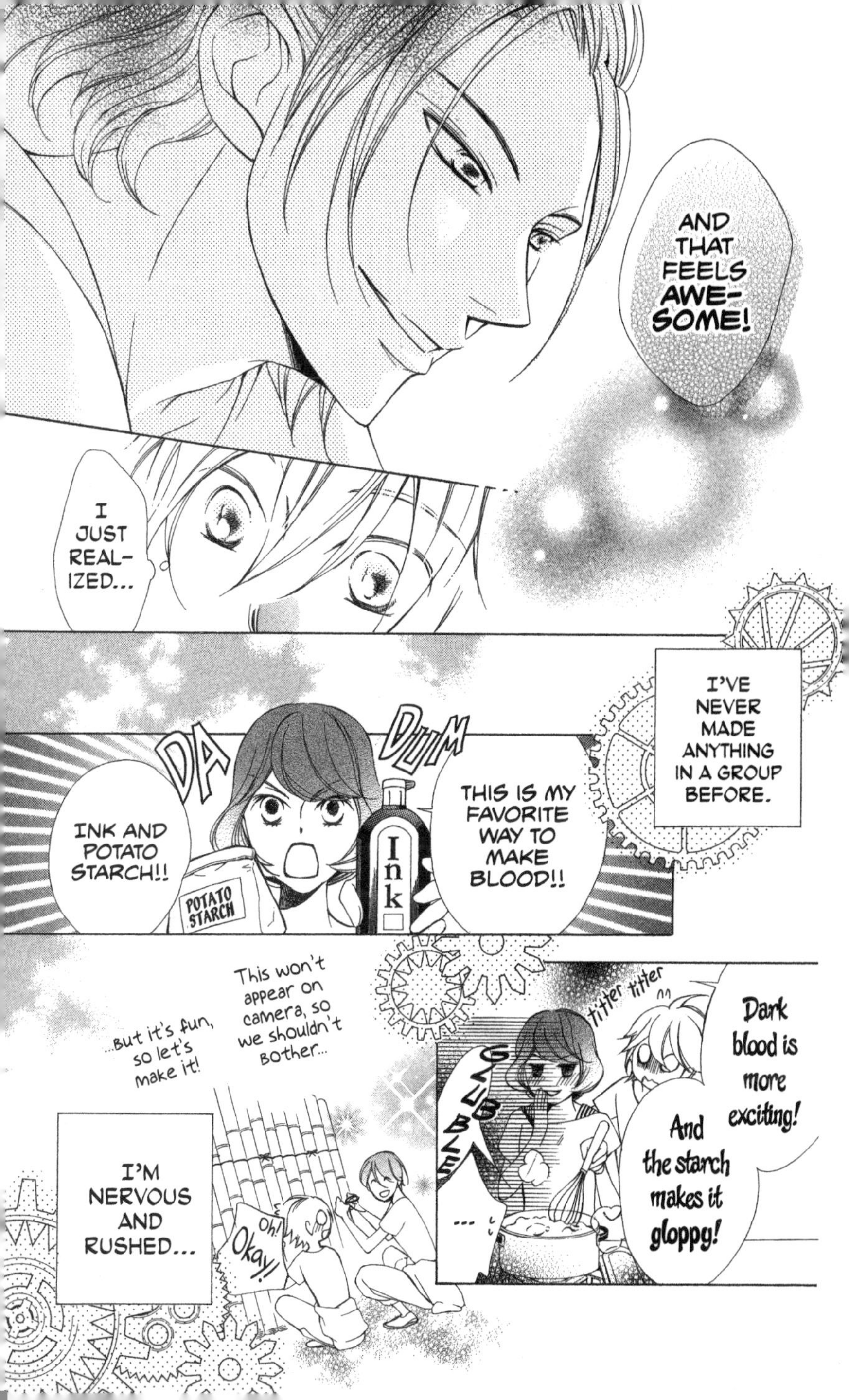
AND THAT FEELS AWESOME!
I JUST REALIZED...
I'VE NEVER MADE ANYTHING IN A GROUP BEFORE.
DA
DUM
THIS IS MY FAVORITE WAY TO MAKE BLOOD!!
INK AND POTATO STARCH!!
Ink
POTATO STARCH
titter titter
Dark blood is more exciting!
And the starch makes it gloppy!
GLUBBLE
...
This won't appear on camera, so we shouldn't bother...
...But it's fun, so let's make it!
Oh! Okay!
I'M NERVOUS AND RUSHED...

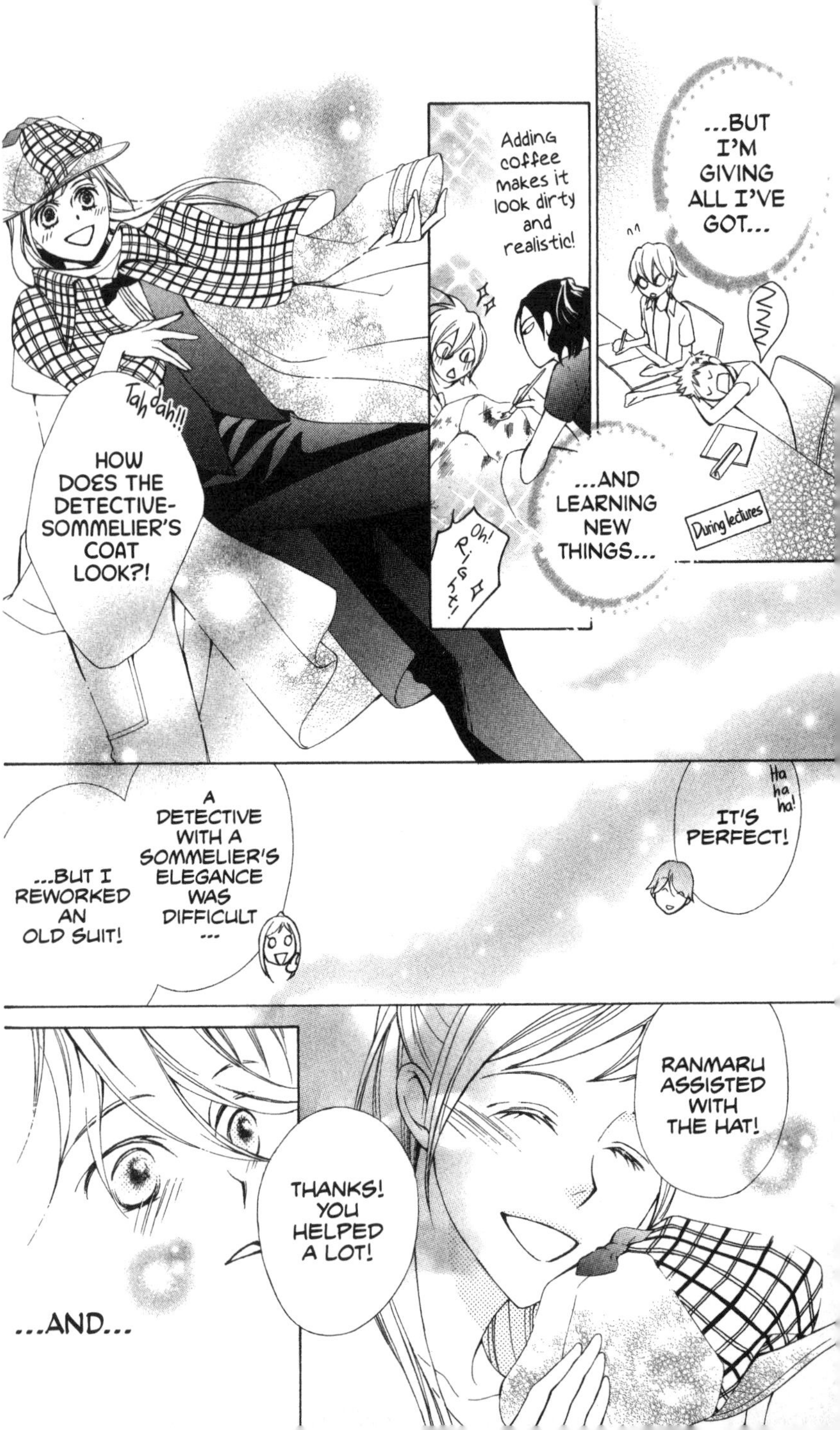
...BUT I'M GIVING ALL I'VE GOT...
During lectures
Adding coffee makes it look dirty and realistic!
Oh! Right!
...AND LEARNING NEW THINGS...
Tah dah!!
HOW DOES THE DETECTIVE-SOMMELIER'S COAT LOOK?!
IT'S PERFECT!
Ha ha ha!
A DETECTIVE WITH A SOMMELIER'S ELEGANCE WAS DIFFICULT ...
...BUT I REWORKED AN OLD SUIT!
RANMARU ASSISTED WITH THE HAT!
THANKS! YOU HELPED A LOT!
...AND...

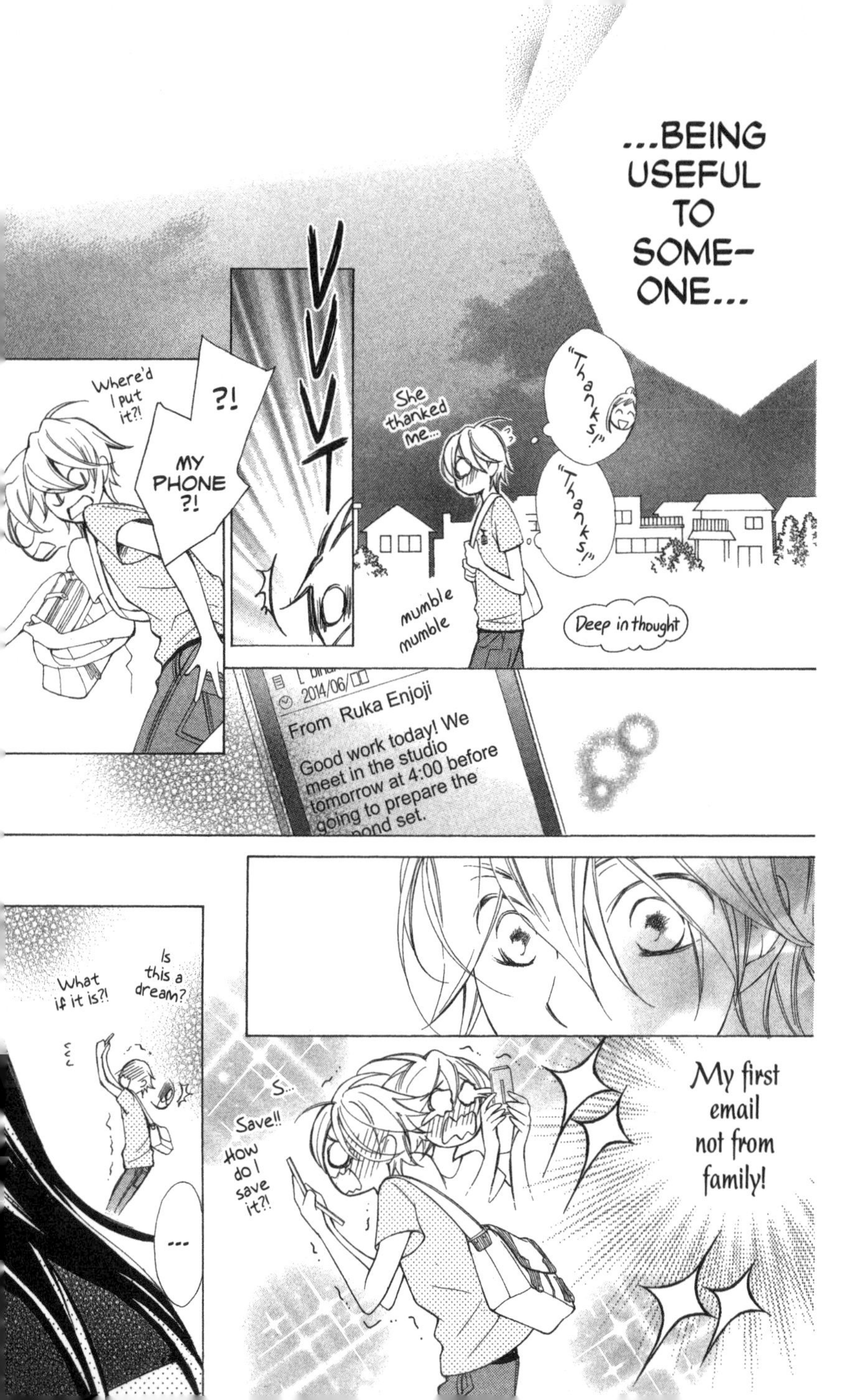
...BEING USEFUL TO SOME-ONE...
"Thanks!"
"Thanks!"
She thanked me...
mumble mumble
Deep in thought
VVVVT
?!
MY PHONE ?!
Where'd I put it?!
From Ruka Enjoji
Good work today! We meet in the studio tomorrow at 4:00 before going to prepare the
My first email not from family!
S...
Save!!
How do I save it?!
Is this a dream?
What if it is?!
...

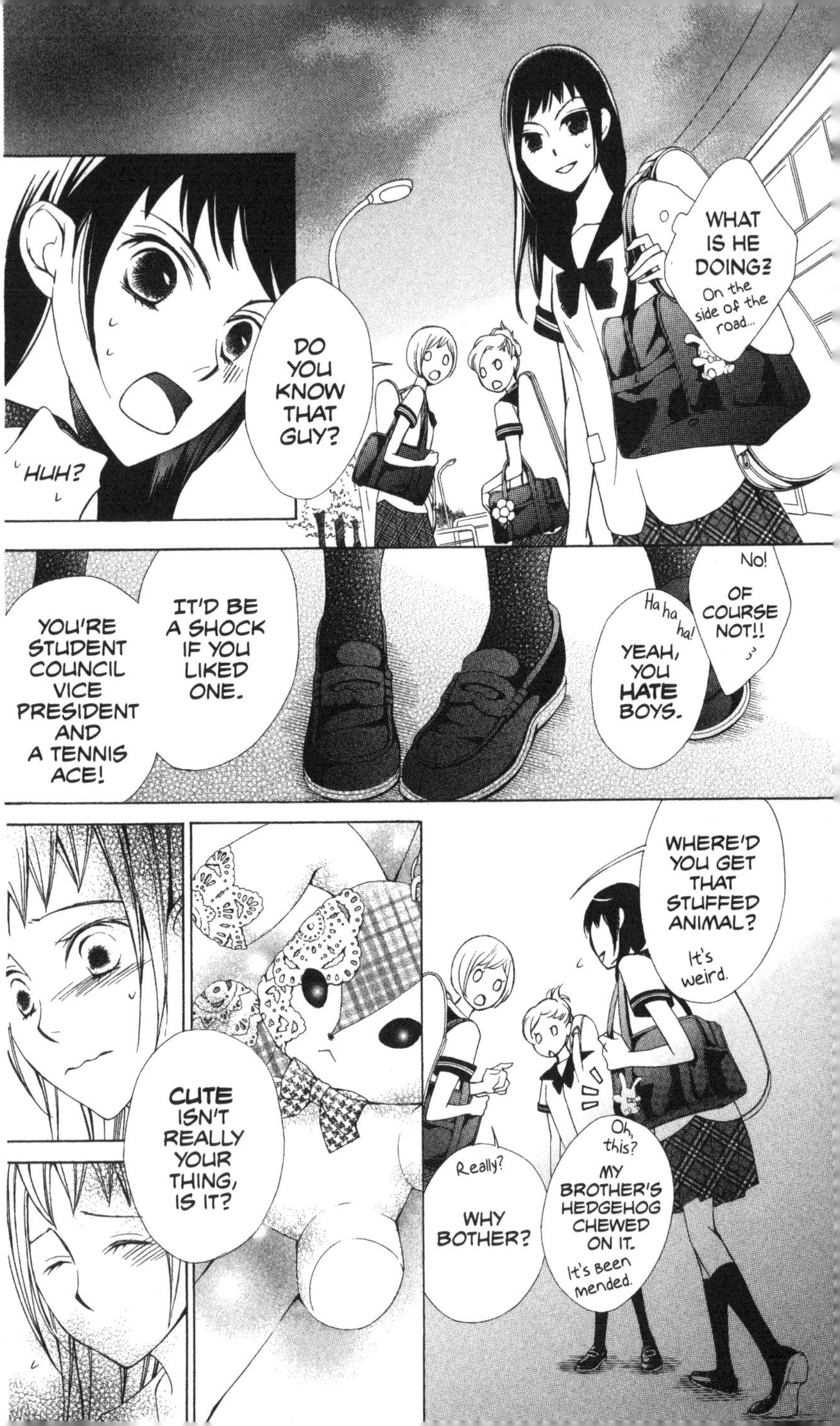
WHAT IS HE DOING? On the side of the road...
DO YOU KNOW THAT GUY?
HUH?
No! OF COURSE NOT!!
Ha ha ha! YEAH, YOU HATE BOYS.
IT'D BE A SHOCK IF YOU LIKED ONE.
YOU'RE STUDENT COUNCIL VICE PRESIDENT AND A TENNIS ACE!
WHERE'D YOU GET THAT STUFFED ANIMAL? It's weird.
Oh, this? MY BROTHER'S HEDGEHOG CHEWED ON IT. It's been mended.
Really? WHY BOTHER?
CUTE ISN'T REALLY YOUR THING, IS IT?

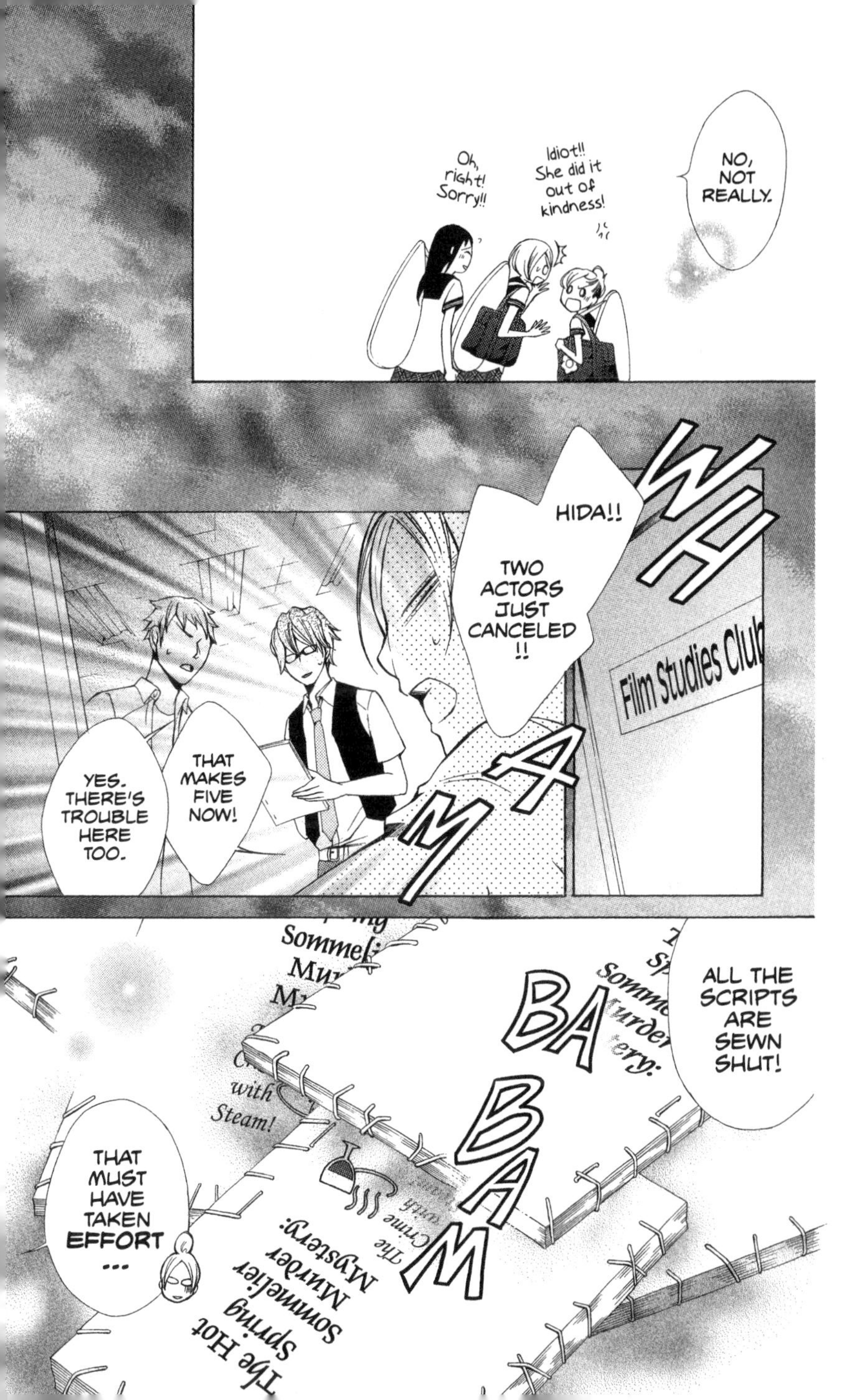
NO, NOT REALLY.
Idiot!! She did it out of kindness!
Oh, right! Sorry!!
WHAM
HIDA!!
TWO ACTORS JUST CANCELED!!
Film Studies Club
THAT MAKES FIVE NOW!
YES. THERE'S TROUBLE HERE TOO.
BABAM
ALL THE SCRIPTS ARE SEWN SHUT!
with Steam!
The Hot Spring Sommelier Murder Mystery:
The Crime with
THAT MUST HAVE TAKEN EFFORT...

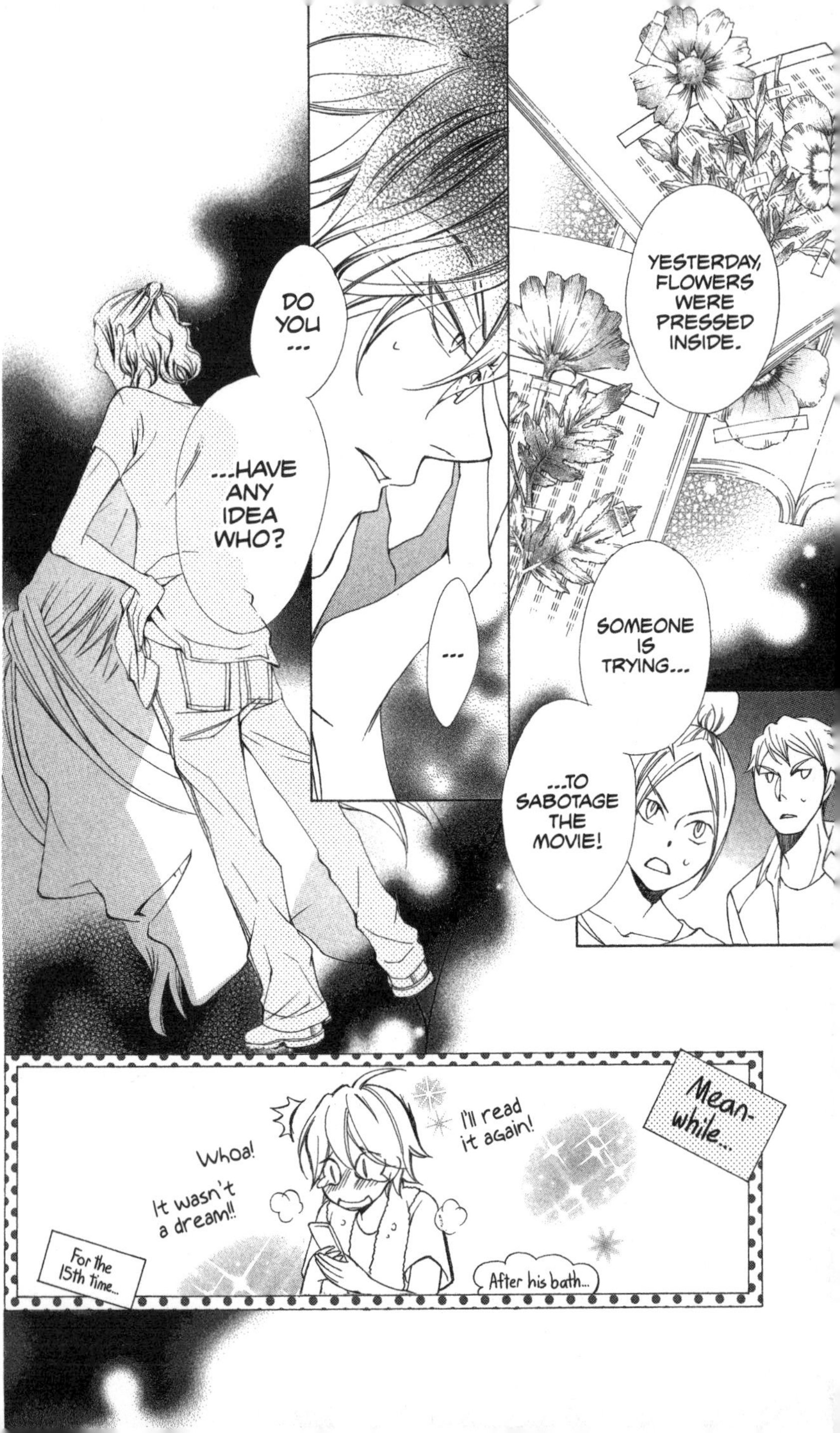
YESTERDAY, FLOWERS WERE PRESSED INSIDE.
SOMEONE IS TRYING...
...TO SABOTAGE THE MOVIE!
...
DO YOU...
...HAVE ANY IDEA WHO?
Mean-while...
I'll read it again!
After his bath...
Whoa!
It wasn't a dream!!
For the 15th time...

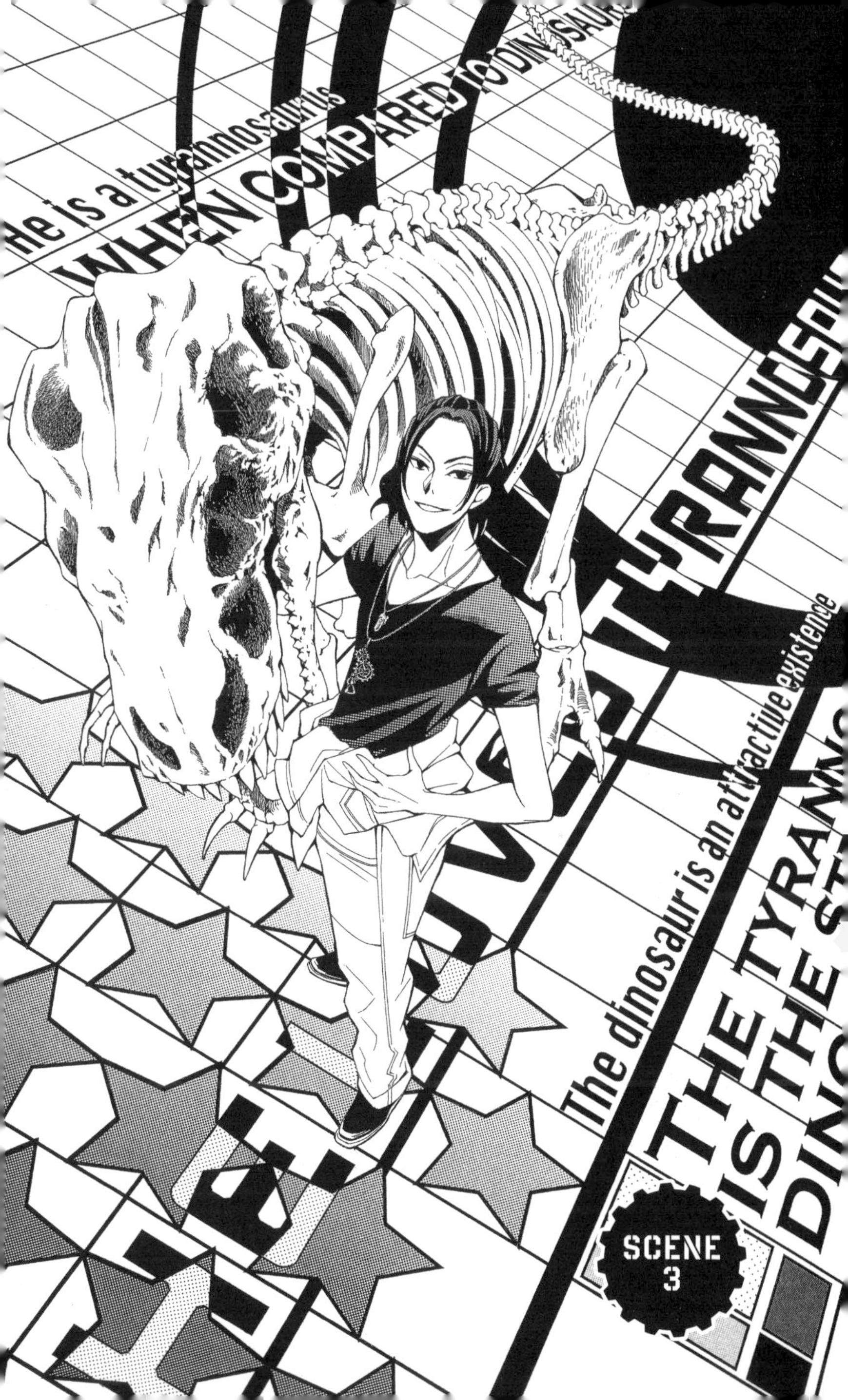
He is a tyrannosaurus
WHEN COMPARED TO
The dinosaur is an attractive existence
SCENE
3

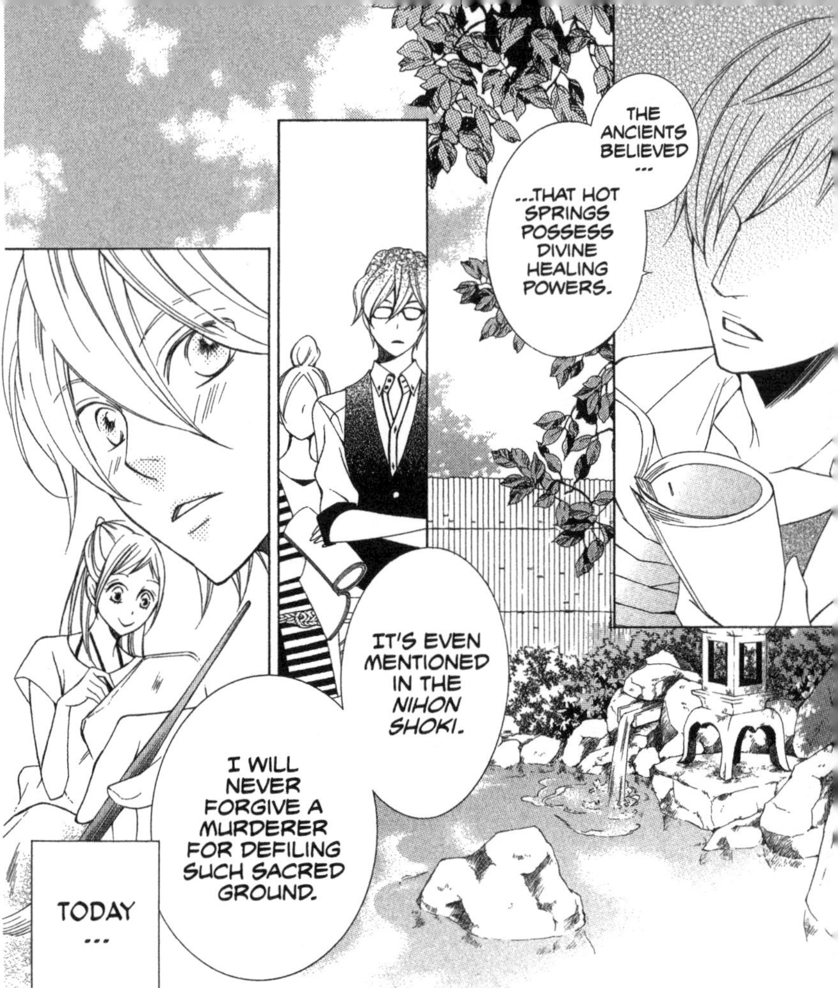
THE ANCIENTS BELIEVED...
...THAT HOT SPRINGS POSSESS DIVINE HEALING POWERS.
IT'S EVEN MENTIONED IN THE *NIHON SHOKI*.
I WILL NEVER FORGIVE A MURDERER FOR DEFILING SUCH SACRED GROUND.
TODAY...

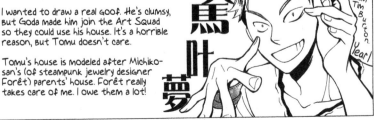

Tomu Tenba

I wanted to draw a real goof. He's clumsy, but Goda made him join the Art Squad so they could use his house. It's a horrible reason, but Tomu doesn't care.

Tomu's house is modeled after Michiko-san's (of steampunk jewelry designer Forêt) parents' house. Forêt really takes care of me. I owe them a lot!

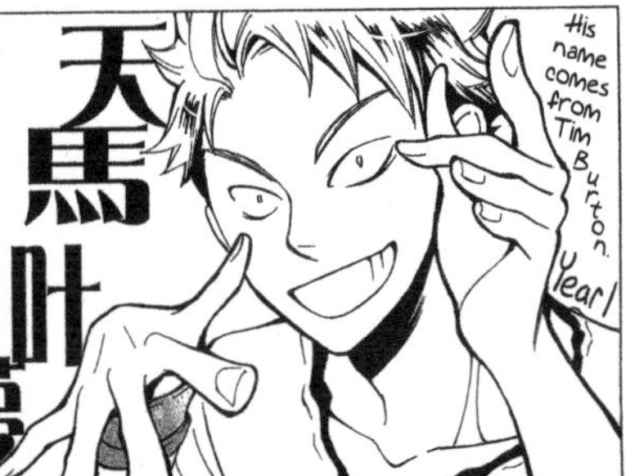
天馬叶夢
His name comes from Tim Burton.
Year 1

Goda's sewing machine is based on Michiko-san's.

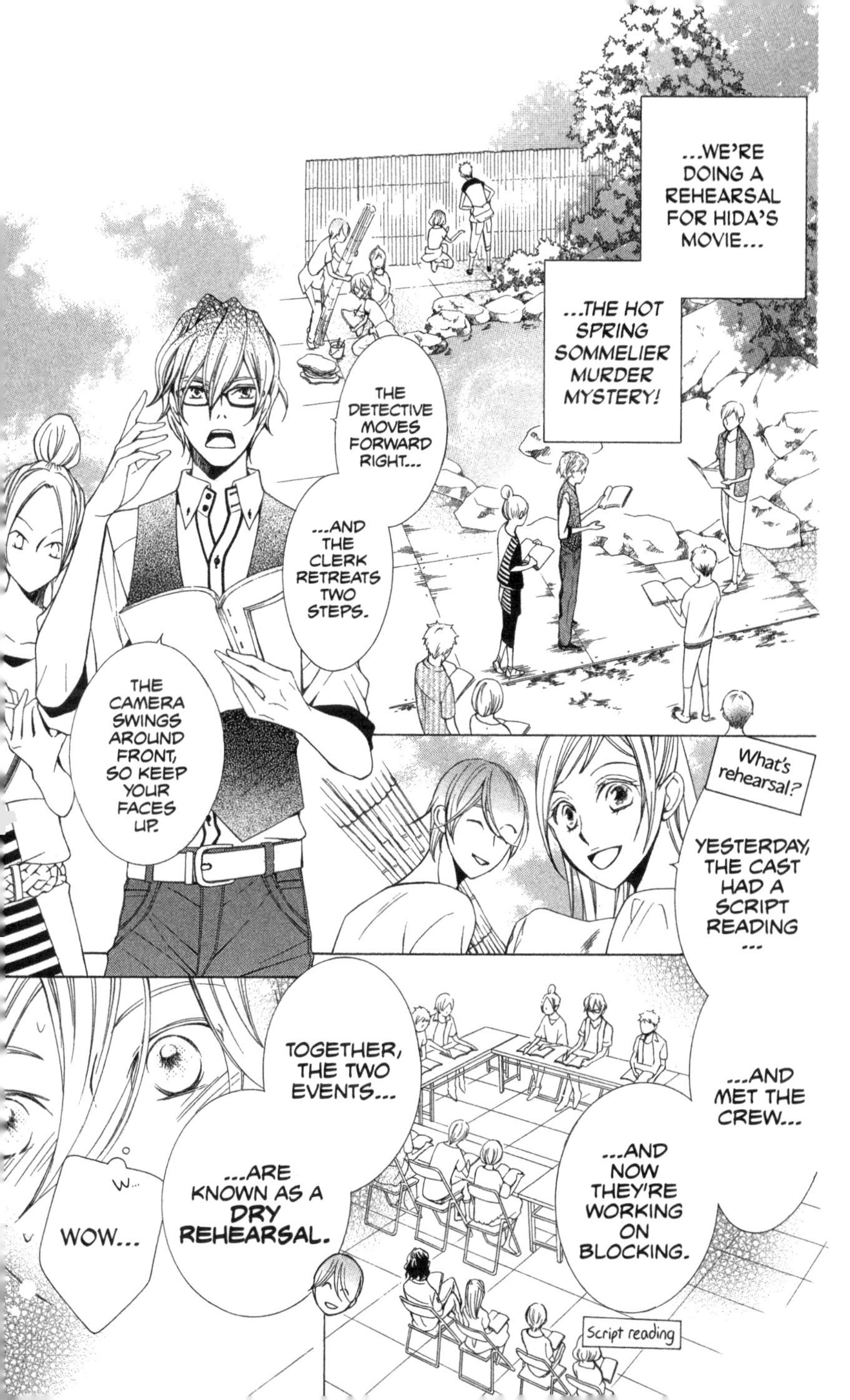
...WE'RE DOING A REHEARSAL FOR HIDA'S MOVIE...
...THE HOT SPRING SOMMELIER MURDER MYSTERY!
THE DETECTIVE MOVES FORWARD RIGHT...
...AND THE CLERK RETREATS TWO STEPS.
THE CAMERA SWINGS AROUND FRONT, SO KEEP YOUR FACES UP.
What's rehearsal?
YESTERDAY, THE CAST HAD A SCRIPT READING...
...AND MET THE CREW...
...AND NOW THEY'RE WORKING ON BLOCKING.
Script reading
TOGETHER, THE TWO EVENTS...
...ARE KNOWN AS A DRY REHEARSAL.
W...
WOW...

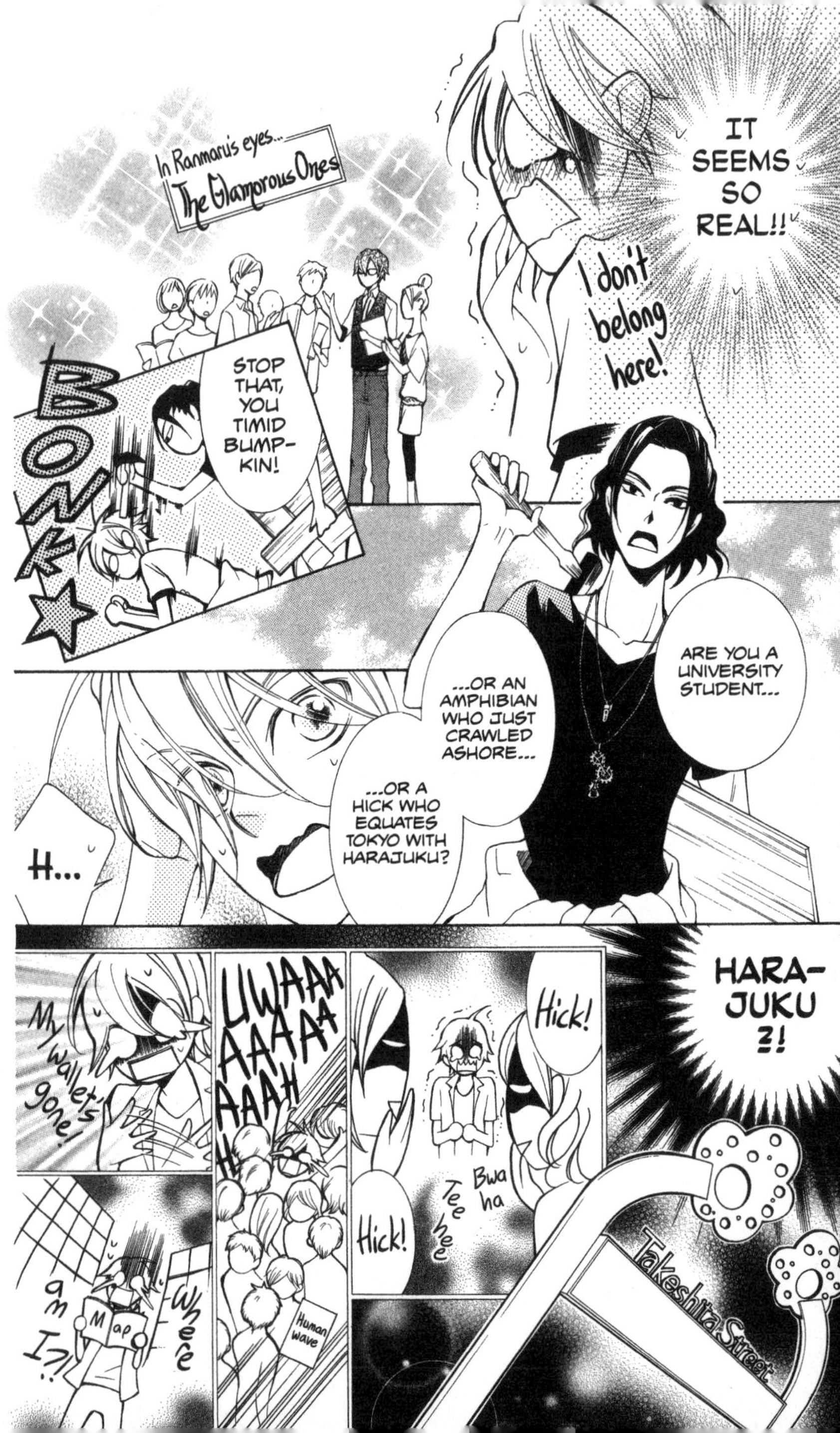
IT SEEMS SO REAL!!
I don't belong here!
In Ranmaru's eyes...
The Glamorous Ones
BONK☆
STOP THAT, YOU TIMID BUMP-KIN!
ARE YOU A UNIVERSITY STUDENT...
...OR AN AMPHIBIAN WHO JUST CRAWLED ASHORE...
...OR A HICK WHO EQUATES TOKYO WITH HARAJUKU?
H...
HARA-JUKU?!
Hick!
Hick!
Bwa ha
Tee hee
Takeshita Street
UWAAAAAAAAAAAH
Human wave
My wallet's gone!
Where am I?!
Map

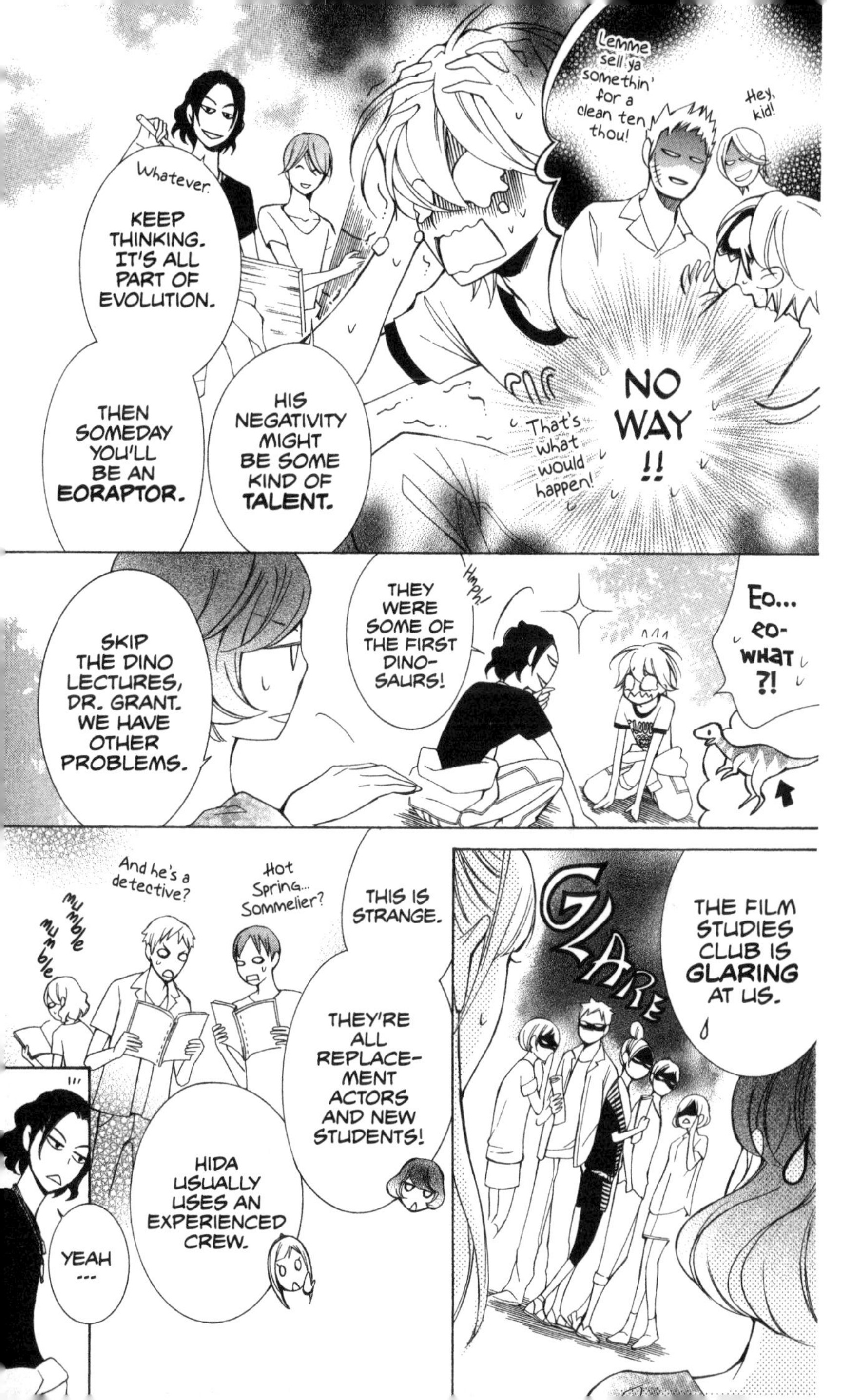
Hey, kid!
Lemme sell ya somethin' for a clean ten thou!
NO WAY!!
That's what would happen!
HIS NEGATIVITY MIGHT BE SOME KIND OF TALENT.
Whatever.
KEEP THINKING. IT'S ALL PART OF EVOLUTION.
THEN SOMEDAY YOU'LL BE AN EORAPTOR.
Eo... eo-WHAT?!
Hmph!
THEY WERE SOME OF THE FIRST DINO-SAURS!
SKIP THE DINO LECTURES, DR. GRANT. WE HAVE OTHER PROBLEMS.
GLARE
THE FILM STUDIES CLUB IS GLARING AT US.
THIS IS STRANGE.
THEY'RE ALL REPLACE-MENT ACTORS AND NEW STUDENTS!
Hot Spring... Sommelier?
And he's a detective?
mumble mumble
HIDA USUALLY USES AN EXPERIENCED CREW.
YEAH...

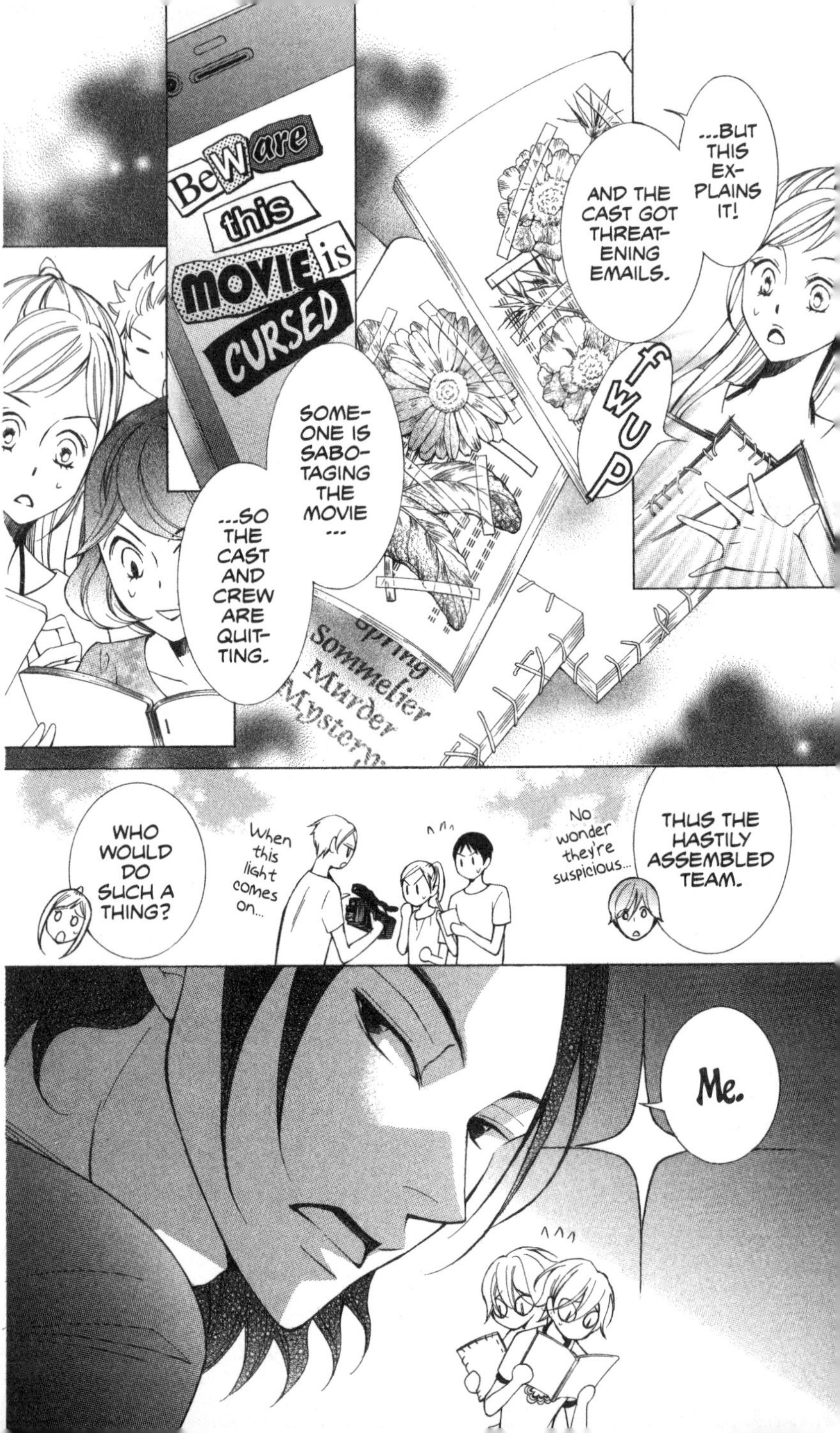
...BUT THIS EX-PLAINS IT!
AND THE CAST GOT THREAT-ENING EMAILS.
FWUP
BeWare this MOVIE is CURSED
SOME-ONE IS SABO-TAGING THE MOVIE...
...SO THE CAST AND CREW ARE QUIT-TING.
Spring Sommelier Murder Mystery
THUS THE HASTILY ASSEMBLED TEAM.
No wonder they're suspicious...
When this light comes on...
WHO WOULD DO SUCH A THING?
Me.

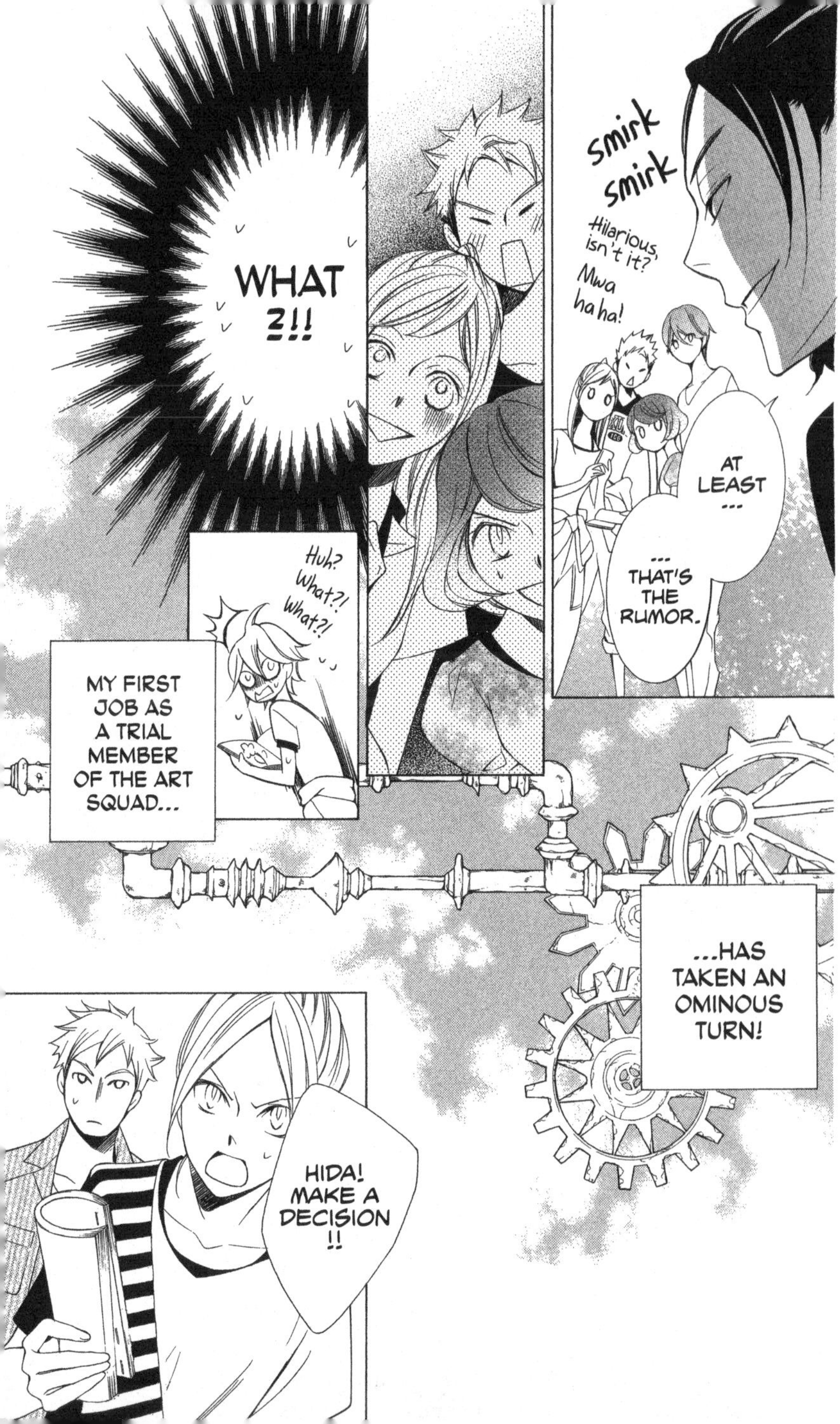
Smirk smirk
Hilarious, isn't it? Mwa ha ha!
AT LEAST...
...THAT'S THE RUMOR.
WHAT ?!!
Huh? What?! What?!
MY FIRST JOB AS A TRIAL MEMBER OF THE ART SQUAD...
...HAS TAKEN AN OMINOUS TURN!
HIDA! MAKE A DECISION !!

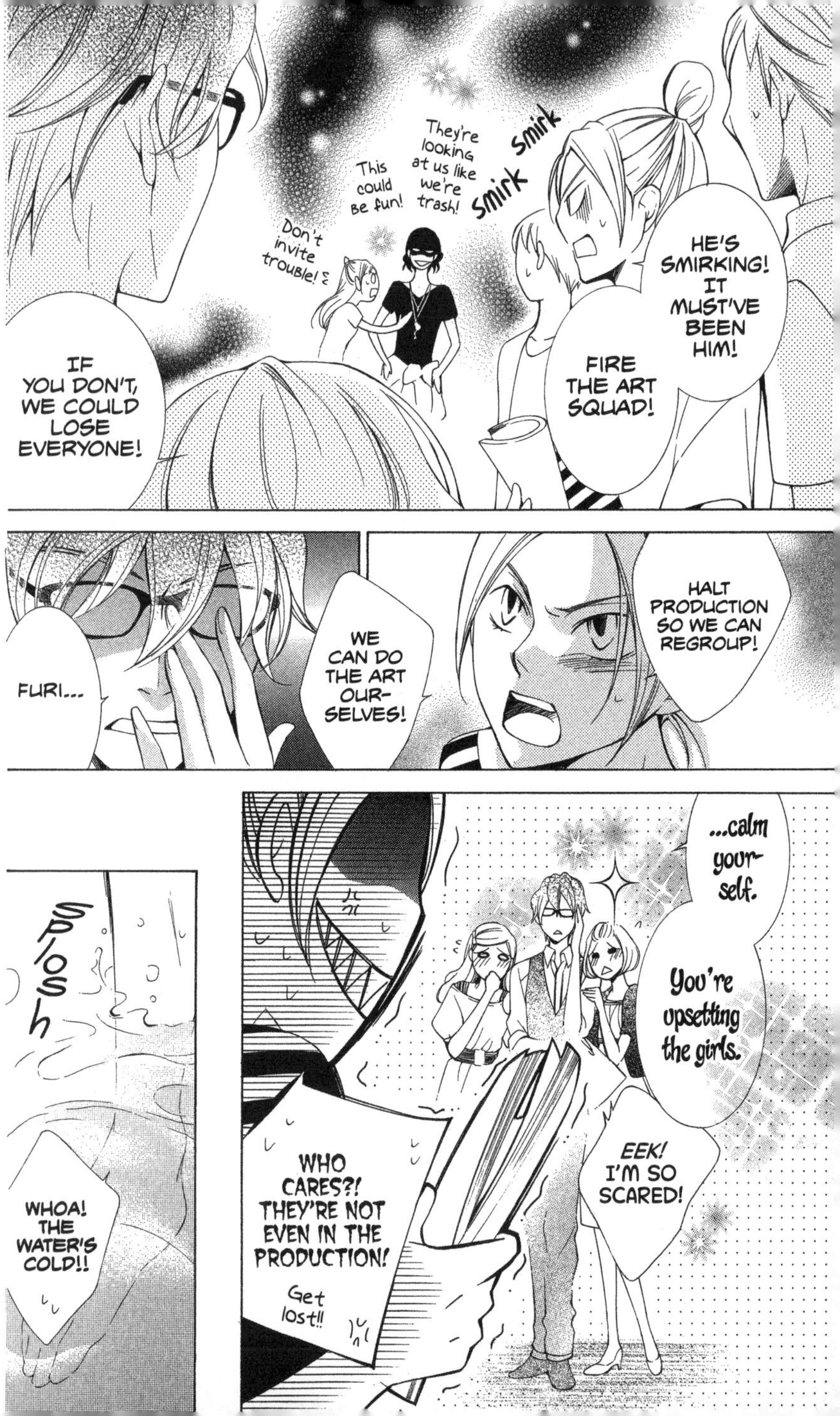
HE'S SMIRKING! IT MUST'VE BEEN HIM!
Smirk
Smirk
They're looking at us like we're trash!
This could be fun!
Don't invite trouble!
FIRE THE ART SQUAD!
IF YOU DON'T, WE COULD LOSE EVERYONE!
HALT PRODUCTION SO WE CAN REGROUP!
WE CAN DO THE ART OURSELVES!
FURI...
...calm yourself.
You're upsetting the girls.
EEK! I'M SO SCARED!
WHO CARES?! THEY'RE NOT EVEN IN THE PRODUCTION!
Get lost!!
Splosh
WHOA! THE WATER'S COLD!!

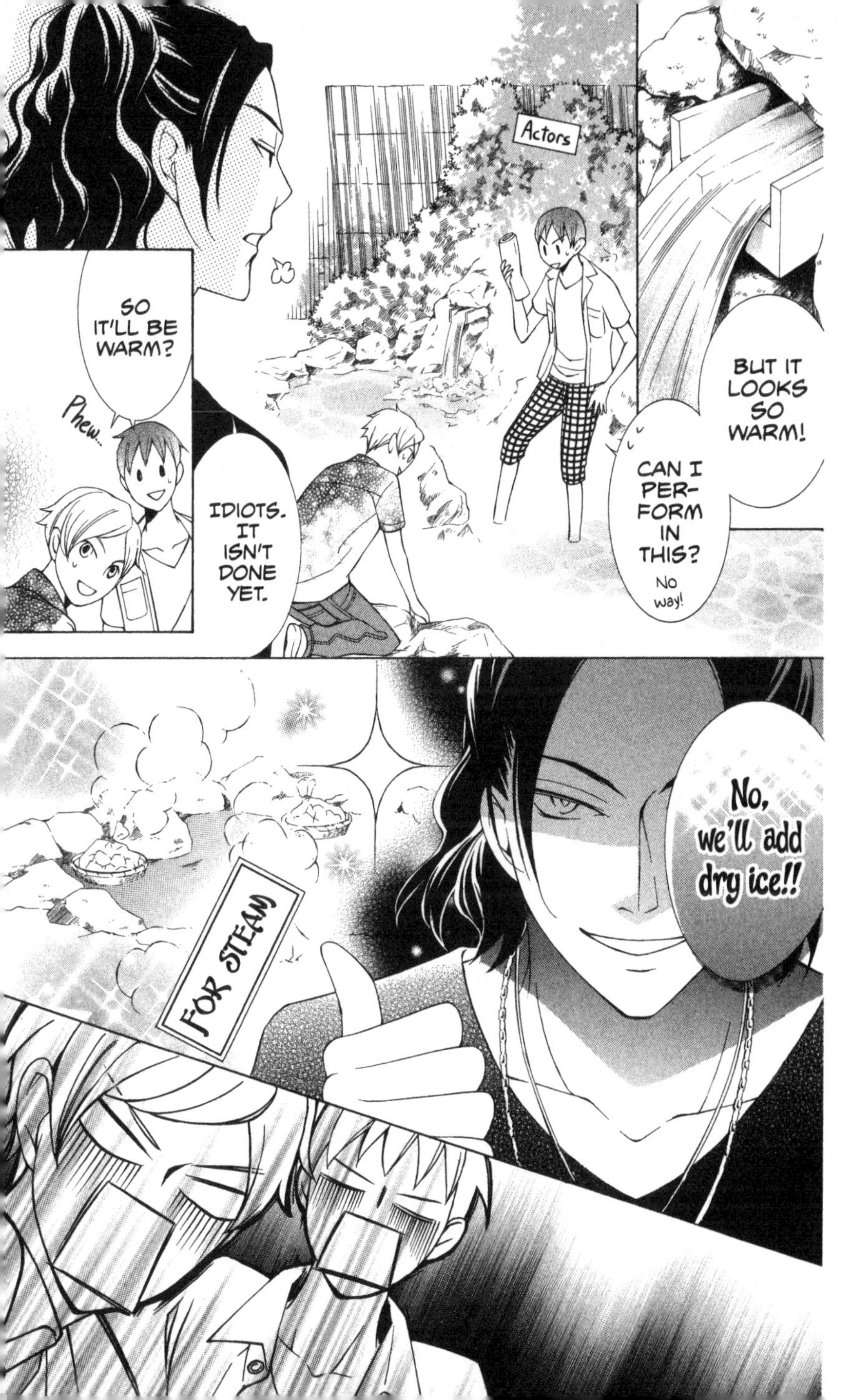
BUT IT LOOKS SO WARM!
Actors
CAN I PERFORM IN THIS?
No way!
SO IT'LL BE WARM?
Phew...
IDIOTS. IT ISN'T DONE YET.
No, we'll add dry ice!!
FOR STEAM

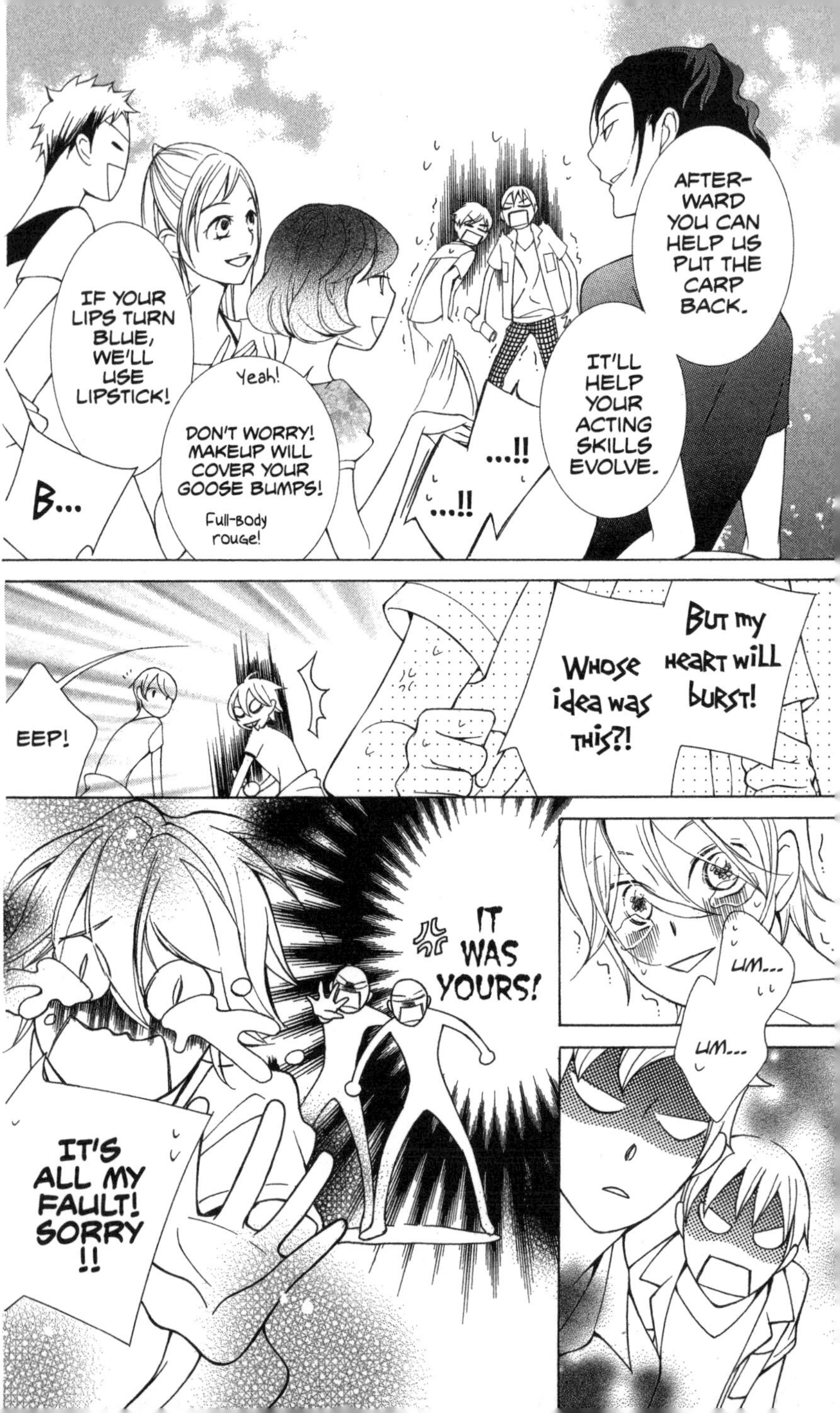
AFTER-WARD YOU CAN HELP US PUT THE CARP BACK.
IT'LL HELP YOUR ACTING SKILLS EVOLVE.
...!!
...!!
Yeah!
DON'T WORRY! MAKEUP WILL COVER YOUR GOOSE BUMPS!
Full-body rouge!
IF YOUR LIPS TURN BLUE, WE'LL USE LIPSTICK!
B...
But my heart will burst!
Whose idea was this?!
EEP!
um...
um...
IT WAS YOURS!
IT'S ALL MY FAULT! SORRY!!

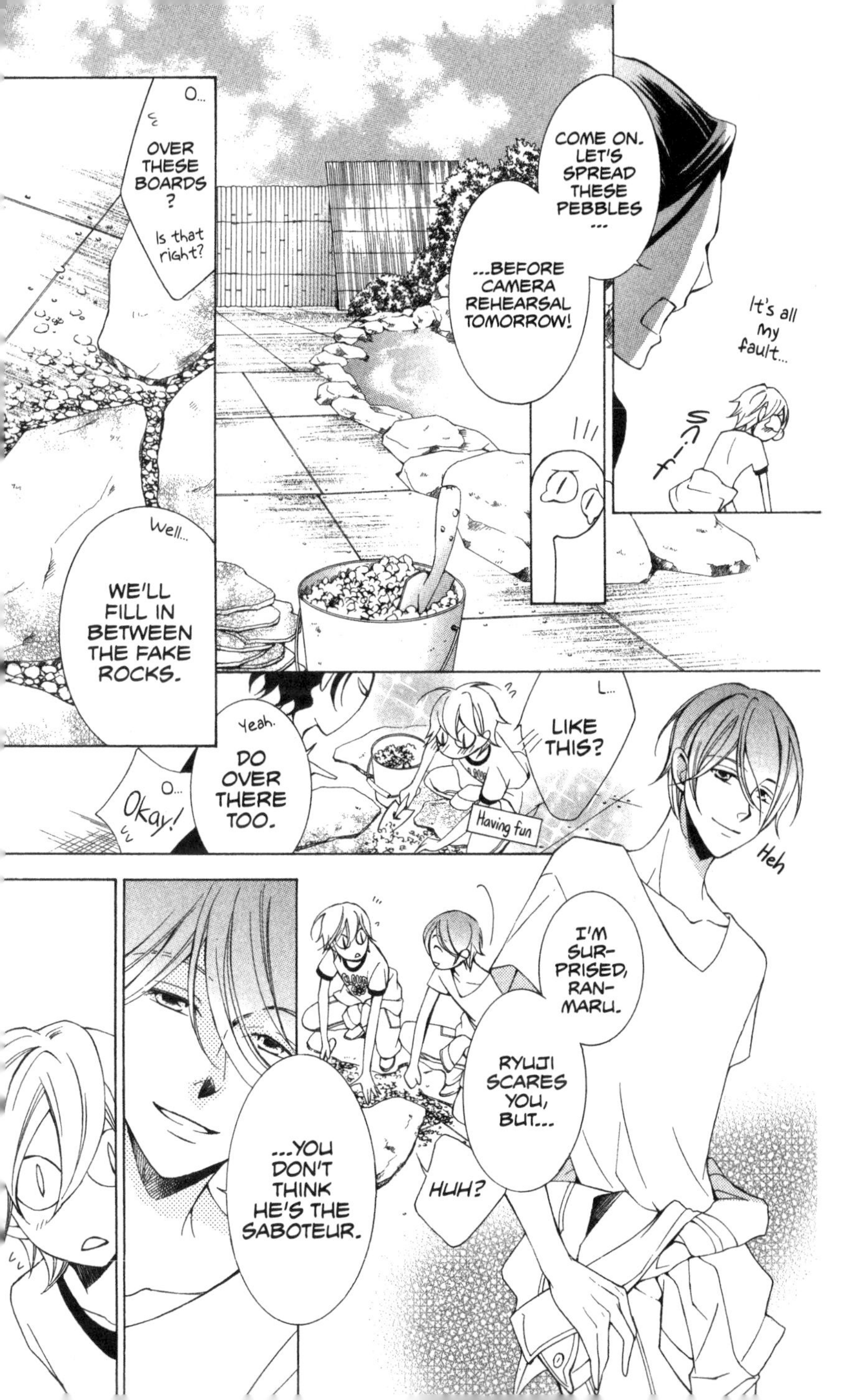

COME ON. LET'S SPREAD THESE PEBBLES...
...BEFORE CAMERA REHEARSAL TOMORROW!
It's all my fault...
Sniff
O... OVER THESE BOARDS?
Is that right?
Well...
WE'LL FILL IN BETWEEN THE FAKE ROCKS.
L... LIKE THIS?
Having fun
Yeah.
DO OVER THERE TOO.
O... Okay!
Heh
I'M SUR-PRISED, RAN-MARU.
RYUJI SCARES YOU, BUT...
HUH?
...YOU DON'T THINK HE'S THE SABOTEUR.

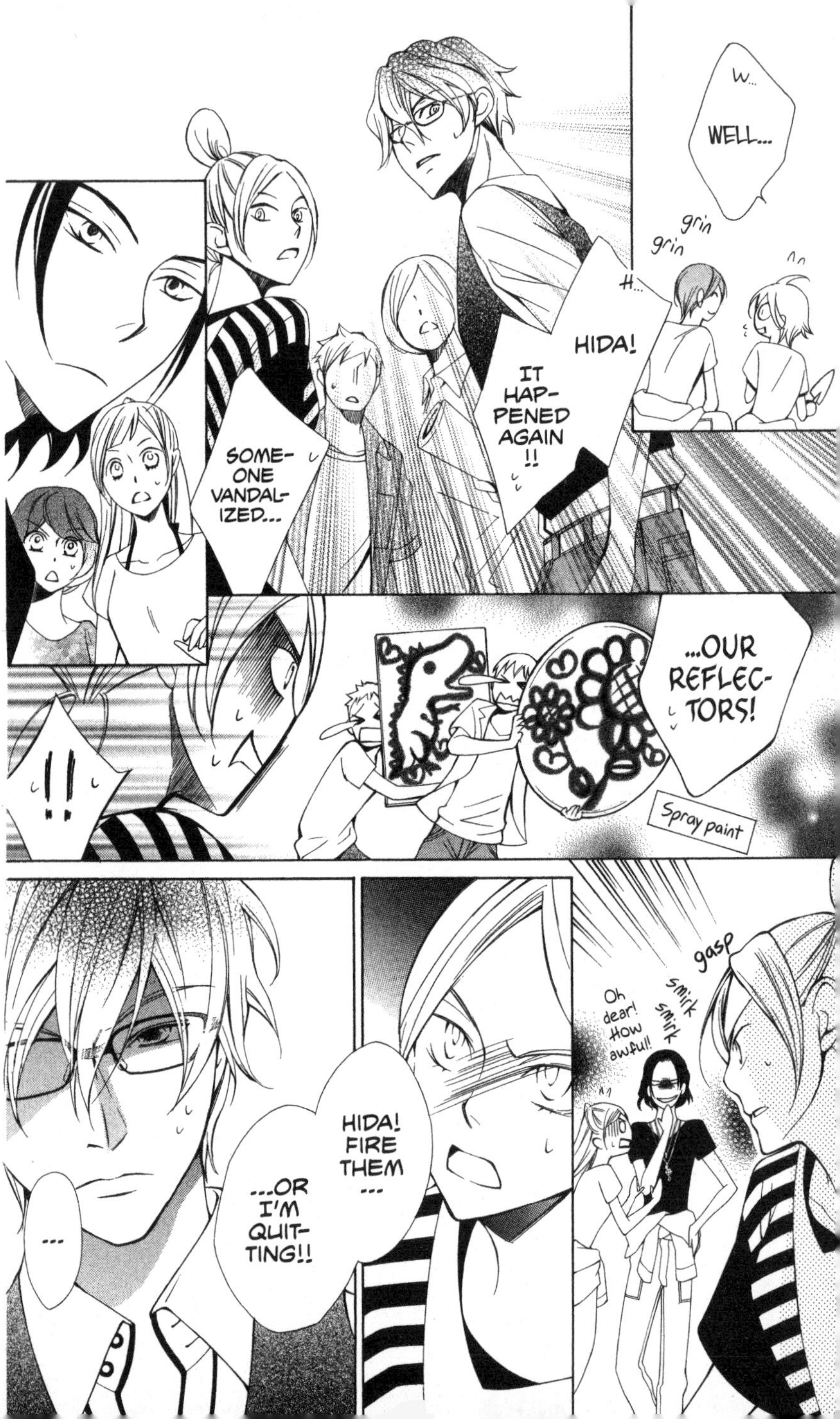
W...
WELL...
grin grin
H...
HIDA!
IT HAP-PENED AGAIN!!
SOME-ONE VANDAL-IZED...
...OUR REFLEC-TORS!
Spray paint
!!
gasp
smirk smirk
Oh dear! How awful!
HIDA! FIRE THEM...
...OR I'M QUIT-TING!!
...

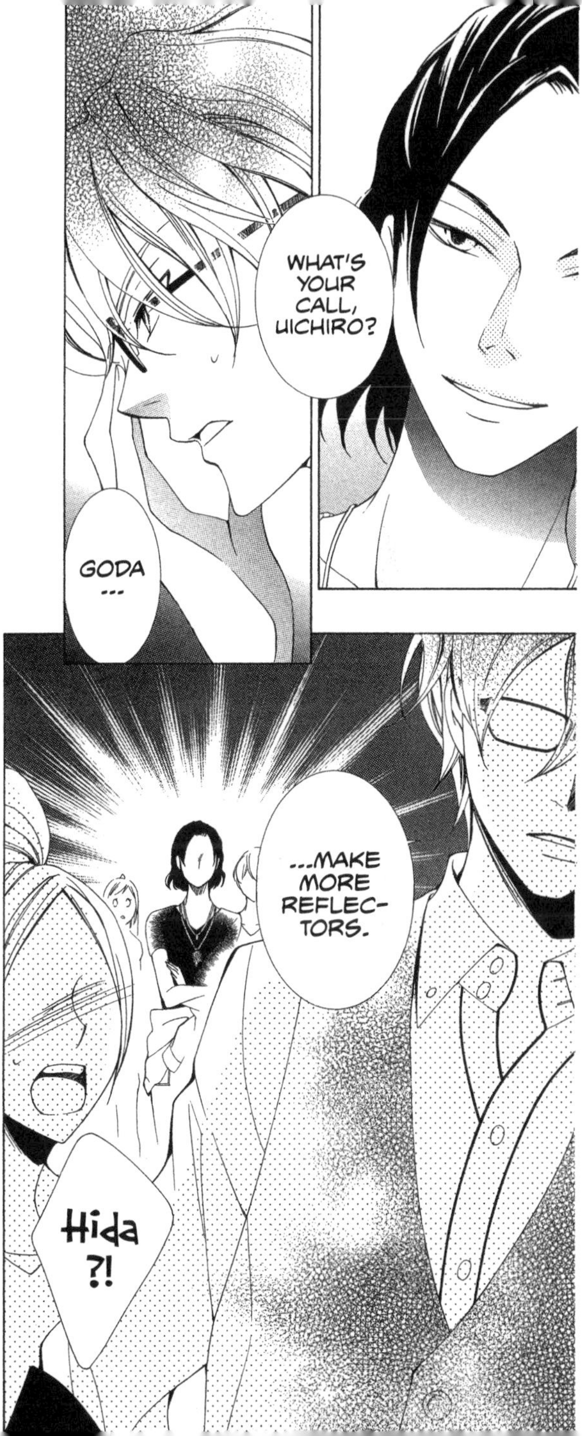
WHAT'S YOUR CALL, UICHIRO?
GODA...
...MAKE MORE REFLECTORS.
Hida?!

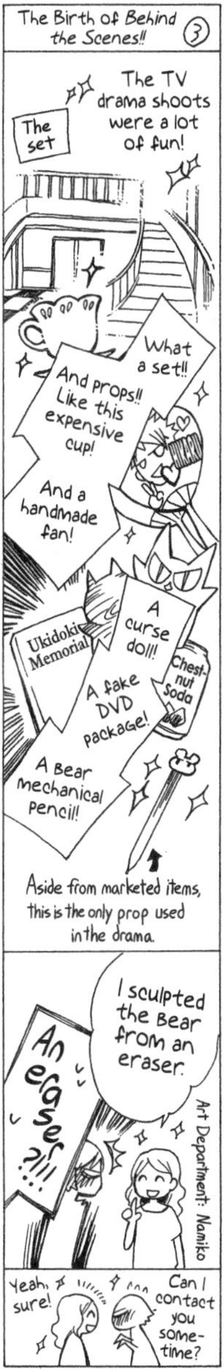
The Birth of Behind the Scenes!! 3
The TV drama shoots were a lot of fun!
The set
What a set!!
And props!! Like this expensive cup!
And a handmade fan!
Ukidoki Memorial
A curse doll!
Chest-nut Soda
A fake DVD package!
A Bear mechanical pencil!
Aside from marketed items, this is the only prop used in the drama.
I sculpted the Bear from an eraser.
An eraser?!!
Art Department: Namiko
Can I contact you some-time?
Yeah, sure!
Already on the attack...

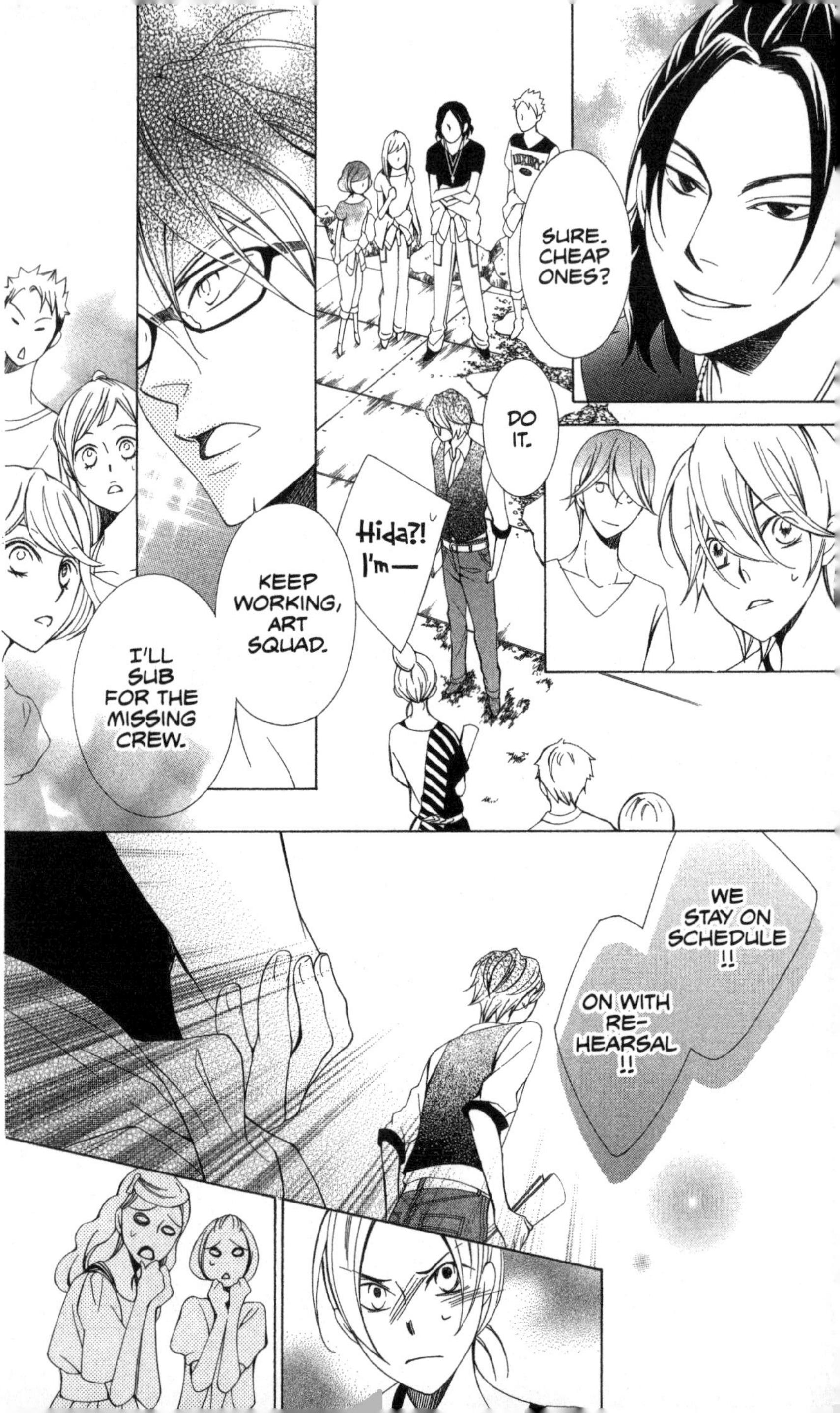
SURE. CHEAP ONES?
DO IT.
Hida?! I'm—
KEEP WORKING, ART SQUAD.
I'LL SUB FOR THE MISSING CREW.
WE STAY ON SCHEDULE !!
ON WITH RE-HEARSAL !!

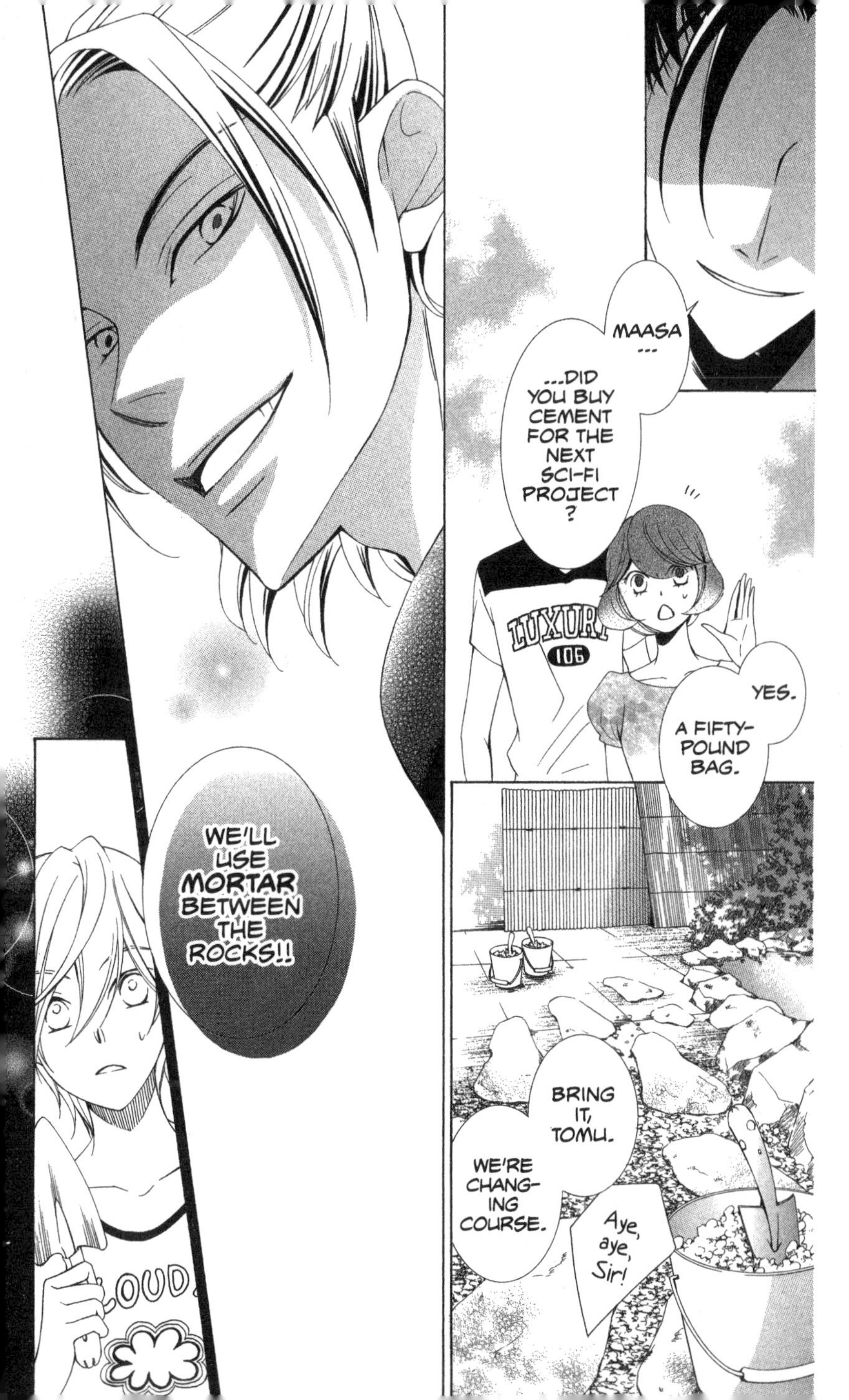
MAASA...
...DID YOU BUY CEMENT FOR THE NEXT SCI-FI PROJECT?
YES.
A FIFTY-POUND BAG.
BRING IT, TOMU.
WE'RE CHANGING COURSE.
Aye, aye, Sir!
WE'LL USE MORTAR BETWEEN THE ROCKS!!
LUXURI
106
LOUD

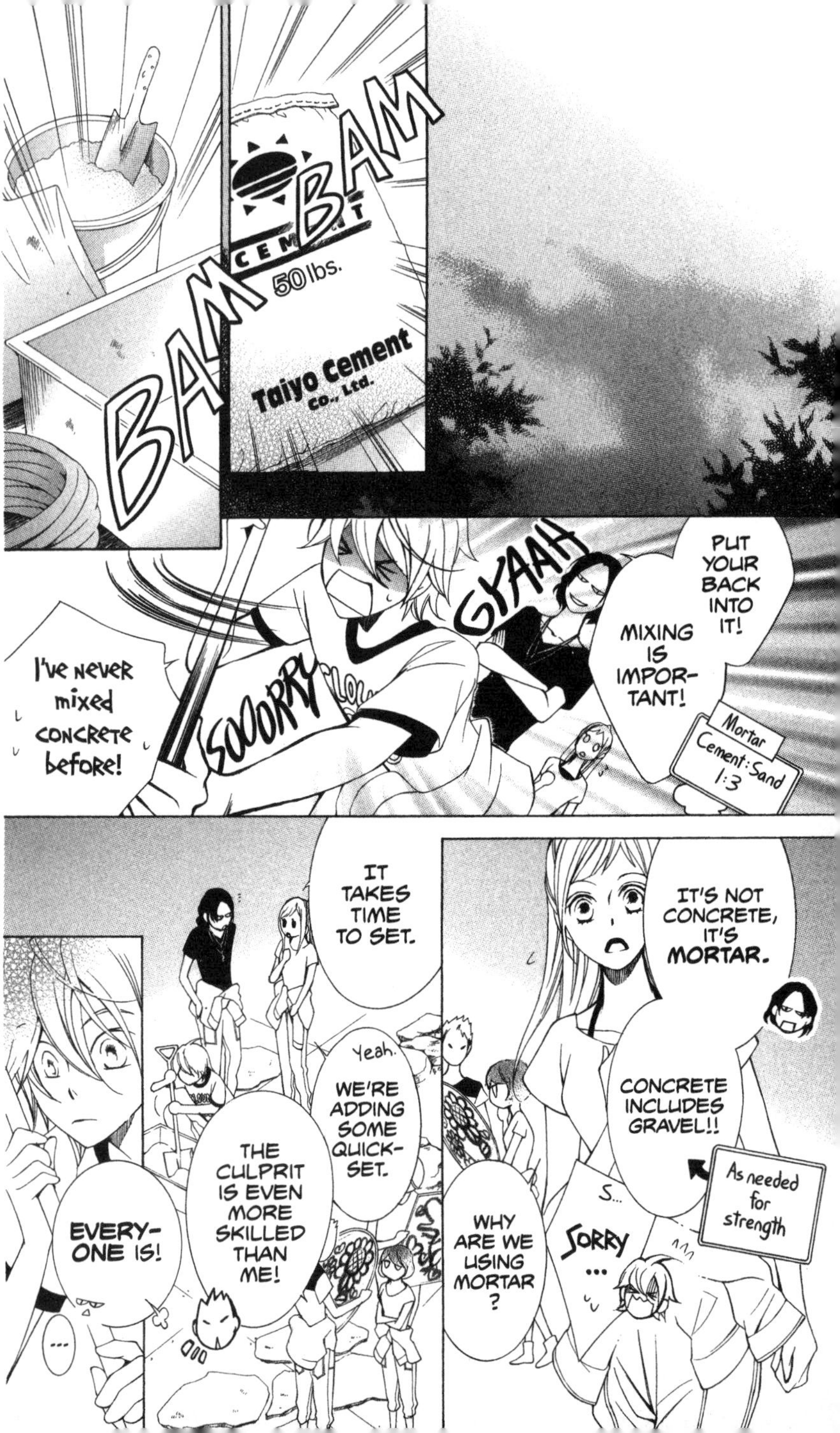
BAM BAM
50 lbs.
Taiyo Cement Co., Ltd.
PUT YOUR BACK INTO IT!
MIXING IS IMPORTANT!
Mortar
Cement : Sand 1:3
GYAAH
SOOORRY
I've never mixed concrete before!
IT'S NOT CONCRETE, IT'S MORTAR.
CONCRETE INCLUDES GRAVEL!!
As needed for strength
S...
SORRY...
WHY ARE WE USING MORTAR?
IT TAKES TIME TO SET.
Yeah.
WE'RE ADDING SOME QUICK-SET.
THE CULPRIT IS EVEN MORE SKILLED THAN ME!
EVERYONE IS!
...

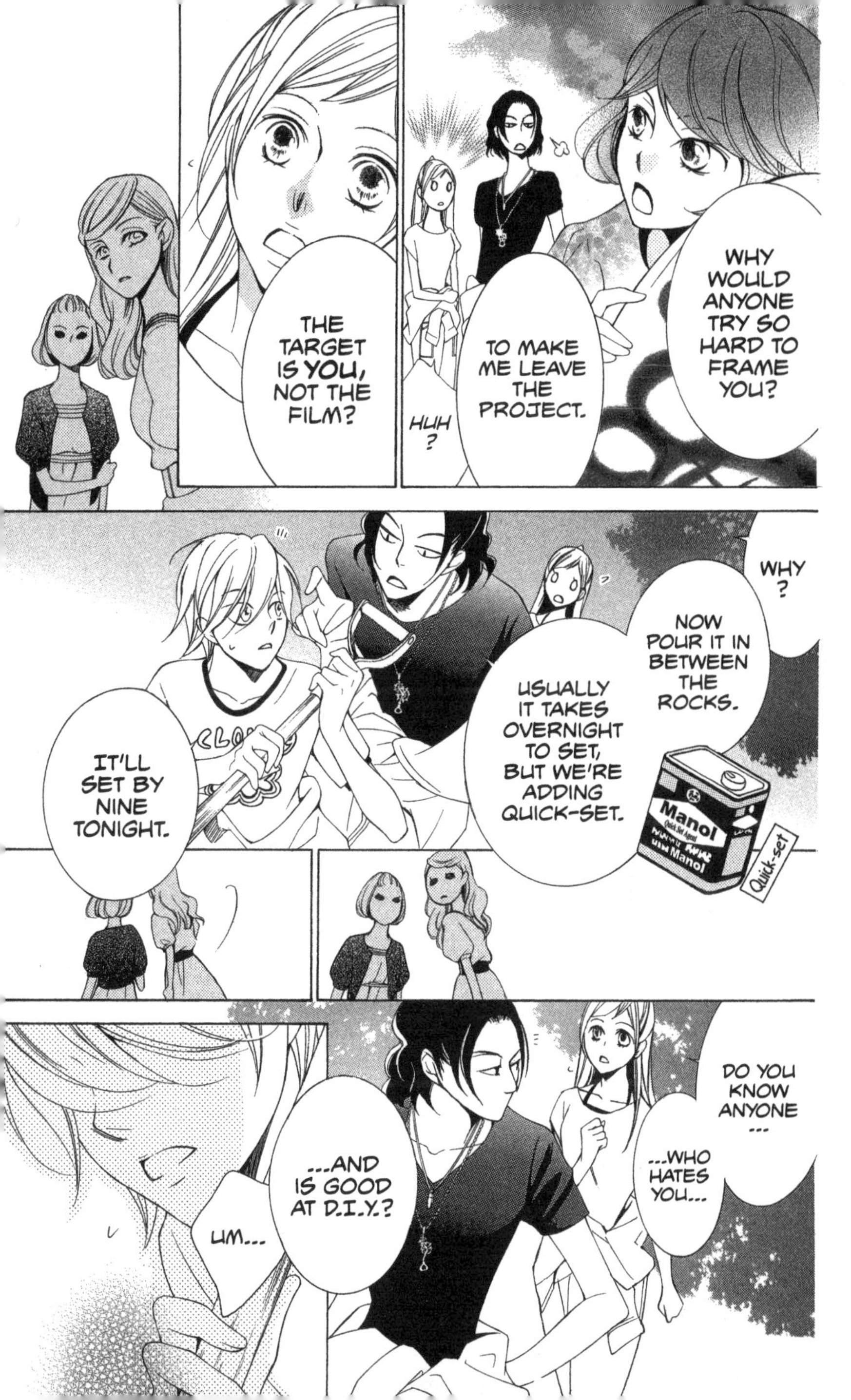
WHY WOULD ANYONE TRY SO HARD TO FRAME YOU?
TO MAKE ME LEAVE THE PROJECT.
HUH?
THE TARGET IS **YOU**, NOT THE FILM?
WHY?
NOW POUR IT IN BETWEEN THE ROCKS.
USUALLY IT TAKES OVERNIGHT TO SET, BUT WE'RE ADDING QUICK-SET.
Manol
Quick-set
IT'LL SET BY NINE TONIGHT.
DO YOU KNOW ANYONE ...
...WHO HATES YOU...
...AND IS GOOD AT D.I.Y.?
UM...

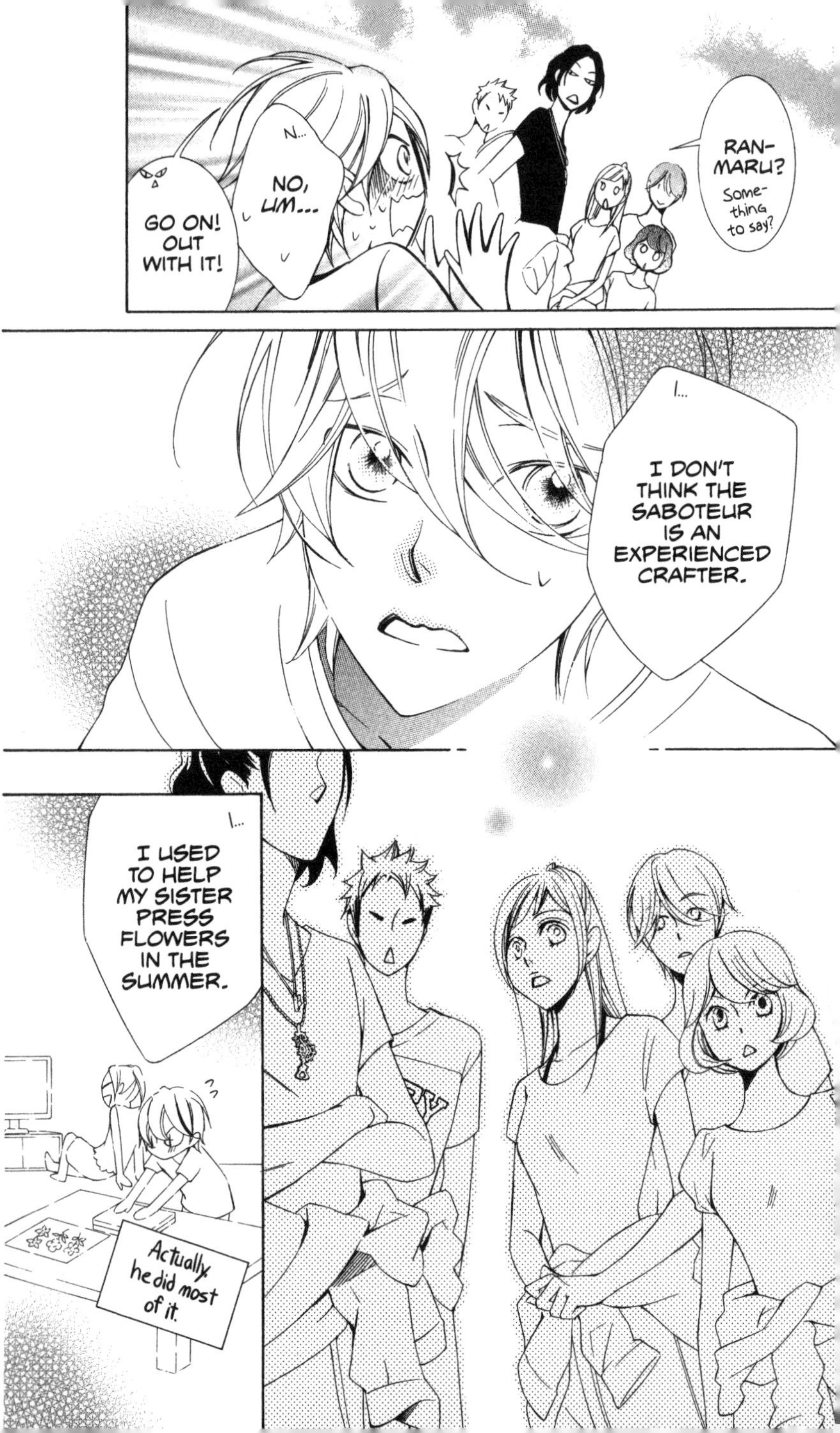
RAN-MARU? Some-thing to say?
N...
NO, UM...
GO ON! OUT WITH IT!
I...
I DON'T THINK THE SABOTEUR IS AN EXPERIENCED CRAFTER.
I...
I USED TO HELP MY SISTER PRESS FLOWERS IN THE SUMMER.
Actually, he did most of it.

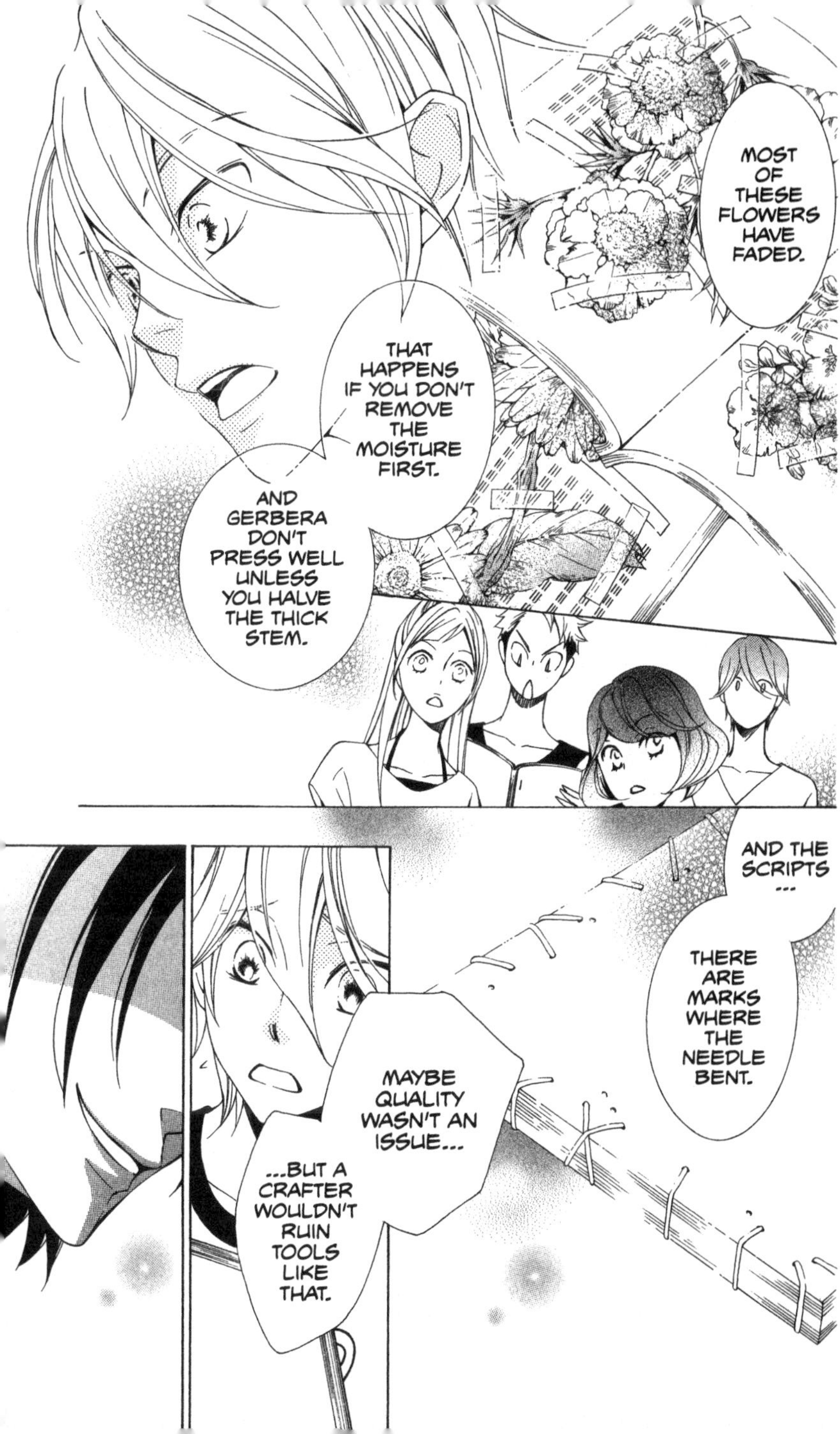
MOST OF THESE FLOWERS HAVE FADED.
THAT HAPPENS IF YOU DON'T REMOVE THE MOISTURE FIRST.
AND GERBERA DON'T PRESS WELL UNLESS YOU HALVE THE THICK STEM.
AND THE SCRIPTS...
THERE ARE MARKS WHERE THE NEEDLE BENT.
MAYBE QUALITY WASN'T AN ISSUE...
...BUT A CRAFTER WOULDN'T RUIN TOOLS LIKE THAT.

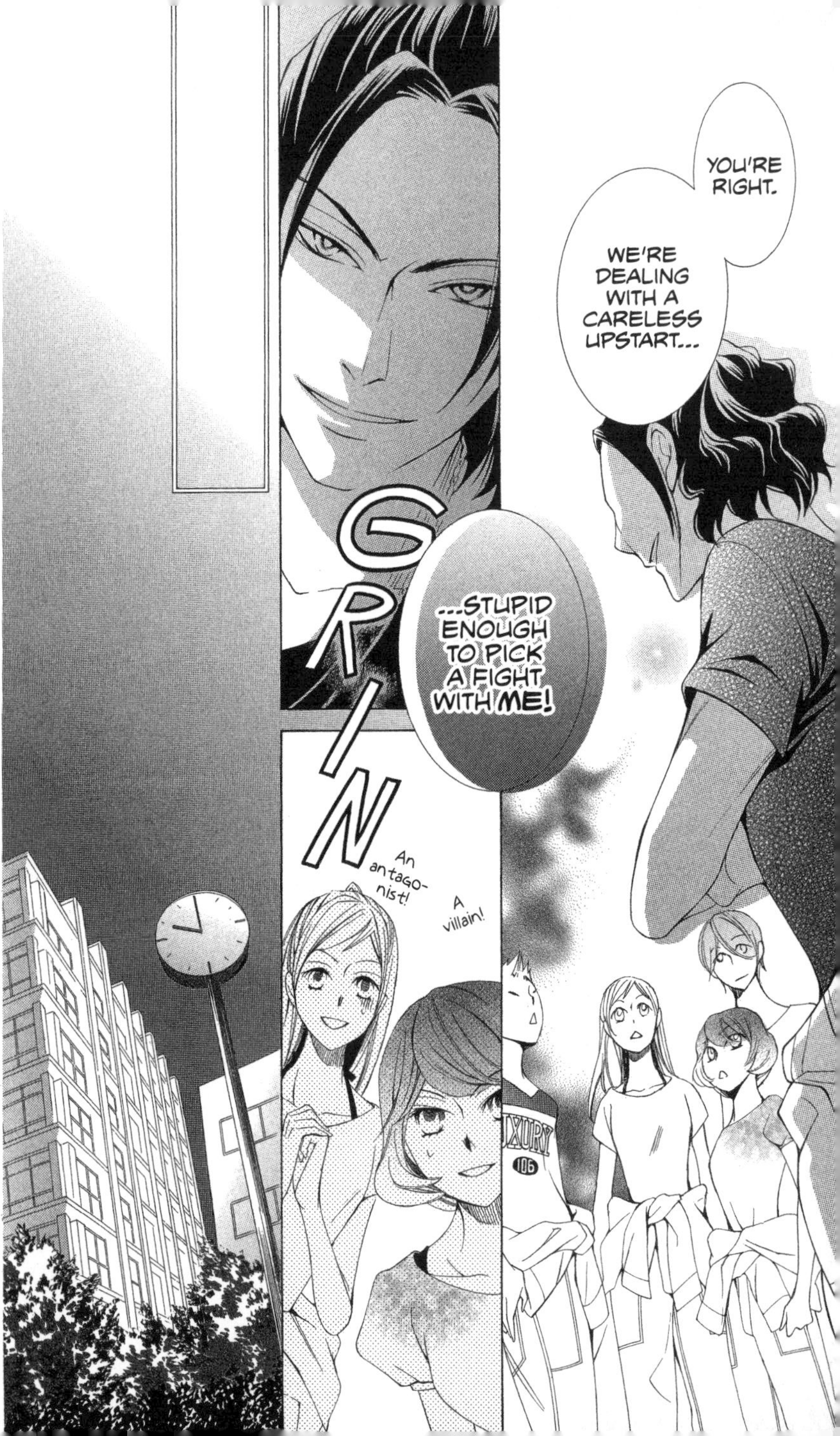
YOU'RE RIGHT.
WE'RE DEALING WITH A CARELESS UPSTART...
...STUPID ENOUGH TO PICK A FIGHT WITH ME!
GRIN
A villain!
An antago-nist!

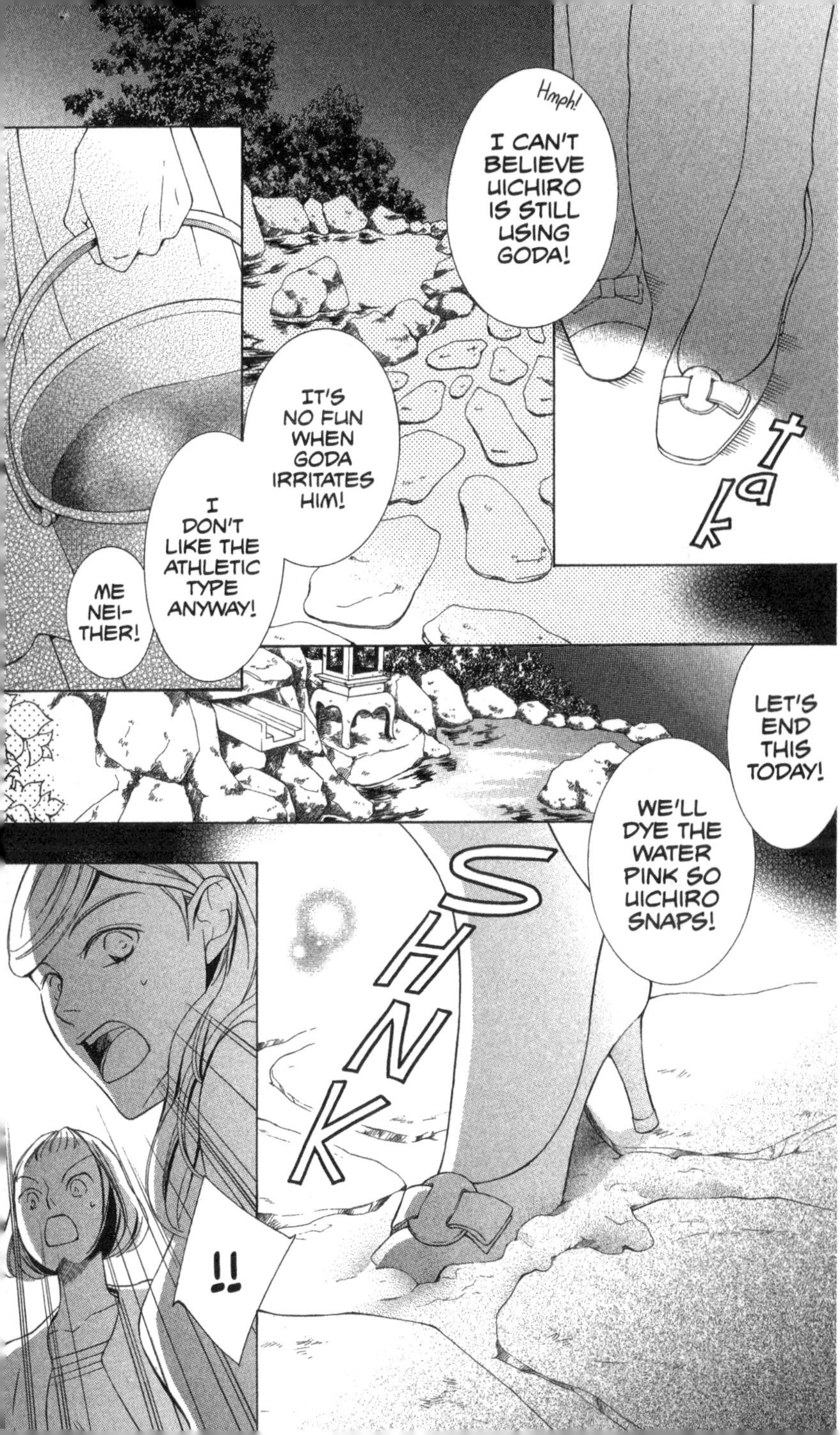
Hmph!
I CAN'T BELIEVE UICHIRO IS STILL USING GODA!
tak
IT'S NO FUN WHEN GODA IRRITATES HIM!
I DON'T LIKE THE ATHLETIC TYPE ANYWAY!
ME NEI-THER!
LET'S END THIS TODAY!
WE'LL DYE THE WATER PINK SO UICHIRO SNAPS!
SHNK
!!

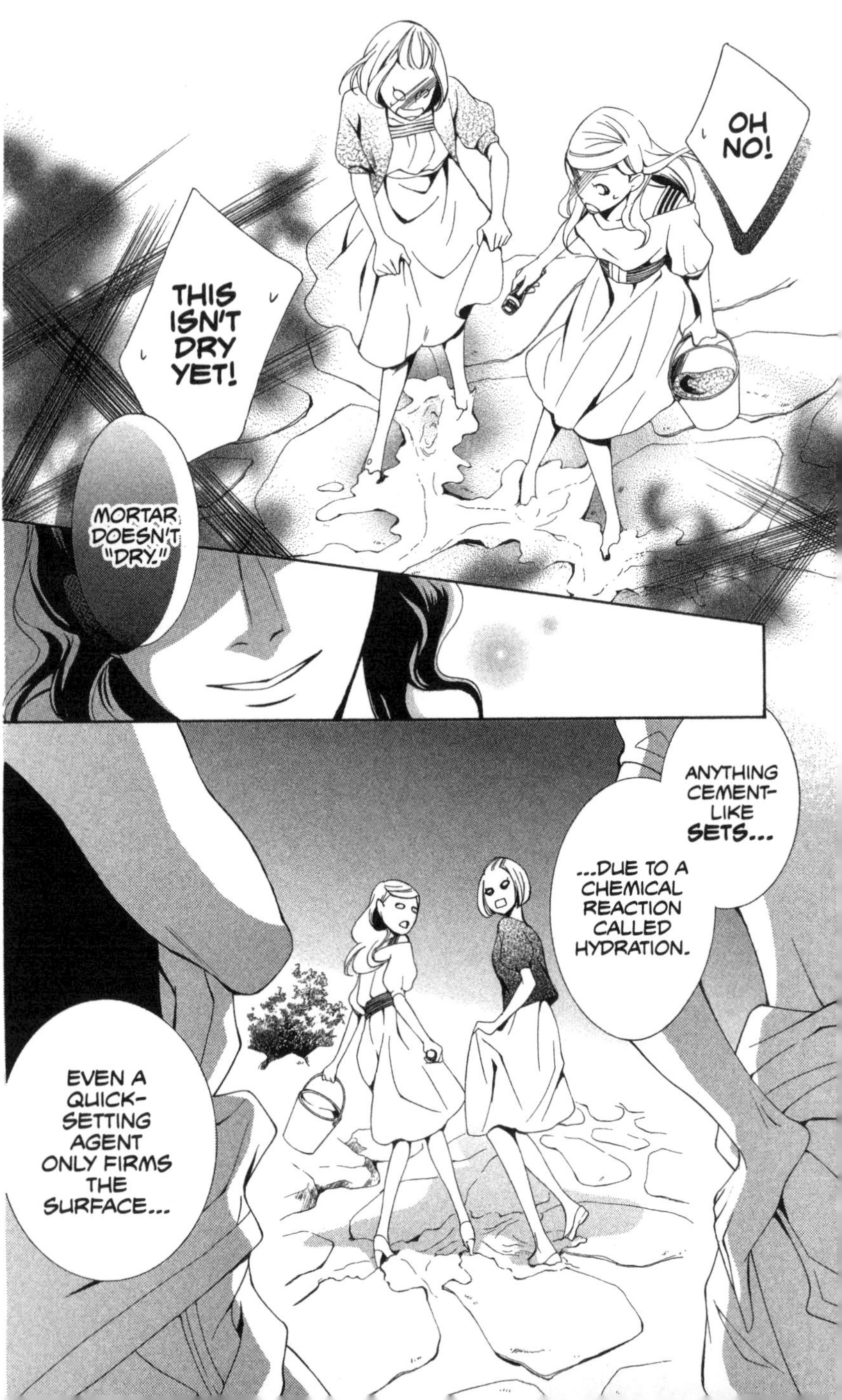
OH NO!
THIS ISN'T DRY YET!
MORTAR DOESN'T "DRY."
ANYTHING CEMENT-LIKE SETS...
...DUE TO A CHEMICAL REACTION CALLED HYDRATION.
EVEN A QUICK-SETTING AGENT ONLY FIRMS THE SURFACE...

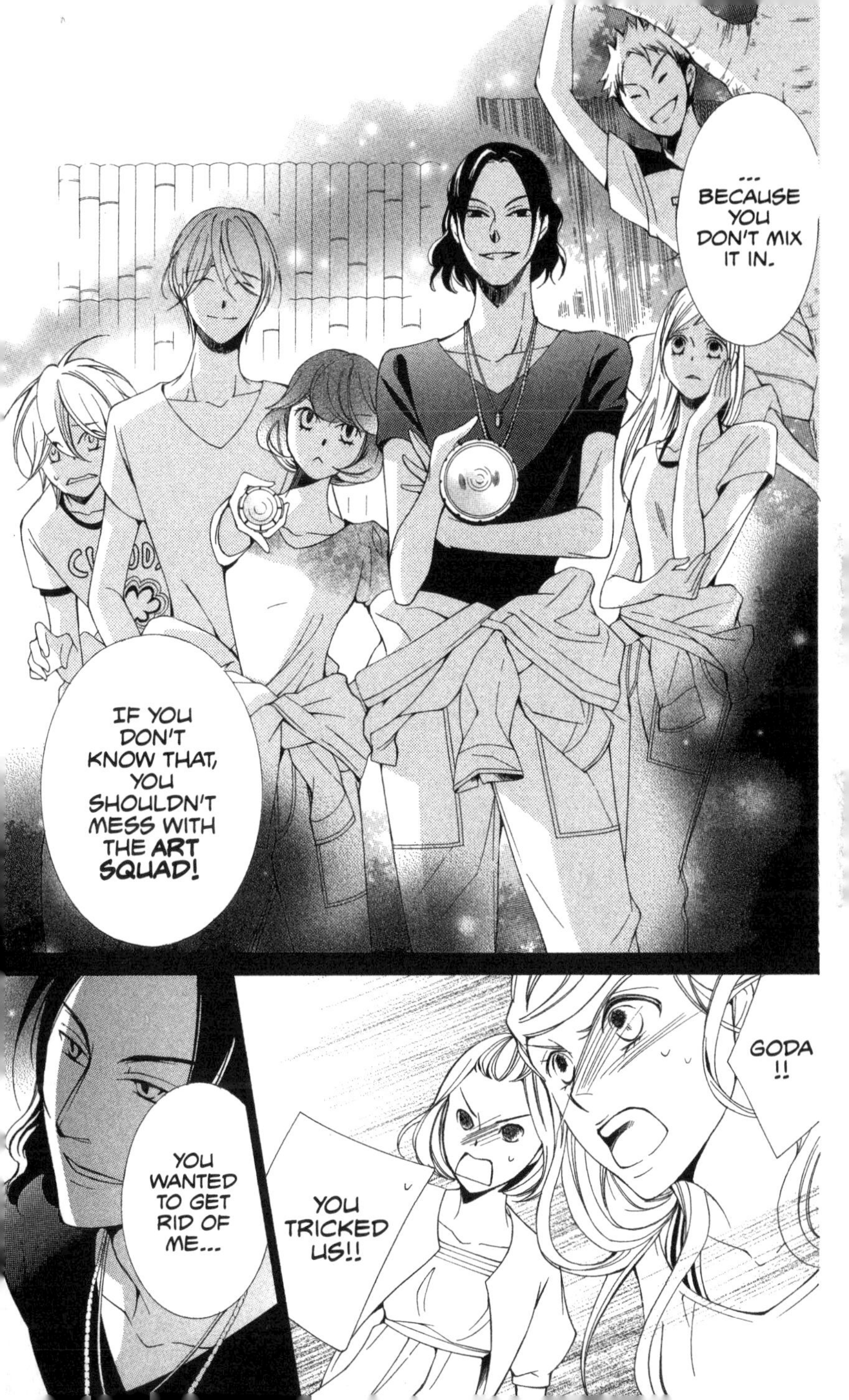
...BECAUSE YOU DON'T MIX IT IN.
IF YOU DON'T KNOW THAT, YOU SHOULDN'T MESS WITH THE ART SQUAD!
GODA !!
YOU TRICKED US!!
YOU WANTED TO GET RID OF ME...

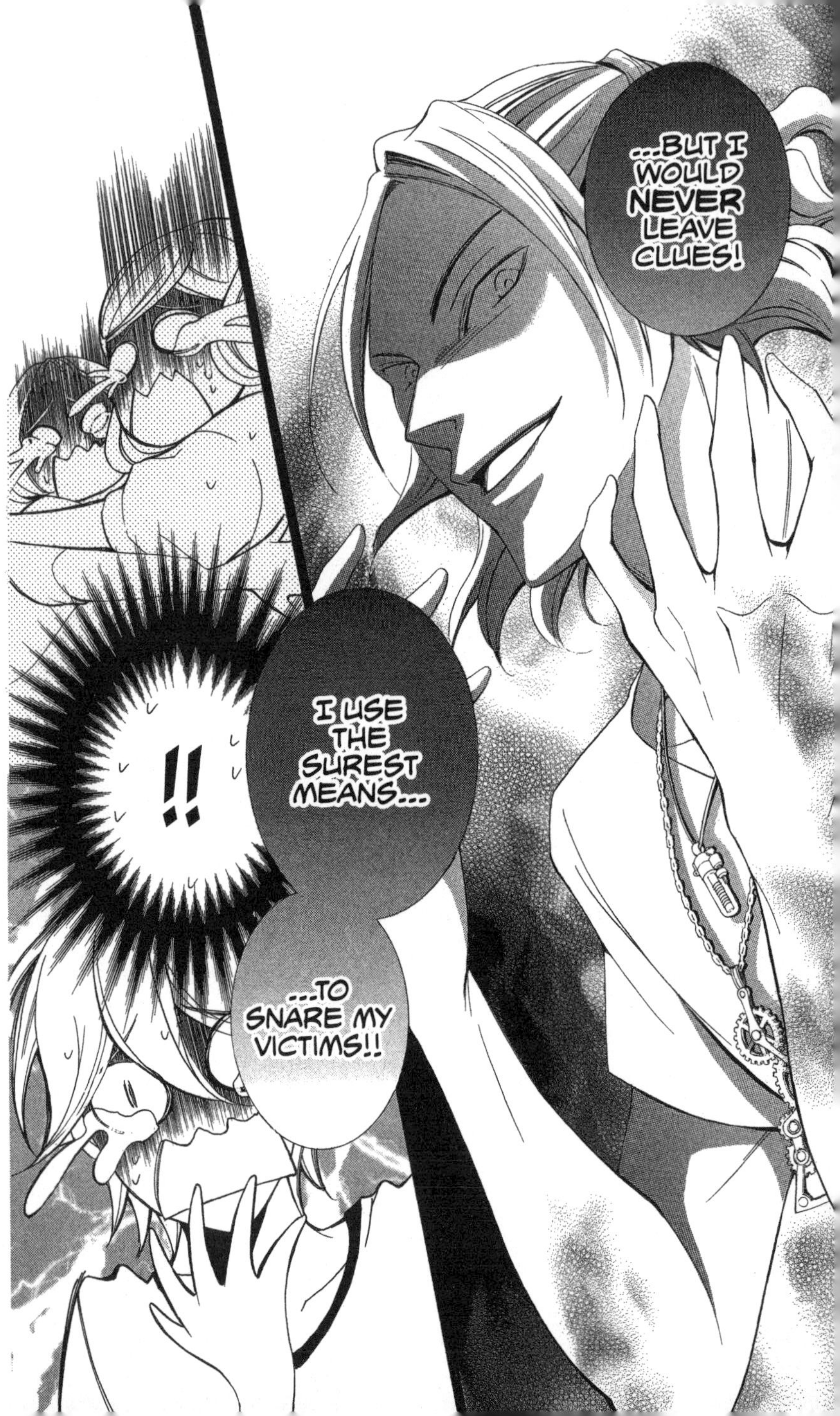
...BUT I WOULD NEVER LEAVE CLUES!
!!
I USE THE SUREST MEANS...
...TO SNARE MY VICTIMS!!

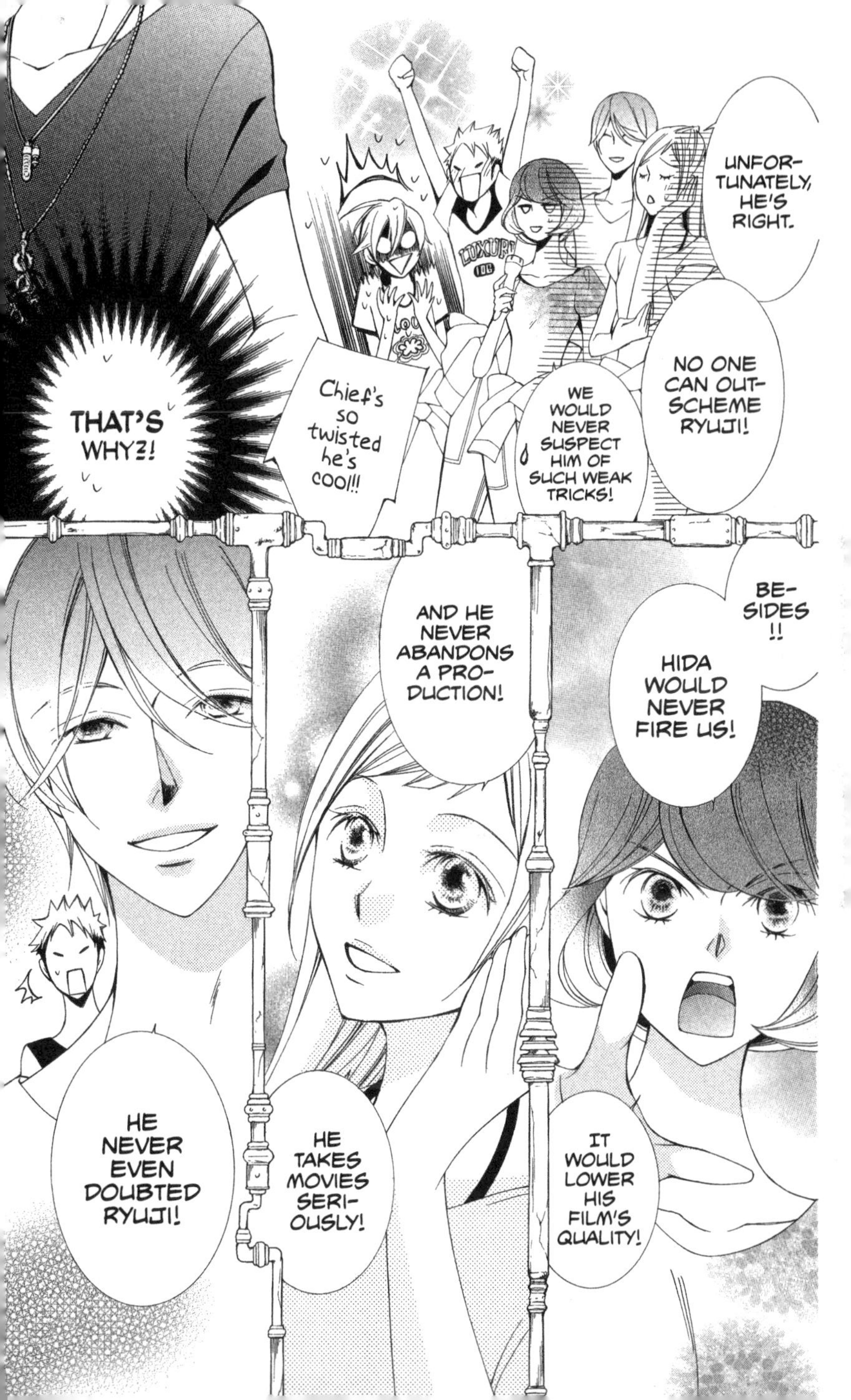
UNFORTUNATELY, HE'S RIGHT.
NO ONE CAN OUT-SCHEME RYUJI!
WE WOULD NEVER SUSPECT HIM OF SUCH WEAK TRICKS!
Chief's so twisted he's cool!!
THAT'S WHY?!
BESIDES!!
HIDA WOULD NEVER FIRE US!
IT WOULD LOWER HIS FILM'S QUALITY!
AND HE NEVER ABANDONS A PRODUCTION!
HE TAKES MOVIES SERIOUSLY!
HE NEVER EVEN DOUBTED RYUJI!

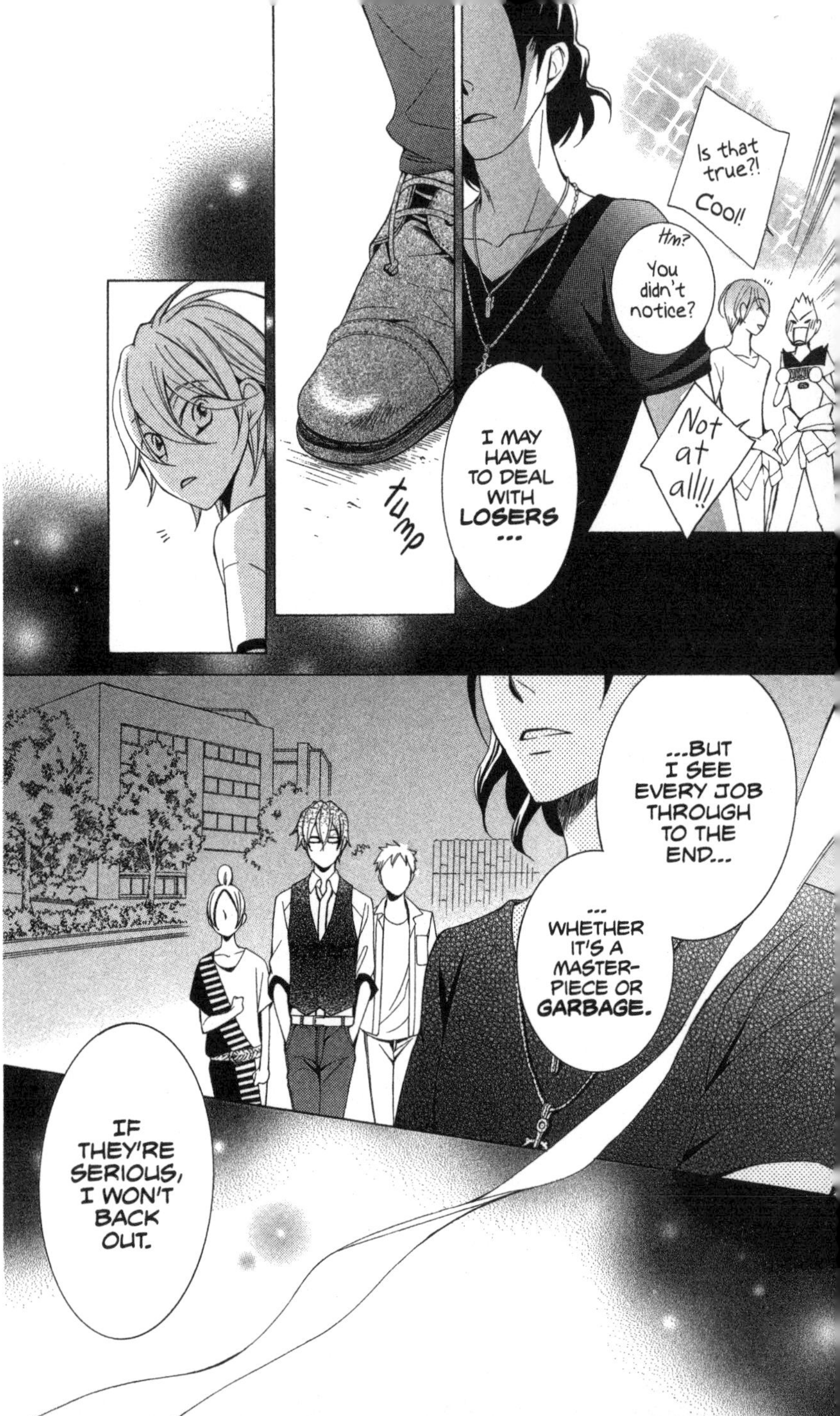
Is that true?! Cool!!
Hm? You didn't notice?
Not at all!!
I MAY HAVE TO DEAL WITH LOSERS...
tump
...BUT I SEE EVERY JOB THROUGH TO THE END...
...WHETHER IT'S A MASTER-PIECE OR GARBAGE.
IF THEY'RE SERIOUS, I WON'T BACK OUT.

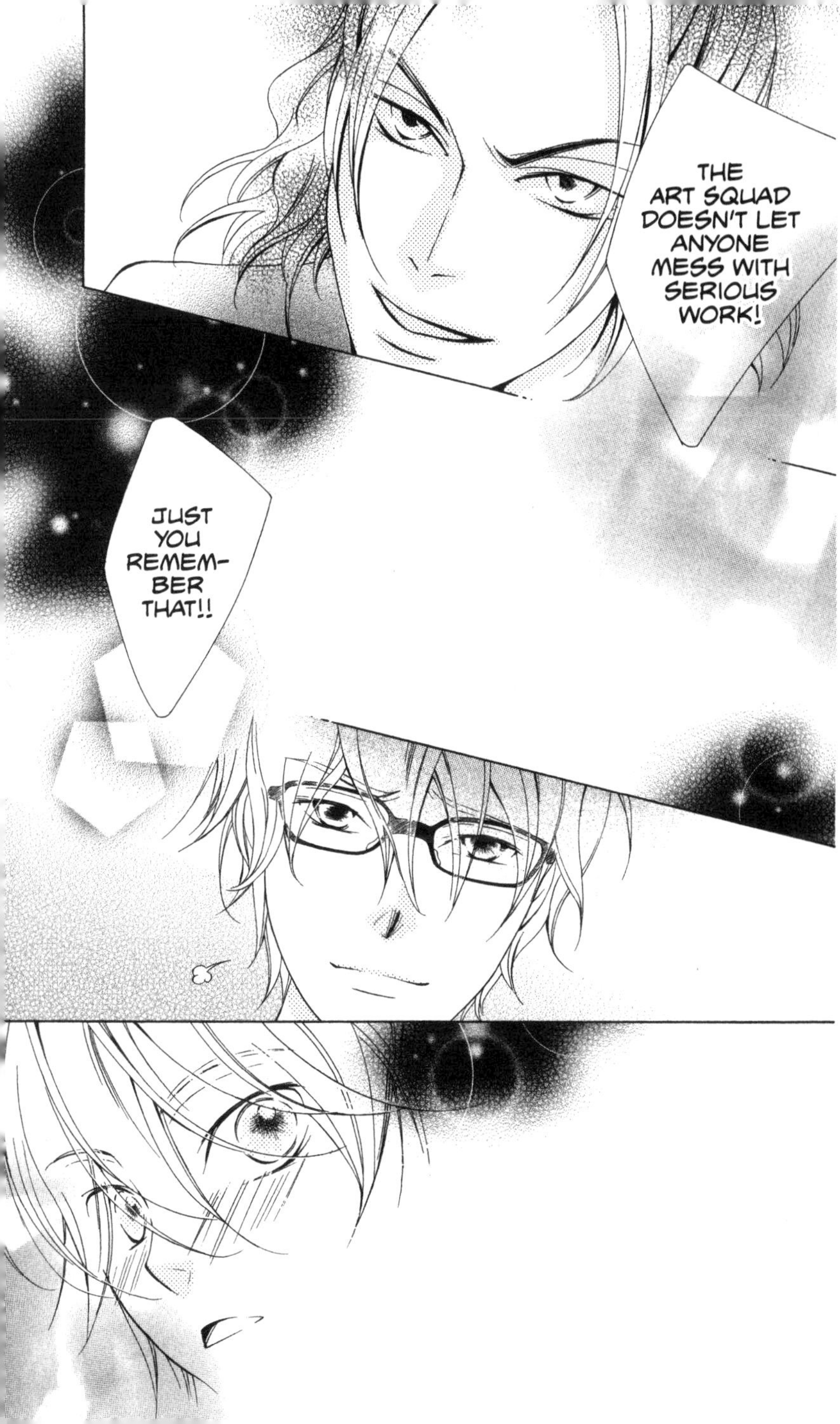
THE ART SQUAD DOESN'T LET ANYONE MESS WITH SERIOUS WORK!
JUST YOU REMEM-BER THAT!!

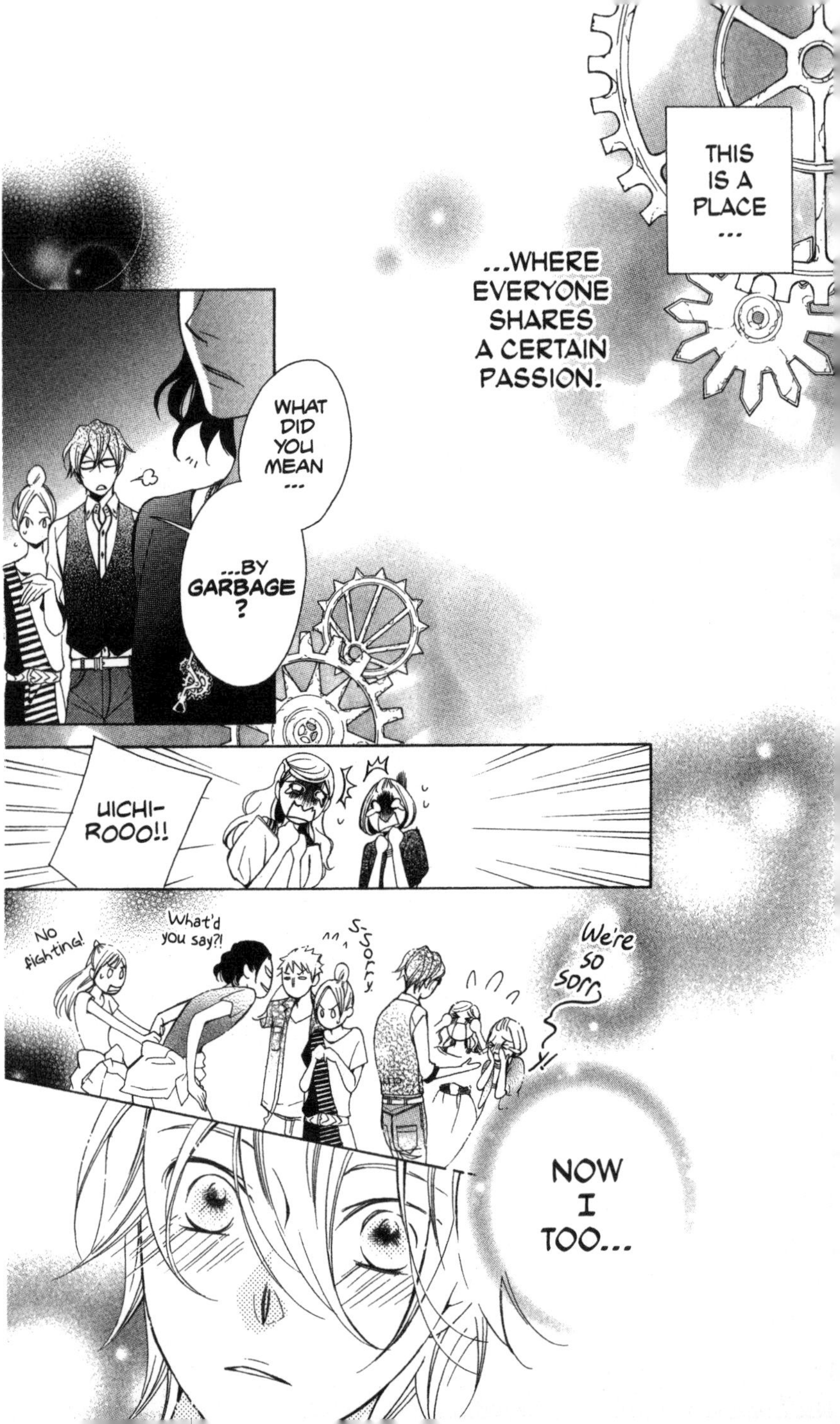
THIS IS A PLACE...
...WHERE EVERYONE SHARES A CERTAIN PASSION.
WHAT DID YOU MEAN...
...BY GARBAGE?
UICHI-ROOO!!
We're so sorry!
S-Sorry.
What'd you say?!
No fighting!
NOW I TOO...

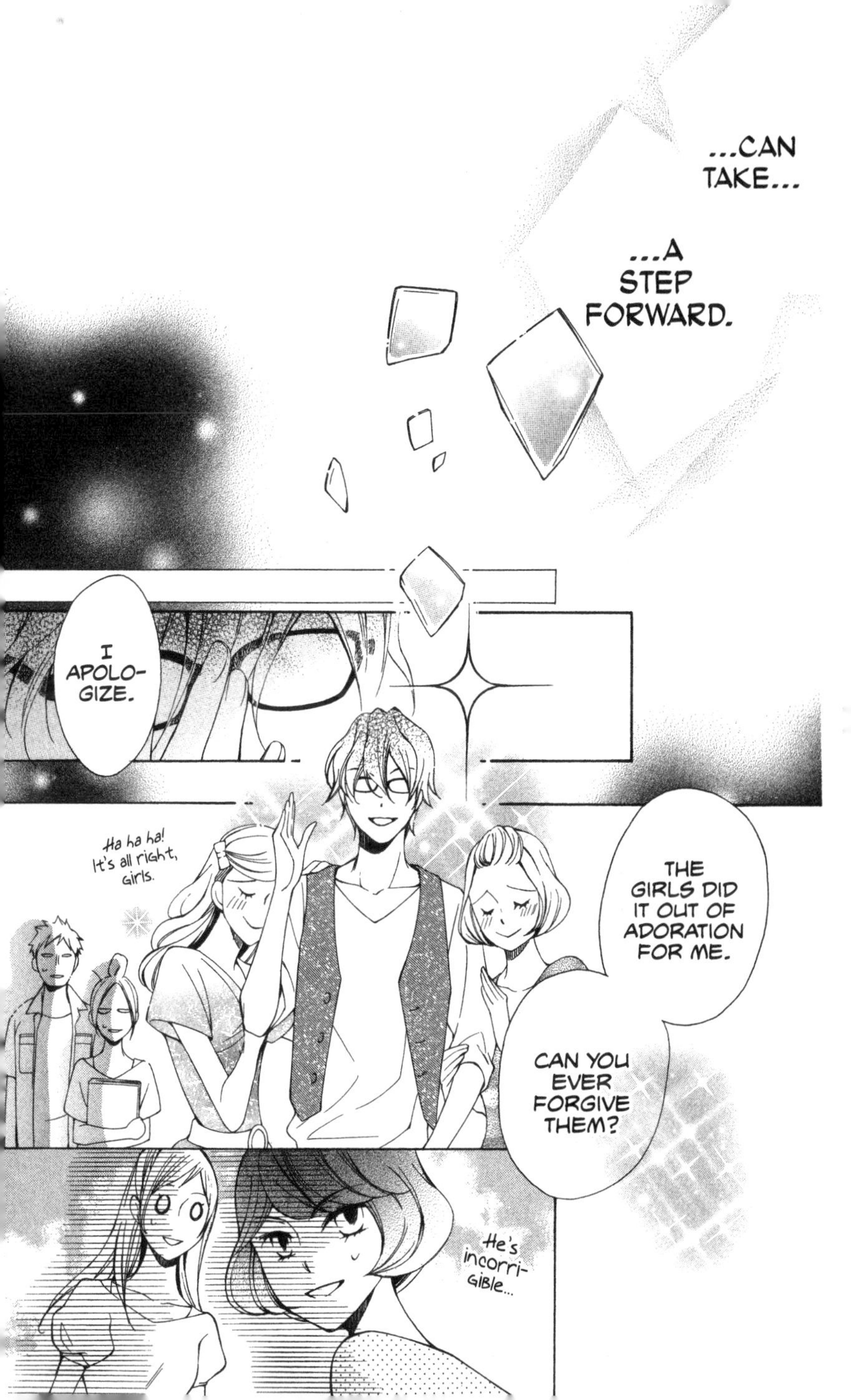
...CAN TAKE...
...A STEP FORWARD.
I APOLOGIZE.
THE GIRLS DID IT OUT OF ADORATION FOR ME.
CAN YOU EVER FORGIVE THEM?
Ha ha ha! It's all right, girls.
He's incorrigible...

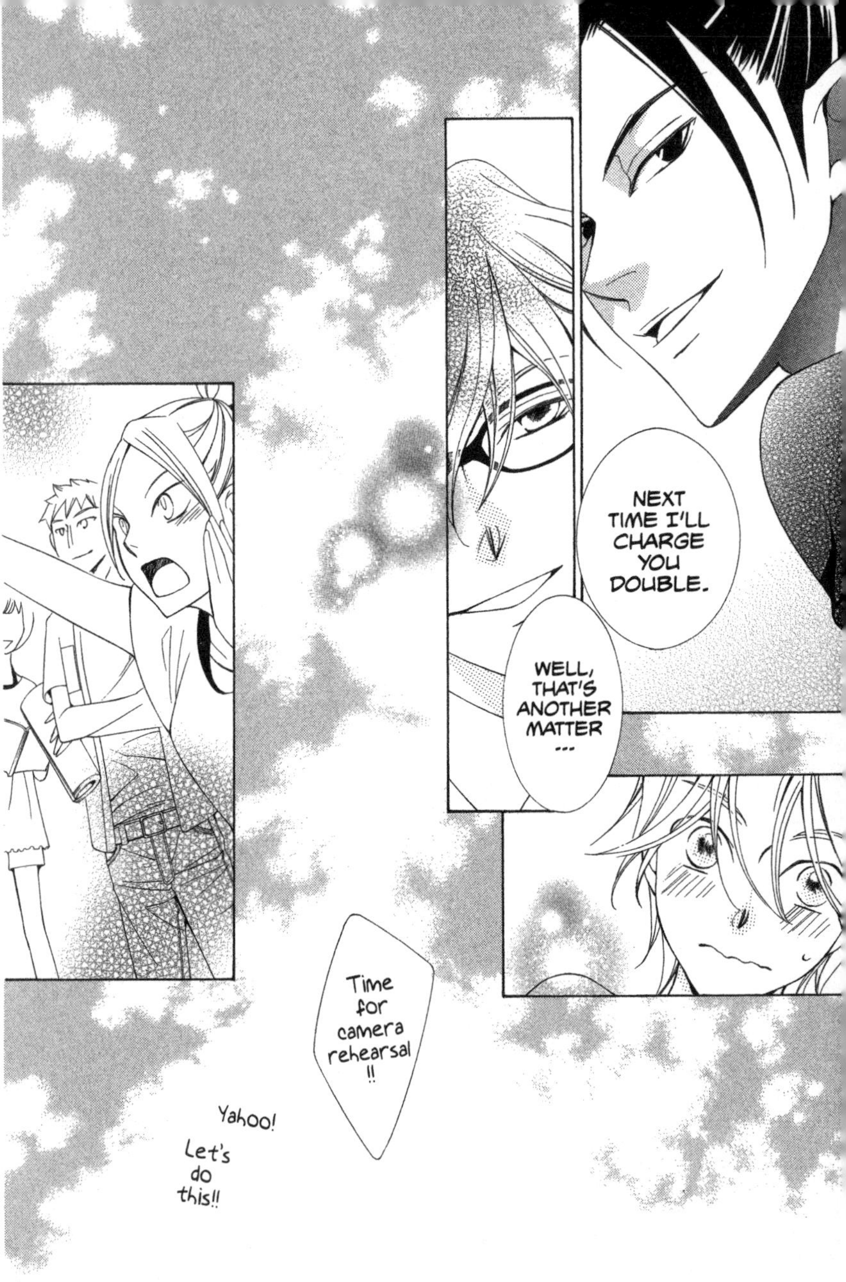
NEXT TIME I'LL CHARGE YOU DOUBLE.
WELL, THAT'S ANOTHER MATTER ...
Time for camera rehearsal !!
Yahoo!
Let's do this!!

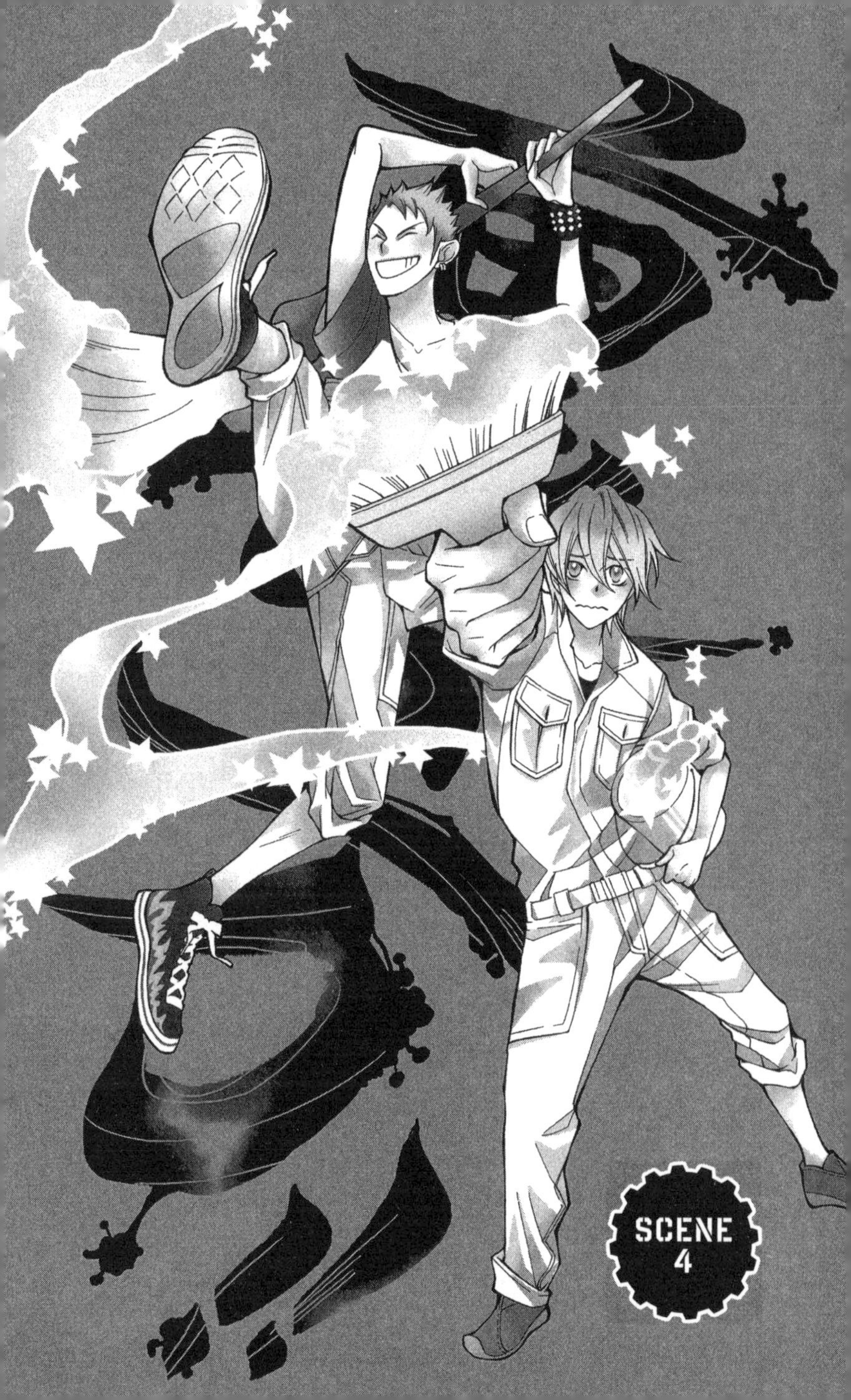
SCENE
4

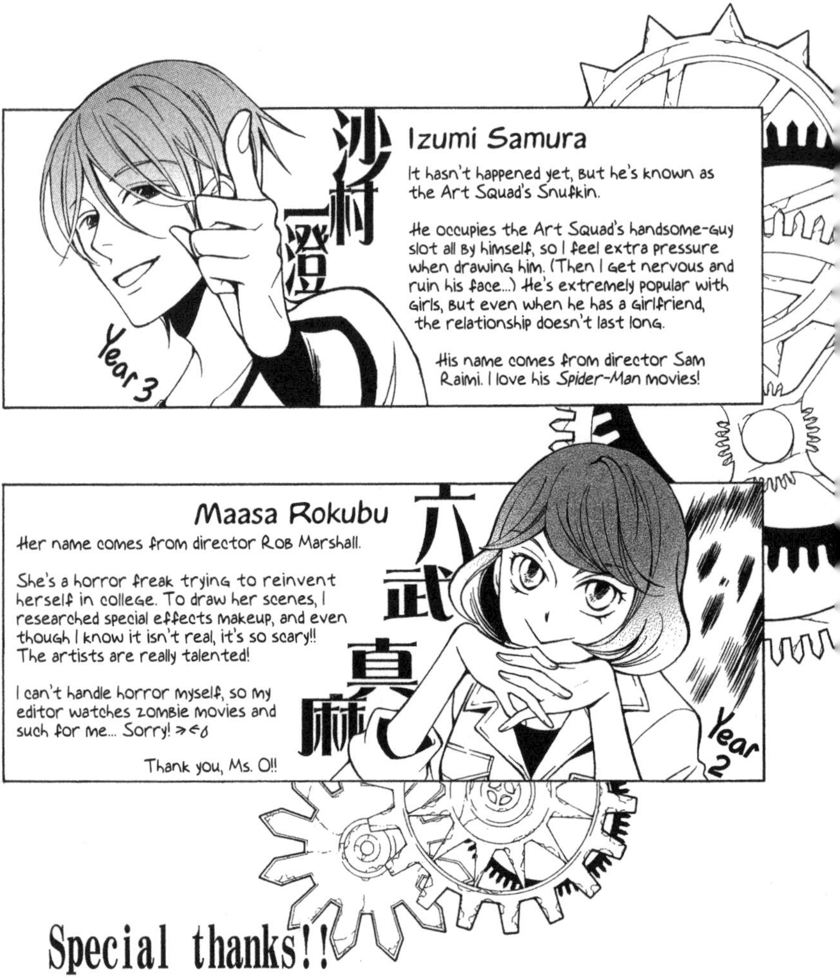
沙村一澄
Izumi Samura
It hasn't happened yet, but he's known as the Art Squad's Snufkin.
He occupies the Art Squad's handsome-guy slot all by himself, so I feel extra pressure when drawing him. (Then I get nervous and ruin his face...) He's extremely popular with girls, but even when he has a girlfriend, the relationship doesn't last long.
His name comes from director Sam Raimi. I love his *Spider-Man* movies!
Year 3
Maasa Rokubu
六武真麻
Her name comes from director Rob Marshall.
She's a horror freak trying to reinvent herself in college. To draw her scenes, I researched special effects makeup, and even though I know it isn't real, it's so scary!! The artists are really talented!
I can't handle horror myself, so my editor watches zombie movies and such for me... Sorry! ><
Thank you, Ms. O!!
Year 2

Special thanks!!

Art Producer YANG-sama, Namiko Yokota-sama, Yasuhito Tachibana-sama, PANTO GRAPH-sama, Forêt-sama, Rodemu-sama, everyone in Sophia Film Makers at Sophia University, Nafumi Sasaki-sama and Shinya Hokimoto-sama.

STAFF: Yui Natsuki, Aya Aomura, Shizuru Shita, Keiko, Umeko and Yutori Hizakura.

Assistants: Shii Tsunokawa-sama, Midori Shiino, Kana-sama, Namiki-sama, Kakeda-sama, Akira Kono-sama and Hitsuji Harumi-sama.

IN ELEMENTARY SCHOOL, I SAW A BLACK-AND-WHITE MOVIE...

...THAT SEARED ITSELF INTO MY MEMORY.

Membership Form

Name: Ranmaru Kurisu

School: Shichikoku University

Department, Year: Humanities and Sciences, Year 1

Student No.:

Email:

GOOD.

NOW YOUR THUMB-PRINT.

inema

Soh Kobora

Her name comes from Sofia Coppola. Her father's name is Fushio Coppola, which is clumsily derived from Francis...

The model for Togezo the hedgehog is Nejiko-chan—who's super cute! The super lovely husky at PANTO GRAPH, which helped me a lot with research, sparked the idea for Tomu's husky, Don. I can't stand it any longer! I want a pet!

But I'm not ready yet...

I want her to play a BIGGER role in the next volume.

High School Year 2

小洞蒼

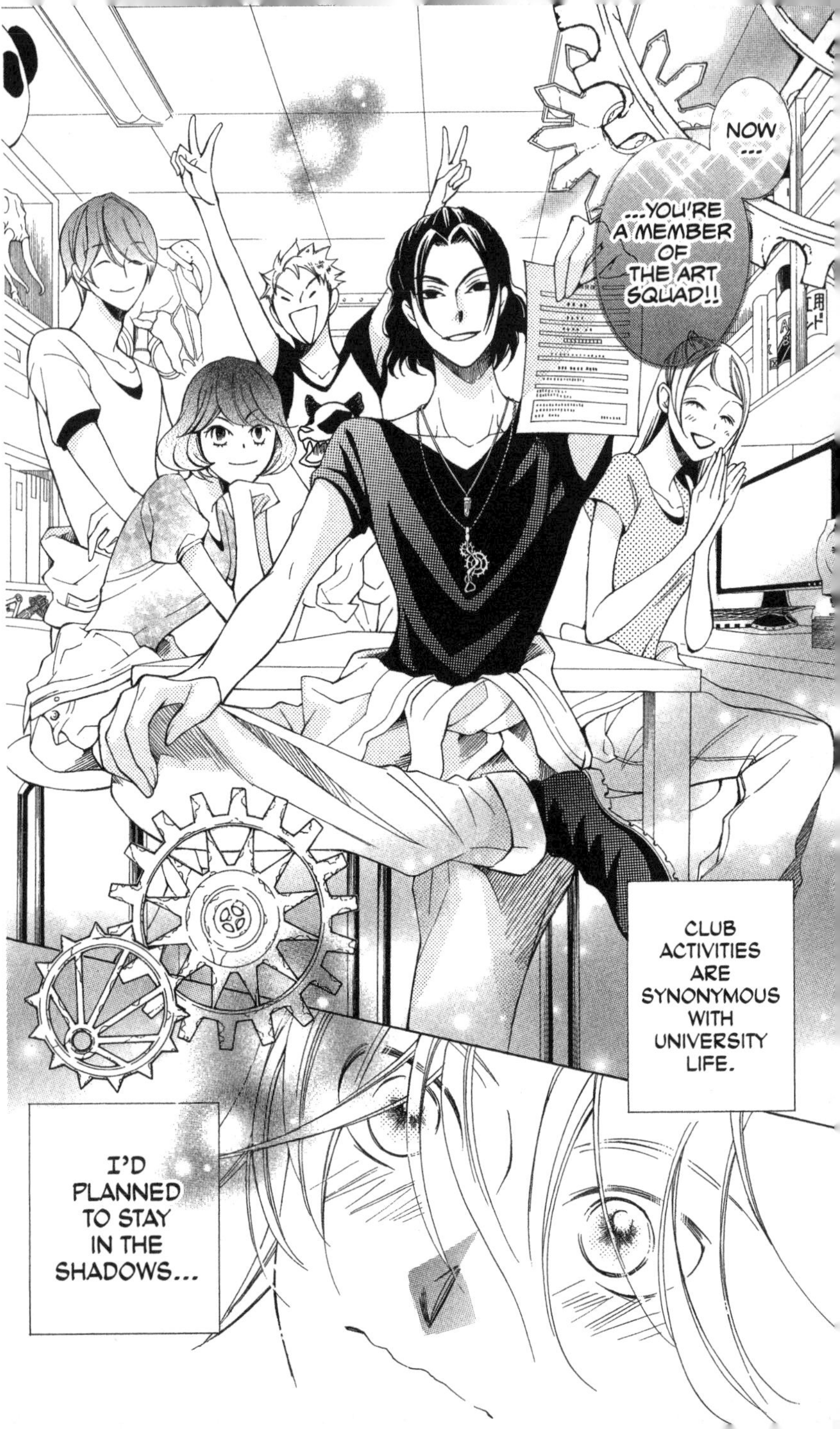
NOW...
...YOU'RE A MEMBER OF THE ART SQUAD!!
CLUB ACTIVITIES ARE SYNONYMOUS WITH UNIVERSITY LIFE.
I'D PLANNED TO STAY IN THE SHADOWS...

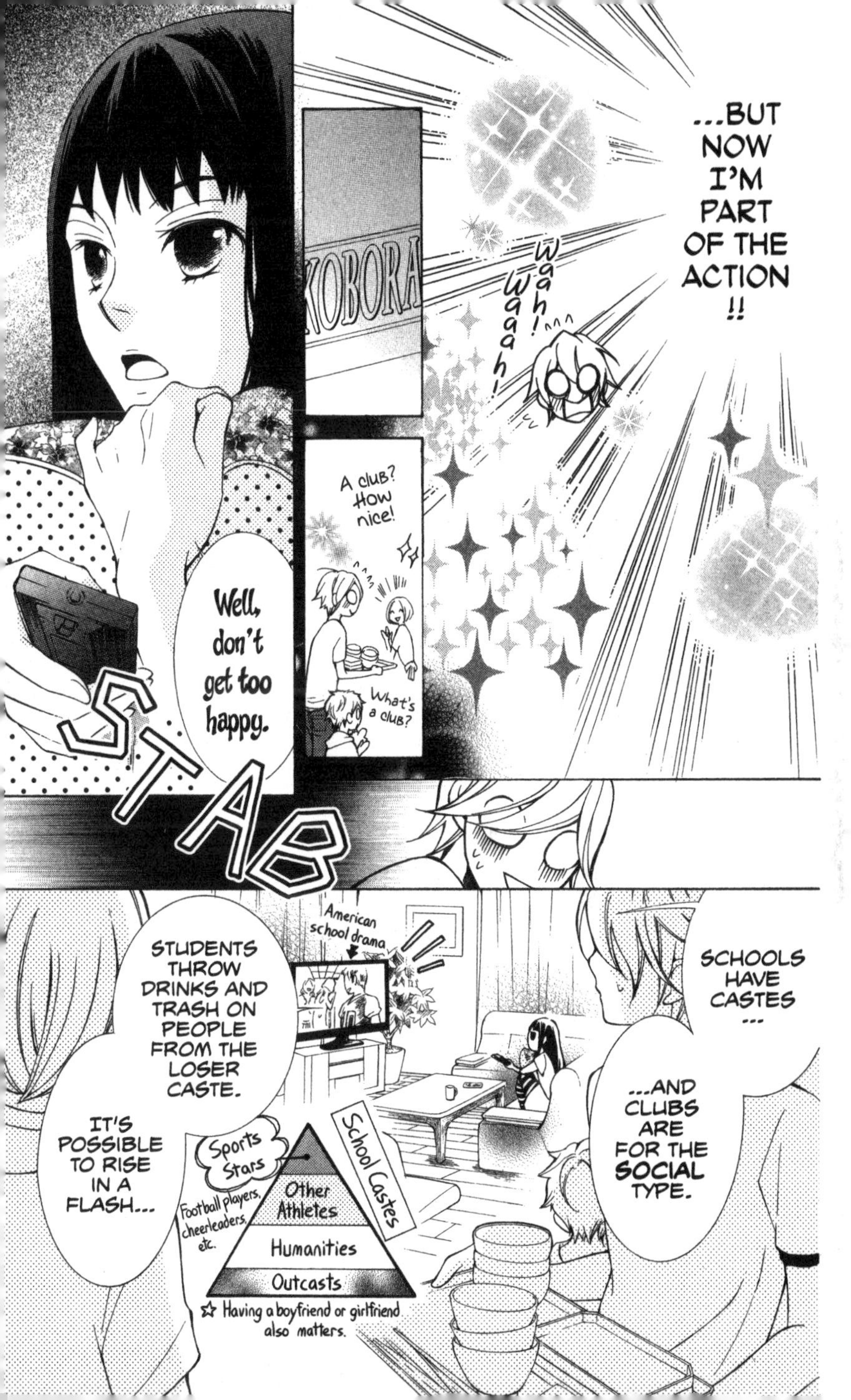
...BUT NOW I'M PART OF THE ACTION!!
Waah! Waaah!
KOBORA
A club? How nice!
What's a club?
Well, don't get too happy.
STAB
SCHOOLS HAVE CASTES...
...AND CLUBS ARE FOR THE SOCIAL TYPE.
American school drama
STUDENTS THROW DRINKS AND TRASH ON PEOPLE FROM THE LOSER CASTE.
IT'S POSSIBLE TO RISE IN A FLASH...
School Castes
Sports Stars
Football players, cheerleaders, etc.
Other Athletes
Humanities
Outcasts
☆ Having a boyfriend or girlfriend also matters.

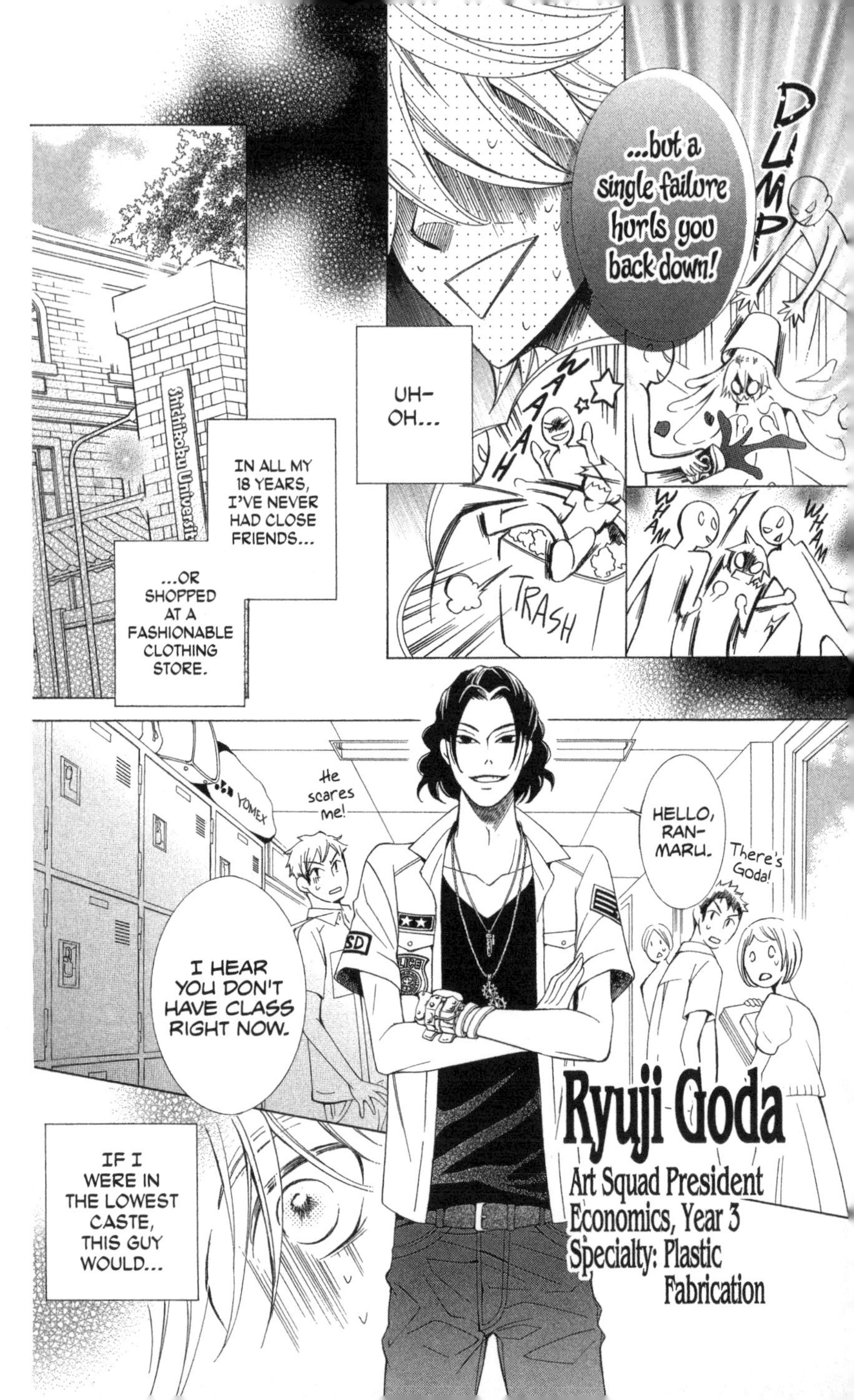

...but a single failure hurls you back down!
DUMP
WHAM
WHAM
WAAAH
TRASH
UH-OH...
Shichikoku Universit
IN ALL MY 18 YEARS, I'VE NEVER HAD CLOSE FRIENDS...
...OR SHOPPED AT A FASHIONABLE CLOTHING STORE.
HELLO, RAN-MARU.
There's Goda!
YOMEX
He scares me!
I HEAR YOU DON'T HAVE CLASS RIGHT NOW.
Ryuji Goda
Art Squad President
Economics, Year 3
Specialty: Plastic Fabrication
IF I WERE IN THE LOWEST CASTE, THIS GUY WOULD...

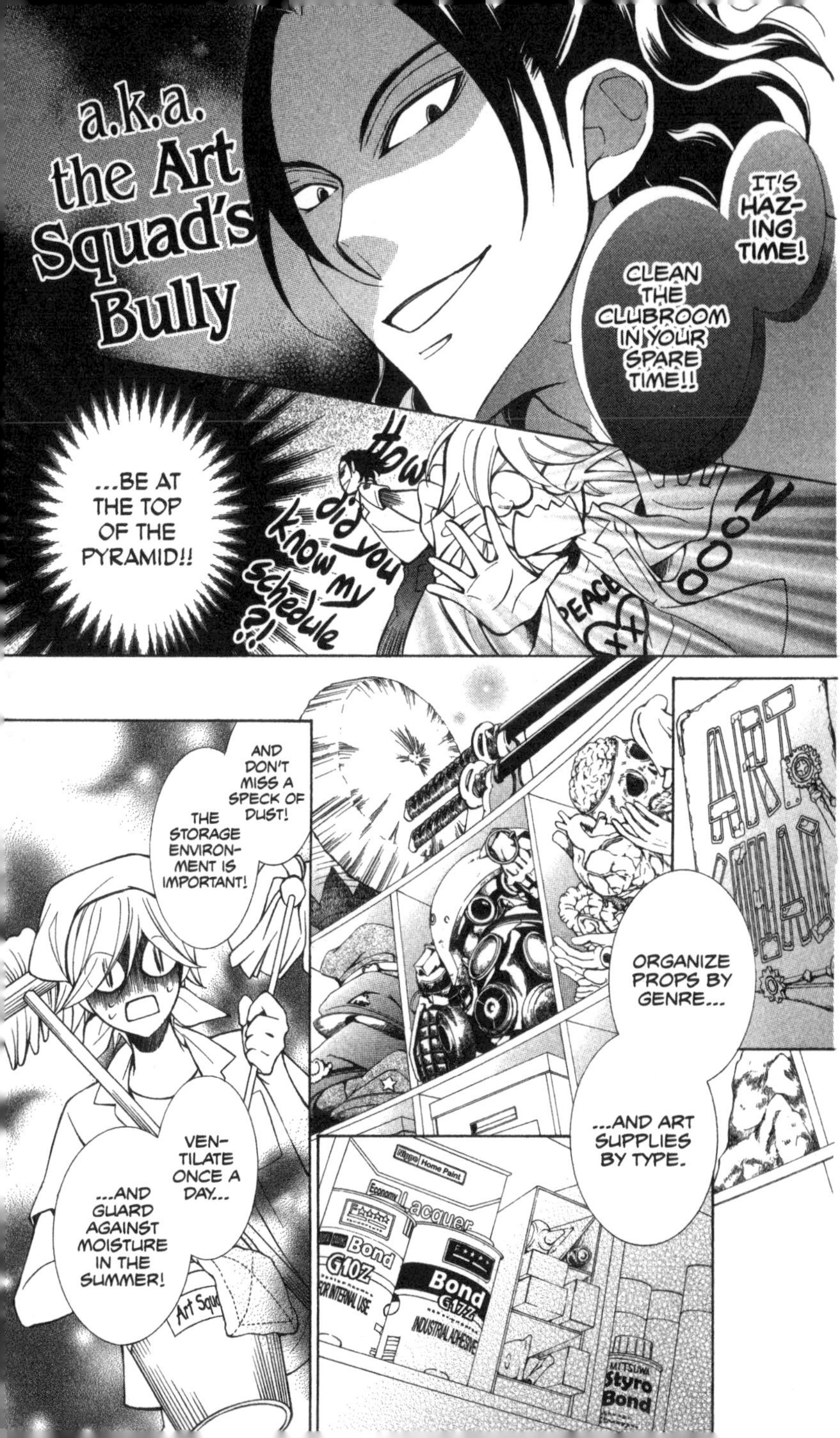
IT'S HAZING TIME!
CLEAN THE CLUBROOM IN YOUR SPARE TIME!!
a.k.a. the Art Squad's Bully
NOOOOO
PEACE
How did you know my schedule?!
...BE AT THE TOP OF THE PYRAMID!!
ORGANIZE PROPS BY GENRE...
...AND ART SUPPLIES BY TYPE.
Nippe Home Paint
Economy Lacquer
Bond G10Z
Bond G17Z
INDUSTRIAL ADHESIVE
MITSUWA Styro Bond
AND DON'T MISS A SPECK OF DUST!
THE STORAGE ENVIRONMENT IS IMPORTANT!
VENTILATE ONCE A DAY...
...AND GUARD AGAINST MOISTURE IN THE SUMMER!

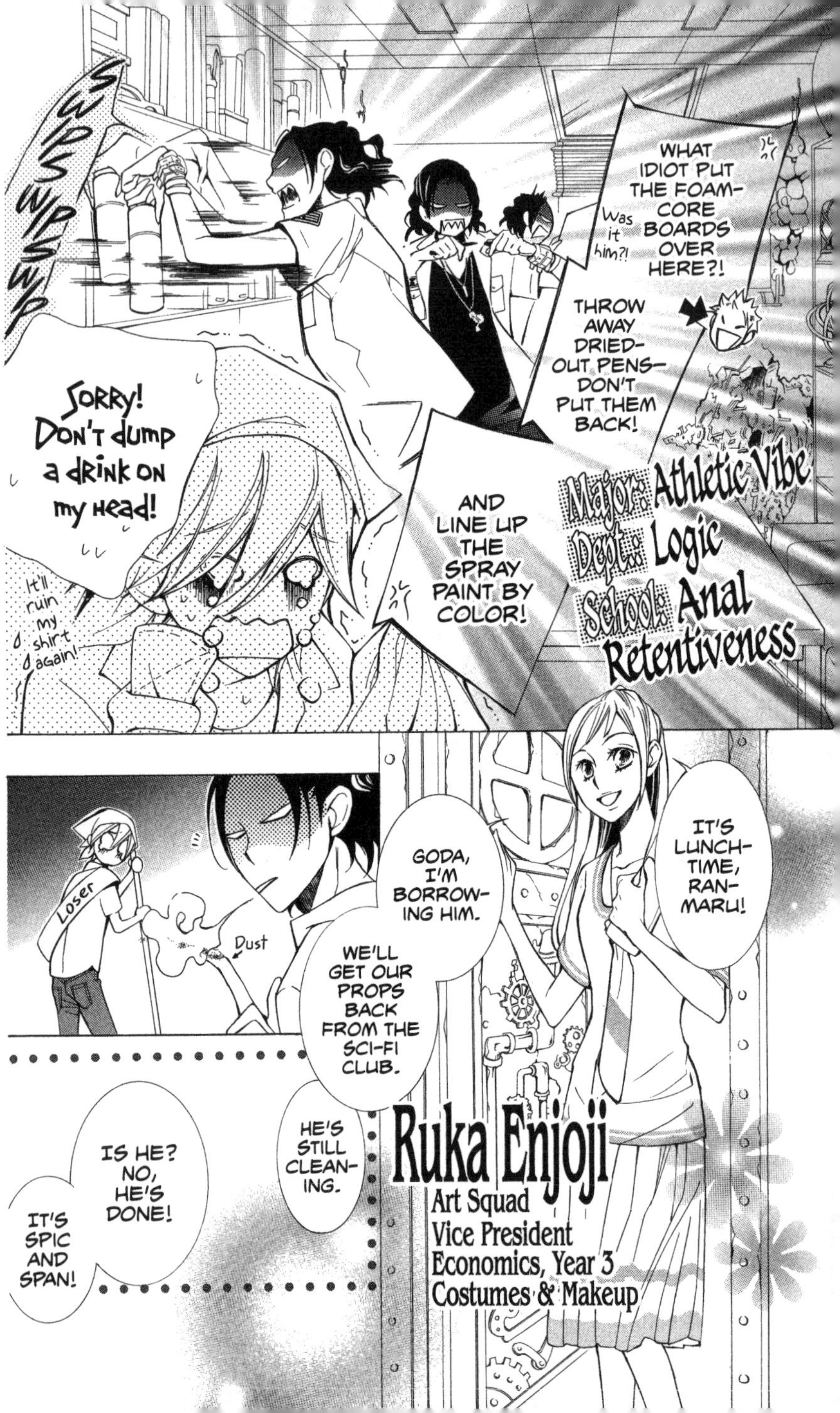
WHAT IDIOT PUT THE FOAM-CORE BOARDS OVER HERE?!
Was it him?!
THROW AWAY DRIED-OUT PENS—DON'T PUT THEM BACK!
AND LINE UP THE SPRAY PAINT BY COLOR!
Major: Athletic Vibe
Dept.: Logic
School: Anal Retentiveness
SWIPSWIPSWIPSWIP
Sorry! Don't dump a drink on my head!
It'll ruin my shirt again!
IT'S LUNCHTIME, RANMARU!
GODA, I'M BORROWING HIM.
WE'LL GET OUR PROPS BACK FROM THE SCI-FI CLUB.
Loser
Dust
Ruka Enjoji
Art Squad
Vice President
Economics, Year 3
Costumes & Makeup
HE'S STILL CLEANING.
IS HE? NO, HE'S DONE!
IT'S SPIC AND SPAN!

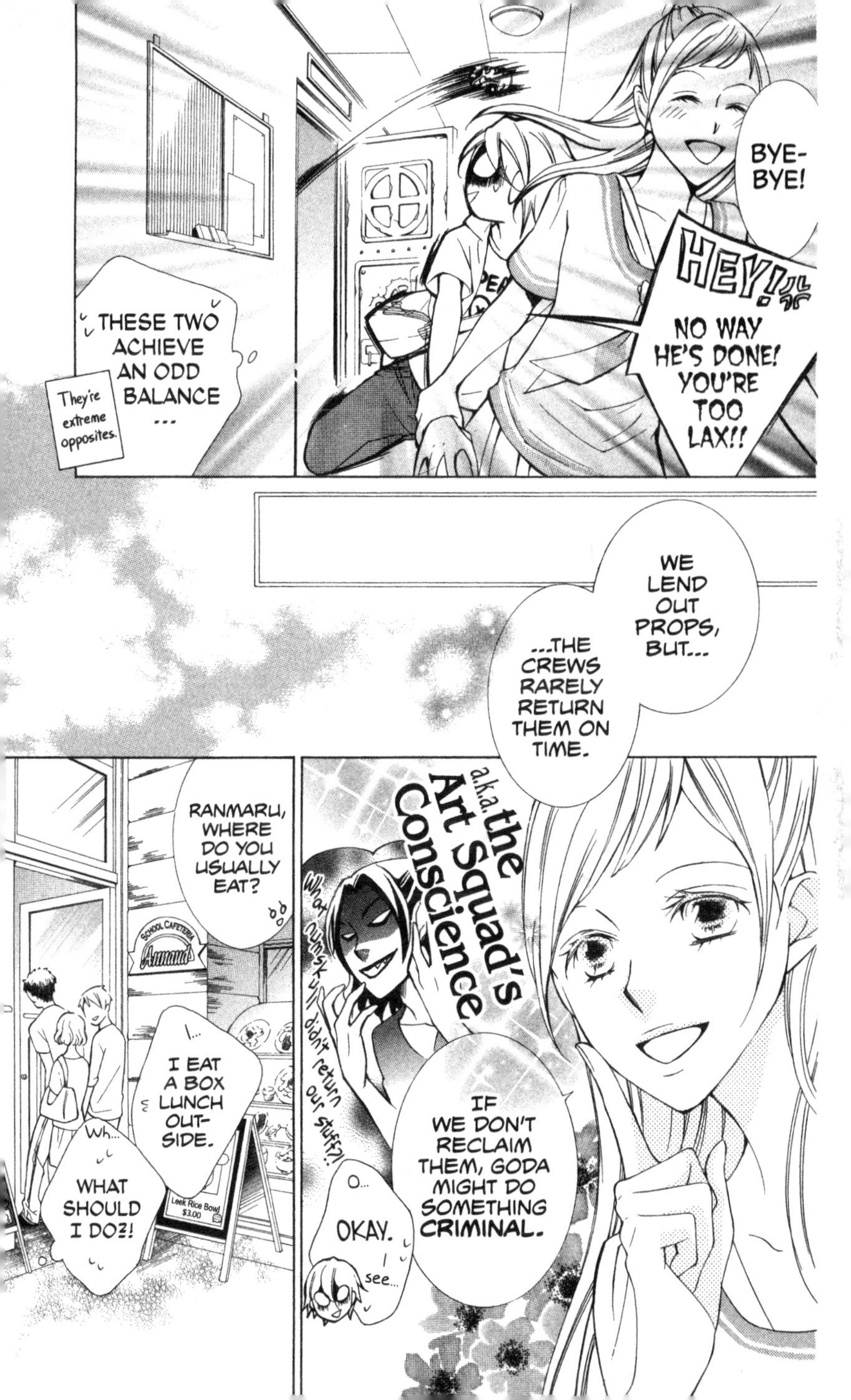
BYE-BYE!
HEY!!
NO WAY HE'S DONE! YOU'RE TOO LAX!!
THESE TWO ACHIEVE AN ODD BALANCE ...
They're extreme opposites.
WE LEND OUT PROPS, BUT...
...THE CREWS RARELY RETURN THEM ON TIME.
a.k.a. the Art Squad's Conscience
What numskull didn't return our stuff?!
IF WE DON'T RECLAIM THEM, GODA MIGHT DO SOMETHING CRIMINAL.
O... OKAY.
I see...
RANMARU, WHERE DO YOU USUALLY EAT?
SCHOOL CAFETERIA
I... I EAT A BOX LUNCH OUTSIDE.
Leek Rice Bowl $3.00
Wh... WHAT SHOULD I DO?!

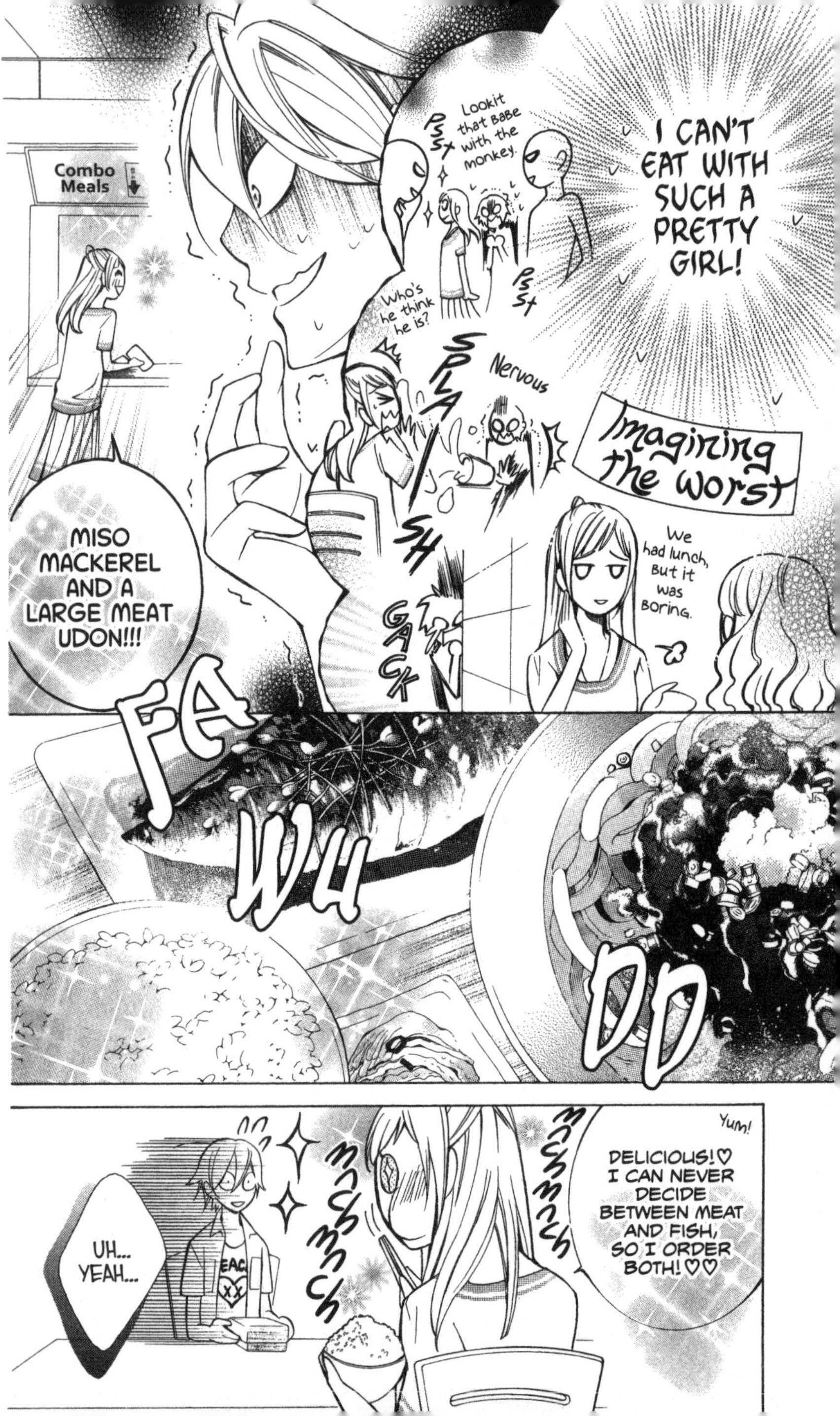
I CAN'T EAT WITH SUCH A PRETTY GIRL!
PSST
Lookit that babe with the monkey.
PSST
Who's he think he is?
Imagining the worst
Nervous
SPLA
SH
GACK
We had lunch, but it was boring.
Combo Meals
MISO MACKEREL AND A LARGE MEAT UDON!!!
FA
WU
DD
Yum!
DELICIOUS!♡ I CAN NEVER DECIDE BETWEEN MEAT AND FISH, SO I ORDER BOTH!♡♡
UH... YEAH...

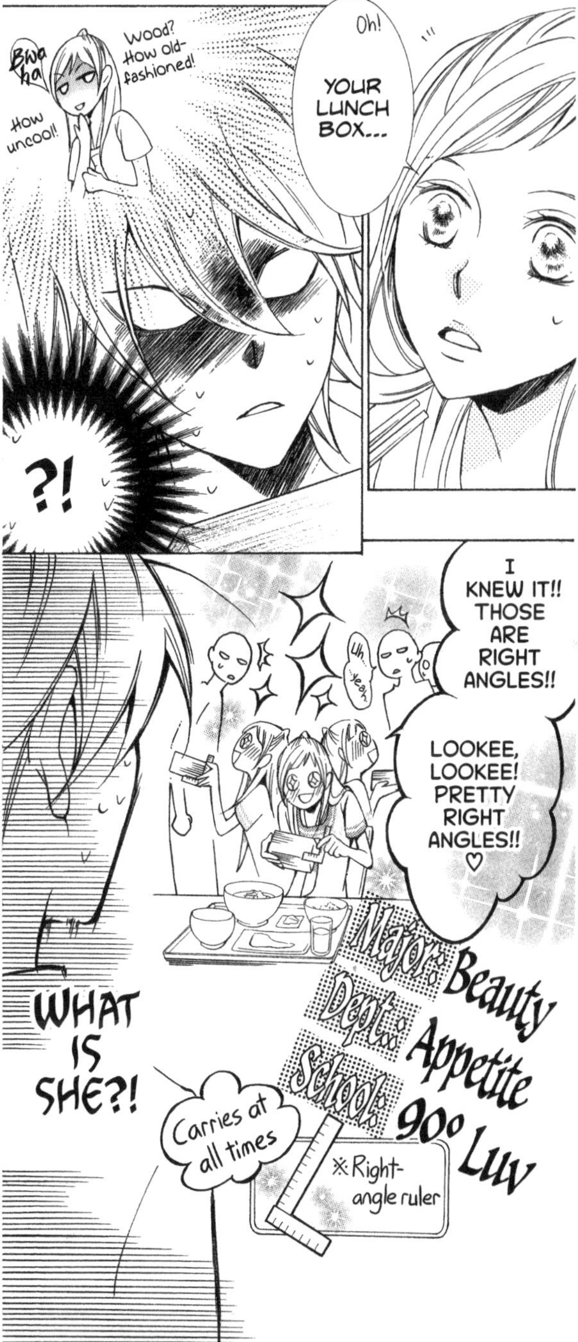
Oh!
YOUR LUNCH BOX...
?!
Bwa ha
Wood? How old-fashioned!
How uncool!
I KNEW IT!! THOSE ARE RIGHT ANGLES!!
LOOKEE, LOOKEE! PRETTY RIGHT ANGLES!! ♡
Uh... yeah
Major: Beauty
Dept.: Appetite
School: 90° Luv
※Right-angle ruler
Carries at all times
WHAT IS SHE?!

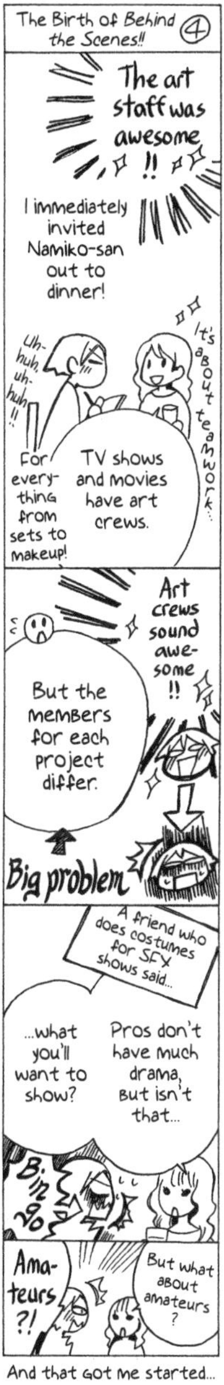
The Birth of Behind the Scenes!! ④
The art staff was awesome!!
I immediately invited Namiko-san out to dinner!
It's about teamwork...
Uh-huh, uh-huh!!
TV shows and movies have art crews.
For everything from sets to makeup!
Art crews sound awesome!!
But the members for each project differ.
Big problem
A friend who does costumes for SFX shows said...
Pros don't have much drama, but isn't that...
...what you'll want to show?
But what about amateurs?
Amateurs?!

And that got me started...

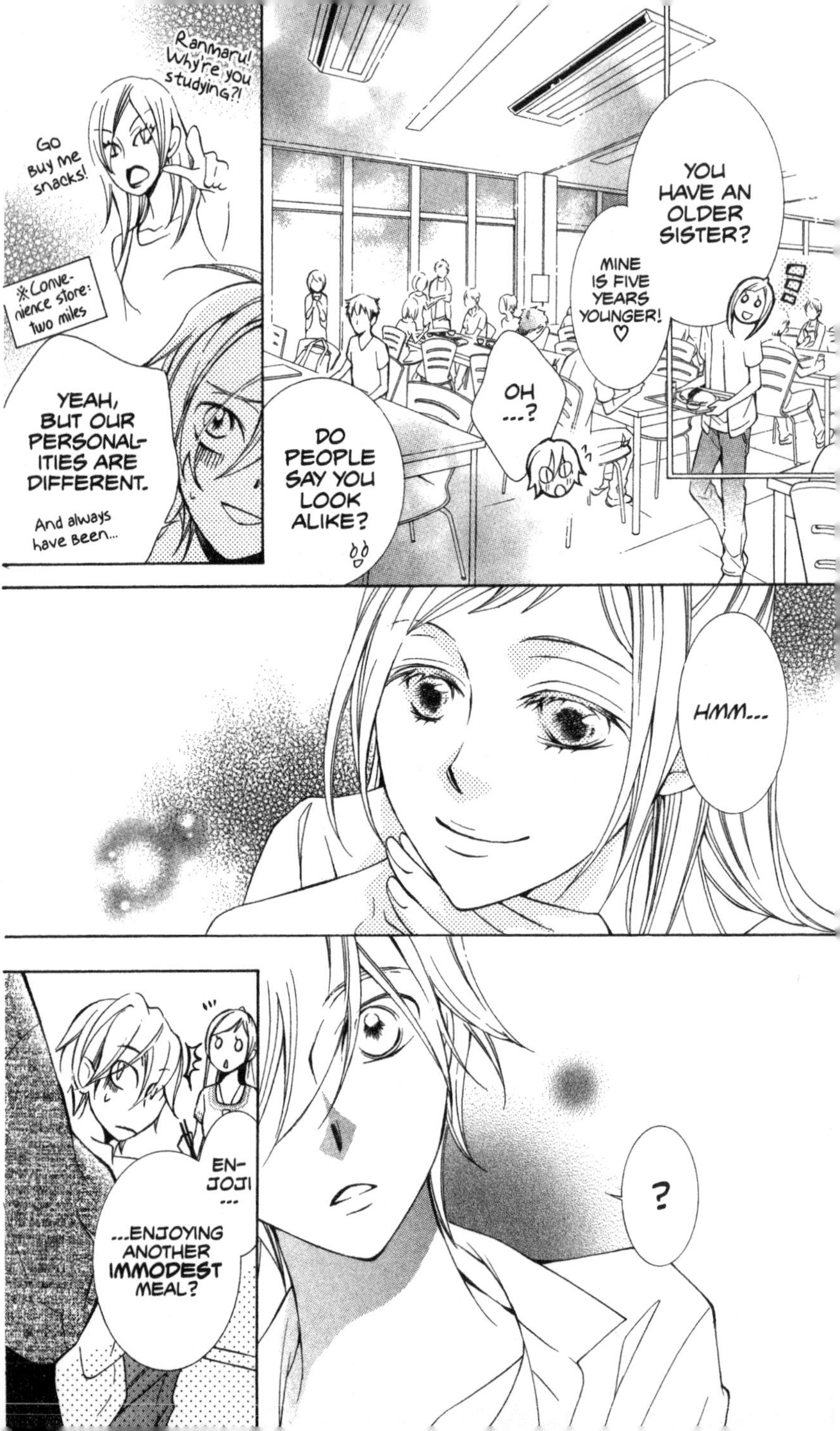
YOU HAVE AN OLDER SISTER?
MINE IS FIVE YEARS YOUNGER! ♡
OH...?
DO PEOPLE SAY YOU LOOK ALIKE?
Ranmaru! Why're you studying?!
Go Buy me snacks!
※Convenience store: two miles
YEAH, BUT OUR PERSONALITIES ARE DIFFERENT.
And always have Been...
HMM...
?
EN-JOJI...
...ENJOYING ANOTHER IMMODEST MEAL?

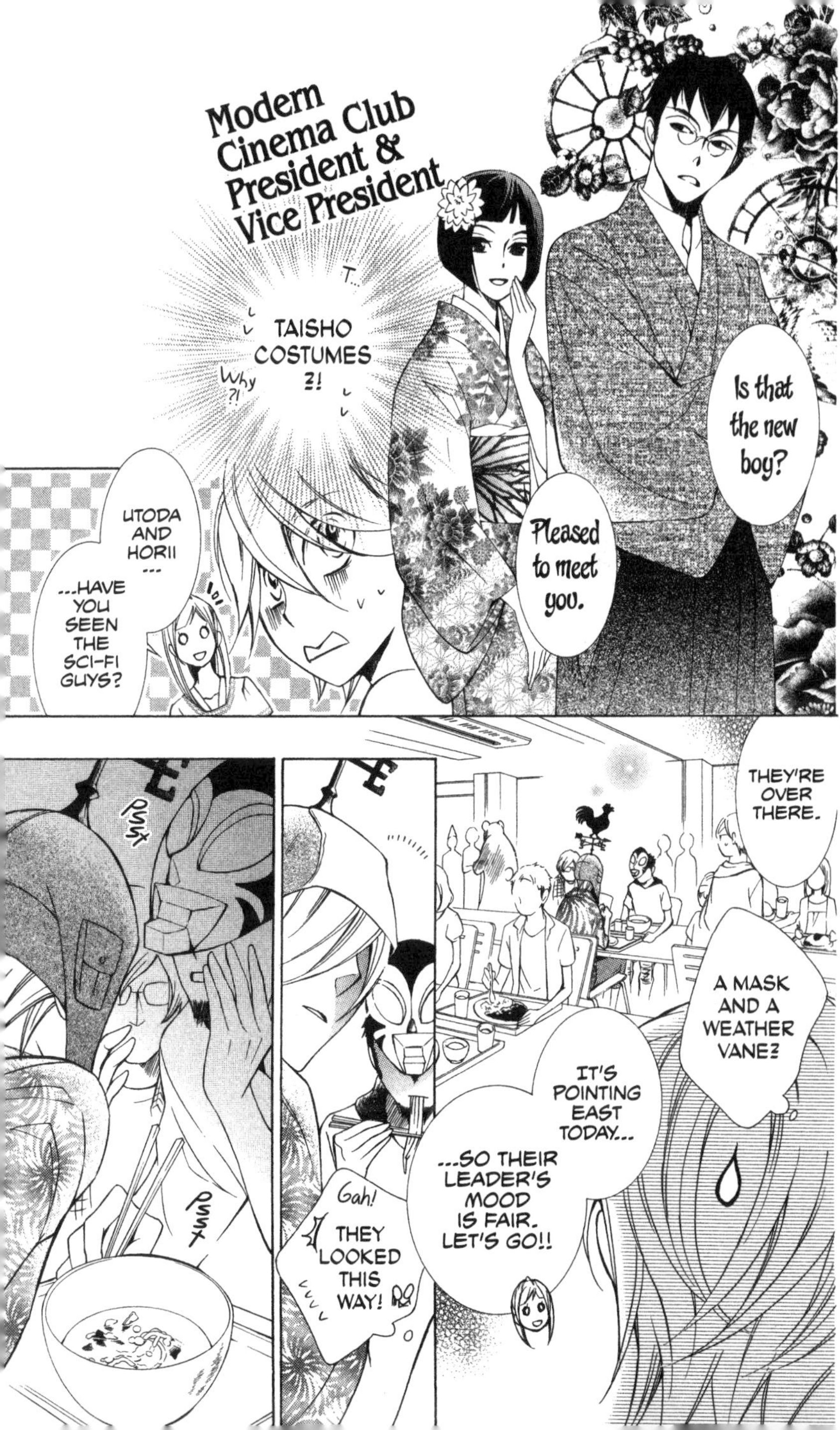
Modern Cinema Club President & Vice President
Is that the new boy?
Pleased to meet you.
T...
TAISHO COSTUMES?!
Why?!
UTODA AND HORII...
...HAVE YOU SEEN THE SCI-FI GUYS?
THEY'RE OVER THERE.
A MASK AND A WEATHER VANE?
IT'S POINTING EAST TODAY...
...SO THEIR LEADER'S MOOD IS FAIR. LET'S GO!!
Gah!
THEY LOOKED THIS WAY!
Psst
Psst

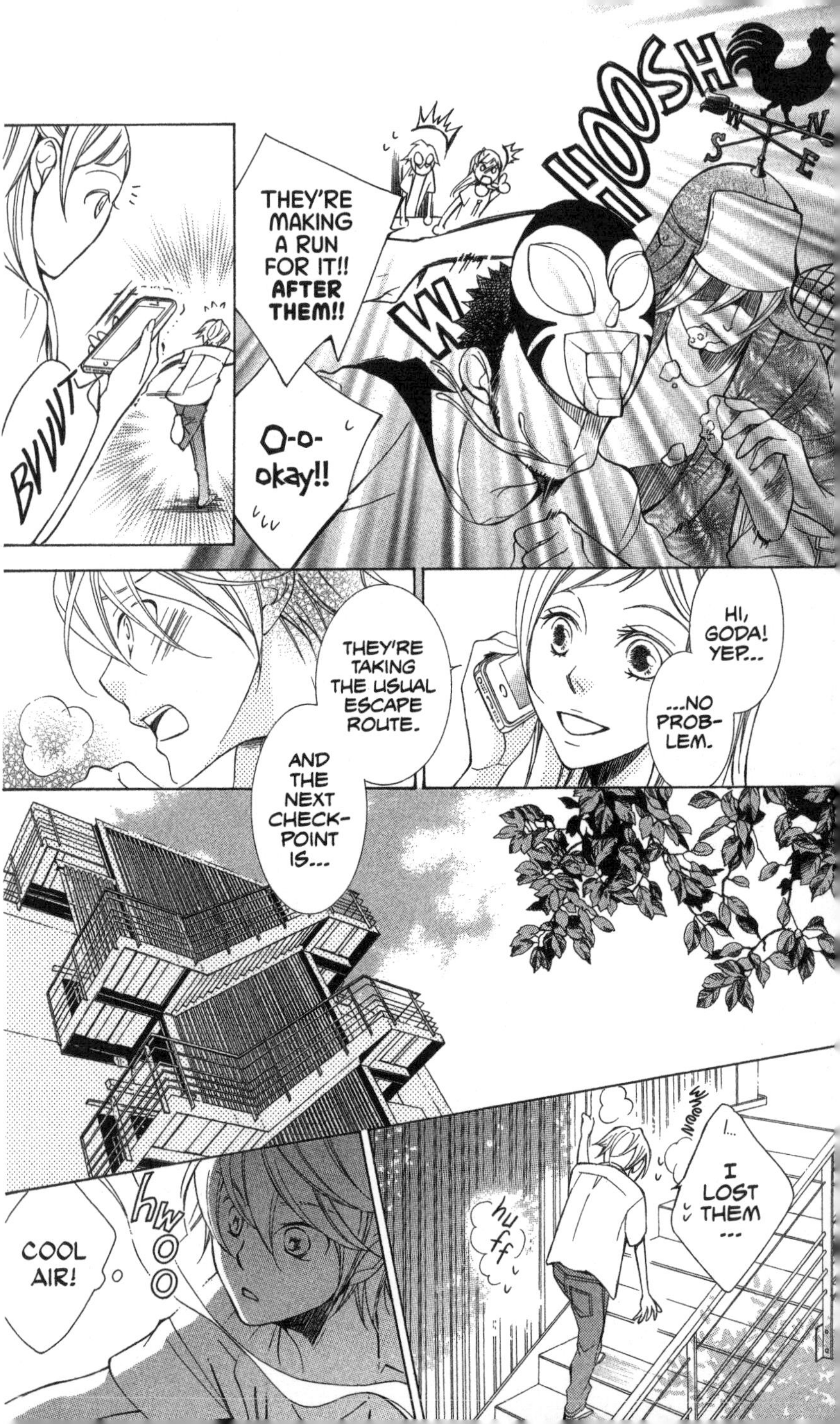
WHOOSH
W!
THEY'RE MAKING A RUN FOR IT!! AFTER THEM!!
O-o-okay!!
BVVVT
HI, GODA! YEP...
...NO PROBLEM.
THEY'RE TAKING THE USUAL ESCAPE ROUTE.
AND THE NEXT CHECKPOINT IS...
whew
I... I LOST THEM...
huff
hwoo
COOL AIR!

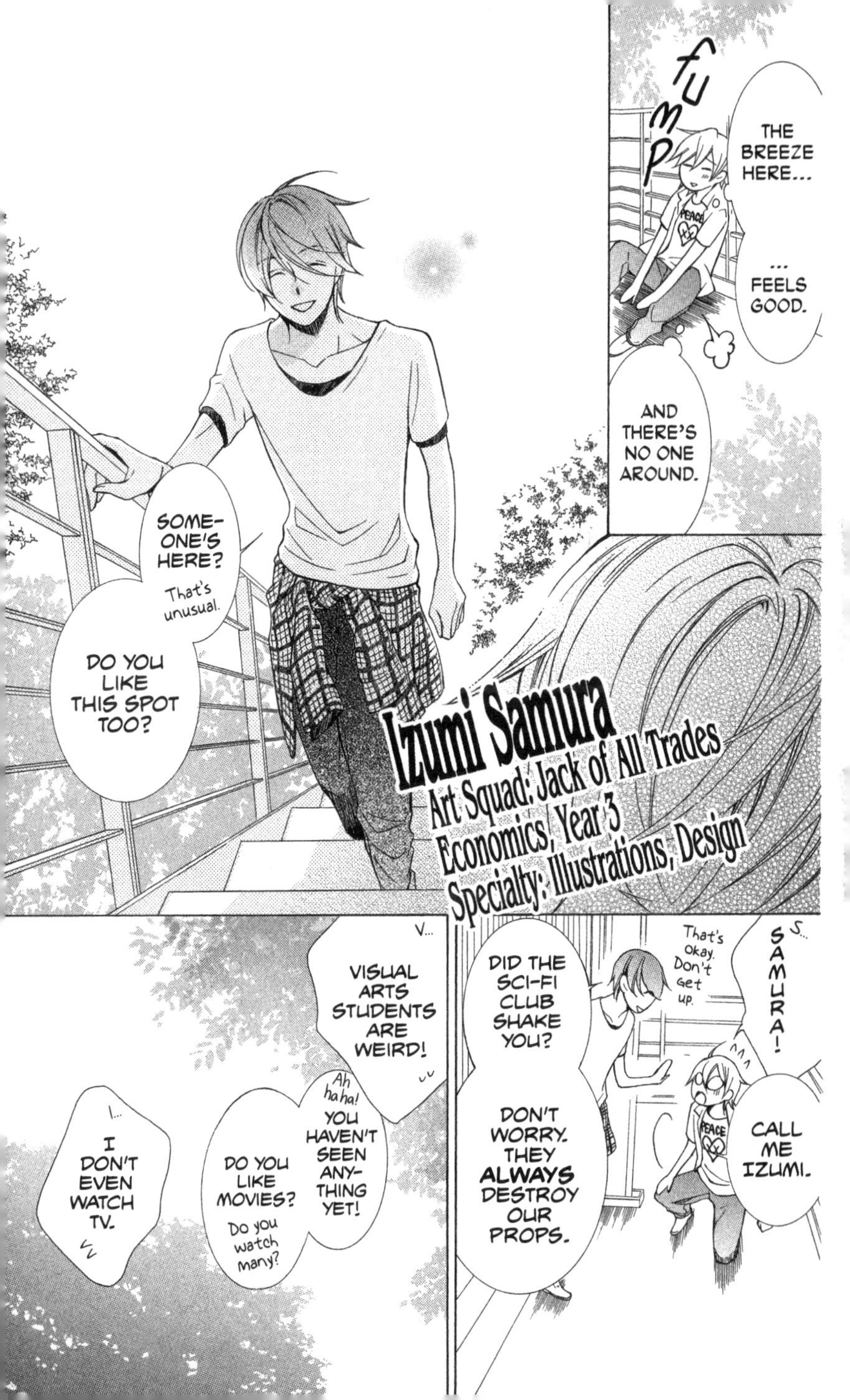
FUMP
THE BREEZE HERE...
... FEELS GOOD.
AND THERE'S NO ONE AROUND.
Izumi Samura
Art Squad: Jack of All Trades
Economics, Year 3
Specialty: Illustrations, Design
SOME-ONE'S HERE?
That's unusual.
DO YOU LIKE THIS SPOT TOO?
S... SAMURA!
That's okay. Don't get up.
DID THE SCI-FI CLUB SHAKE YOU?
CALL ME IZUMI.
DON'T WORRY. THEY ALWAYS DESTROY OUR PROPS.
V...
VISUAL ARTS STUDENTS ARE WEIRD!
Ah haha!
YOU HAVEN'T SEEN ANY-THING YET!
DO YOU LIKE MOVIES?
Do you watch many?
I...
I DON'T EVEN WATCH TV.

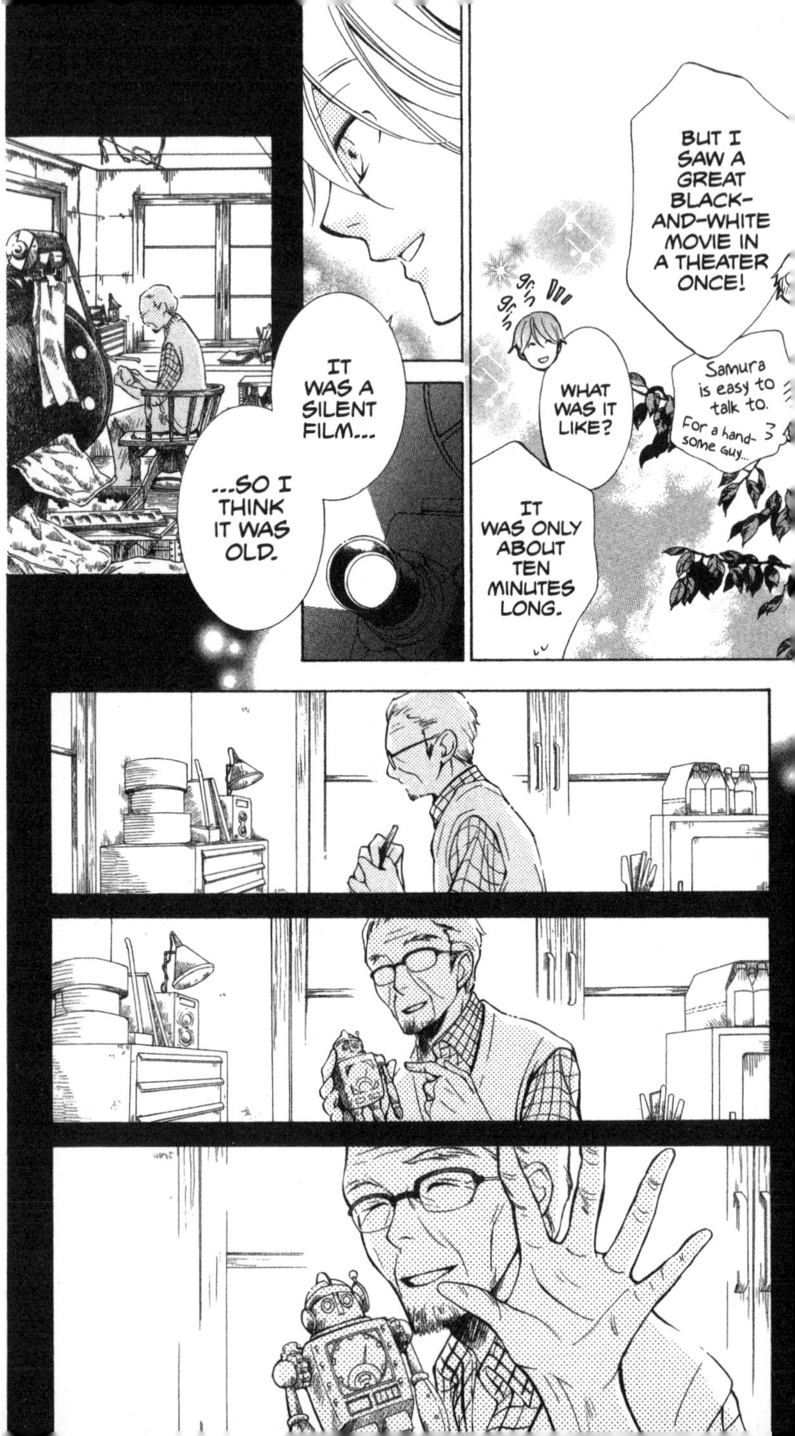
BUT I SAW A GREAT BLACK-AND-WHITE MOVIE IN A THEATER ONCE!
grin grin
Samura is easy to talk to.
For a hand-some guy...
WHAT WAS IT LIKE?
IT WAS ONLY ABOUT TEN MINUTES LONG.
IT WAS A SILENT FILM...
...SO I THINK IT WAS OLD.

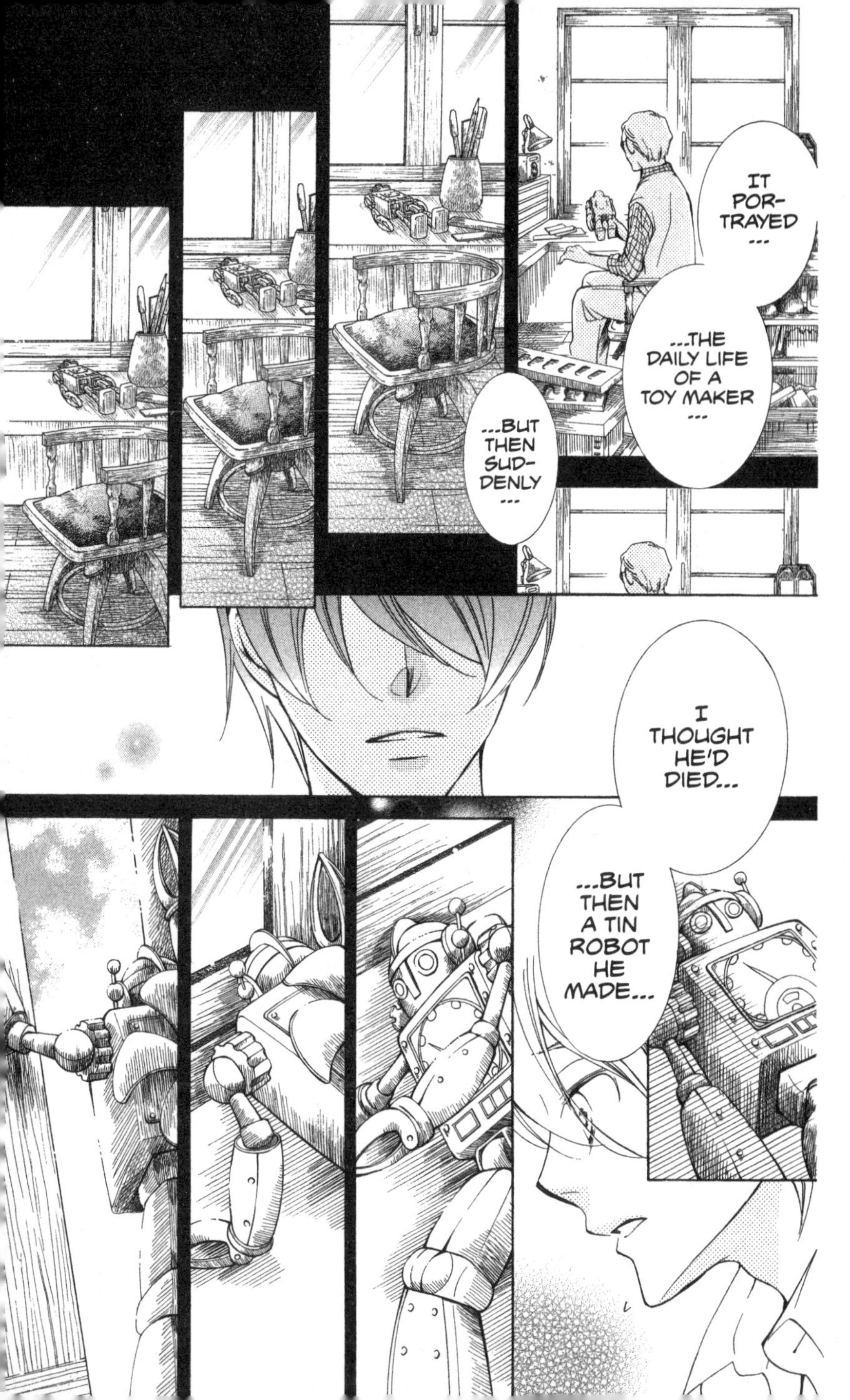
IT POR-TRAYED...
...THE DAILY LIFE OF A TOY MAKER...
...BUT THEN SUD-DENLY...
I THOUGHT HE'D DIED...
...BUT THEN A TIN ROBOT HE MADE...

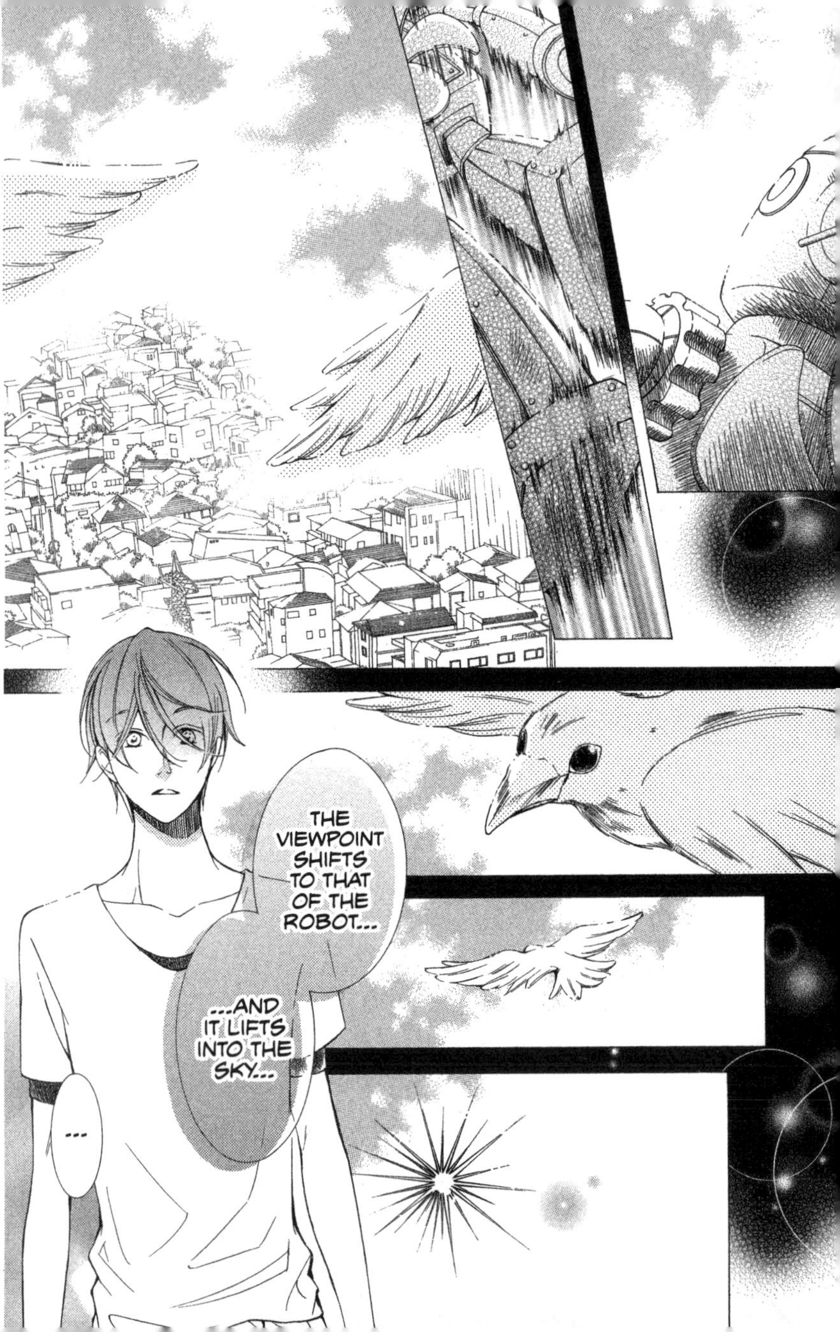
THE VIEWPOINT SHIFTS TO THAT OF THE ROBOT...
...AND IT LIFTS INTO THE SKY...
...

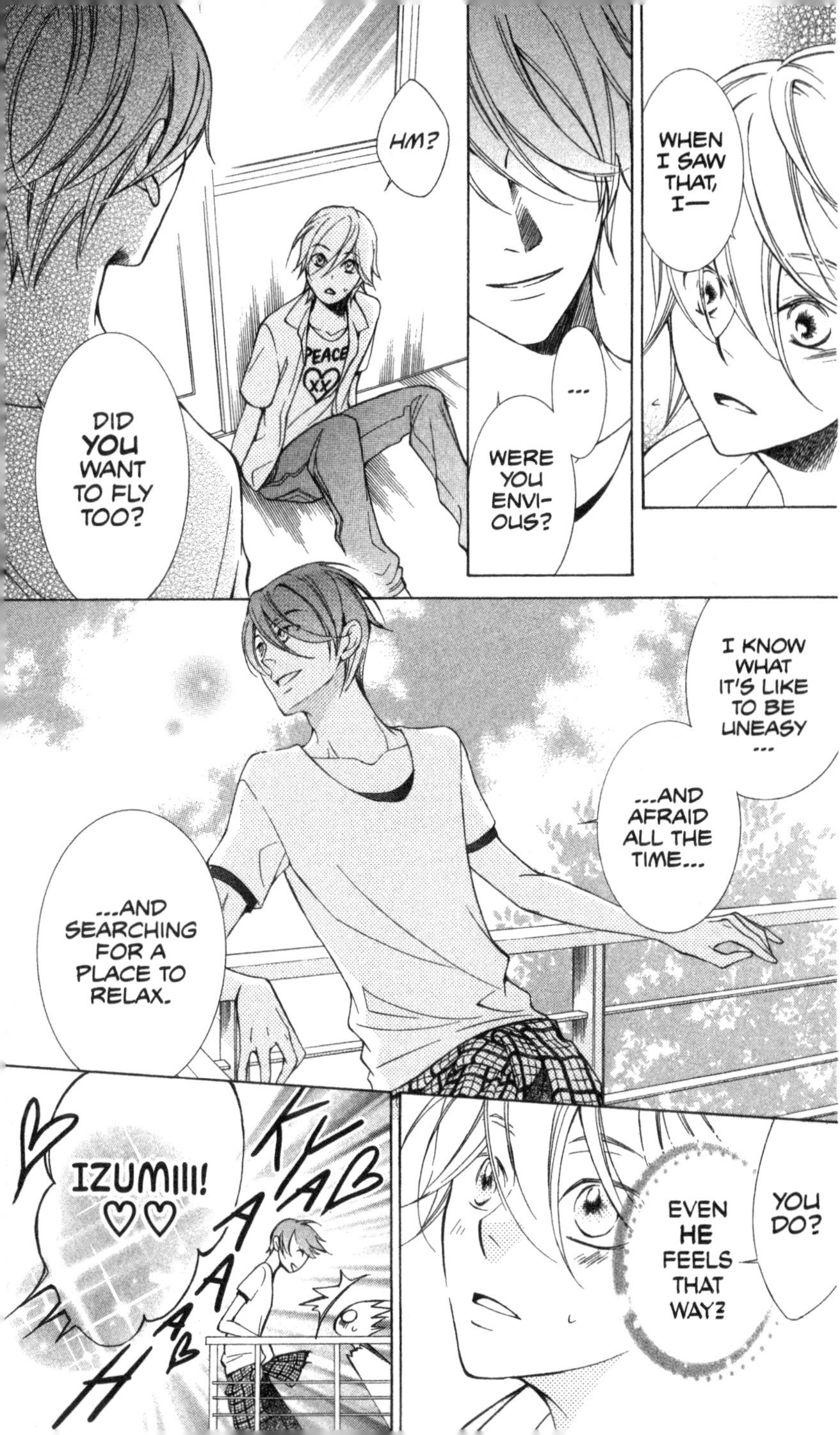
WHEN I SAW THAT, I—
...
WERE YOU ENVIOUS?
HM?
DID YOU WANT TO FLY TOO?
I KNOW WHAT IT'S LIKE TO BE UNEASY...
...AND AFRAID ALL THE TIME...
...AND SEARCHING FOR A PLACE TO RELAX.
YOU DO?
EVEN HE FEELS THAT WAY?
IZUMIIII! ♡♡
KYAAAAAH

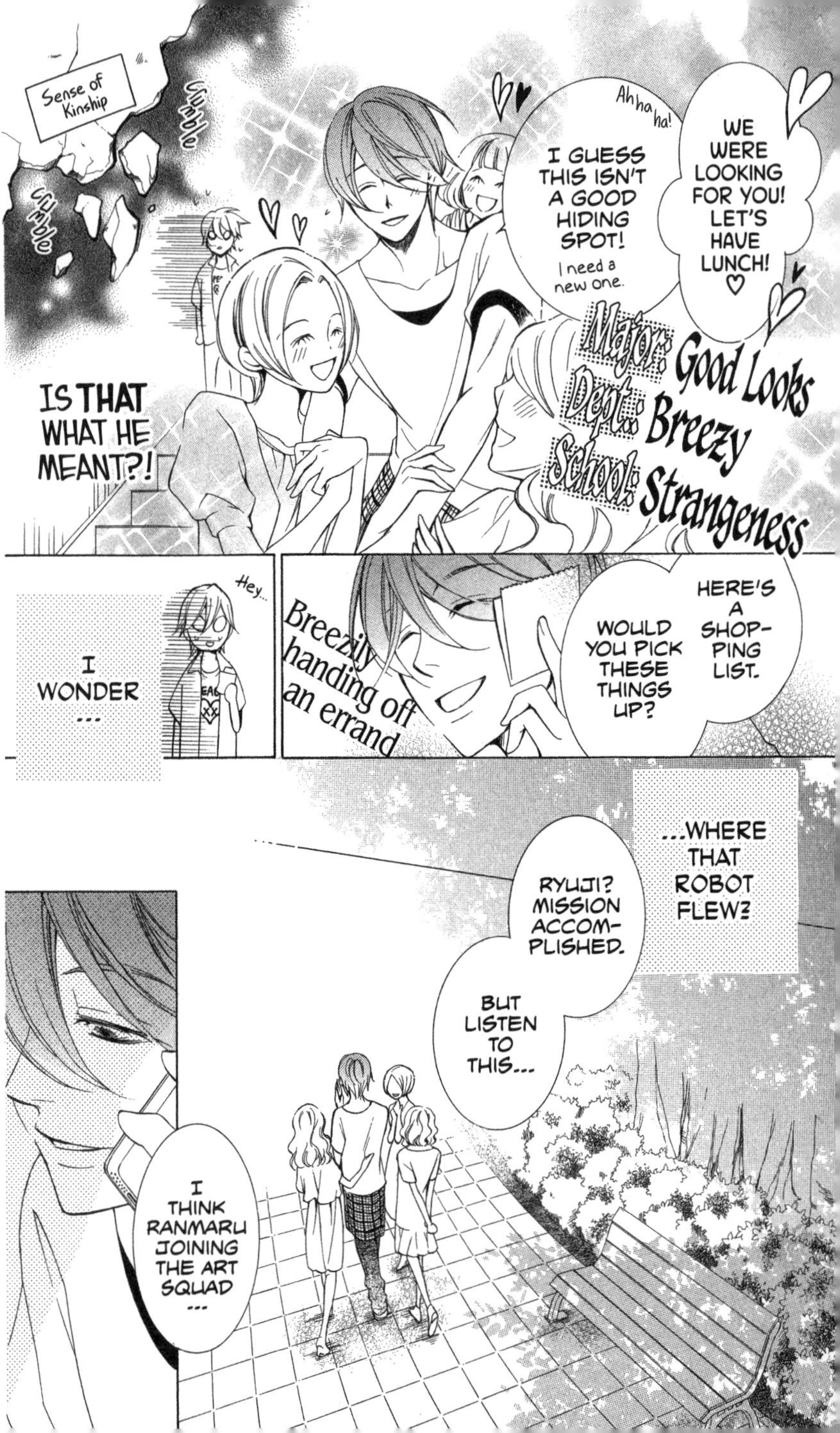
WE WERE LOOKING FOR YOU! LET'S HAVE LUNCH! ♡
Ahhaha!
I GUESS THIS ISN'T A GOOD HIDING SPOT!
I need a new one.
Major: Good Looks
Dept.: Breezy
School: Strangeness
Sense of Kinship
Crumble
Crumble
IS THAT WHAT HE MEANT?!
HERE'S A SHOPPING LIST.
WOULD YOU PICK THESE THINGS UP?
Breezily handing off an errand
Hey...
I WONDER...
...WHERE THAT ROBOT FLEW?
RYUJI? MISSION ACCOMPLISHED.
BUT LISTEN TO THIS...
I THINK RANMARU JOINING THE ART SQUAD...

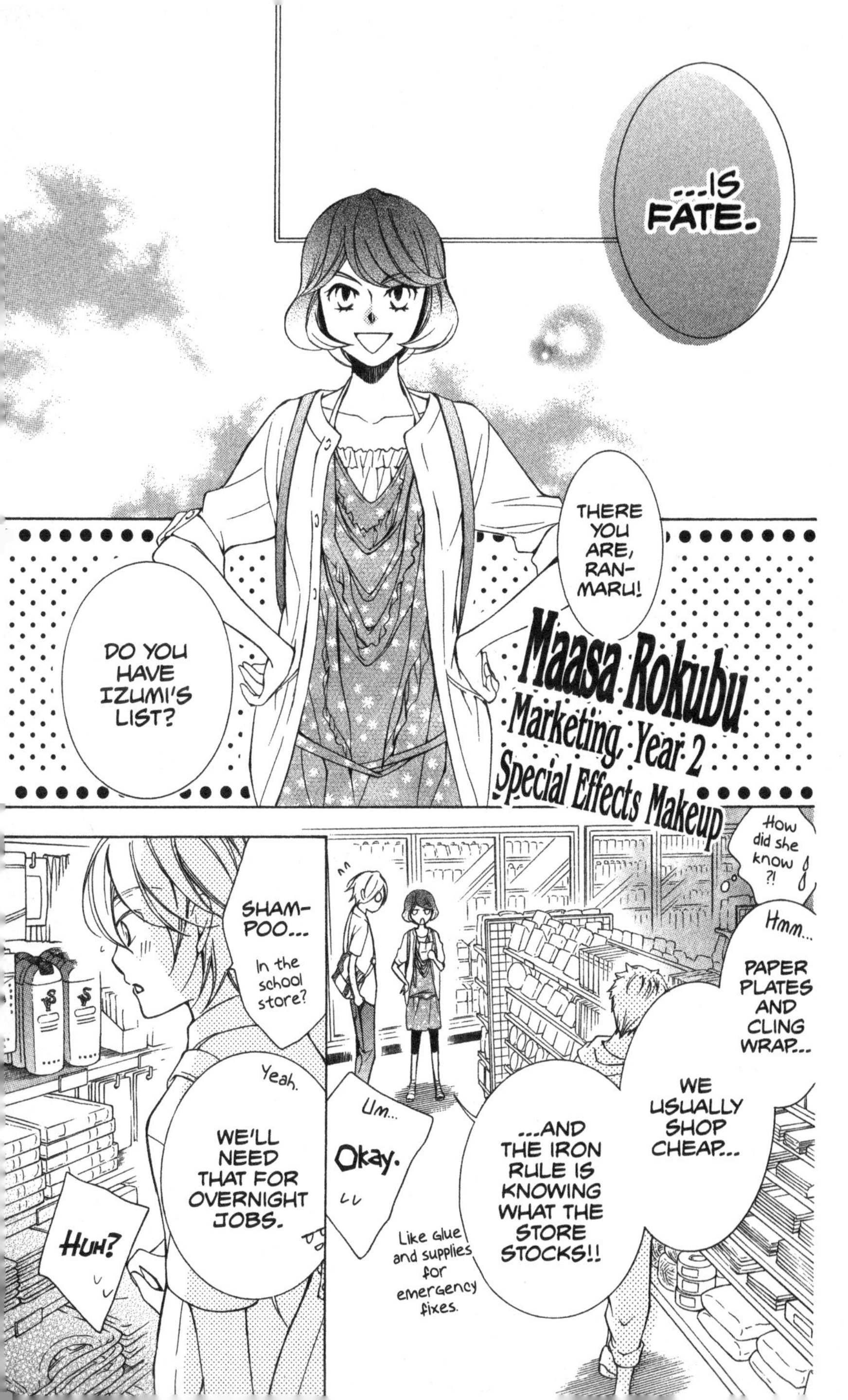
...IS FATE.
THERE YOU ARE, RAN-MARU!
DO YOU HAVE IZUMI'S LIST?
Maasa Rokubu
Marketing, Year 2
Special Effects Makeup
How did she know ?!
Hmm...
PAPER PLATES AND CLING WRAP...
WE USUALLY SHOP CHEAP...
...AND THE IRON RULE IS KNOWING WHAT THE STORE STOCKS!!
Um...
Okay.
Like Glue and supplies for emergency fixes.
SHAM-POO...
In the school store?
Yeah.
WE'LL NEED THAT FOR OVERNIGHT JOBS.
HUH?

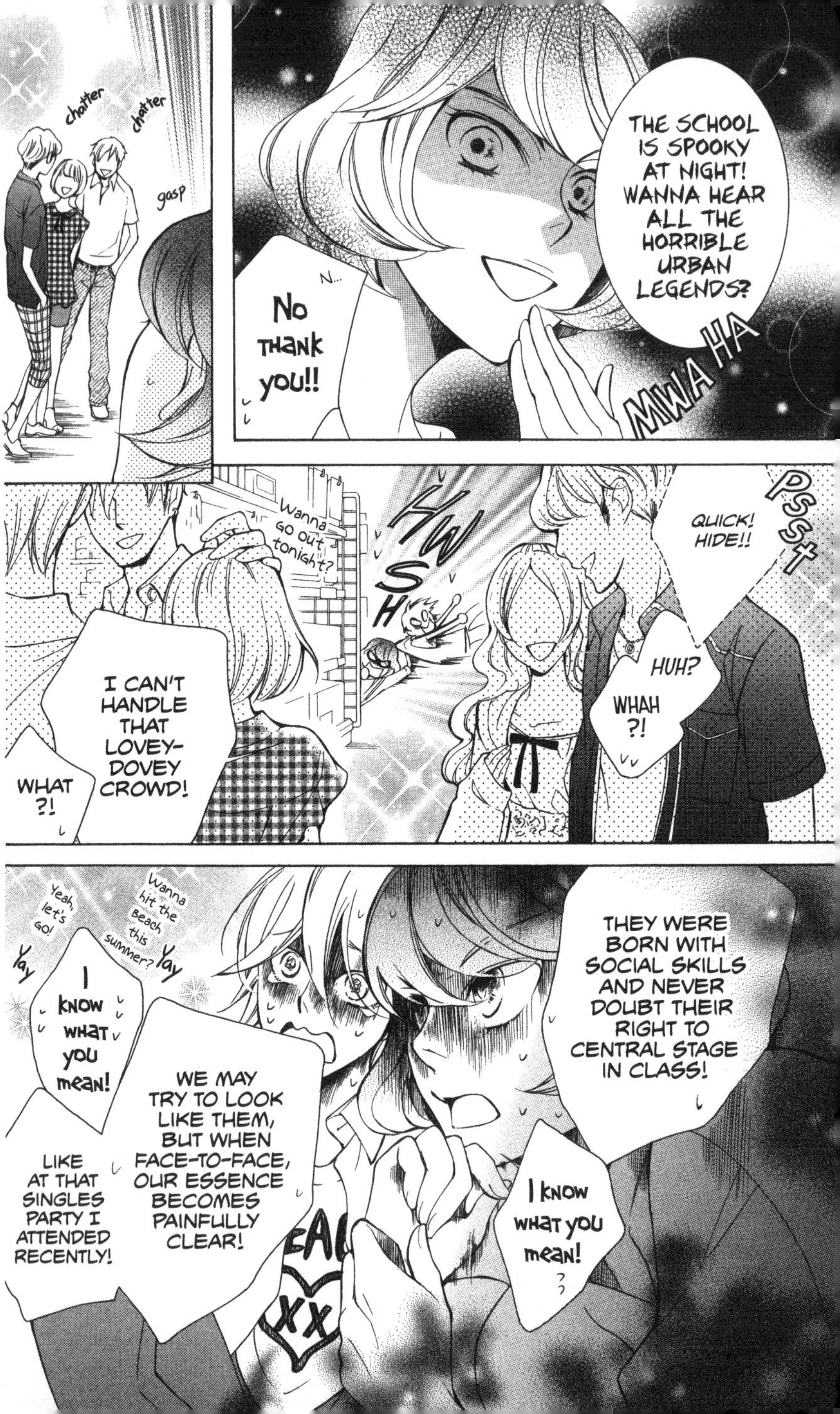
THE SCHOOL IS SPOOKY AT NIGHT! WANNA HEAR ALL THE HORRIBLE URBAN LEGENDS?
MWA HA
N...
No thank you!!
chatter
chatter
gasp
PSST
QUICK! HIDE!!
HUH?
WHAH ?!
HWSH
Wanna go out tonight?
I CAN'T HANDLE THAT LOVEY-DOVEY CROWD!
WHAT ?!
THEY WERE BORN WITH SOCIAL SKILLS AND NEVER DOUBT THEIR RIGHT TO CENTRAL STAGE IN CLASS!
I know what you mean!
WE MAY TRY TO LOOK LIKE THEM, BUT WHEN FACE-TO-FACE, OUR ESSENCE BECOMES PAINFULLY CLEAR!
Wanna hit the beach this summer?
Yeah, let's go!
Yay
Yay
I know what you mean!
LIKE AT THAT SINGLES PARTY I ATTENDED RECENTLY!

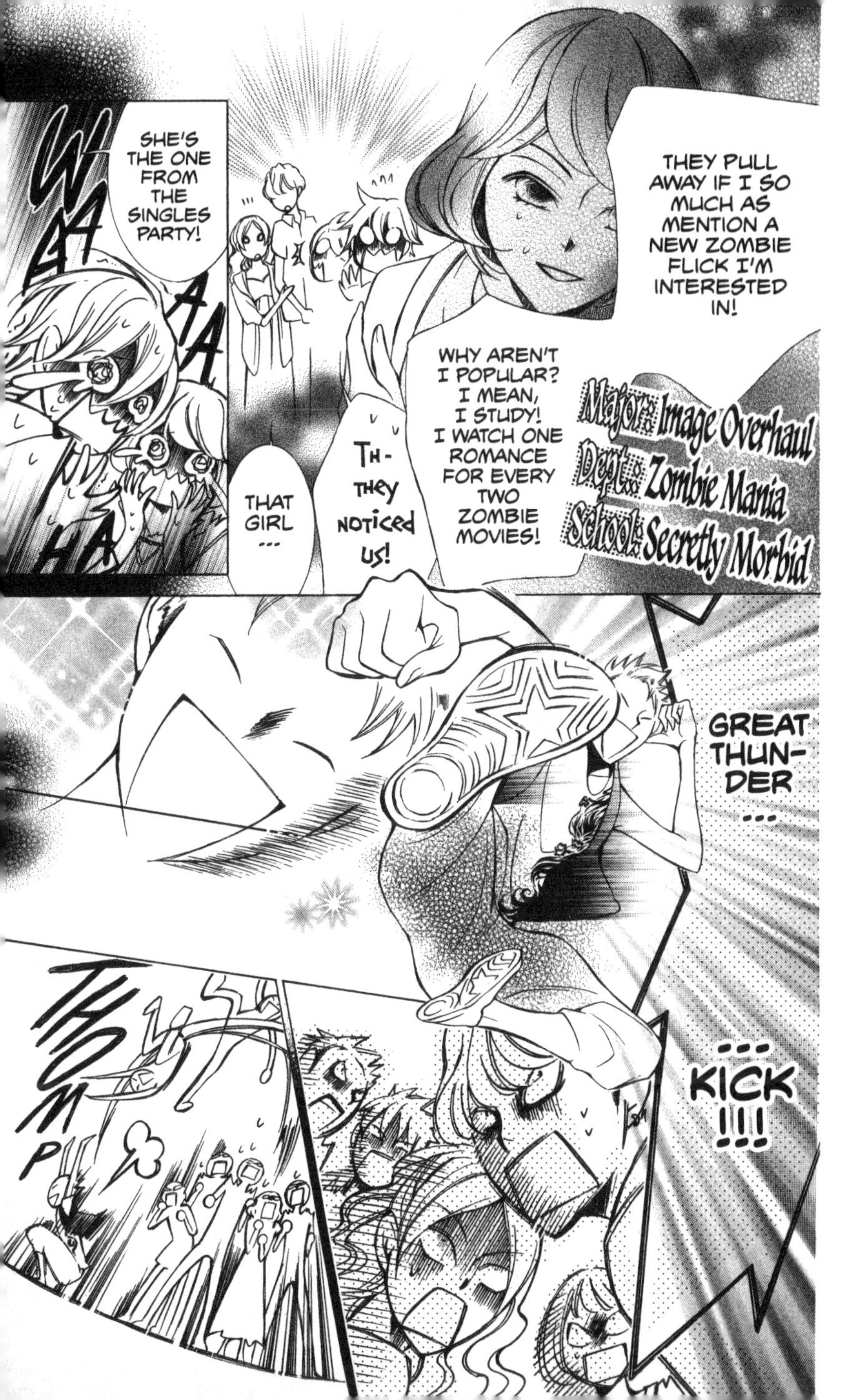
THEY PULL AWAY IF I SO MUCH AS MENTION A NEW ZOMBIE FLICK I'M INTERESTED IN!
WHY AREN'T I POPULAR? I MEAN, I STUDY! I WATCH ONE ROMANCE FOR EVERY TWO ZOMBIE MOVIES!
Major: Image Overhaul
Dept.: Zombie Mania
School: Secretly Morbid
TH-THEY NOTICED US!
THAT GIRL...
SHE'S THE ONE FROM THE SINGLES PARTY!
WAAAAHA
GREAT THUNDER...
...KICK!!!
THOMP

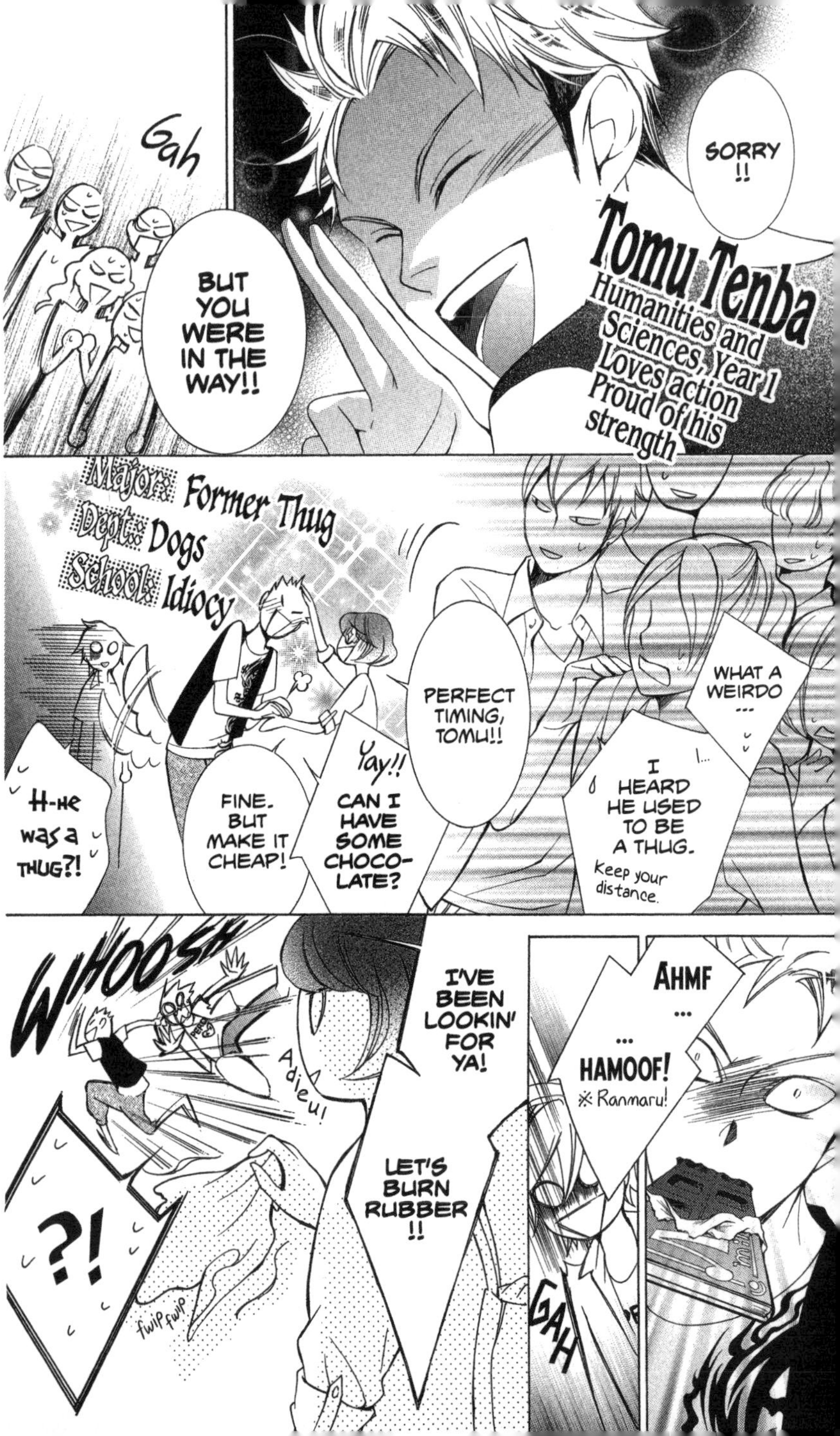
SORRY!!
Tomu Tenba
Humanities and Sciences, Year 1
Loves action
Proud of his strength
BUT YOU WERE IN THE WAY!!
Gah
WHAT A WEIRDO...
I... I HEARD HE USED TO BE A THUG.
Keep your distance.
PERFECT TIMING, TOMU!!
Yay!! CAN I HAVE SOME CHOCOLATE?
FINE. BUT MAKE IT CHEAP!
Major: Former Thug
Dept.: Dogs
School: Idiocy
H-he was a thug?!
AHMF... ...HAMOOF!
※Ranmaru!
GAH
I'VE BEEN LOOKIN' FOR YA!
LET'S BURN RUBBER!!
Adieu!
WHOOSH
?!
fwip fwip

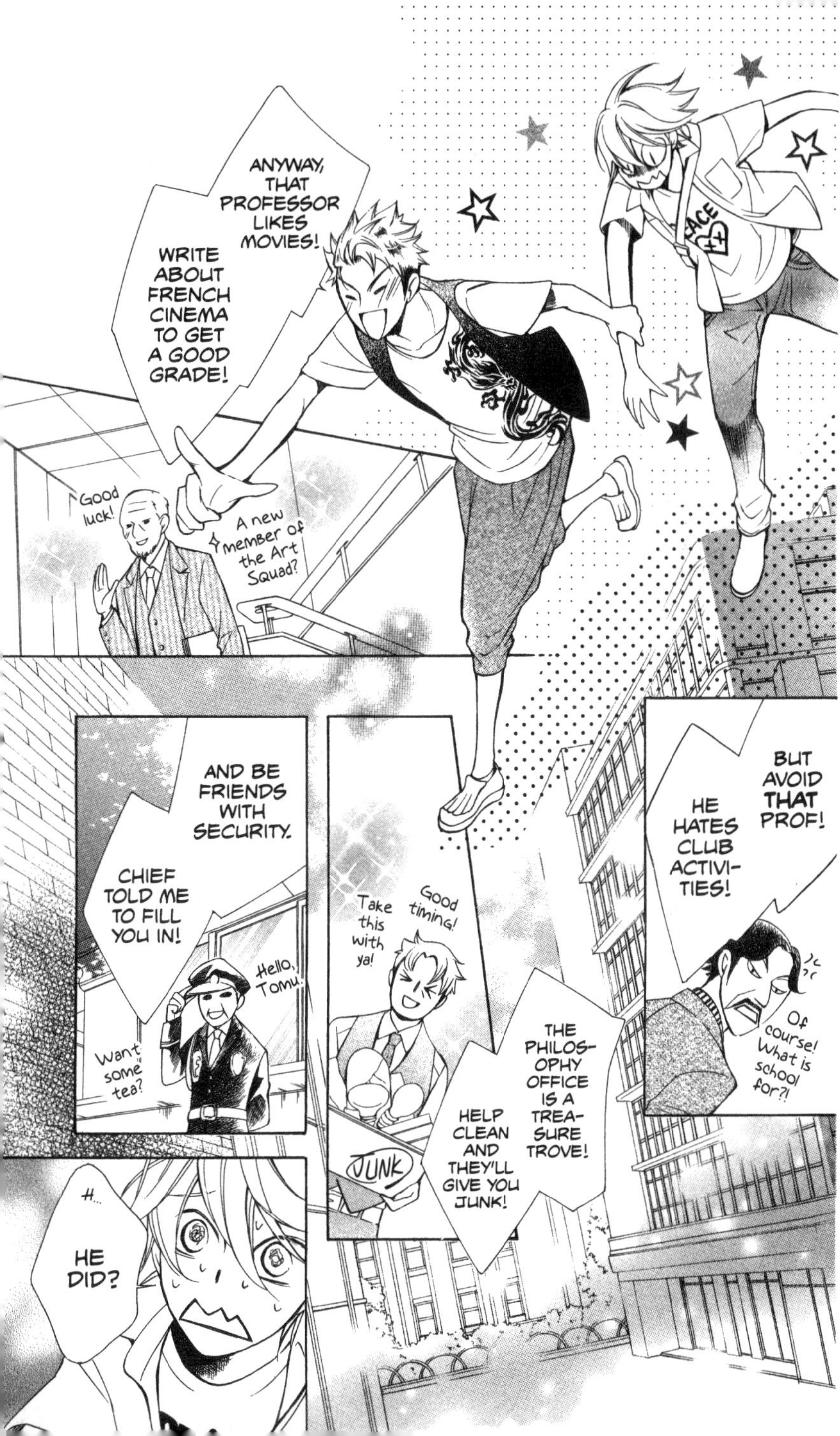
ANYWAY, THAT PROFESSOR LIKES MOVIES!
WRITE ABOUT FRENCH CINEMA TO GET A GOOD GRADE!
A new member of the Art Squad?
Good luck!
BUT AVOID THAT PROF!
HE HATES CLUB ACTIVI-TIES!
Of course! What is school for?!
THE PHILOS-OPHY OFFICE IS A TREA-SURE TROVE!
HELP CLEAN AND THEY'LL GIVE YOU JUNK!
Good timing!
Take this with ya!
JUNK
AND BE FRIENDS WITH SECURITY.
CHIEF TOLD ME TO FILL YOU IN!
Hello, Tomu!
Want some tea?
H...
HE DID?

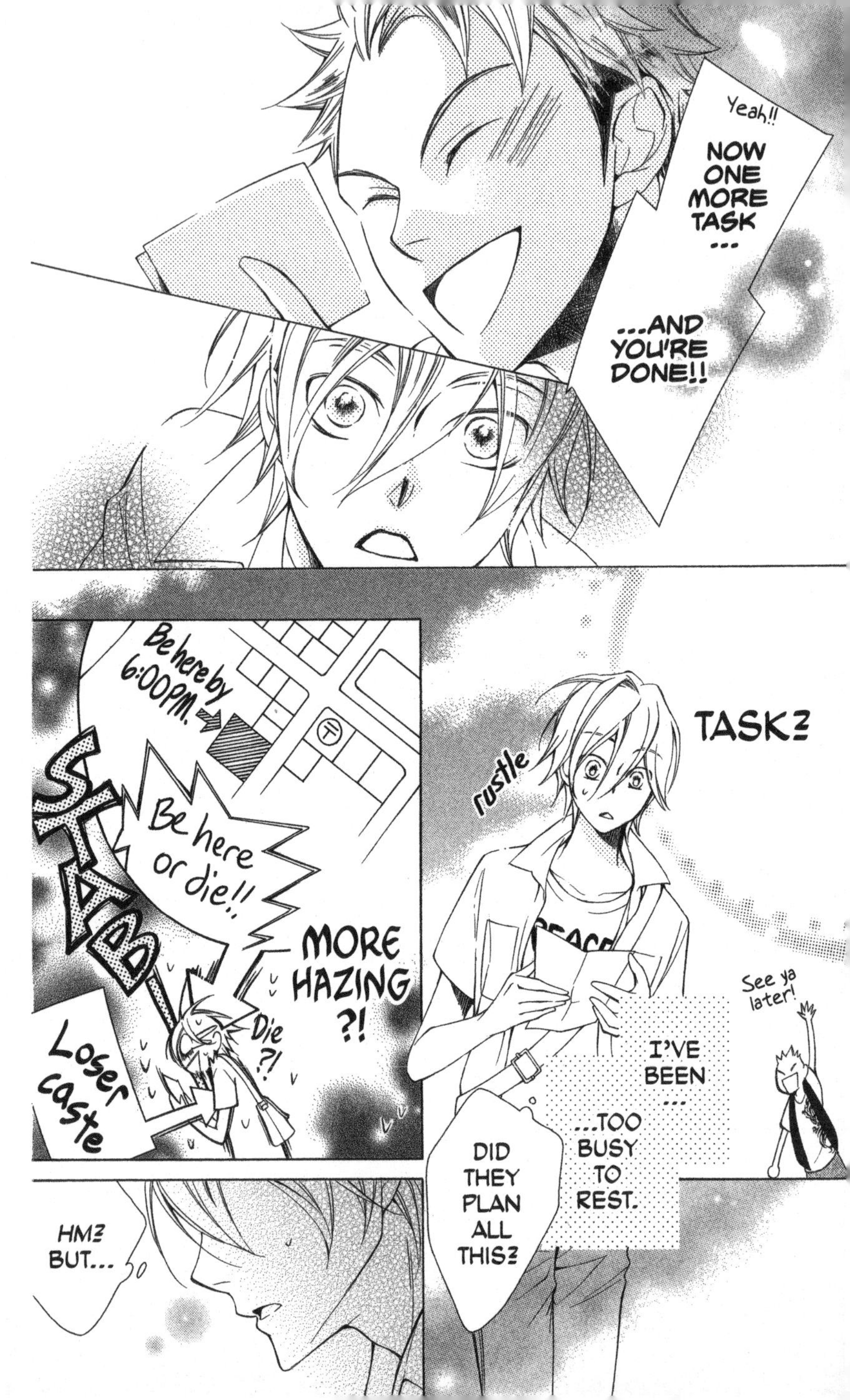
Yeah!!
NOW ONE MORE TASK...
...AND YOU'RE DONE!!
TASK?
rustle
See ya later!
Be here by 6:00PM.
STAB
Be here or die!!
MORE HAZING?!
Die?!
Loser caste
I'VE BEEN...
...TOO BUSY TO REST.
DID THEY PLAN ALL THIS?
HM? BUT...

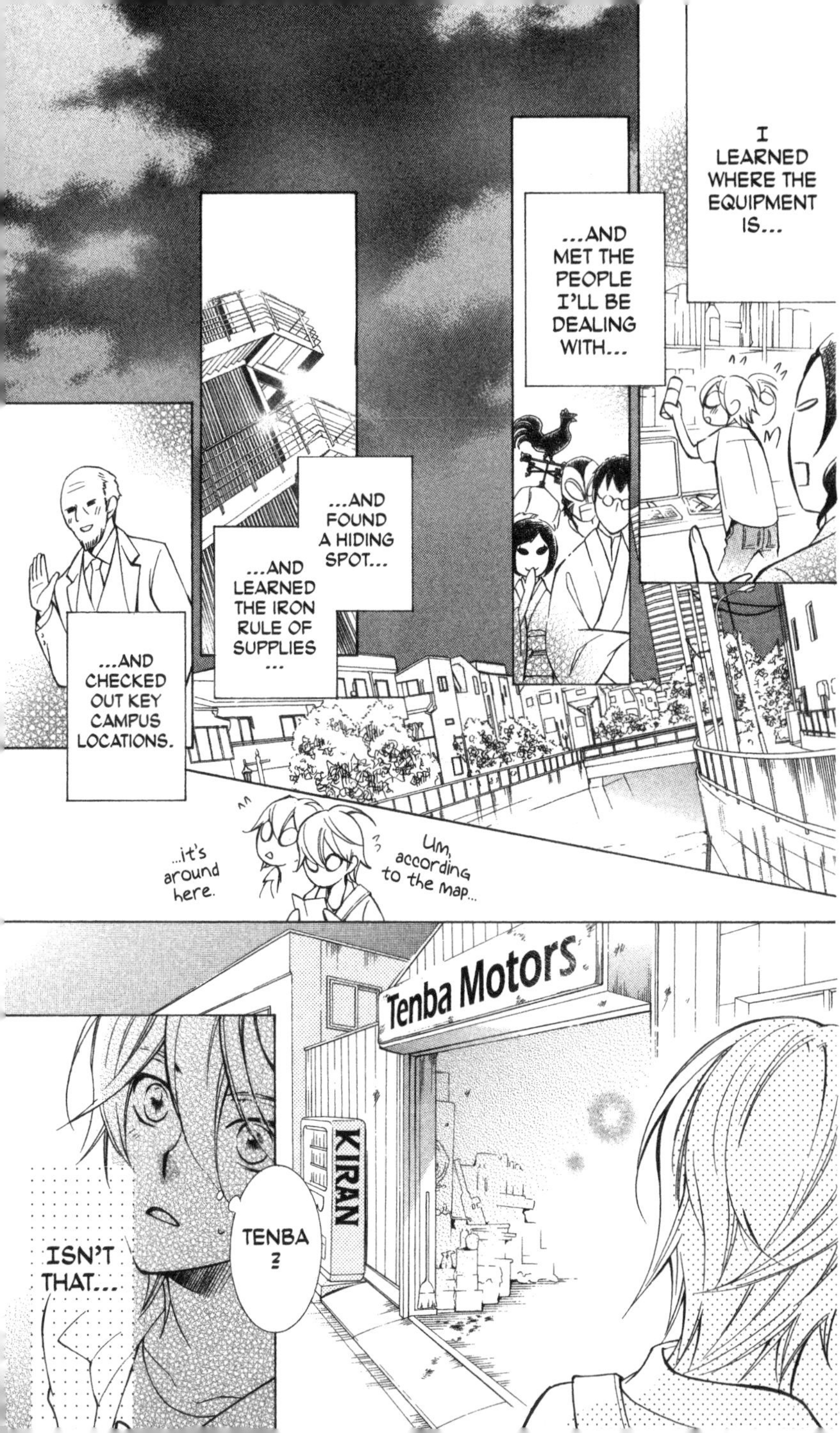
I LEARNED WHERE THE EQUIPMENT IS...
...AND MET THE PEOPLE I'LL BE DEALING WITH...
...AND FOUND A HIDING SPOT...
...AND LEARNED THE IRON RULE OF SUPPLIES...
...AND CHECKED OUT KEY CAMPUS LOCATIONS.
Um, according to the map...
...it's around here.
Tenba Motors
KIRAN
TENBA?
ISN'T THAT...

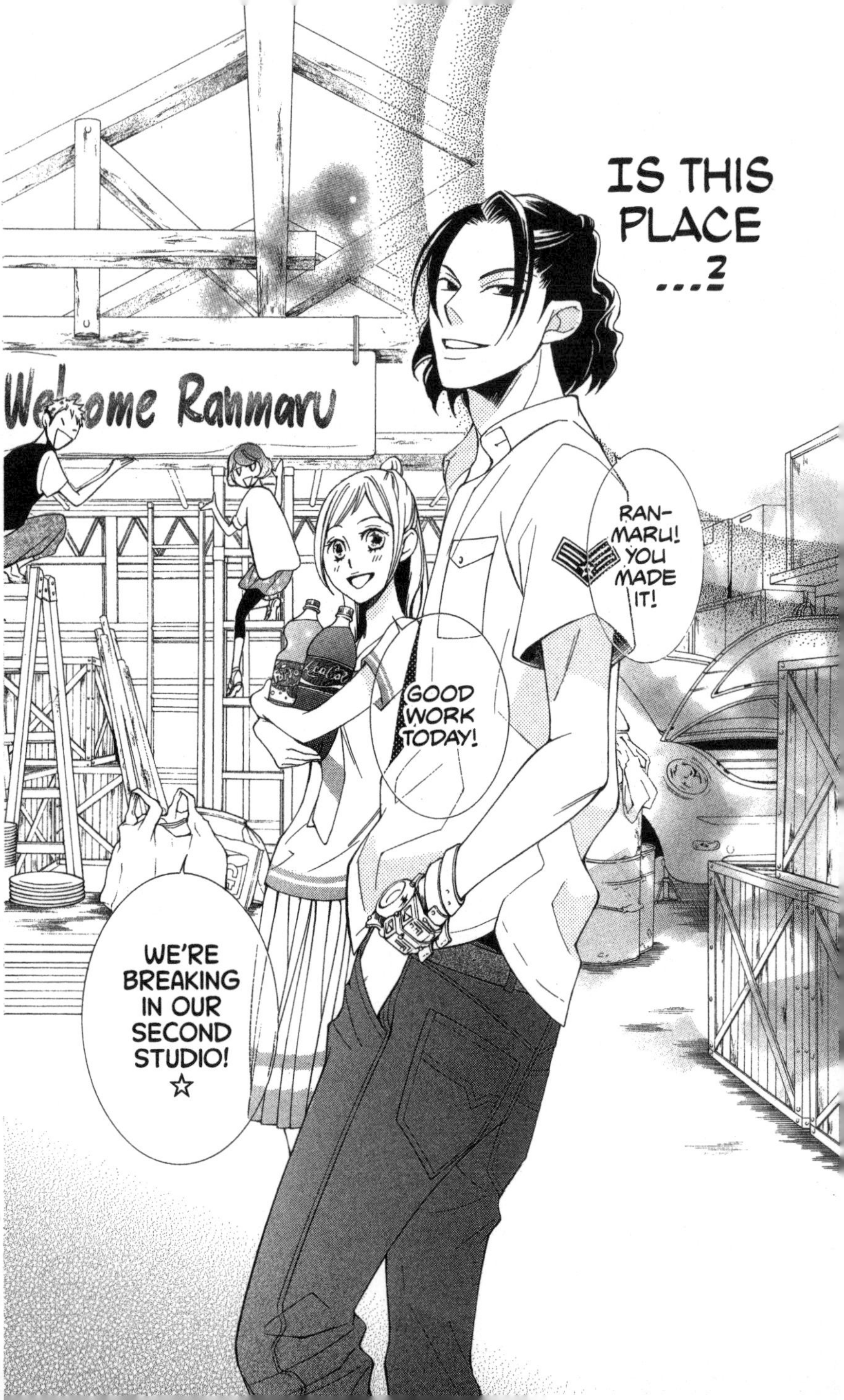
IS THIS PLACE ...?
Welcome Ranmaru
RAN-MARU! YOU MADE IT!
GOOD WORK TODAY!
WE'RE BREAKING IN OUR SECOND STUDIO! ☆

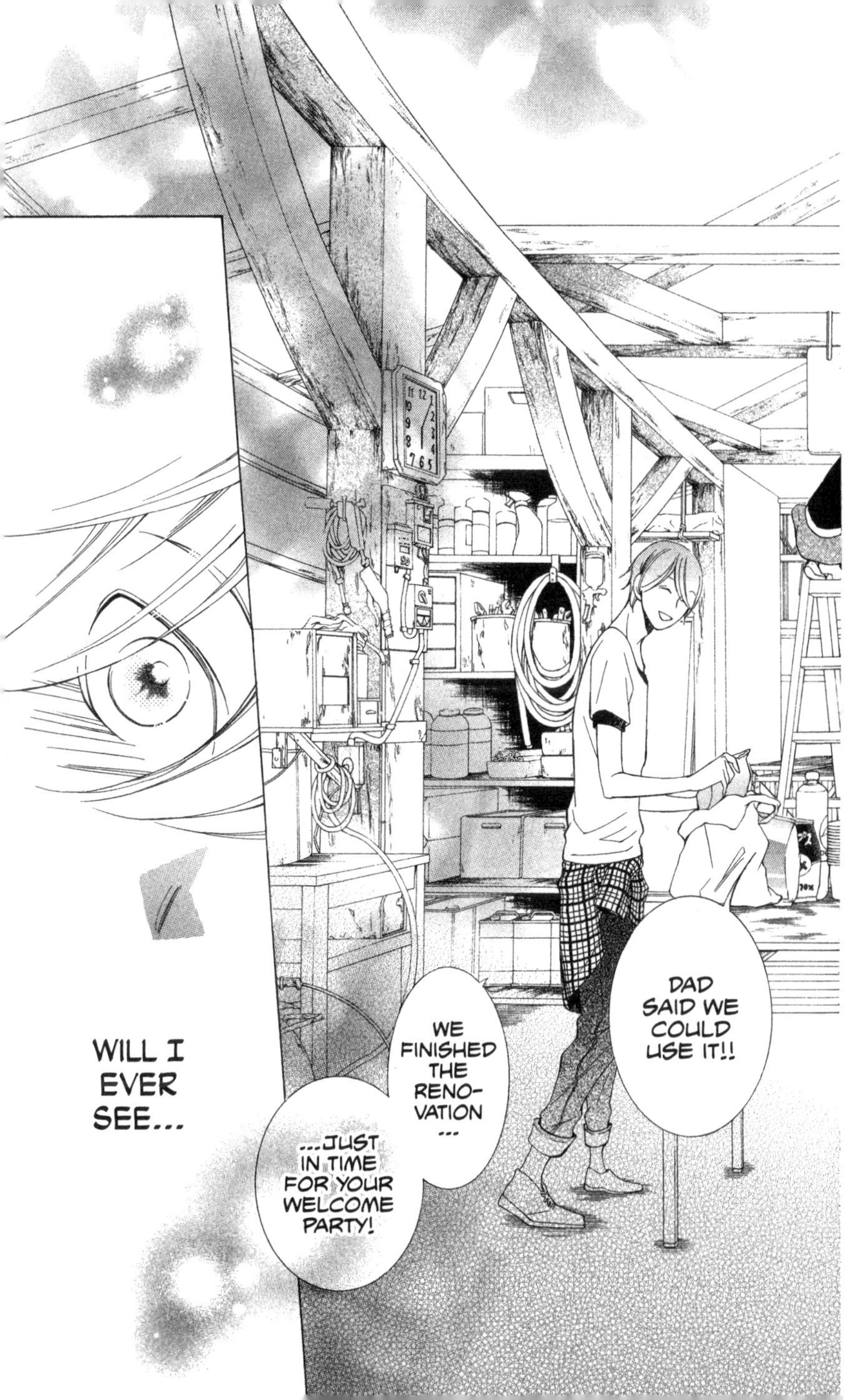
DAD SAID WE COULD USE IT!!
WE FINISHED THE RENOVATION...
...JUST IN TIME FOR YOUR WELCOME PARTY!
WILL I EVER SEE...

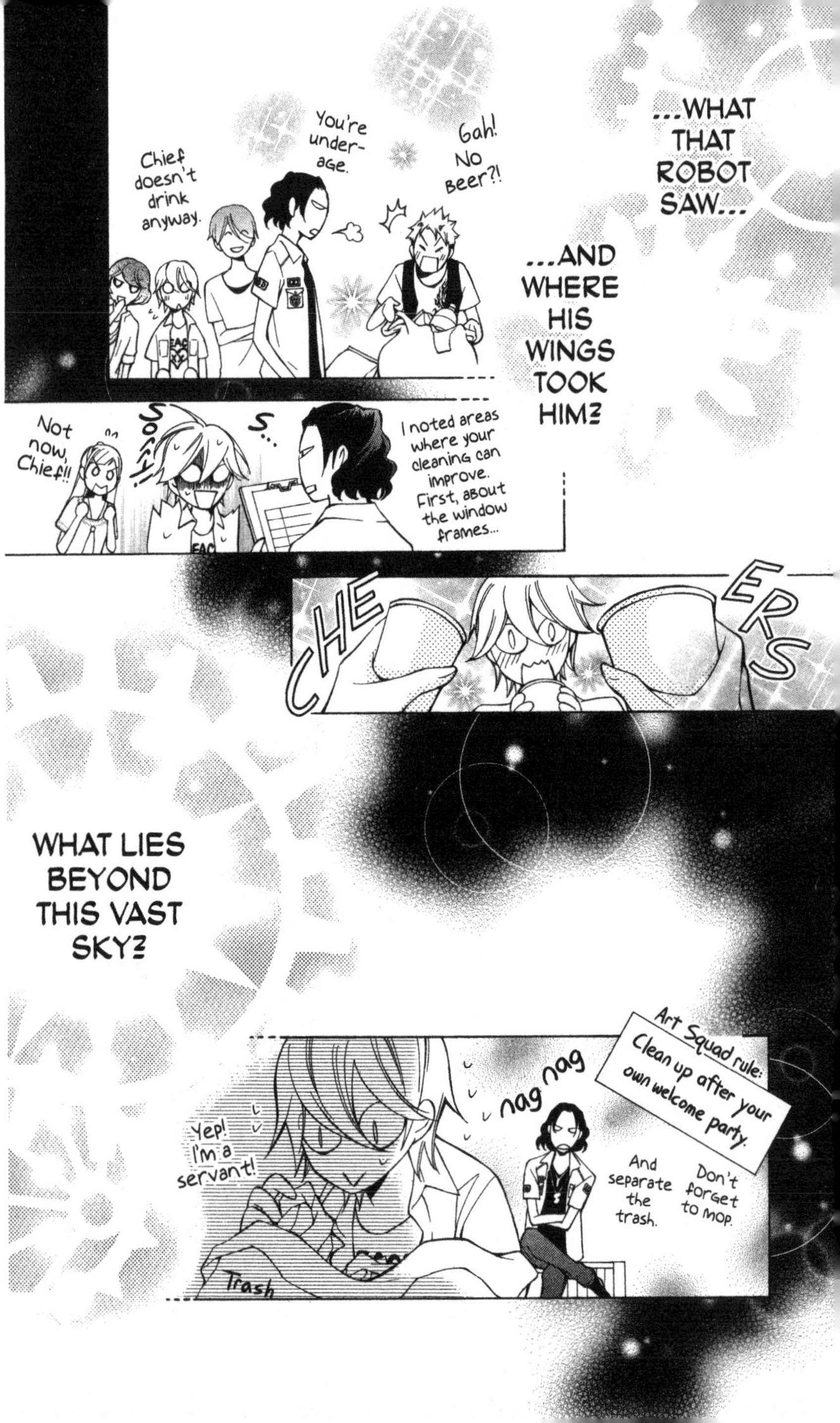
...WHAT THAT ROBOT SAW...
Gah! No Beer?!
You're under-age.
Chief doesn't drink anyway.
...AND WHERE HIS WINGS TOOK HIM?
I noted areas where your cleaning can improve. First, about the window frames...
S...
Sorry!
Not now, Chief!!
CHEERS
WHAT LIES BEYOND THIS VAST SKY?
Art Squad rule: Clean up after your own welcome party.
Don't forget to mop.
And separate the trash.
nag nag
Yep! I'm a servant!
Trash

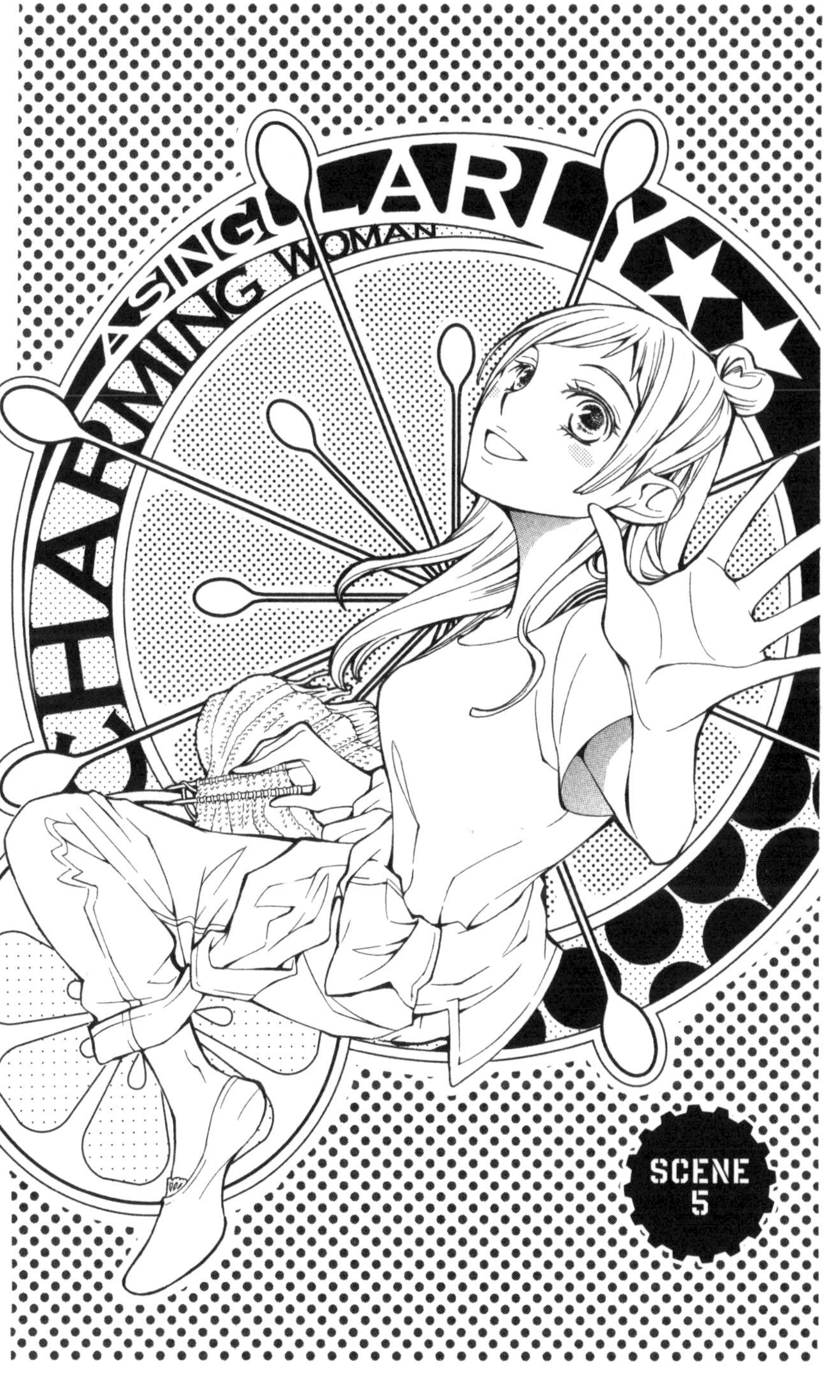
A SINGULARLY CHARMING WOMAN
SCENE 5

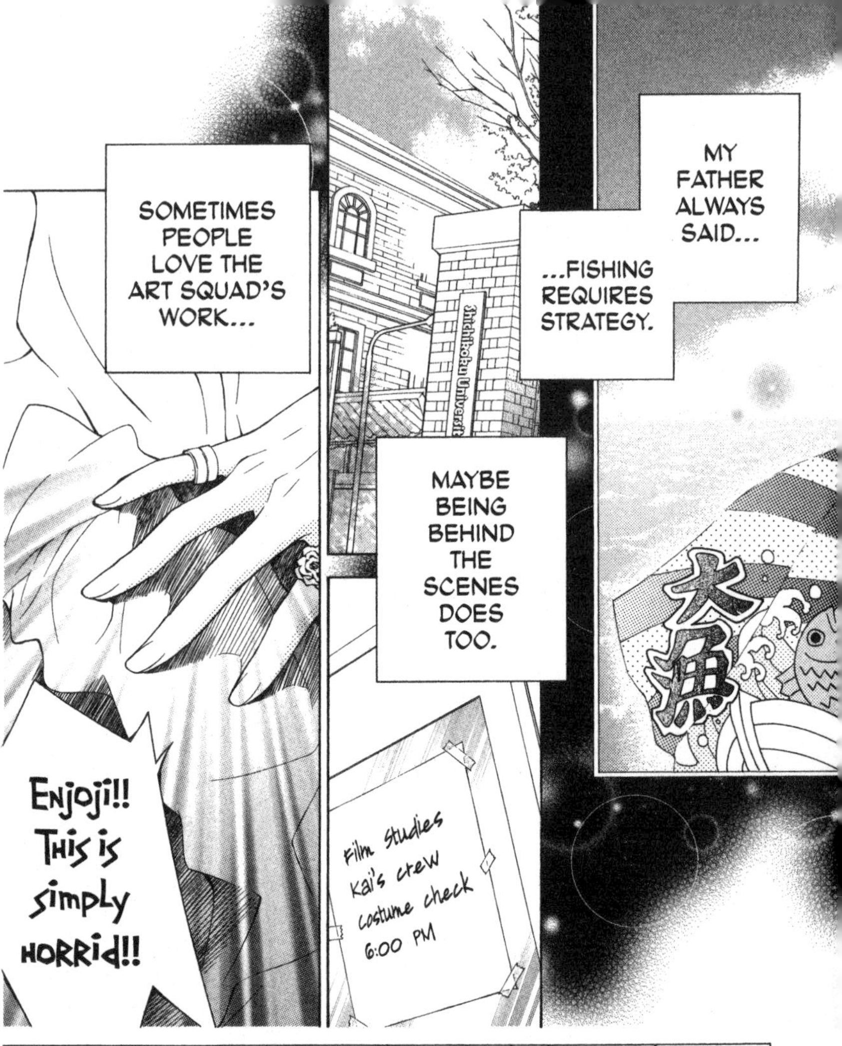
MY FATHER ALWAYS SAID...
...FISHING REQUIRES STRATEGY.
Shichifuku University
MAYBE BEING BEHIND THE SCENES DOES TOO.
Film studies
Kai's crew
costume check
6:00 PM
SOMETIMES PEOPLE LOVE THE ART SQUAD'S WORK...
Enjoji!! This is simply horrid!!

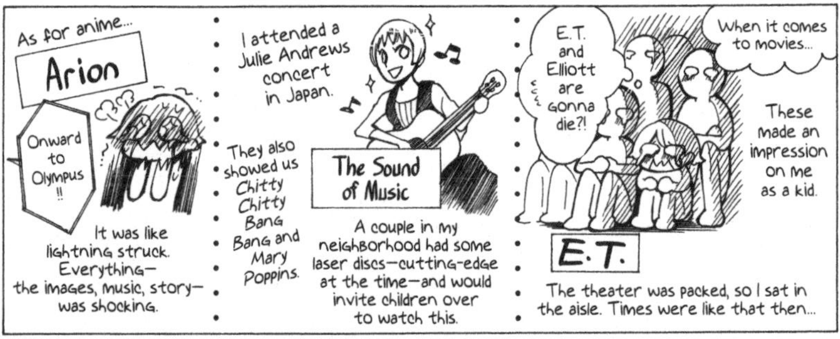
When it comes to movies...
These made an impression on me as a kid.
E.T. and Elliott are gonna die?!
E.T.
The theater was packed, so I sat in the aisle. Times were like that then...
I attended a Julie Andrews concert in Japan.
The Sound of Music
A couple in my neighborhood had some laser discs—cutting-edge at the time—and would invite children over to watch this.
They also showed us Chitty Chitty Bang Bang and Mary Poppins.
As for anime...
Arion
Onward to Olympus !!
It was like lightning struck. Everything—the images, music, story—was shocking.

I've always been the type to get obsessed with stuff...

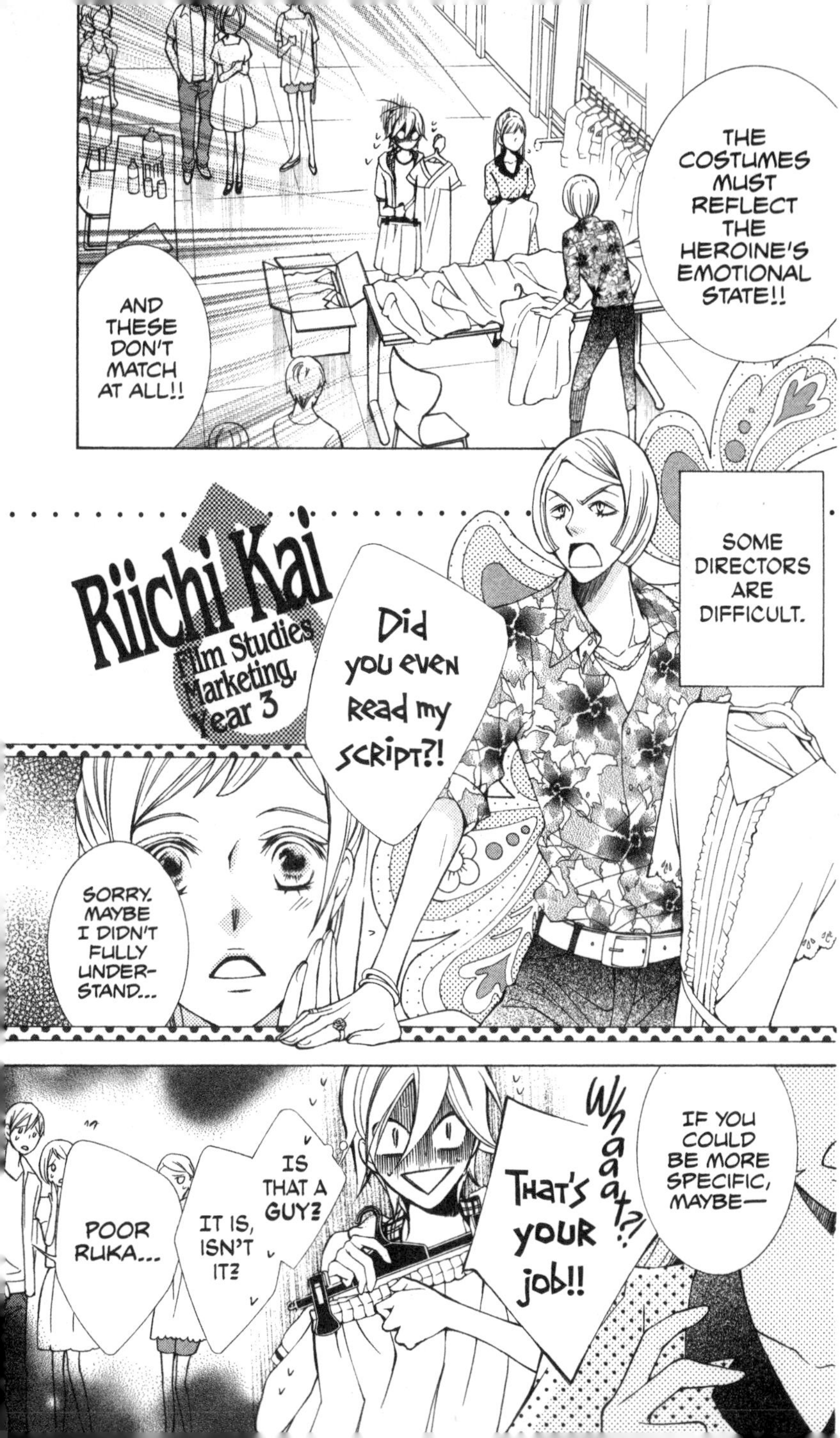

THE COSTUMES MUST REFLECT THE HEROINE'S EMOTIONAL STATE!!
AND THESE DON'T MATCH AT ALL!!
SOME DIRECTORS ARE DIFFICULT.
Riichi Kai
Film Studies Marketing, Year 3
Did you even read my script?!
SORRY. MAYBE I DIDN'T FULLY UNDER-STAND...
IF YOU COULD BE MORE SPECIFIC, MAYBE—
Whaaat?!
That's your job!!
IS THAT A GUY?
IT IS, ISN'T IT?
POOR RUKA...

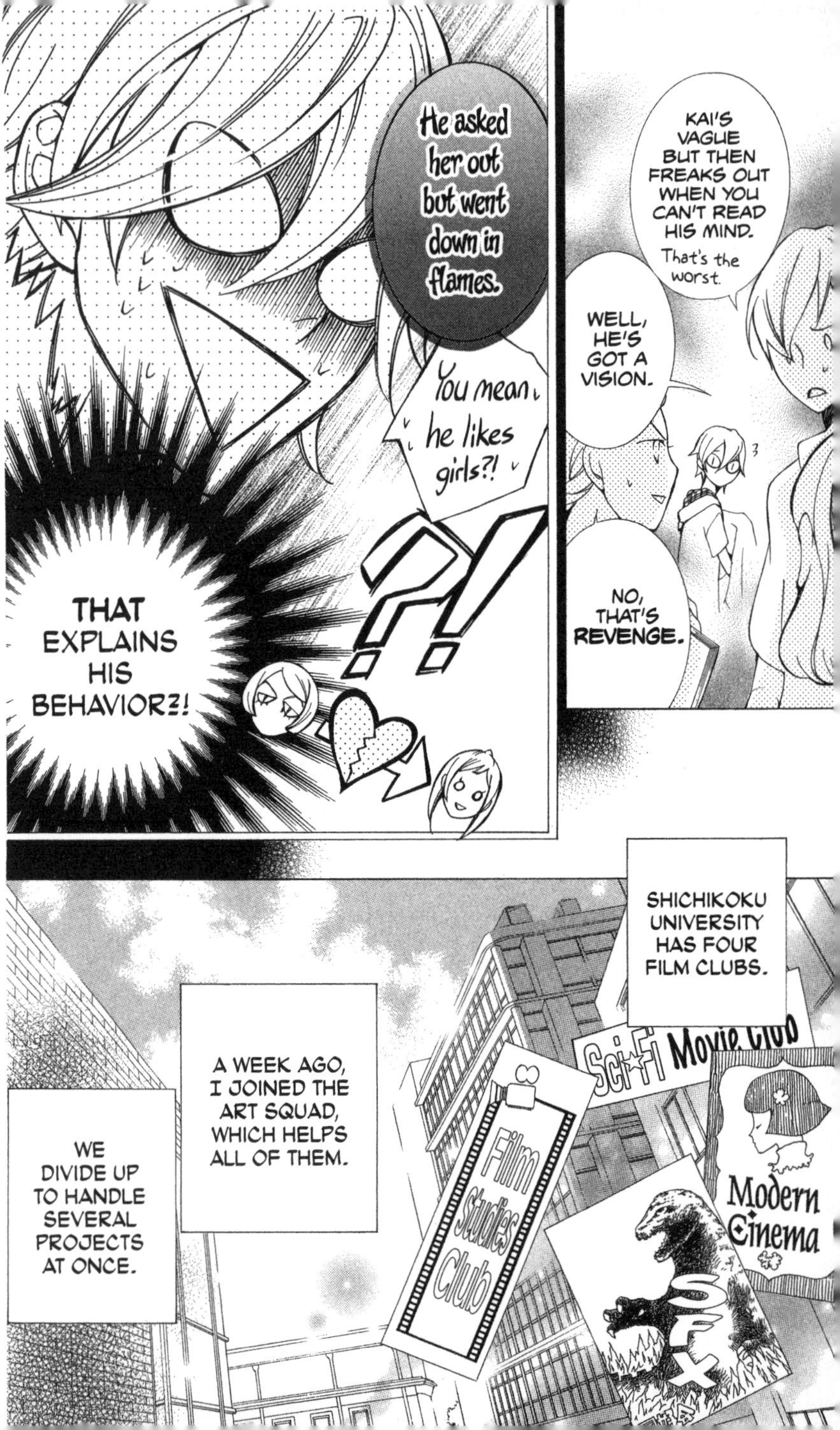
KAI'S VAGUE BUT THEN FREAKS OUT WHEN YOU CAN'T READ HIS MIND.
That's the worst.
WELL, HE'S GOT A VISION.
NO, THAT'S REVENGE.
He asked her out but went down in flames.
You mean he likes girls?!
?!
THAT EXPLAINS HIS BEHAVIOR?!
SHICHIKOKU UNIVERSITY HAS FOUR FILM CLUBS.
Sci☆Fi Movie Club
Modern Cinema
SFX
Film Studies Club
A WEEK AGO, I JOINED THE ART SQUAD, WHICH HELPS ALL OF THEM.
WE DIVIDE UP TO HANDLE SEVERAL PROJECTS AT ONCE.

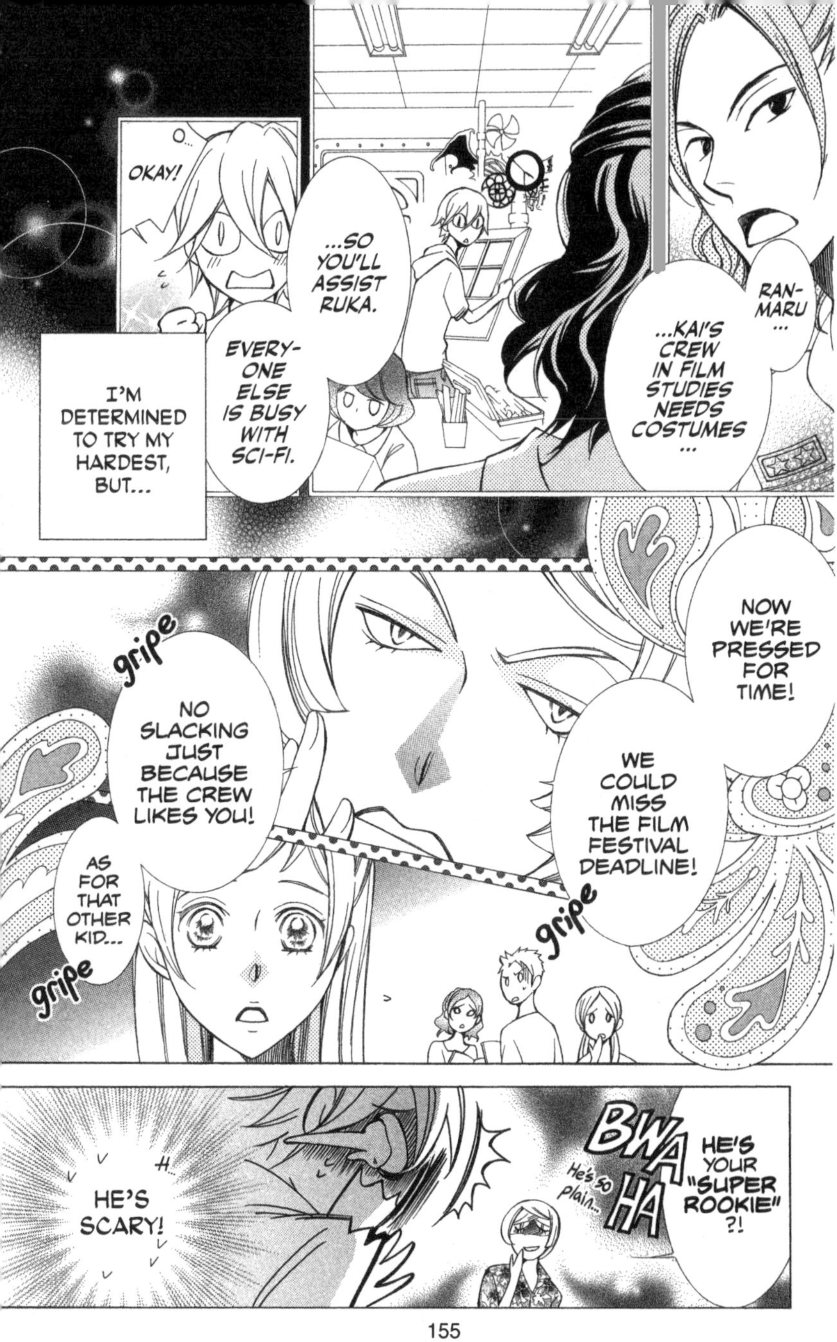
RAN-MARU...
...KAI'S CREW IN FILM STUDIES NEEDS COSTUMES...
...SO YOU'LL ASSIST RUKA.
EVERY-ONE ELSE IS BUSY WITH SCI-FI.
O...
OKAY!
I'M DETERMINED TO TRY MY HARDEST, BUT...
NOW WE'RE PRESSED FOR TIME!
WE COULD MISS THE FILM FESTIVAL DEADLINE!
gripe
NO SLACKING JUST BECAUSE THE CREW LIKES YOU!
gripe
AS FOR THAT OTHER KID...
gripe
HE'S YOUR "SUPER ROOKIE"?!
BWA HA
He's so plain...
H...
HE'S SCARY!

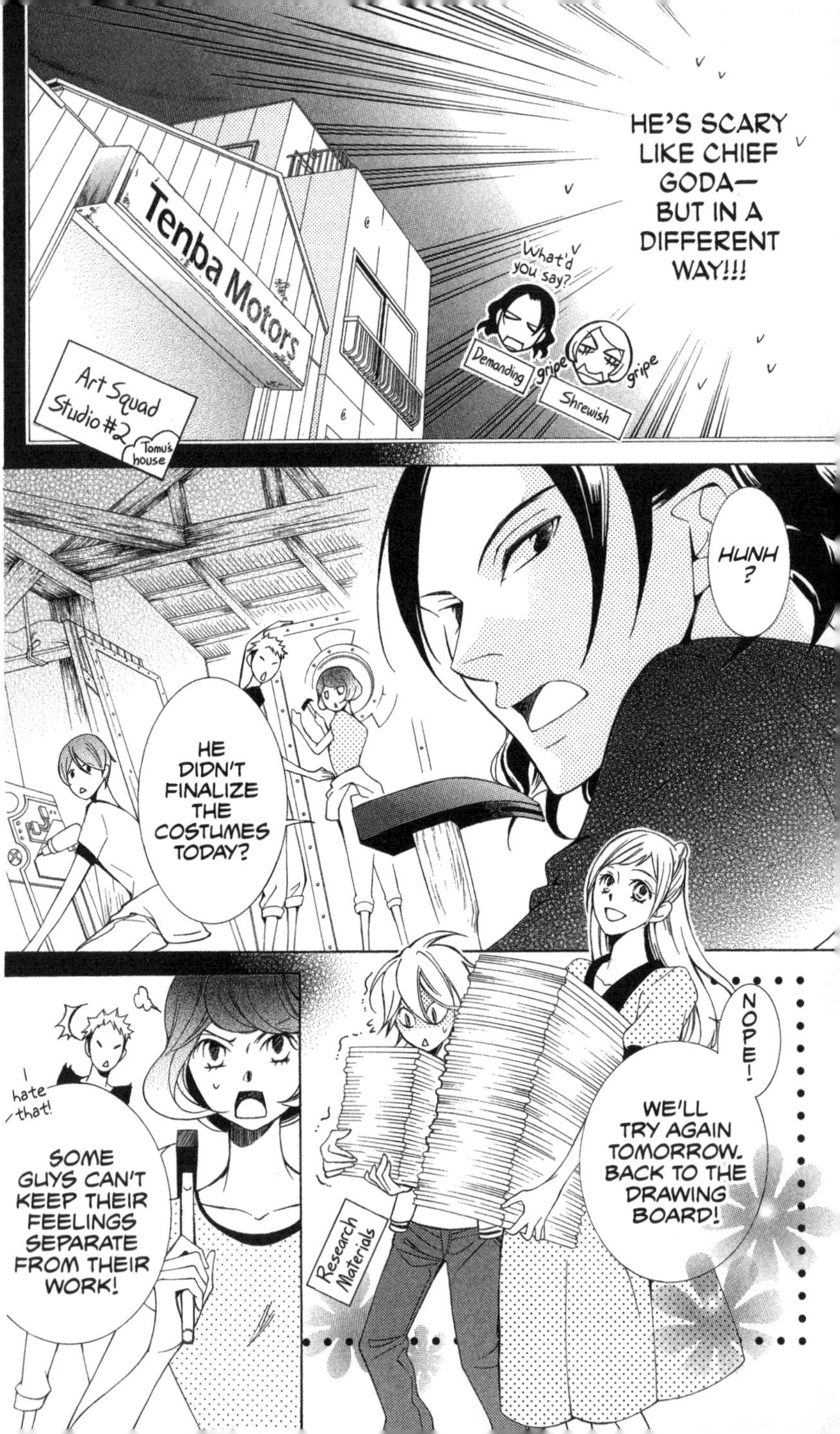
HE'S SCARY LIKE CHIEF GODA—BUT IN A DIFFERENT WAY!!!
What'd you say?
Demanding
gripe
Shrewish
gripe
Tenba Motors
Art Squad Studio #2
Tomu's house
HUNH?
HE DIDN'T FINALIZE THE COSTUMES TODAY?
NOPE!
WE'LL TRY AGAIN TOMORROW. BACK TO THE DRAWING BOARD!
Research Materials
SOME GUYS CAN'T KEEP THEIR FEELINGS SEPARATE FROM THEIR WORK!
I hate that!

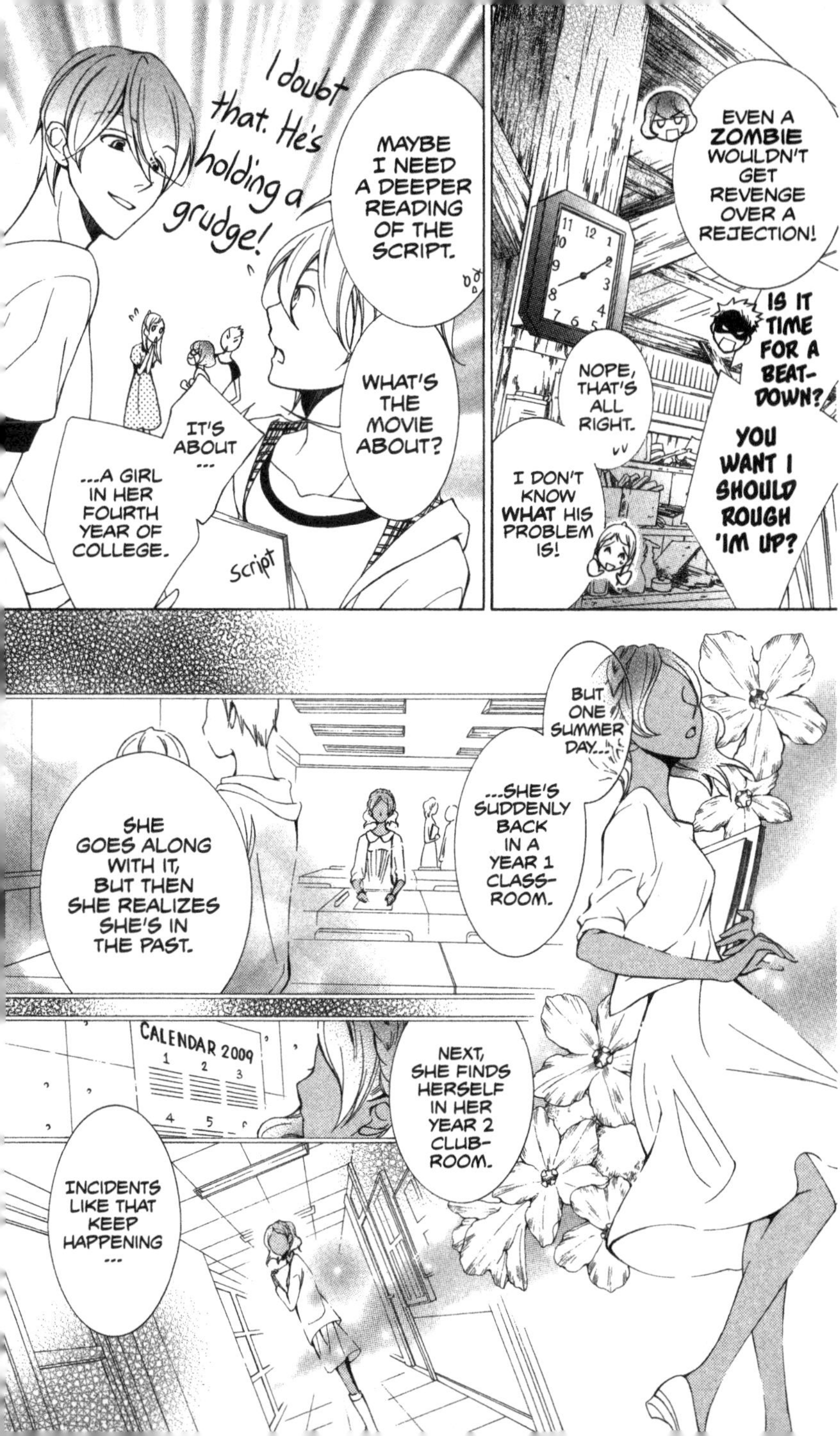
EVEN A ZOMBIE WOULDN'T GET REVENGE OVER A REJECTION!
IS IT TIME FOR A BEAT-DOWN?
YOU WANT I SHOULD ROUGH 'IM UP?
NOPE, THAT'S ALL RIGHT.
I DON'T KNOW WHAT HIS PROBLEM IS!
MAYBE I NEED A DEEPER READING OF THE SCRIPT.
I doubt that. He's holding a grudge!
WHAT'S THE MOVIE ABOUT?
IT'S ABOUT ...
...A GIRL IN HER FOURTH YEAR OF COLLEGE.
Script
BUT ONE SUMMER DAY...
...SHE'S SUDDENLY BACK IN A YEAR 1 CLASSROOM.
SHE GOES ALONG WITH IT, BUT THEN SHE REALIZES SHE'S IN THE PAST.
CALENDAR 2009
NEXT, SHE FINDS HERSELF IN HER YEAR 2 CLUBROOM.
INCIDENTS LIKE THAT KEEP HAPPENING ...

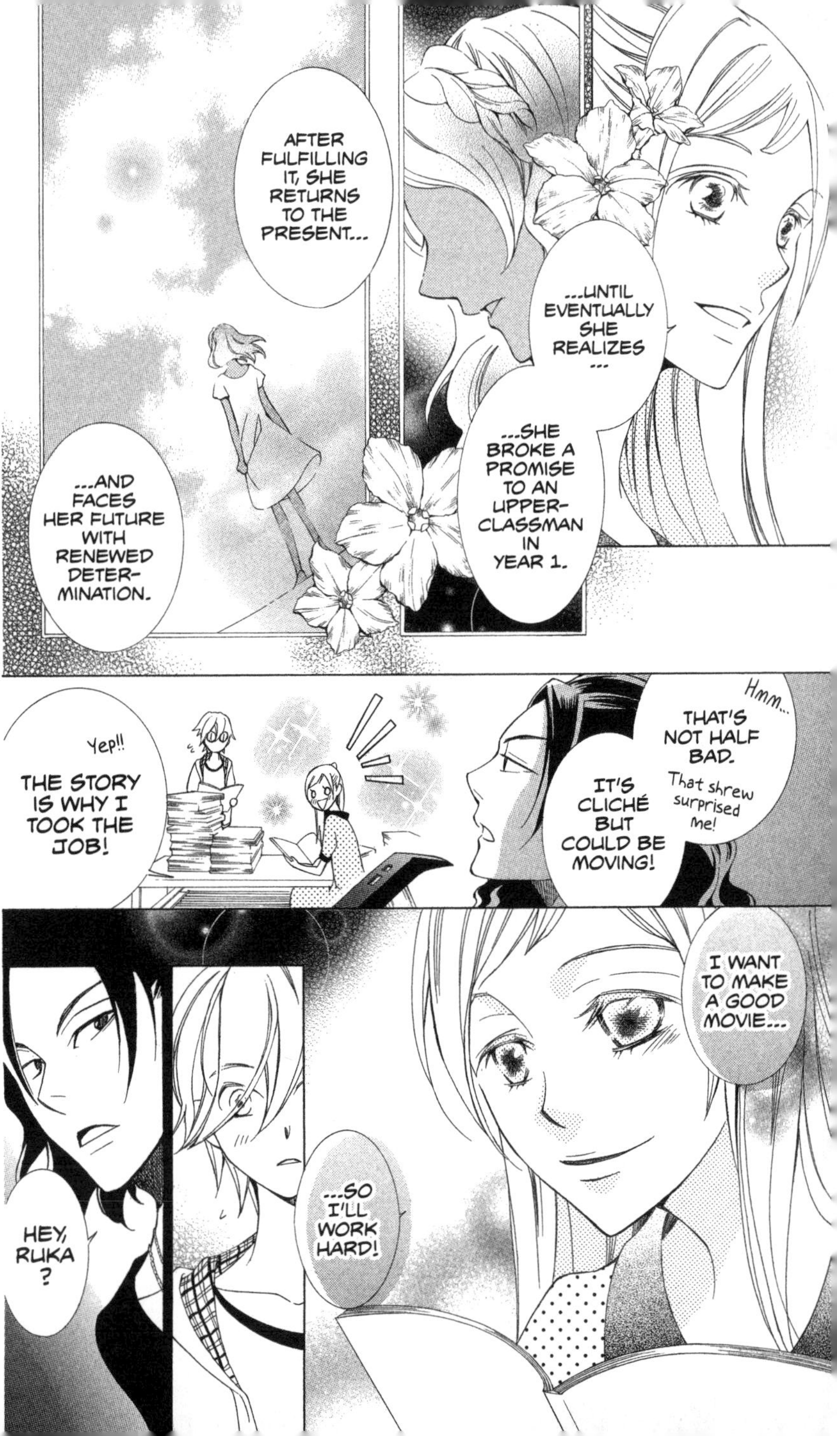
...UNTIL EVENTUALLY SHE REALIZES...
...SHE BROKE A PROMISE TO AN UPPER-CLASSMAN IN YEAR 1.
AFTER FULFILLING IT, SHE RETURNS TO THE PRESENT...
...AND FACES HER FUTURE WITH RENEWED DETER-MINATION.
Hmm...
THAT'S NOT HALF BAD.
That shrew surprised me!
IT'S CLICHÉ BUT COULD BE MOVING!
Yep!!
THE STORY IS WHY I TOOK THE JOB!
I WANT TO MAKE A GOOD MOVIE...
...SO I'LL WORK HARD!
HEY, RUKA?

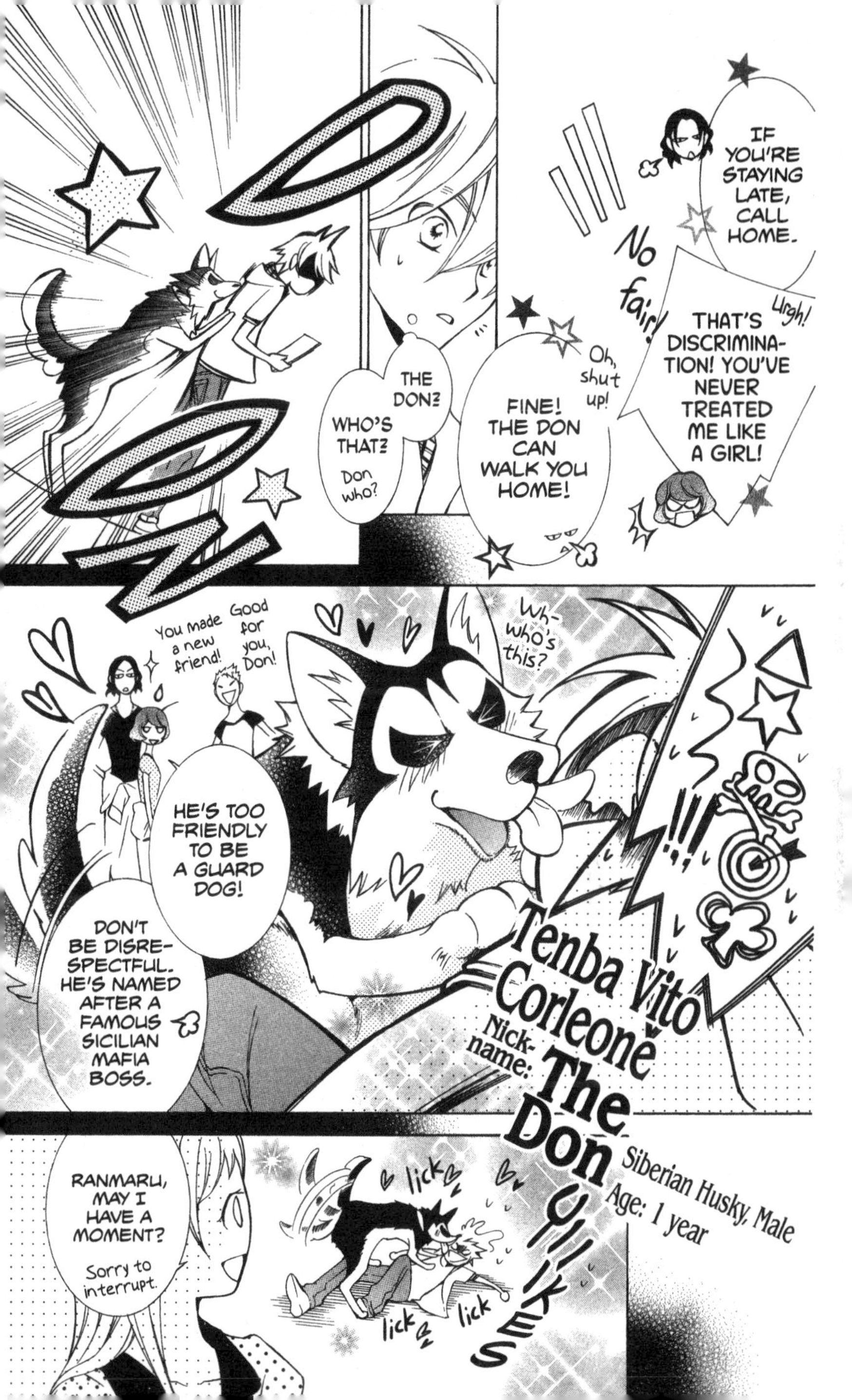
IF YOU'RE STAYING LATE, CALL HOME.
Urgh!
THAT'S DISCRIMINATION! YOU'VE NEVER TREATED ME LIKE A GIRL!
No fair!
Oh, shut up!
FINE! THE DON CAN WALK YOU HOME!
THE DON?
WHO'S THAT?
Don who?
DON
Wh-who's this?
Tenba Vito Corleone
Nickname: The Don
Siberian Husky, Male
Age: 1 year
Good for you, Don!
You made a new friend!
HE'S TOO FRIENDLY TO BE A GUARD DOG!
DON'T BE DISRESPECTFUL. HE'S NAMED AFTER A FAMOUS SICILIAN MAFIA BOSS.
YIKES
lick
lick
lick
lick
RANMARU, MAY I HAVE A MOMENT?
Sorry to interrupt.

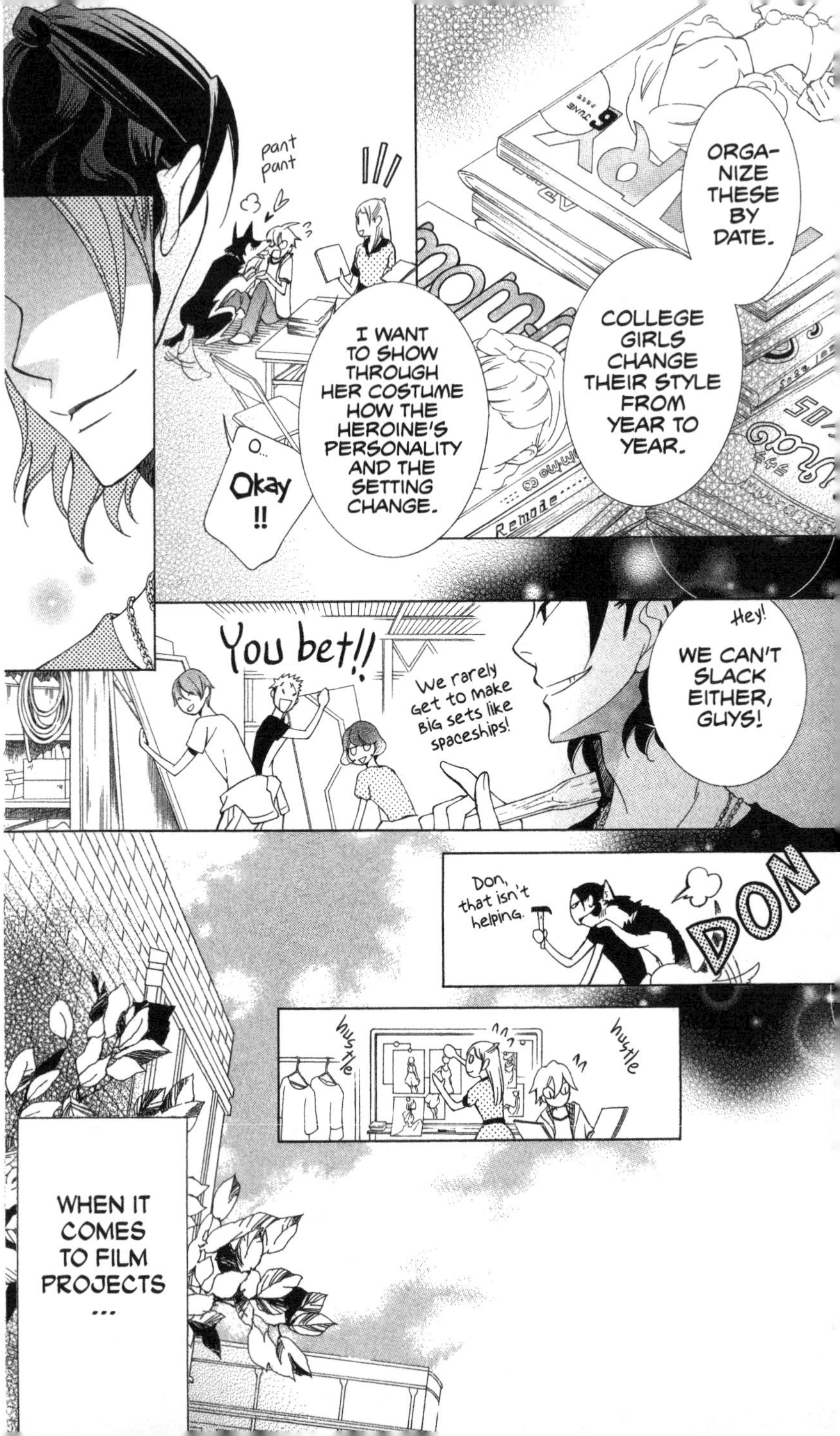
ORGA-NIZE THESE BY DATE.
COLLEGE GIRLS CHANGE THEIR STYLE FROM YEAR TO YEAR.
I WANT TO SHOW THROUGH HER COSTUME HOW THE HEROINE'S PERSONALITY AND THE SETTING CHANGE.
pant pant
O... Okay!!
Hey!
WE CAN'T SLACK EITHER, GUYS!
We rarely get to make big sets like spaceships!
You bet!!
DON
Don, that isn't helping.
hustle
hustle
WHEN IT COMES TO FILM PROJECTS...

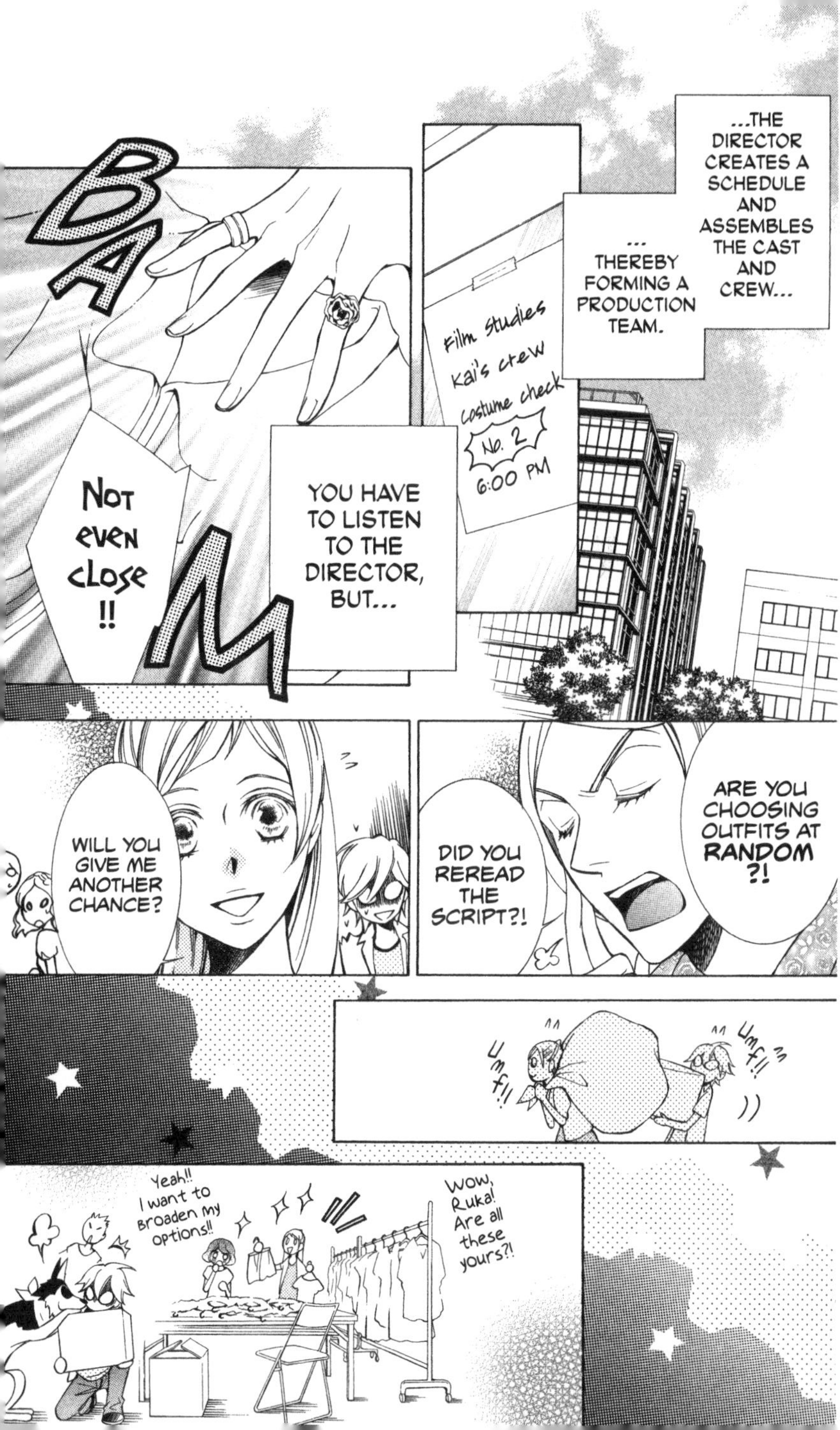
...THE DIRECTOR CREATES A SCHEDULE AND ASSEMBLES THE CAST AND CREW...
...THEREBY FORMING A PRODUCTION TEAM.
Film Studies
Kai's crew
costume check
No. 2
6:00 PM
YOU HAVE TO LISTEN TO THE DIRECTOR, BUT...
BAM
Not even close!!
ARE YOU CHOOSING OUTFITS AT RANDOM?!
DID YOU REREAD THE SCRIPT?!
WILL YOU GIVE ME ANOTHER CHANCE?
Umf!!
Umf!!
Wow, Ruka! Are all these yours?!
Yeah!! I want to broaden my options!!

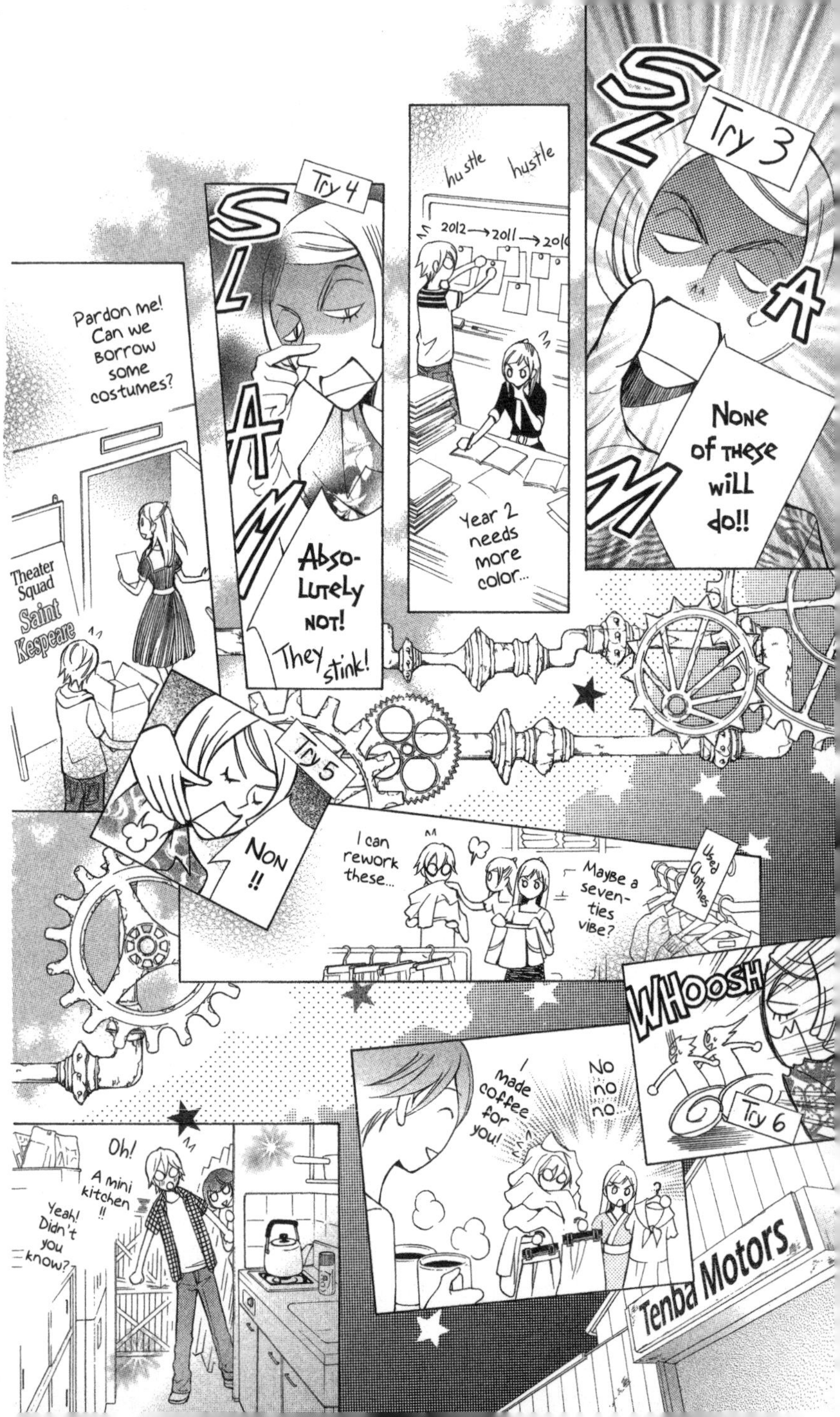
Try 3
SLAM
None of these will do!!
hustle hustle
2012 → 2011 → 2010
Year 2 needs more color...
Try 4
SLAM
Absolutely NOT!
They stink!
Pardon me! Can we borrow some costumes?
Theater Squad
Saint Kespeare
Try 5
NON!!
Used Clothes
Maybe a seventies vibe?
I can rework these...
WHOOSH
Try 6
No no no
I made coffee for you!
Tenba Motors
Oh!
A mini kitchen!!
Yeah! Didn't you know?

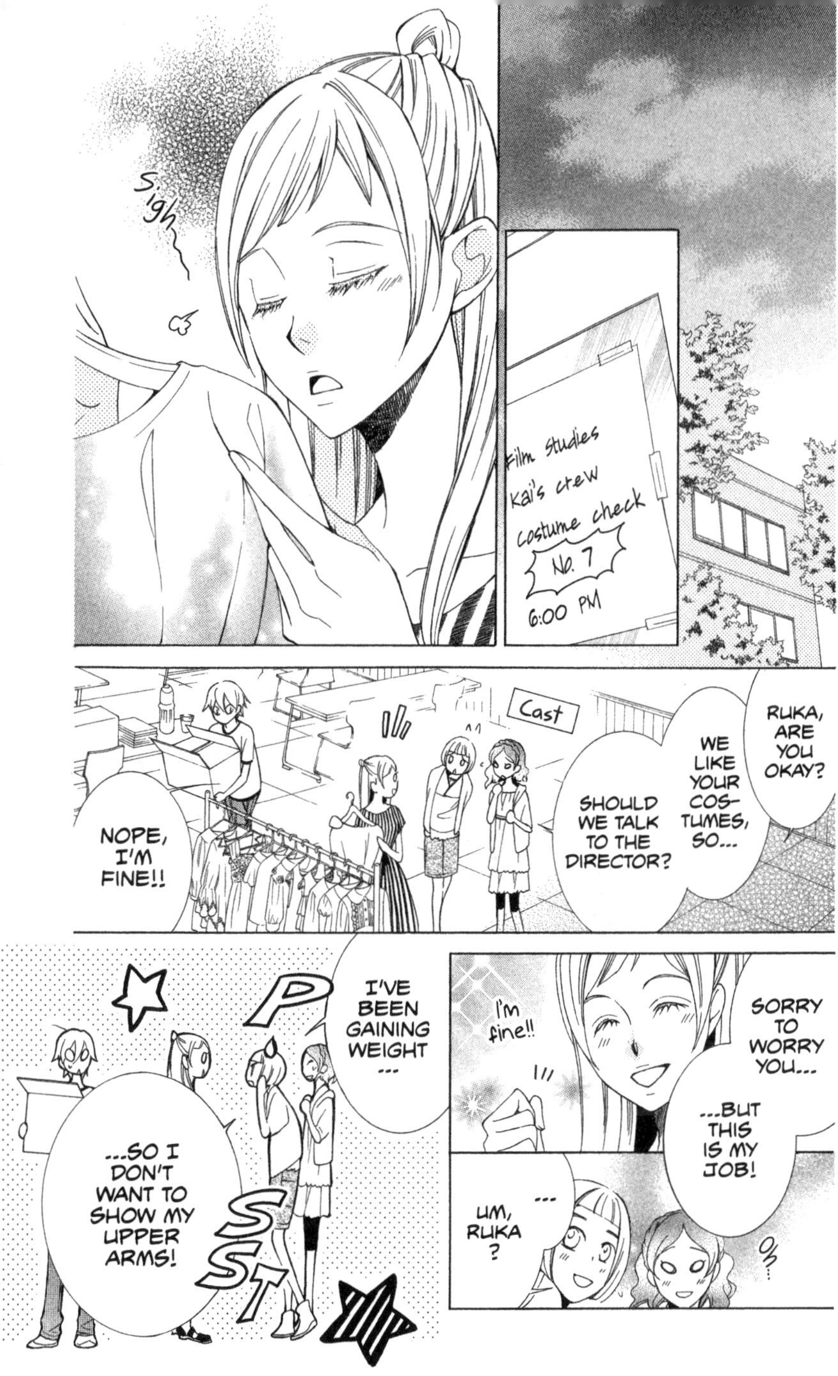
Film studies
Kai's crew
costume check
No. 7
6:00 PM
Sigh
RUKA, ARE YOU OKAY?
WE LIKE YOUR COS-TUMES, SO...
SHOULD WE TALK TO THE DIRECTOR?
Cast
NOPE, I'M FINE!!
SORRY TO WORRY YOU...
I'm fine!!
...BUT THIS IS MY JOB!
Oh...
...
UM, RUKA?
I'VE BEEN GAINING WEIGHT...
PSST
...SO I DON'T WANT TO SHOW MY UPPER ARMS!

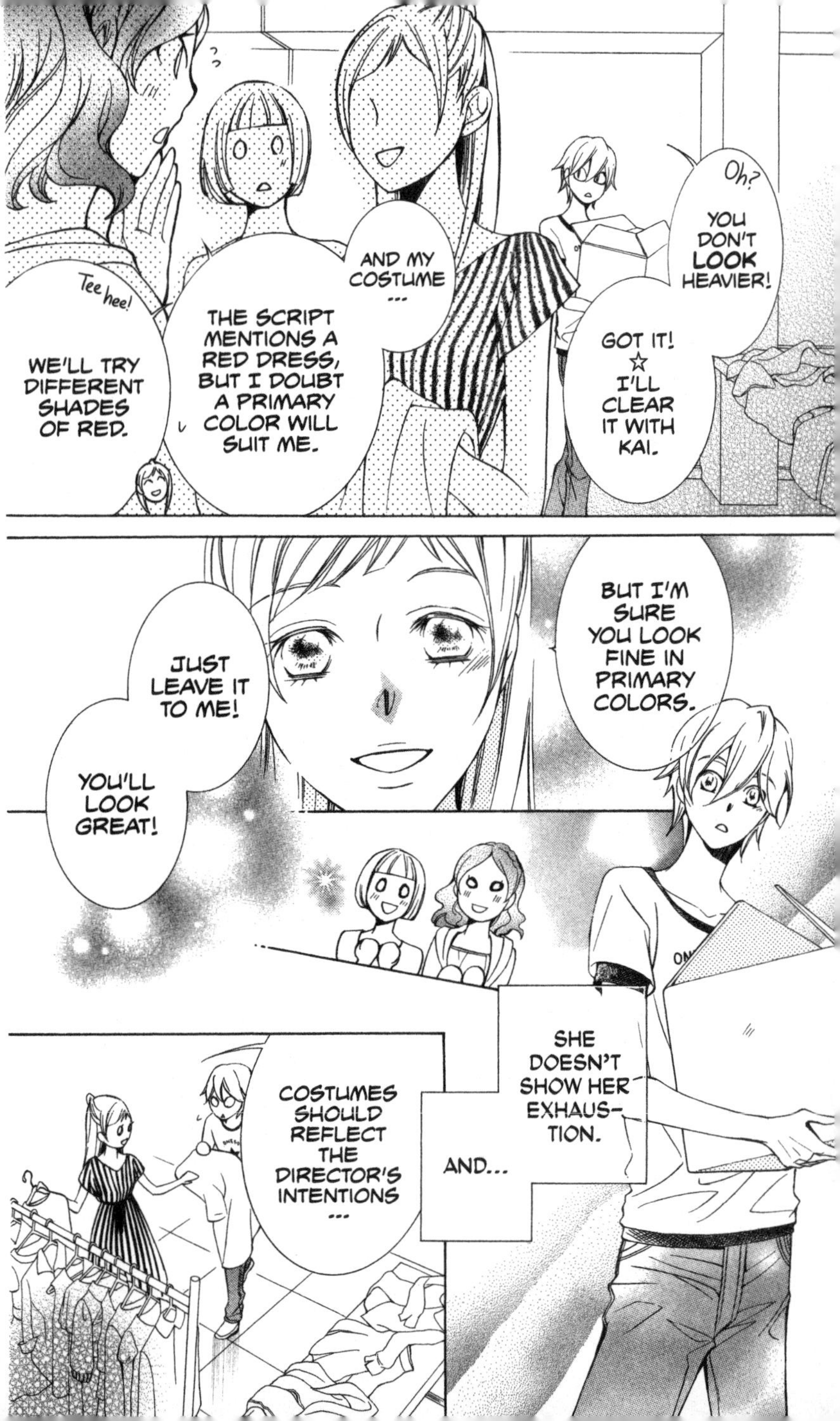
Oh?
YOU DON'T LOOK HEAVIER!
GOT IT! ☆ I'LL CLEAR IT WITH KAI.
AND MY COSTUME ...
THE SCRIPT MENTIONS A RED DRESS, BUT I DOUBT A PRIMARY COLOR WILL SUIT ME.
Tee hee!
WE'LL TRY DIFFERENT SHADES OF RED.
BUT I'M SURE YOU LOOK FINE IN PRIMARY COLORS.
JUST LEAVE IT TO ME!
YOU'LL LOOK GREAT!
SHE DOESN'T SHOW HER EXHAUS-TION.
AND...
COSTUMES SHOULD REFLECT THE DIRECTOR'S INTENTIONS ...

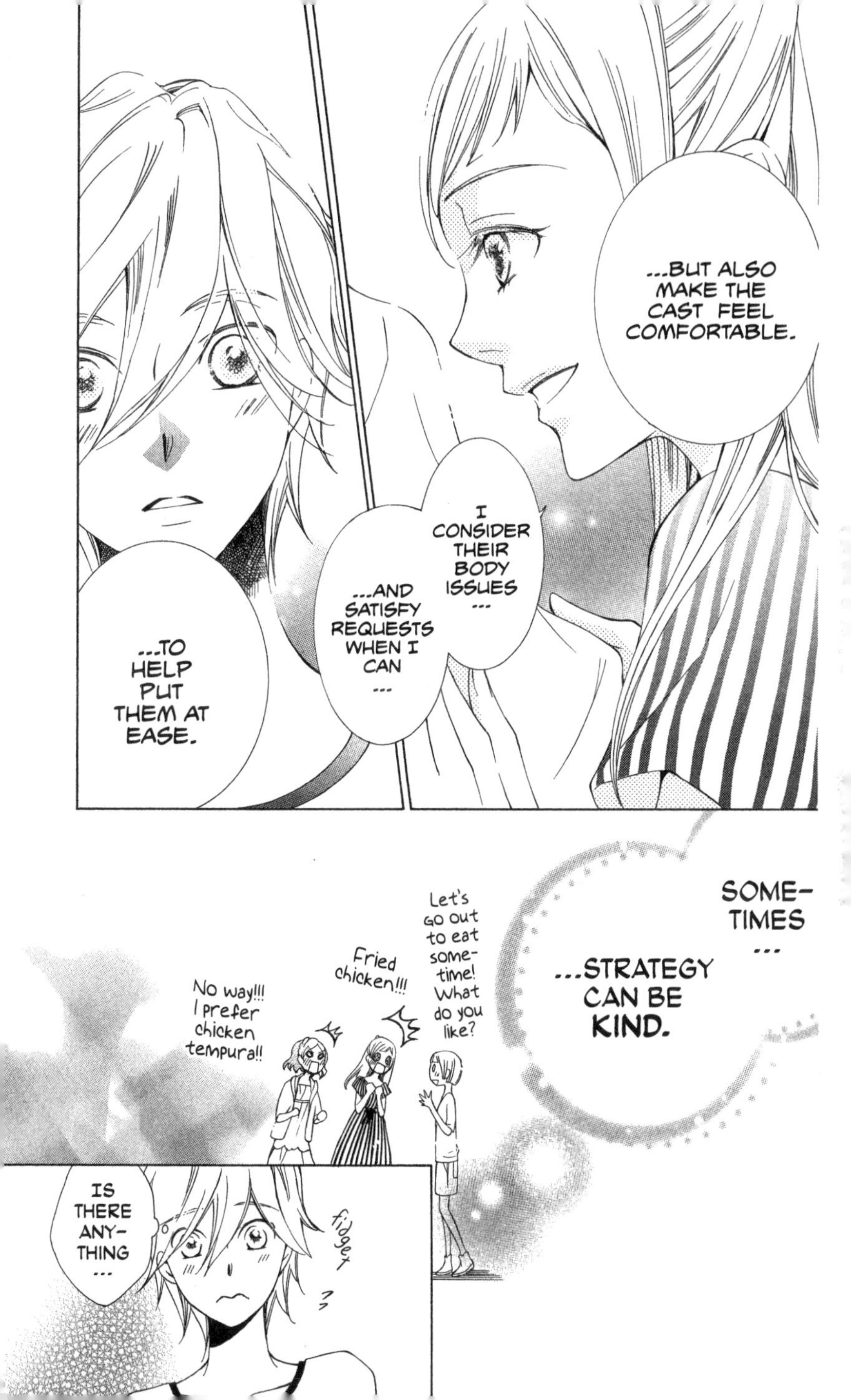
...BUT ALSO MAKE THE CAST FEEL COMFORTABLE.
I CONSIDER THEIR BODY ISSUES...
...AND SATISFY REQUESTS WHEN I CAN...
...TO HELP PUT THEM AT EASE.
SOME-TIMES...
...STRATEGY CAN BE KIND.
Let's go out to eat some-time! What do you like?
Fried chicken!!!
No way!!! I prefer chicken tempura!!
fidget
IS THERE ANY-THING...

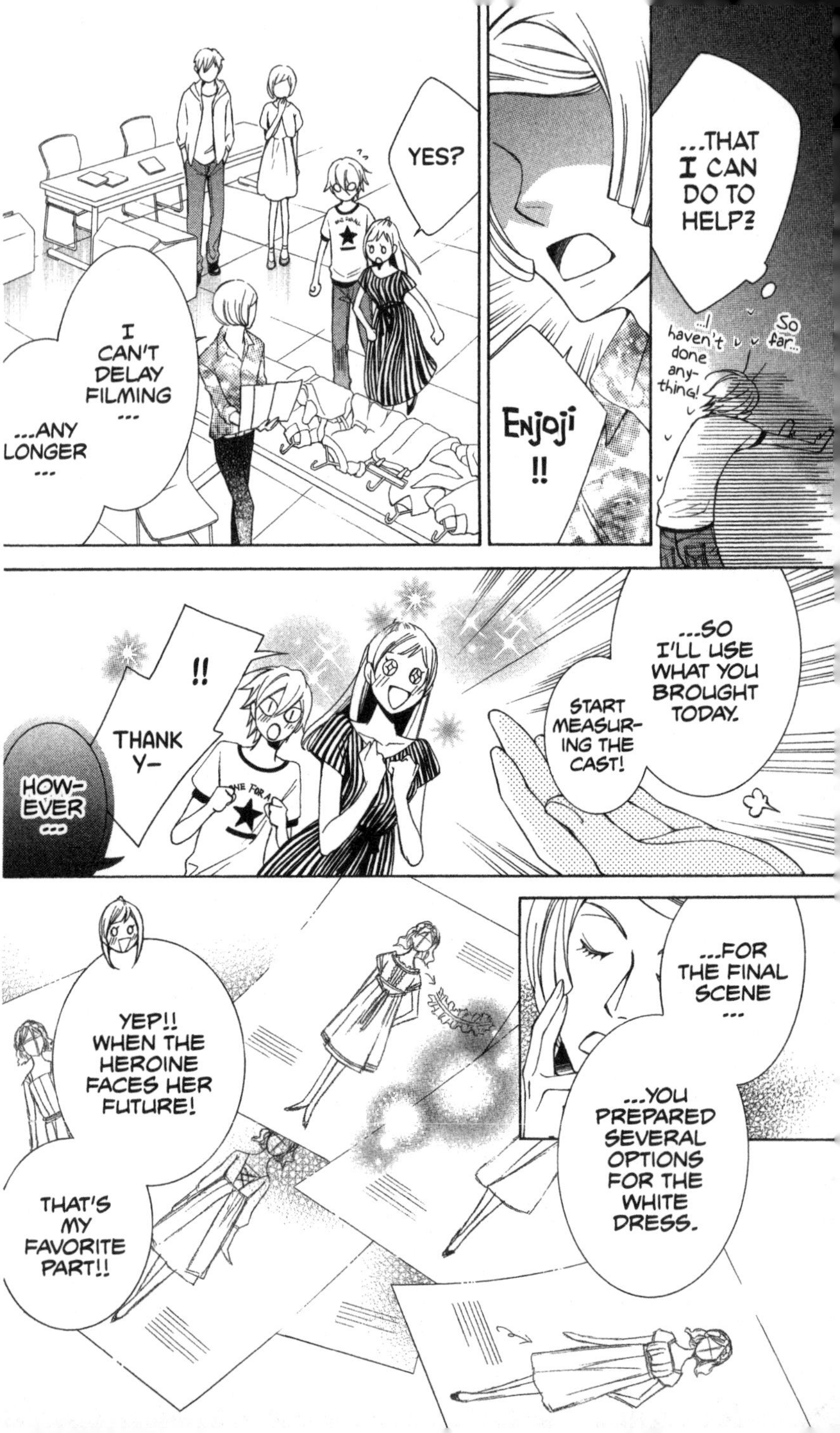
...THAT I CAN DO TO HELP?
So far...
...I haven't done anything!
Enjoji!!
YES?
I CAN'T DELAY FILMING...
...ANY LONGER...
...SO I'LL USE WHAT YOU BROUGHT TODAY.
START MEASURING THE CAST!
!!
THANK Y—
HOWEVER...
...FOR THE FINAL SCENE...
...YOU PREPARED SEVERAL OPTIONS FOR THE WHITE DRESS.
YEP!! WHEN THE HEROINE FACES HER FUTURE!
THAT'S MY FAVORITE PART!!

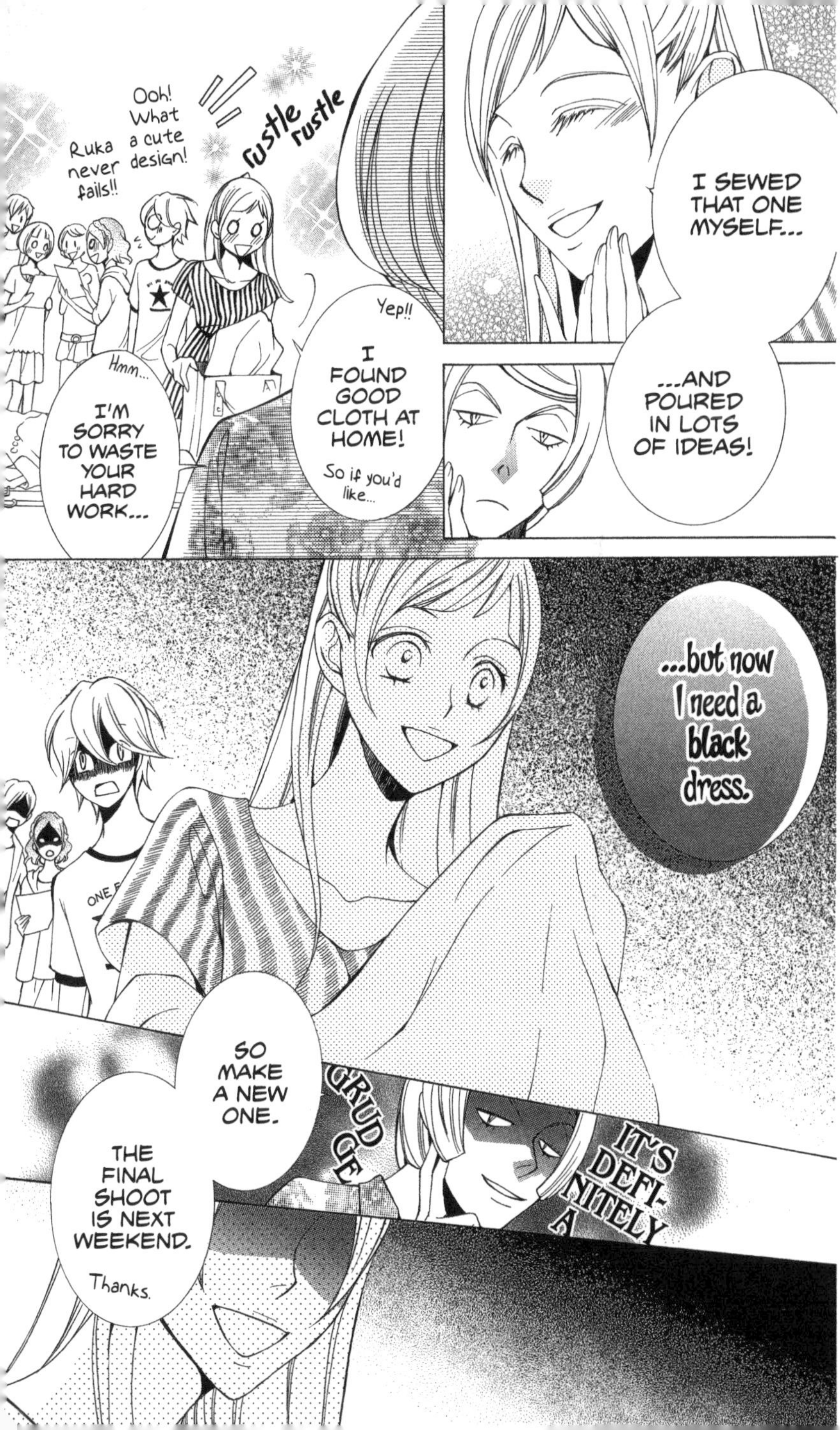
I SEWED THAT ONE MYSELF...
...AND POURED IN LOTS OF IDEAS!
Yep!! I FOUND GOOD CLOTH AT HOME! So if you'd like...
rustle rustle
Ooh! What a cute design!
Ruka never fails!!
Hmm... I'M SORRY TO WASTE YOUR HARD WORK...
...but now I need a black dress.
IT'S DEFINITELY A
GRUDGE
SO MAKE A NEW ONE.
THE FINAL SHOOT IS NEXT WEEKEND. Thanks.

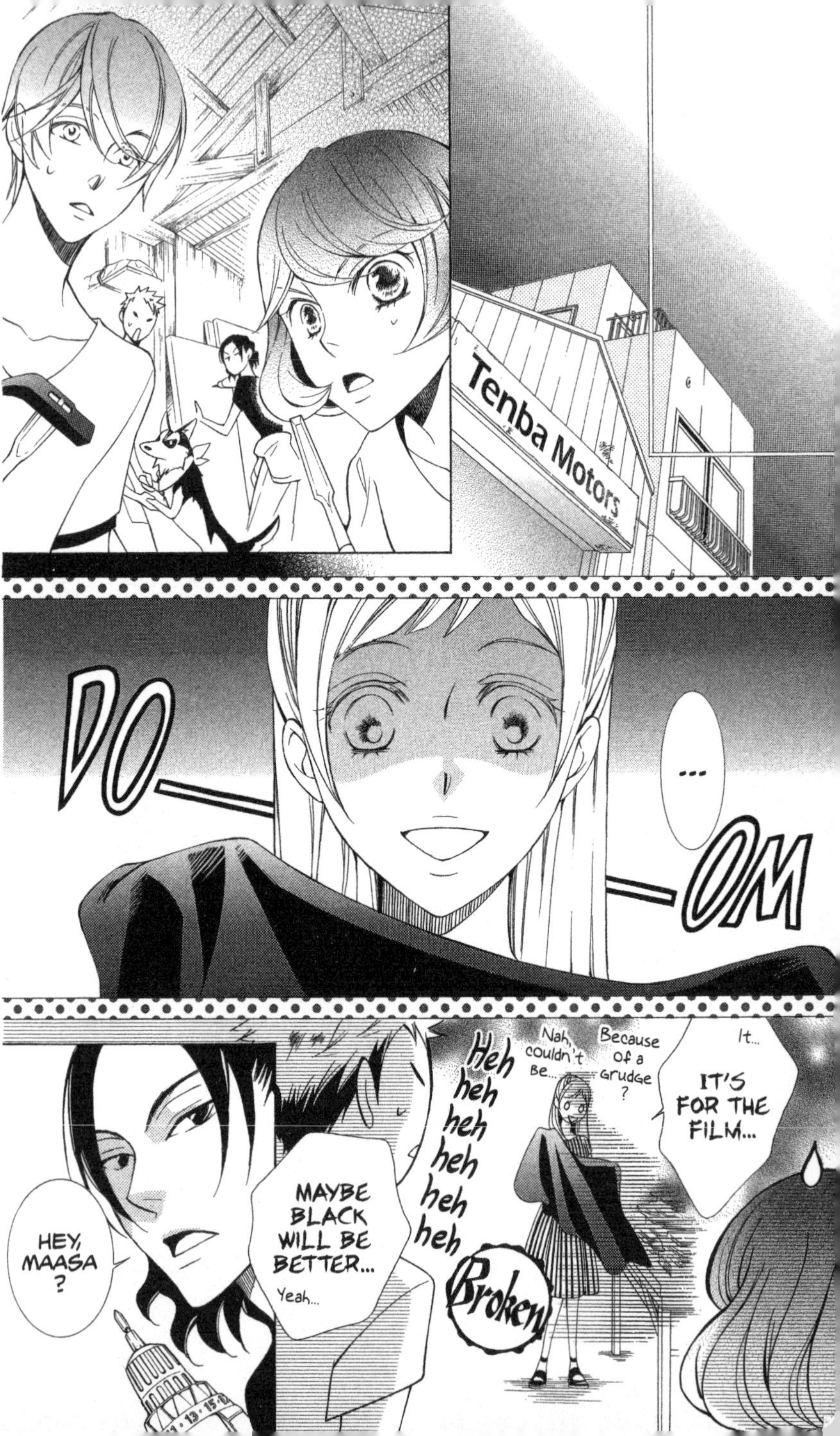

Tenba Motors
...
DO—OM
It...
IT'S FOR THE FILM...
Because of a grudge?
Nah, couldn't be...
Heh heh heh heh heh heh heh
Broken
MAYBE BLACK WILL BE BETTER...
Yeah...
HEY, MAASA?

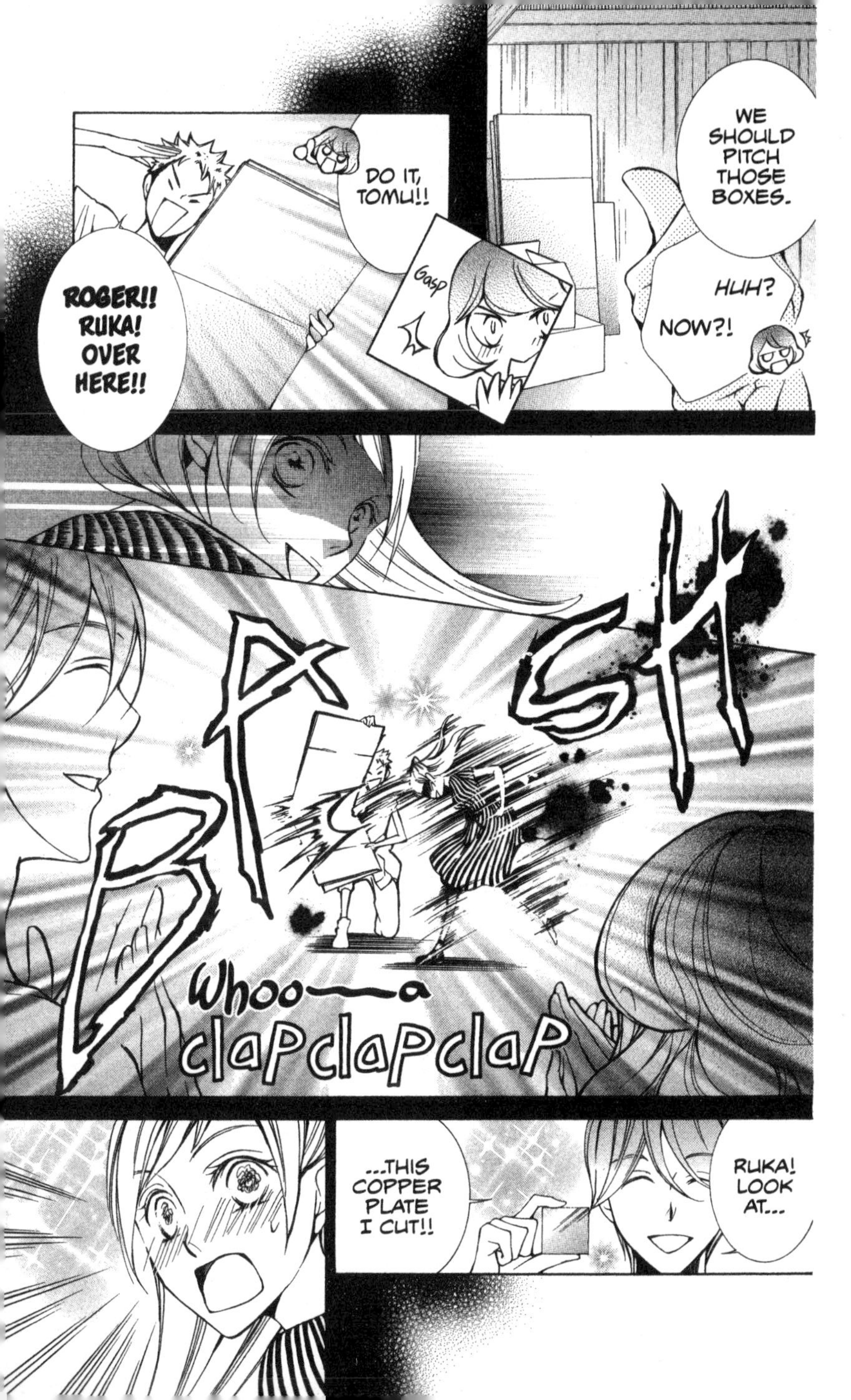

WE SHOULD PITCH THOSE BOXES.
HUH?
NOW?!
Gasp
DO IT, TOMU!!
ROGER!! RUKA! OVER HERE!!
BAPSH
Whoo—a
clapclapclap
RUKA! LOOK AT...
...THIS COPPER PLATE I CUT!!

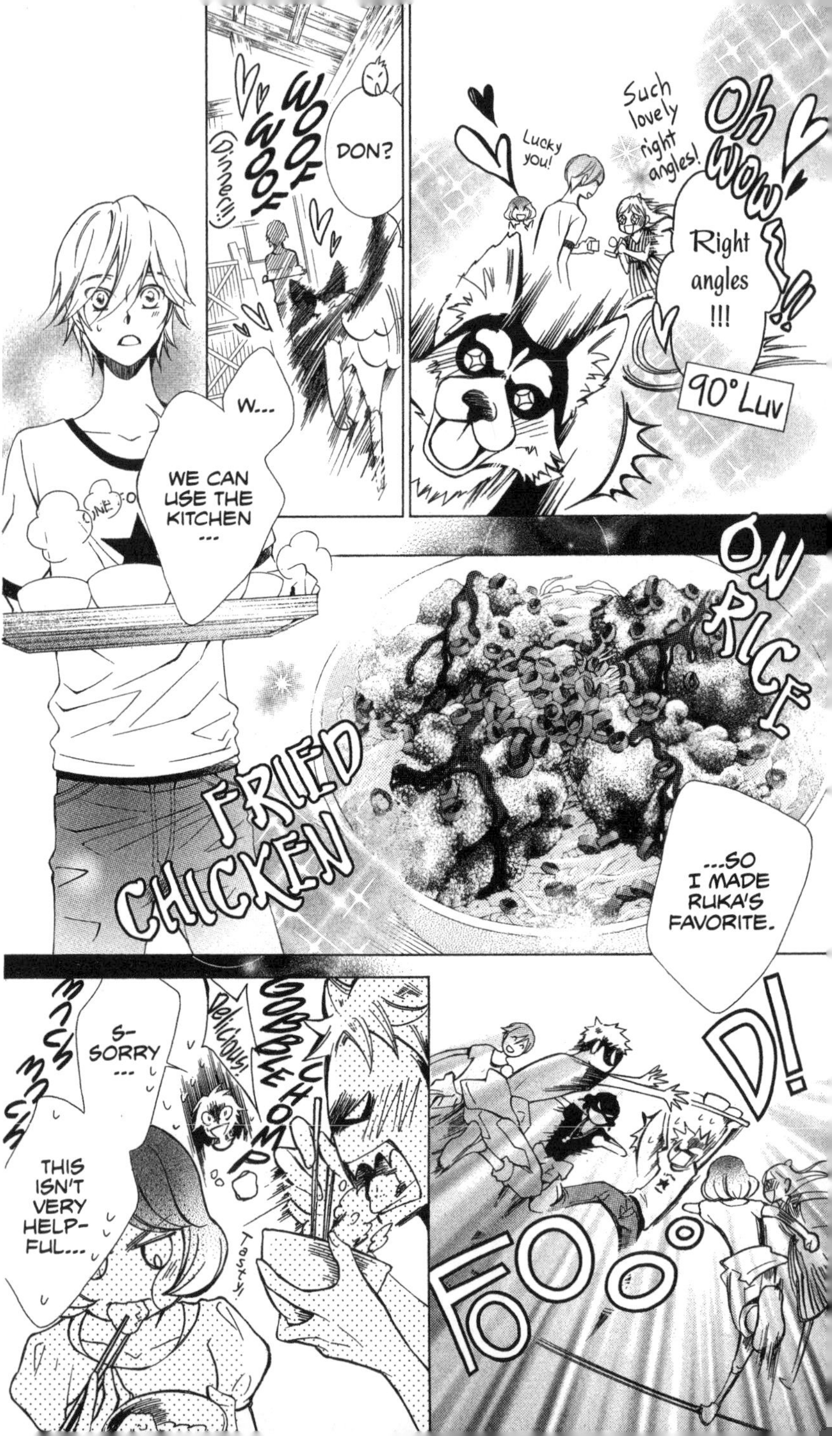
Oh wow~!!
Right angles !!!
90° Luv
Such lovely right angles!
Lucky you!
DON?
WOOF WOOF
(Dinner!!)
W...
WE CAN USE THE KITCHEN ---
...SO I MADE RUKA'S FAVORITE.
FRIED CHICKEN
ON RICE
FOOOOOD!
GOBBLE CHOMP
Delicious!
Tasty!
S-SORRY ---
MUNCH MUNCH
THIS ISN'T VERY HELPFUL...

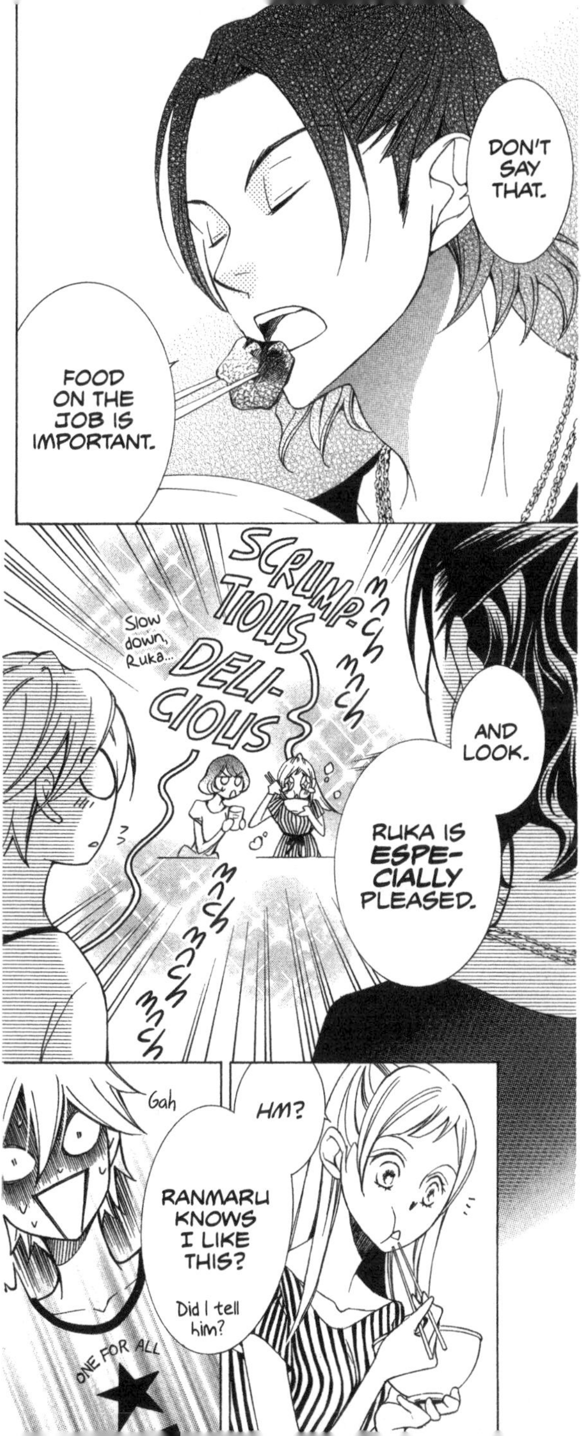
DON'T SAY THAT.
FOOD ON THE JOB IS IMPORTANT.
AND LOOK.
RUKA IS **ESPECIALLY** PLEASED.
SCRUMPTIOUS
mnch mnch mnch
DELICIOUS
Slow down, Ruka...
mnch mnch mnch mnch
HM?
RANMARU KNOWS I LIKE THIS?
Did I tell him?
Gah
ONE FOR ALL

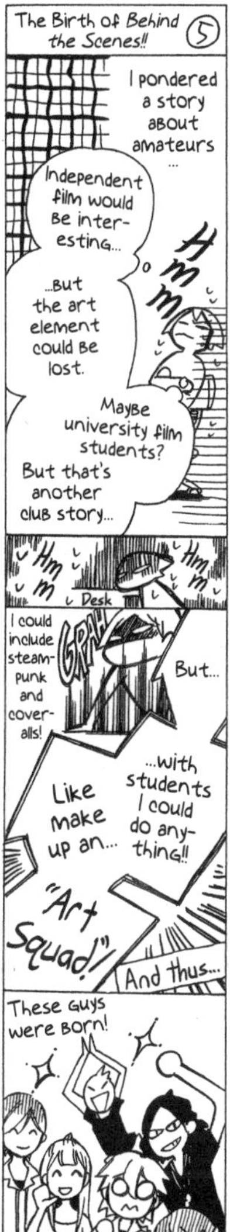
The Birth of Behind the Scenes!! 5
I pondered a story about amateurs...
Independent film would be interesting...
...But the art element could be lost.
HMM
Maybe university film students?
But that's another club story...
Hm m
Hm m
Desk
I could include steampunk and coveralls!
GRAH
But...
Like make up an...
...with students I could do anything!!
"Art Squad!"
And thus...
These guys were born!
Treat them well!!!

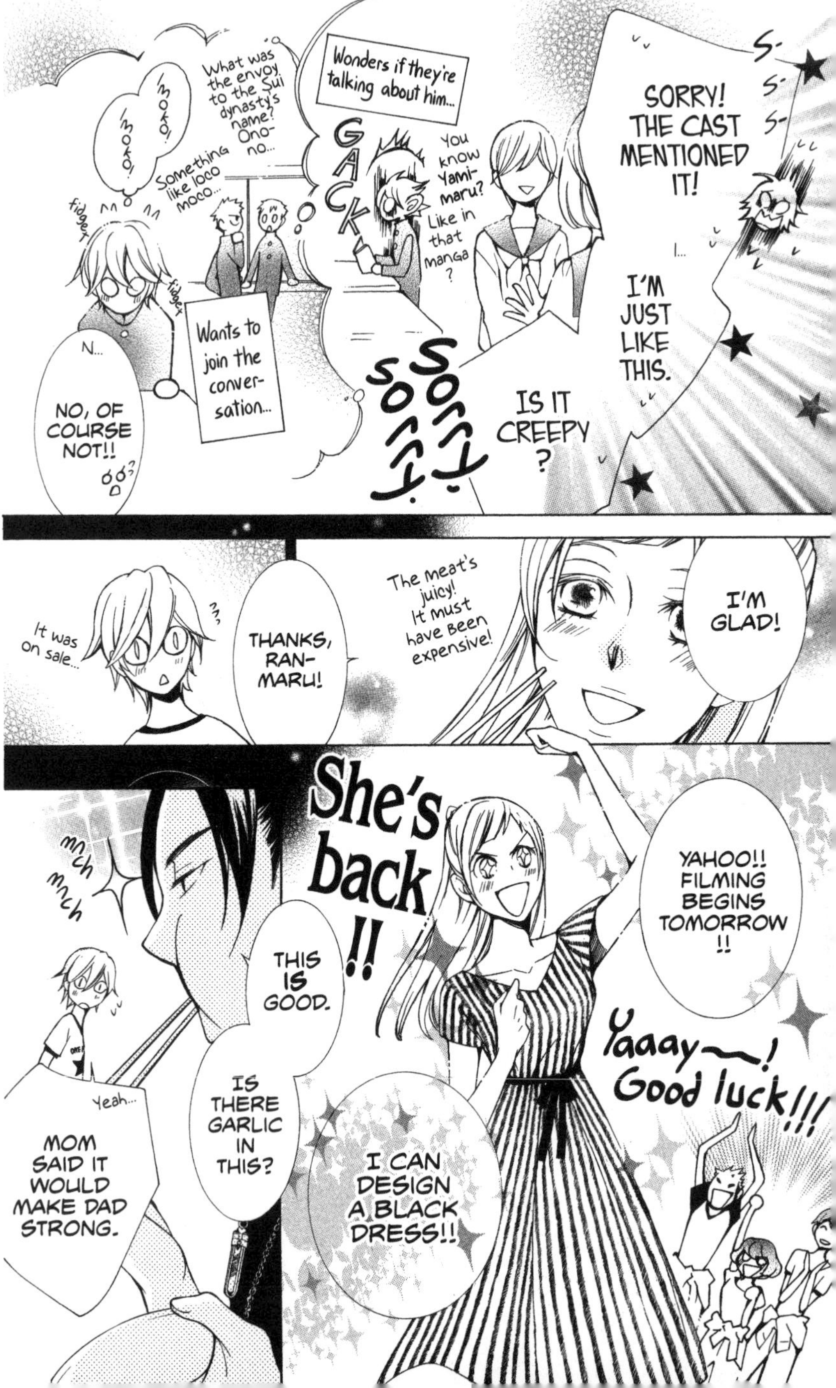
S- S- S-
SORRY! THE CAST MENTIONED IT!
I... I'M JUST LIKE THIS.
IS IT CREEPY?
Sorry sorry
You know Yami-maru? Like in that manga?
GACK
Wonders if they're talking about him...
What was the envoy to the Sui dynasty's name? Ono-no...
Something like loco moco...
Moko! Moko!
fidget fidget
Wants to join the conversation...
N... NO, OF COURSE NOT!!
I'M GLAD!
The meat's juicy! It must have been expensive!
THANKS, RAN-MARU!
It was on sale...
YAHOO!! FILMING BEGINS TOMORROW!!
She's back!!
Yaaay—! Good luck!!!
I CAN DESIGN A BLACK DRESS!!
THIS IS GOOD.
mnch mnch
IS THERE GARLIC IN THIS?
Yeah...
MOM SAID IT WOULD MAKE DAD STRONG.

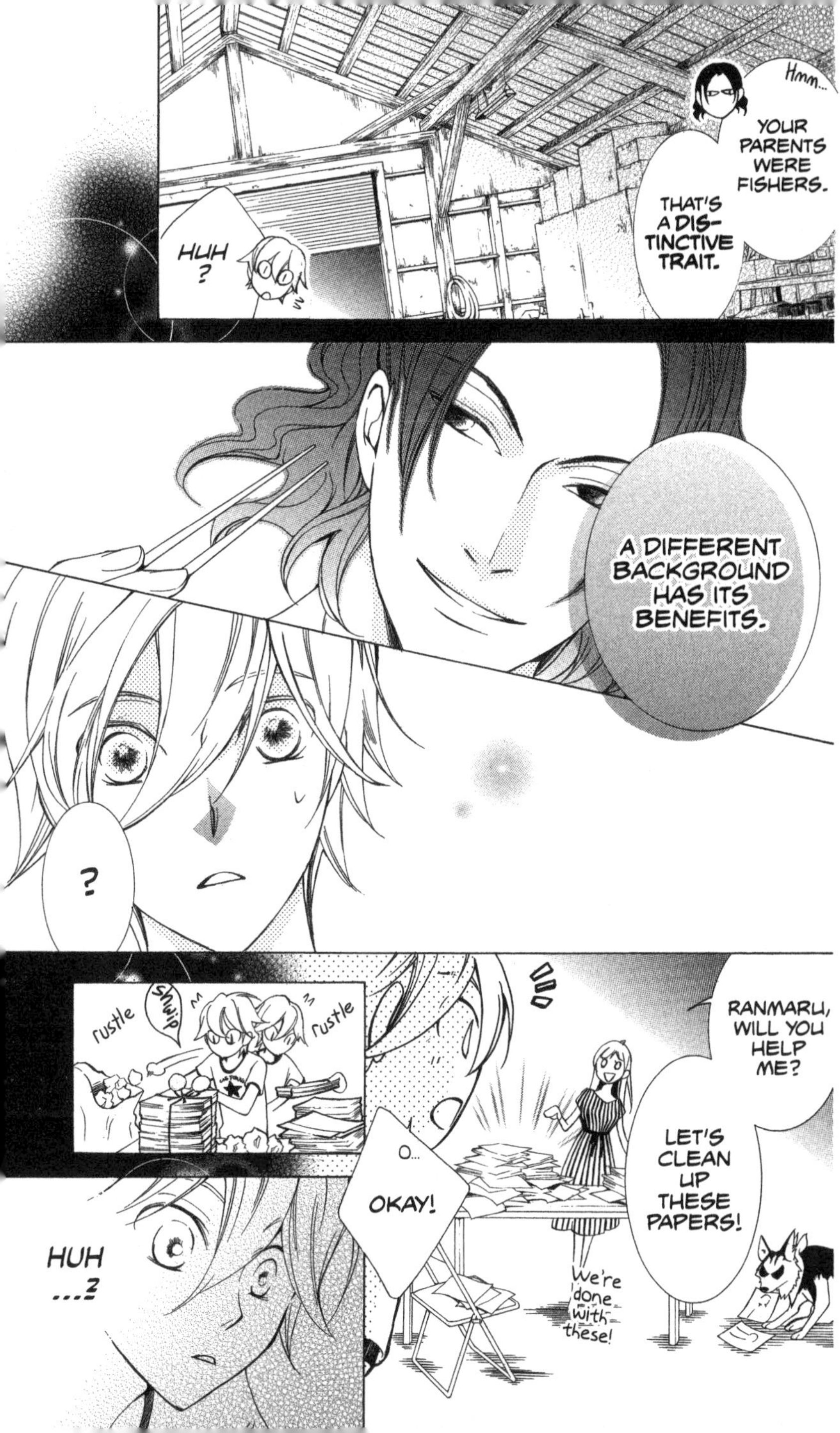
Hmm...
YOUR PARENTS WERE FISHERS.
THAT'S A DIS-TINCTIVE TRAIT.
HUH?
A DIFFERENT BACKGROUND HAS ITS BENEFITS.
?
RANMARU, WILL YOU HELP ME?
LET'S CLEAN UP THESE PAPERS!
We're done with these!
O... OKAY!
rustle
shwip
rustle
HUH ...?

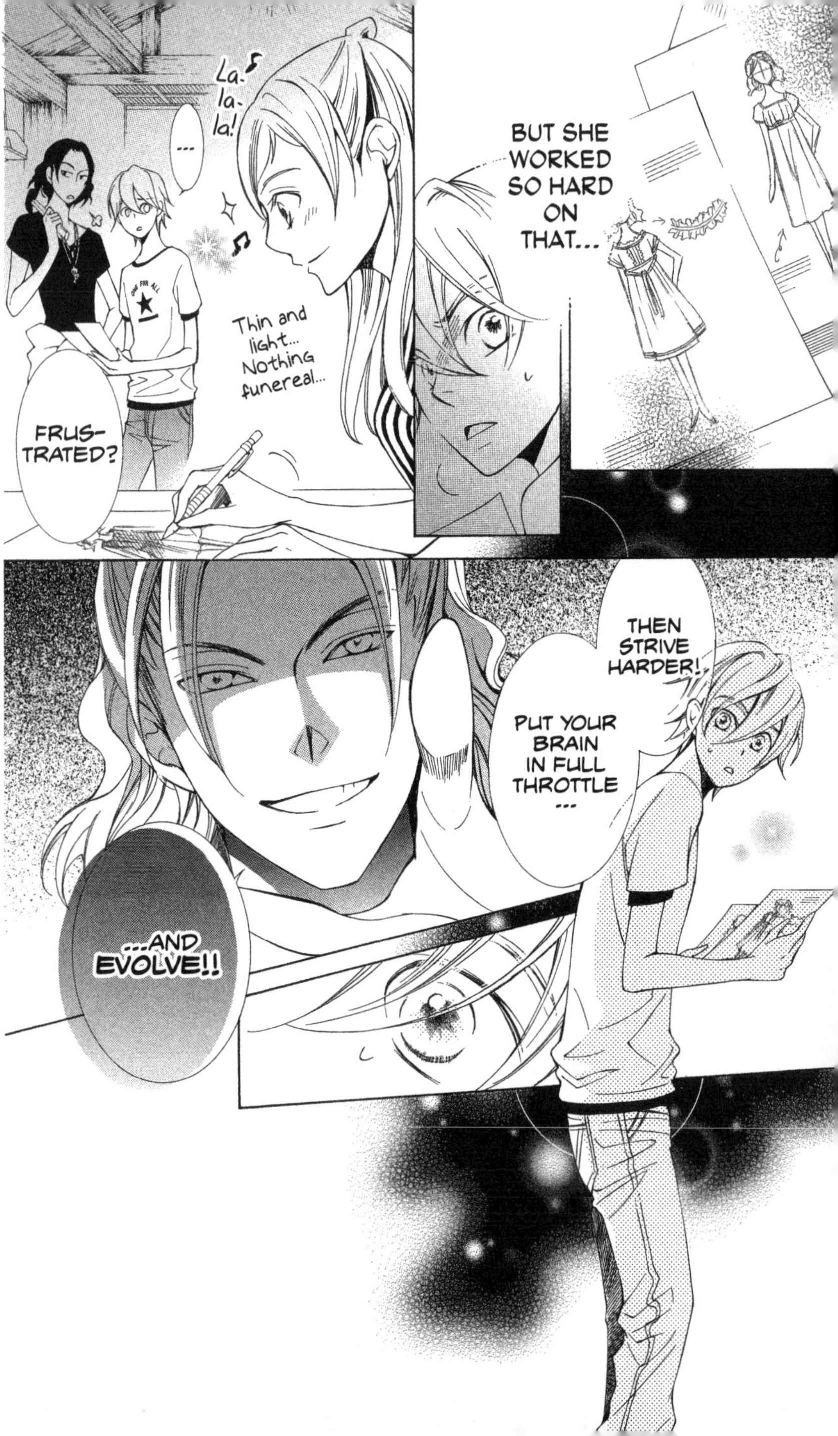
BUT SHE WORKED SO HARD ON THAT...
La-la-la!
...
Thin and light... Nothing funereal...
FRUS-TRATED?
THEN STRIVE HARDER!
PUT YOUR BRAIN IN FULL THROTTLE ...
...AND EVOLVE!!

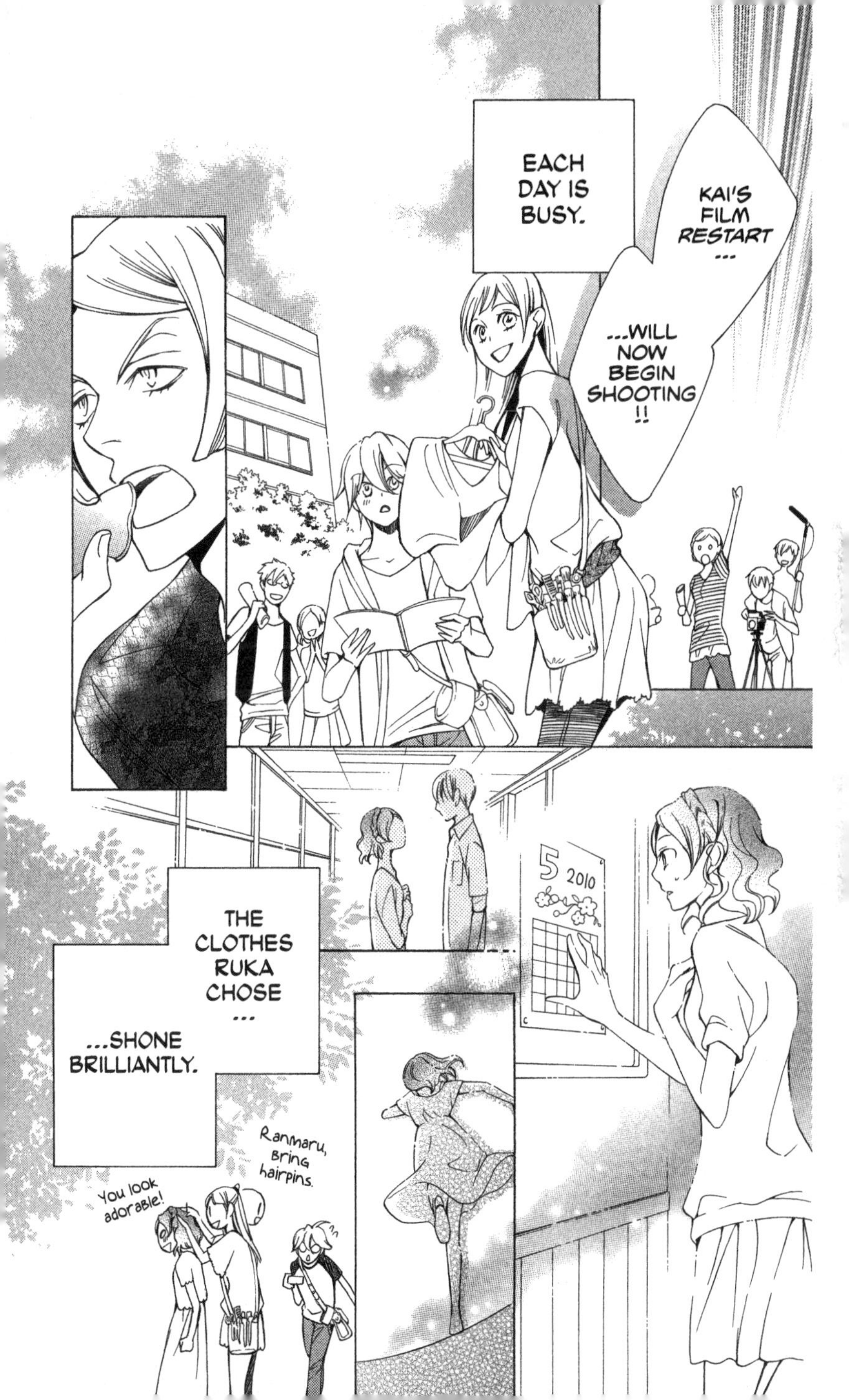
KAI'S FILM RESTART...
...WILL NOW BEGIN SHOOTING!!
EACH DAY IS BUSY.
THE CLOTHES RUKA CHOSE...
...SHONE BRILLIANTLY.
Ranmaru, bring hairpins.
You look adorable!

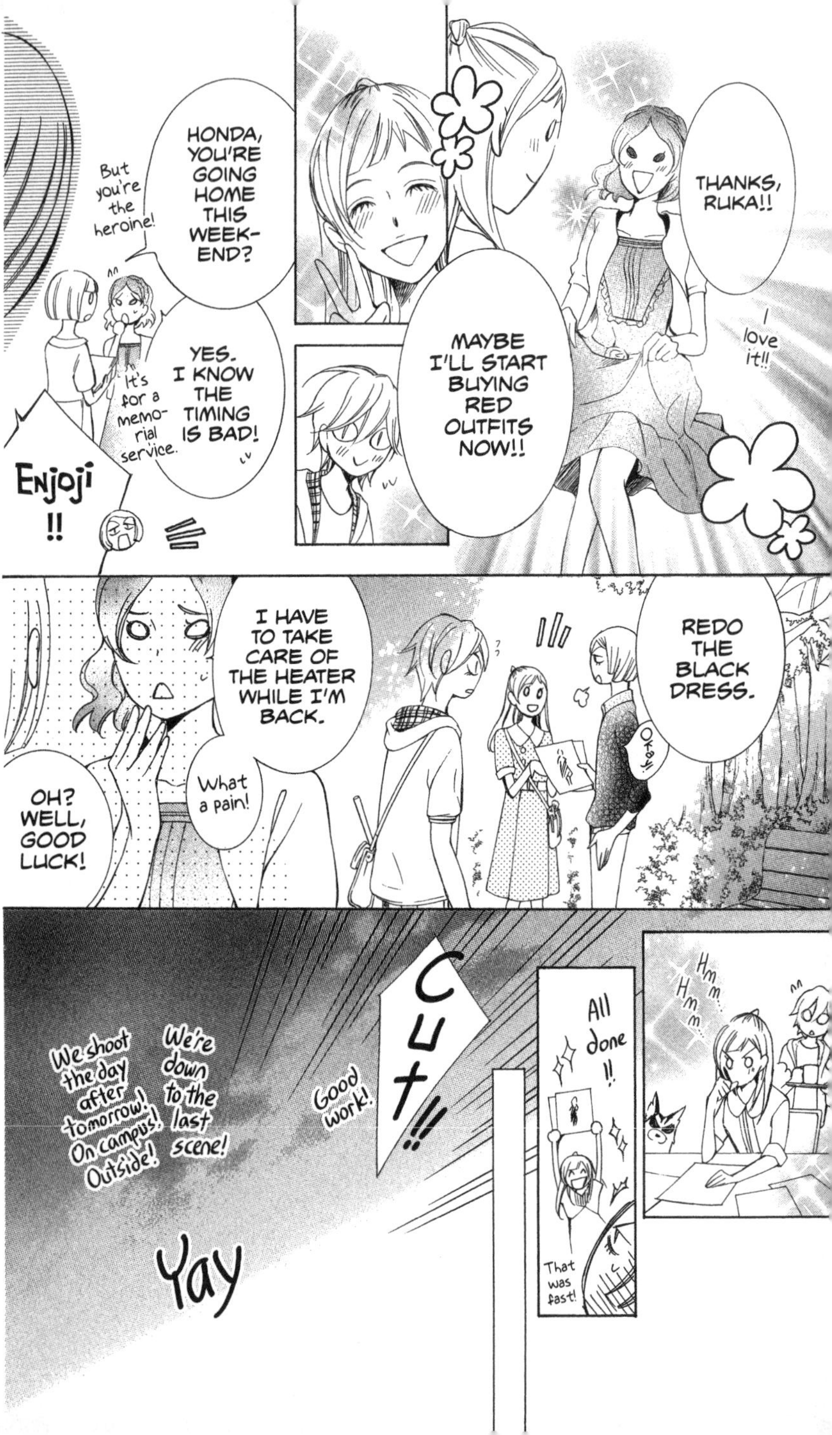
THANKS, RUKA!!
I love it!!
MAYBE I'LL START BUYING RED OUTFITS NOW!!
HONDA, YOU'RE GOING HOME THIS WEEK-END?
But you're the heroine!
YES. I KNOW THE TIMING IS BAD!
It's for a memo-rial service.
Enjoji!!
REDO THE BLACK DRESS.
Okay!
I HAVE TO TAKE CARE OF THE HEATER WHILE I'M BACK.
What a pain!
OH? WELL, GOOD LUCK!
Hmm Hmm...
All done!!
That was fast!
Cut!!
Good work!
We're down to the last scene!
We shoot the day after tomorrow! On campus! Outside!
Yay

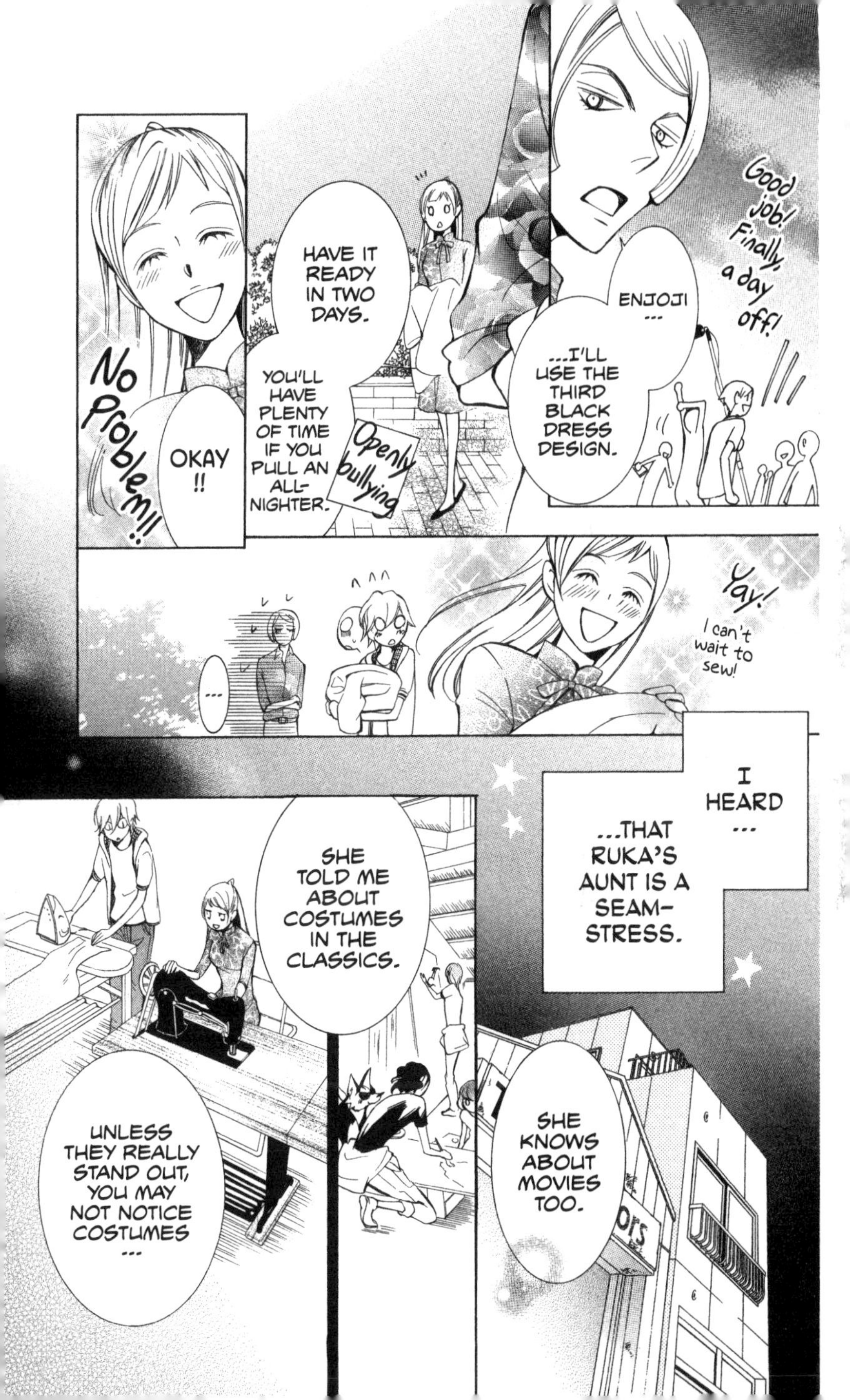
ENJOJI...
...I'LL USE THE THIRD BLACK DRESS DESIGN.
Good job! Finally, a day off!
HAVE IT READY IN TWO DAYS.
YOU'LL HAVE PLENTY OF TIME IF YOU PULL AN ALL-NIGHTER.
Openly bullying
OKAY!!
No Problem!!
Yay!
I can't wait to sew!
...
I HEARD...
...THAT RUKA'S AUNT IS A SEAM-STRESS.
SHE KNOWS ABOUT MOVIES TOO.
SHE TOLD ME ABOUT COSTUMES IN THE CLASSICS.
UNLESS THEY REALLY STAND OUT, YOU MAY NOT NOTICE COSTUMES...

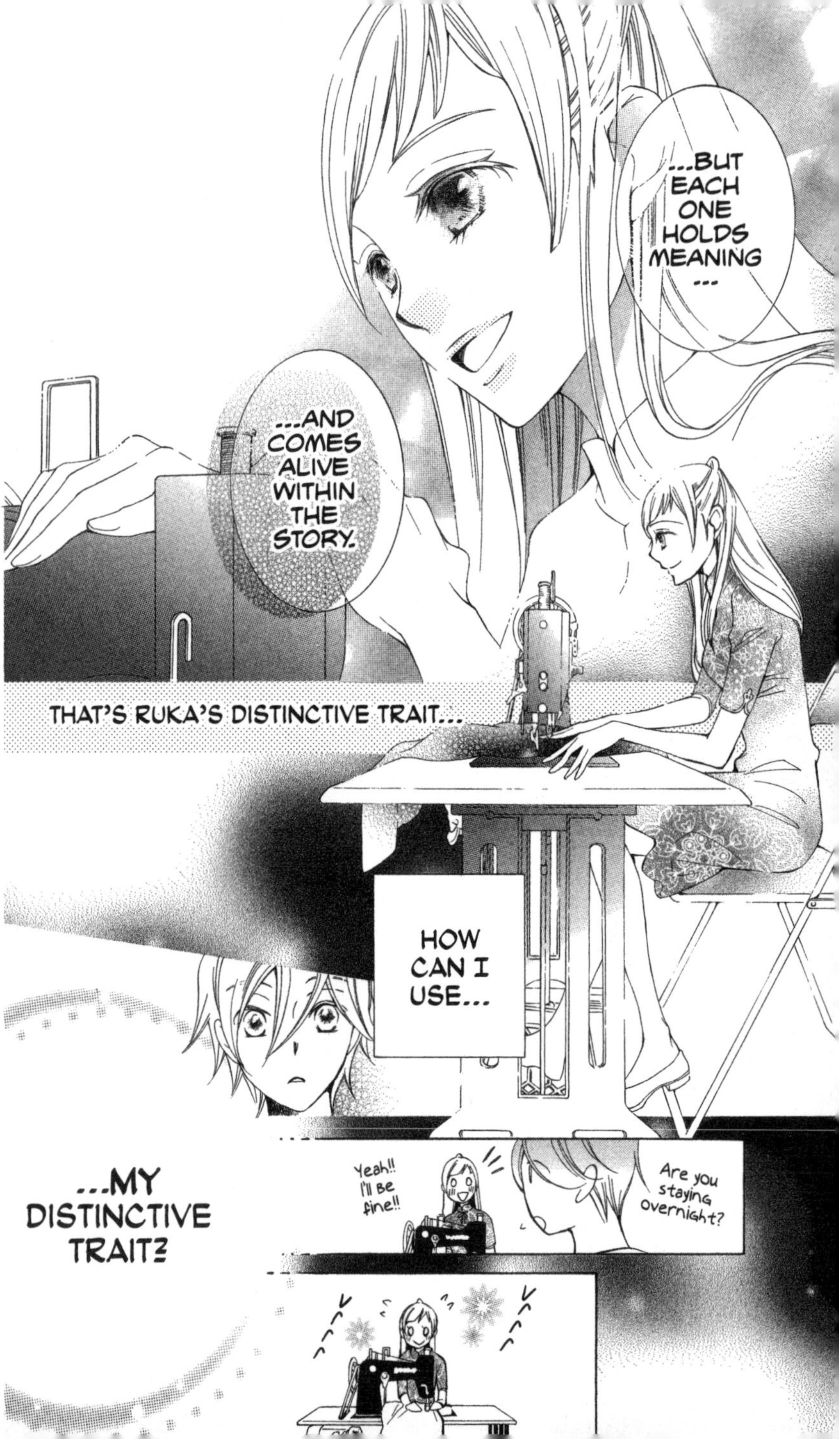
...BUT EACH ONE HOLDS MEANING...
...AND COMES ALIVE WITHIN THE STORY.
THAT'S RUKA'S DISTINCTIVE TRAIT...
HOW CAN I USE...
...MY DISTINCTIVE TRAIT?
Are you staying overnight?
Yeah!! I'll be fine!!

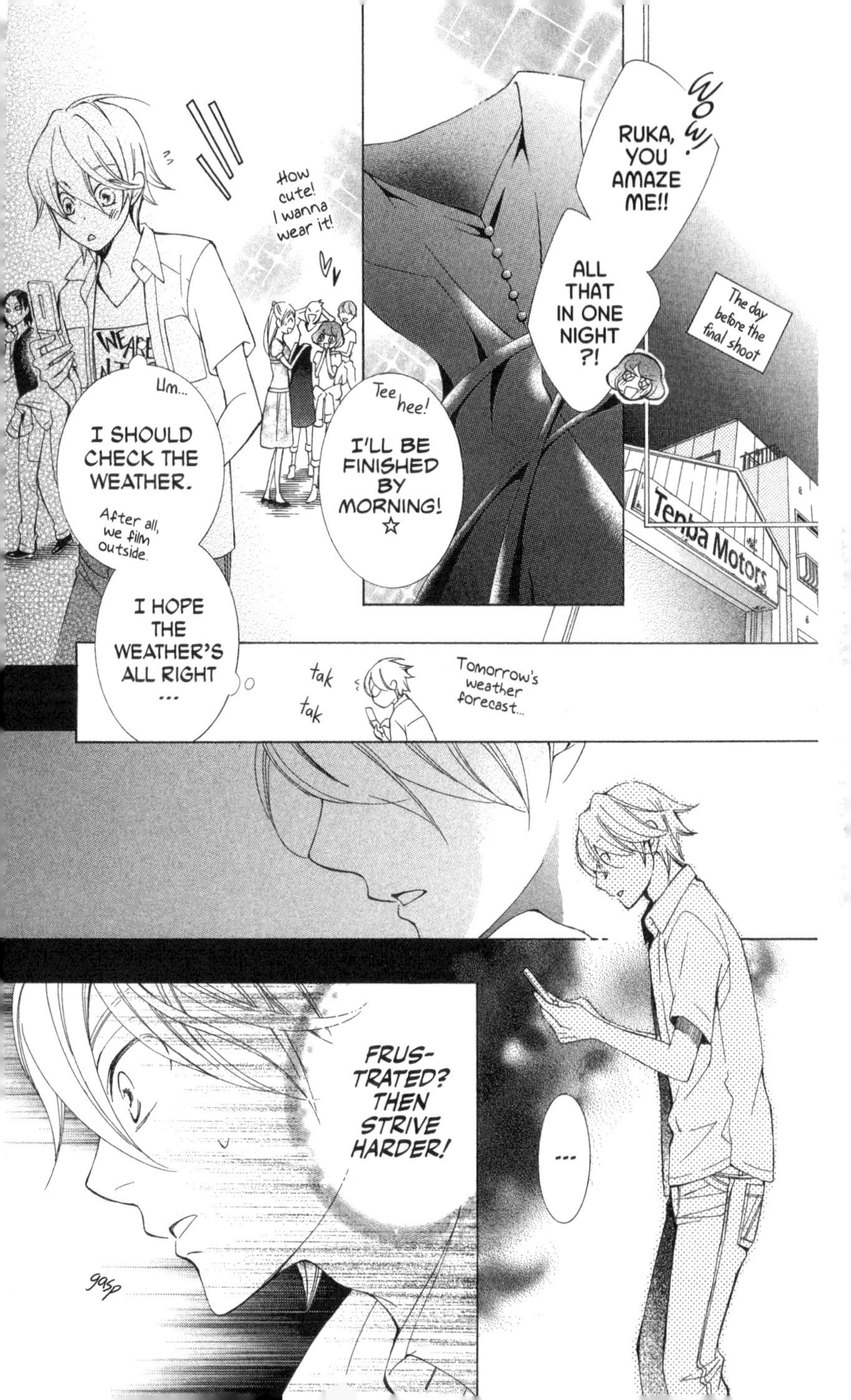
The day before the final shoot
WOW!
RUKA, YOU AMAZE ME!!
ALL THAT IN ONE NIGHT?!
Tee hee!
I'LL BE FINISHED BY MORNING! ☆
How cute! I wanna wear it!
Um...
I SHOULD CHECK THE WEATHER.
After all, we film outside.
I HOPE THE WEATHER'S ALL RIGHT...
Tomorrow's weather forecast...
tak
tak
...
FRUS-TRATED? THEN STRIVE HARDER!
gasp

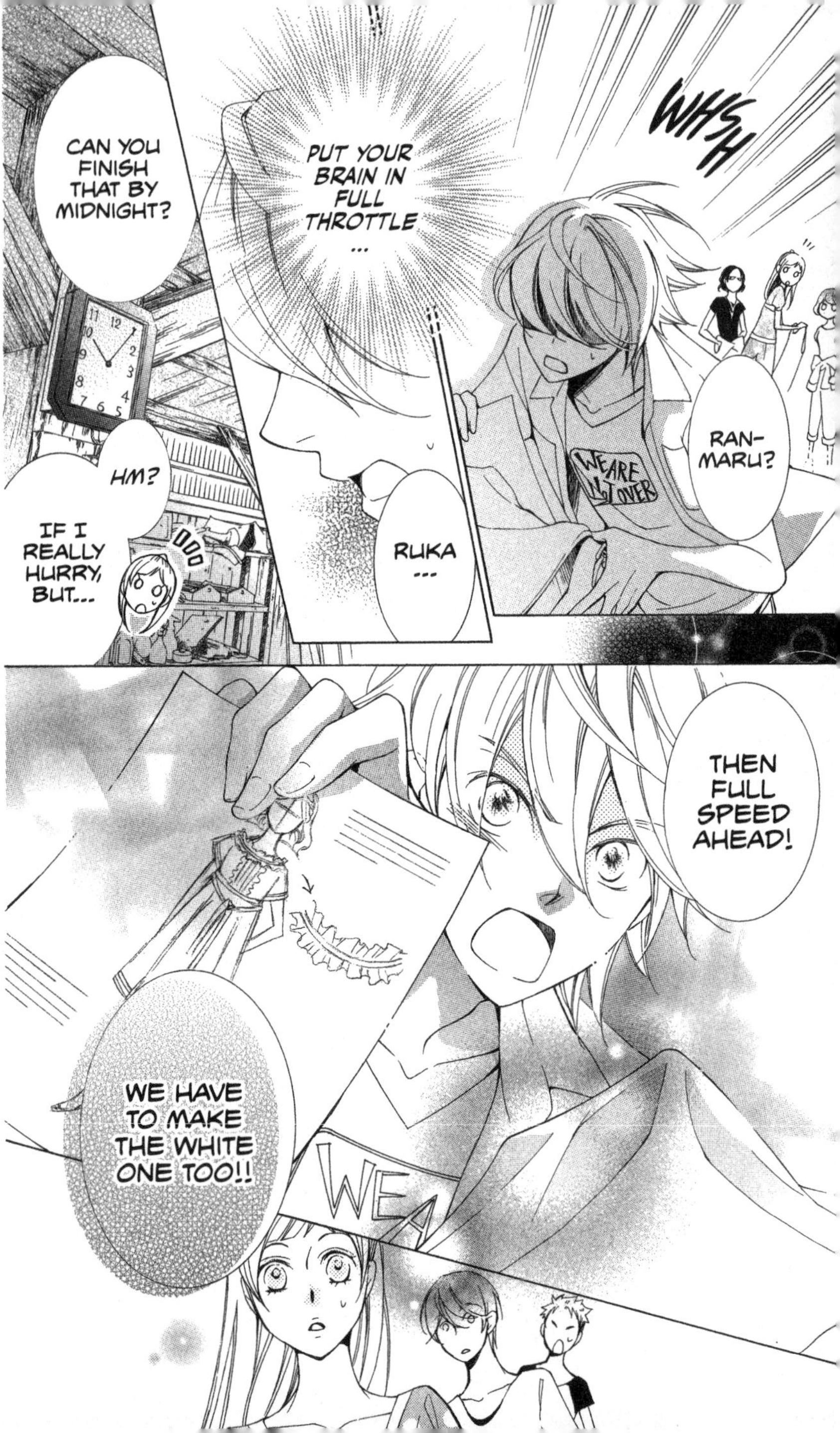
WHSH
RAN-MARU?
PUT YOUR BRAIN IN FULL THROTTLE...
RUKA...
CAN YOU FINISH THAT BY MIDNIGHT?
HM?
IF I REALLY HURRY, BUT...
THEN FULL SPEED AHEAD!
WE HAVE TO MAKE THE WHITE ONE TOO!!

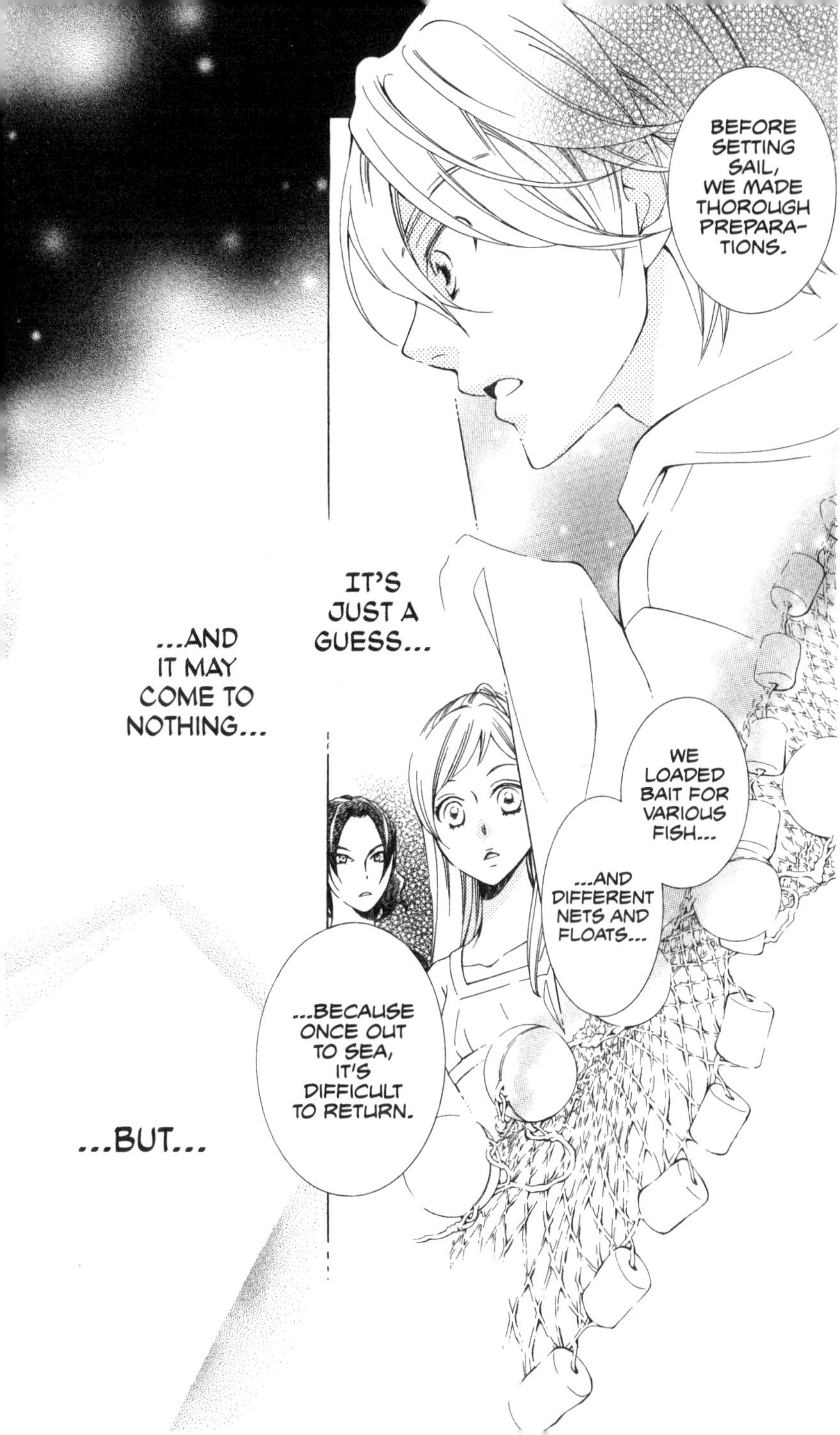
BEFORE SETTING SAIL, WE MADE THOROUGH PREPARATIONS.
WE LOADED BAIT FOR VARIOUS FISH...
...AND DIFFERENT NETS AND FLOATS...
...BECAUSE ONCE OUT TO SEA, IT'S DIFFICULT TO RETURN.
IT'S JUST A GUESS...
...AND IT MAY COME TO NOTHING...
...BUT...

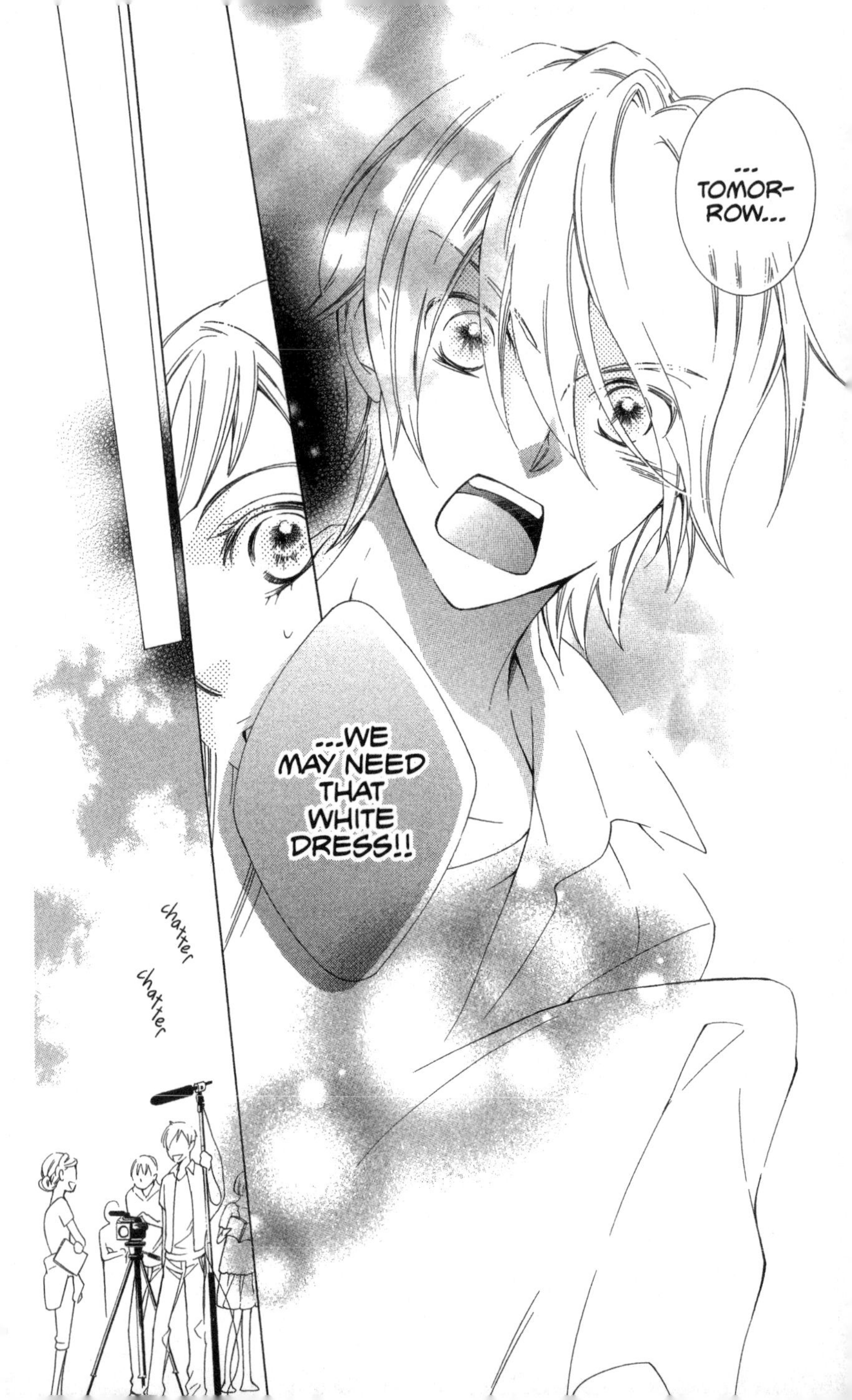
...
TOMORROW...
...WE MAY NEED THAT WHITE DRESS!!
chatter chatter

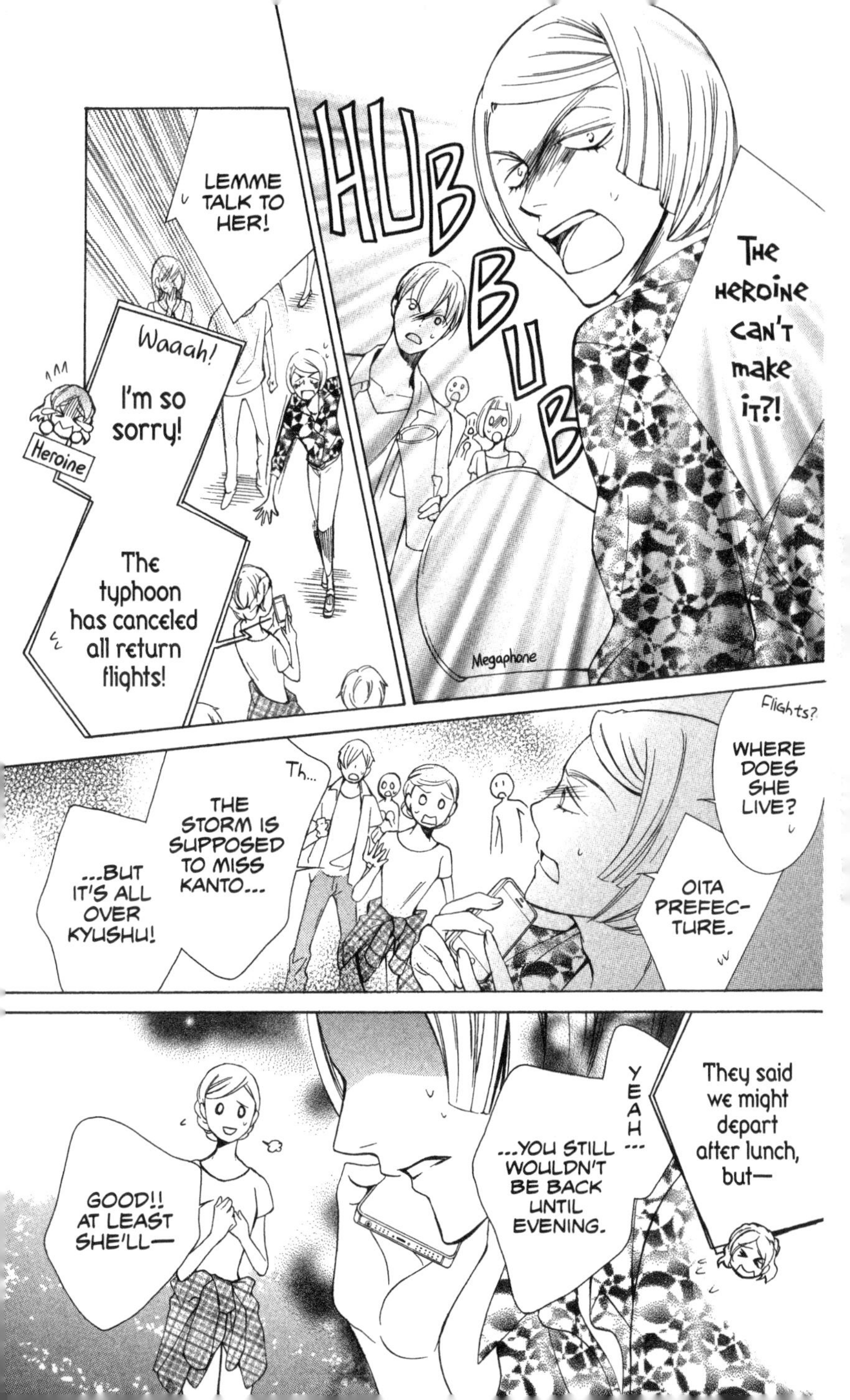

The heroine can't make it?!
HUBBUB
Megaphone
LEMME TALK TO HER!
Waaah!
I'm so sorry!
Heroine
The typhoon has canceled all return flights!
Flights?
WHERE DOES SHE LIVE?
OITA PREFECTURE.
Th...
THE STORM IS SUPPOSED TO MISS KANTO...
...BUT IT'S ALL OVER KYUSHU!
They said we might depart after lunch, but—
YEAH...
...YOU STILL WOULDN'T BE BACK UNTIL EVENING.
GOOD!! AT LEAST SHE'LL—

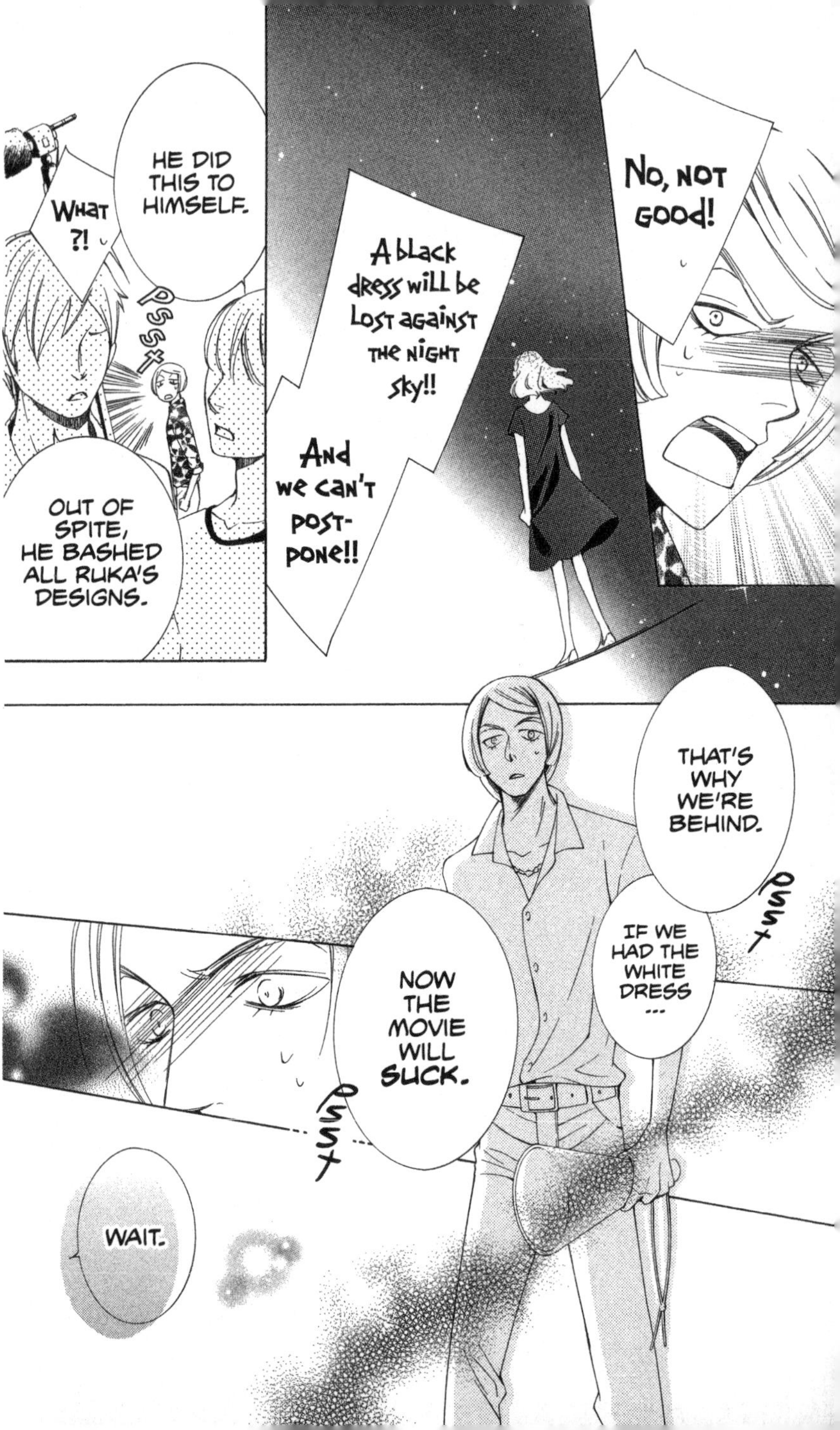
No, NOT GOOD!
A black dress will be lost against the night sky!!
And we can't postpone!!
HE DID THIS TO HIMSELF.
WHAT ?!
PSST
OUT OF SPITE, HE BASHED ALL RUKA'S DESIGNS.
THAT'S WHY WE'RE BEHIND.
PSST
IF WE HAD THE WHITE DRESS...
NOW THE MOVIE WILL SUCK.
PSST
WAIT.

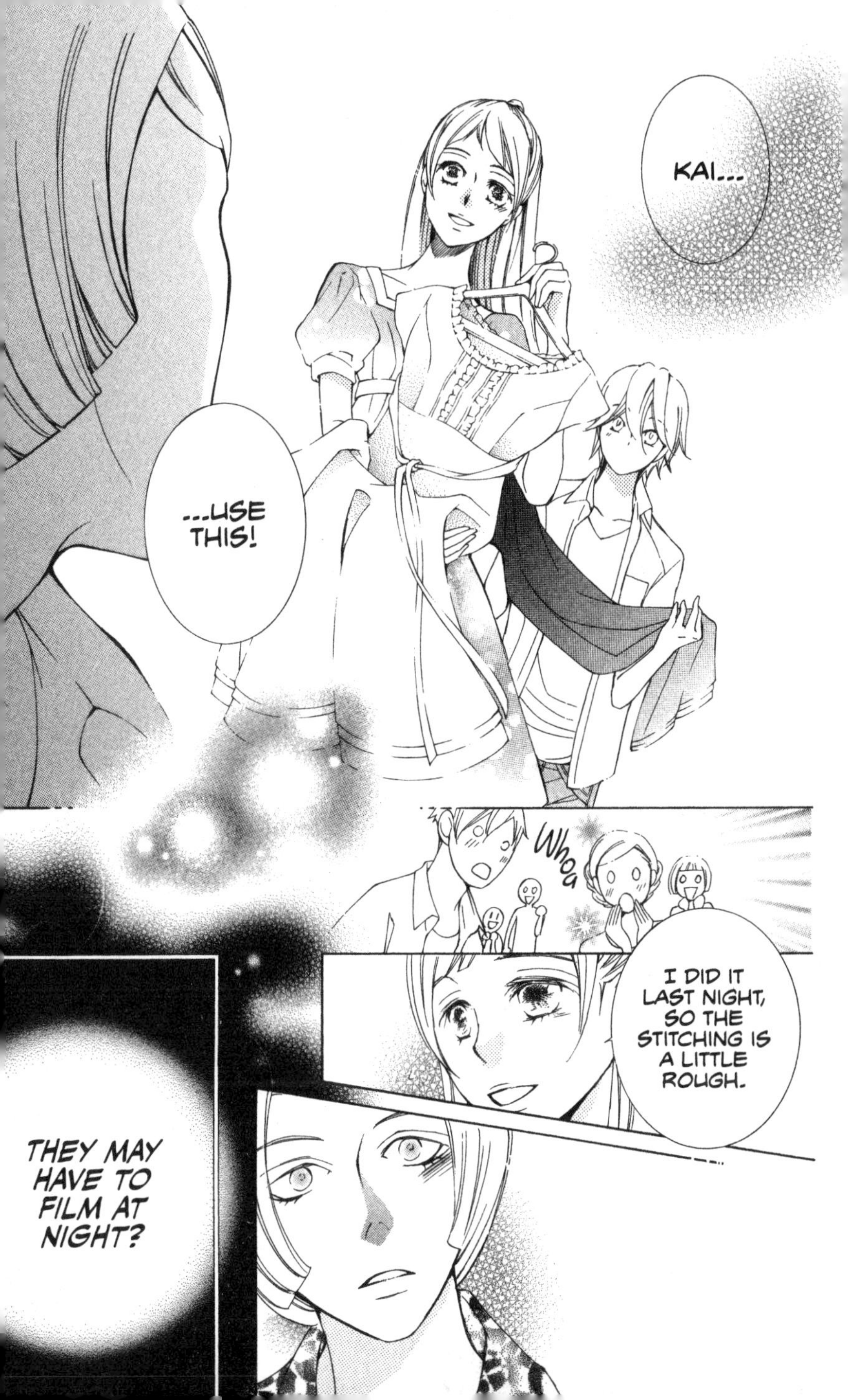
KAI...
...USE THIS!
Whoa
I DID IT LAST NIGHT, SO THE STITCHING IS A LITTLE ROUGH.
THEY MAY HAVE TO FILM AT NIGHT?

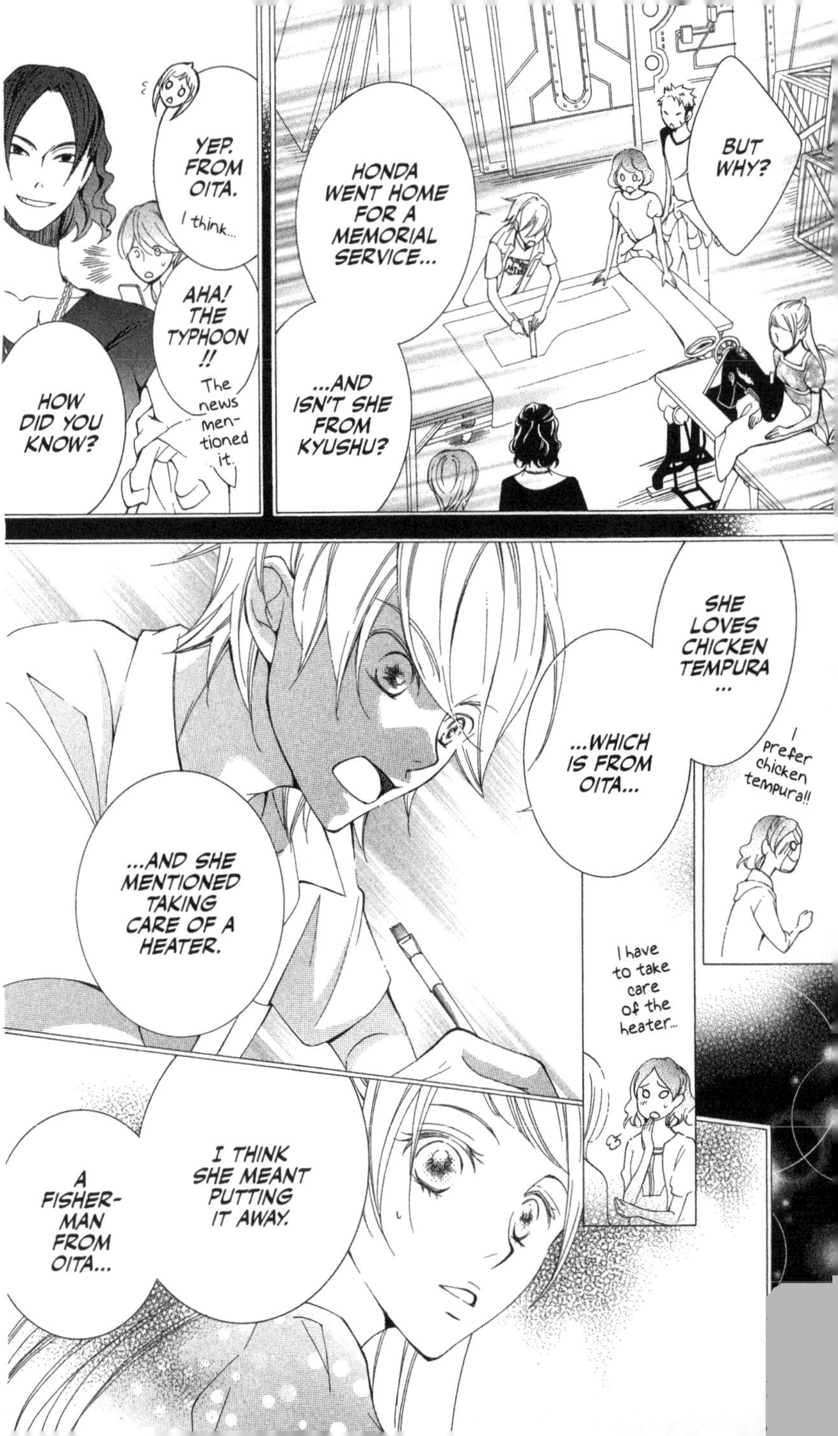
BUT WHY?
HONDA WENT HOME FOR A MEMORIAL SERVICE...
...AND ISN'T SHE FROM KYUSHU?
YEP. FROM OITA.
I think...
AHA! THE TYPHOON!!
The news mentioned it.
HOW DID YOU KNOW?
SHE LOVES CHICKEN TEMPURA...
...WHICH IS FROM OITA...
I prefer chicken tempura!!
...AND SHE MENTIONED TAKING CARE OF A HEATER.
I have to take care of the heater...
I THINK SHE MEANT PUTTING IT AWAY.
A FISHERMAN FROM OITA...

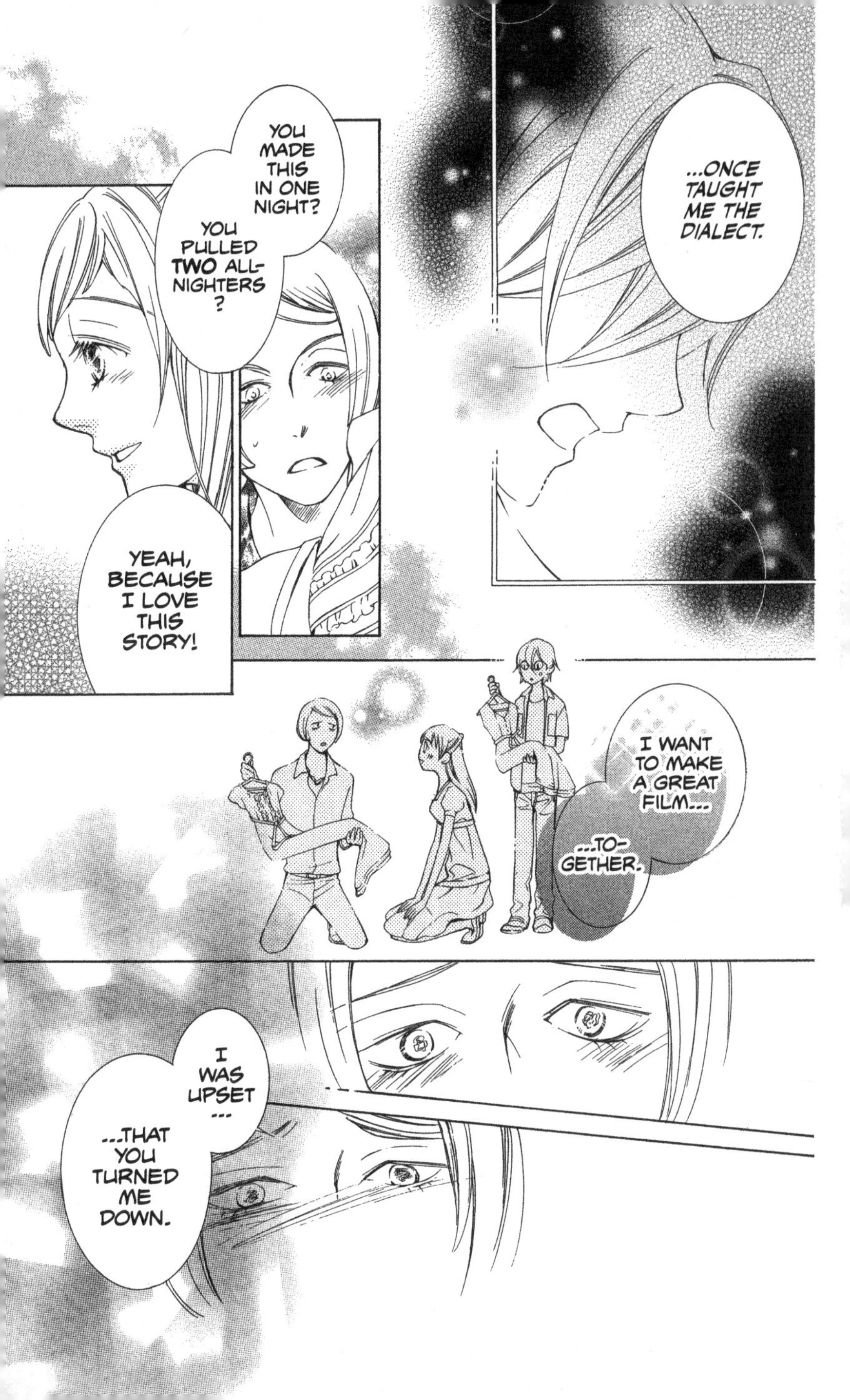
...ONCE TAUGHT ME THE DIALECT.
YOU MADE THIS IN ONE NIGHT?
YOU PULLED TWO ALL-NIGHTERS?
YEAH, BECAUSE I LOVE THIS STORY!
I WANT TO MAKE A GREAT FILM...
...TO-GETHER.
I WAS UPSET...
...THAT YOU TURNED ME DOWN.

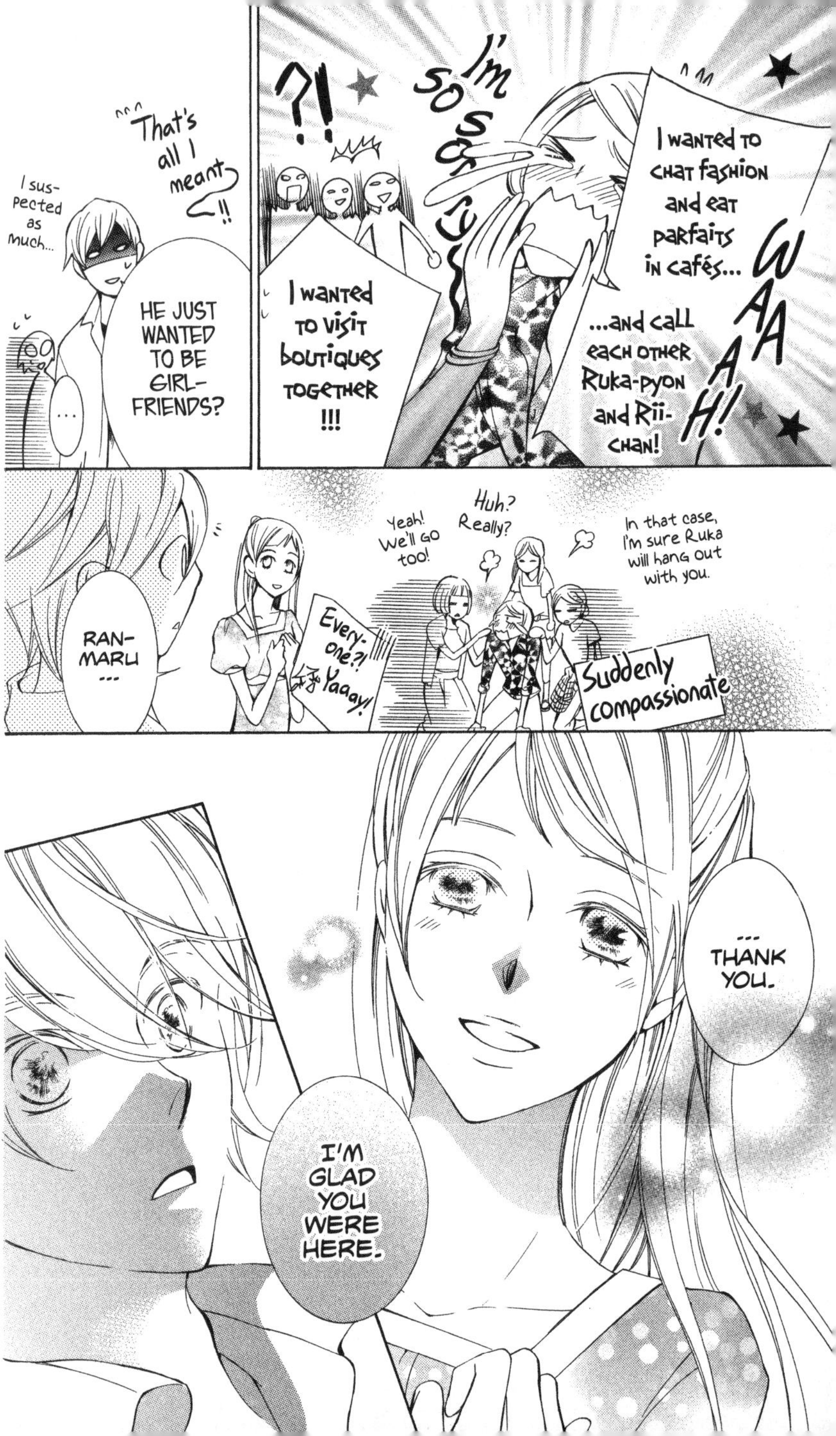
I'm so sorry!
I wanted to chat fashion and eat parfaits in cafés...
WAAAH!
...and call each other Ruka-pyon and Rii-chan!
?!
I wanted to visit boutiques together!!!
That's all I meant!!
I suspected as much...
HE JUST WANTED TO BE GIRLFRIENDS?
...
In that case, I'm sure Ruka will hang out with you.
Huh? Really?
Yeah! We'll go too!
Suddenly compassionate
Everyone?! Yaaay!
RANMARU...
...THANK YOU.
I'M GLAD YOU WERE HERE.

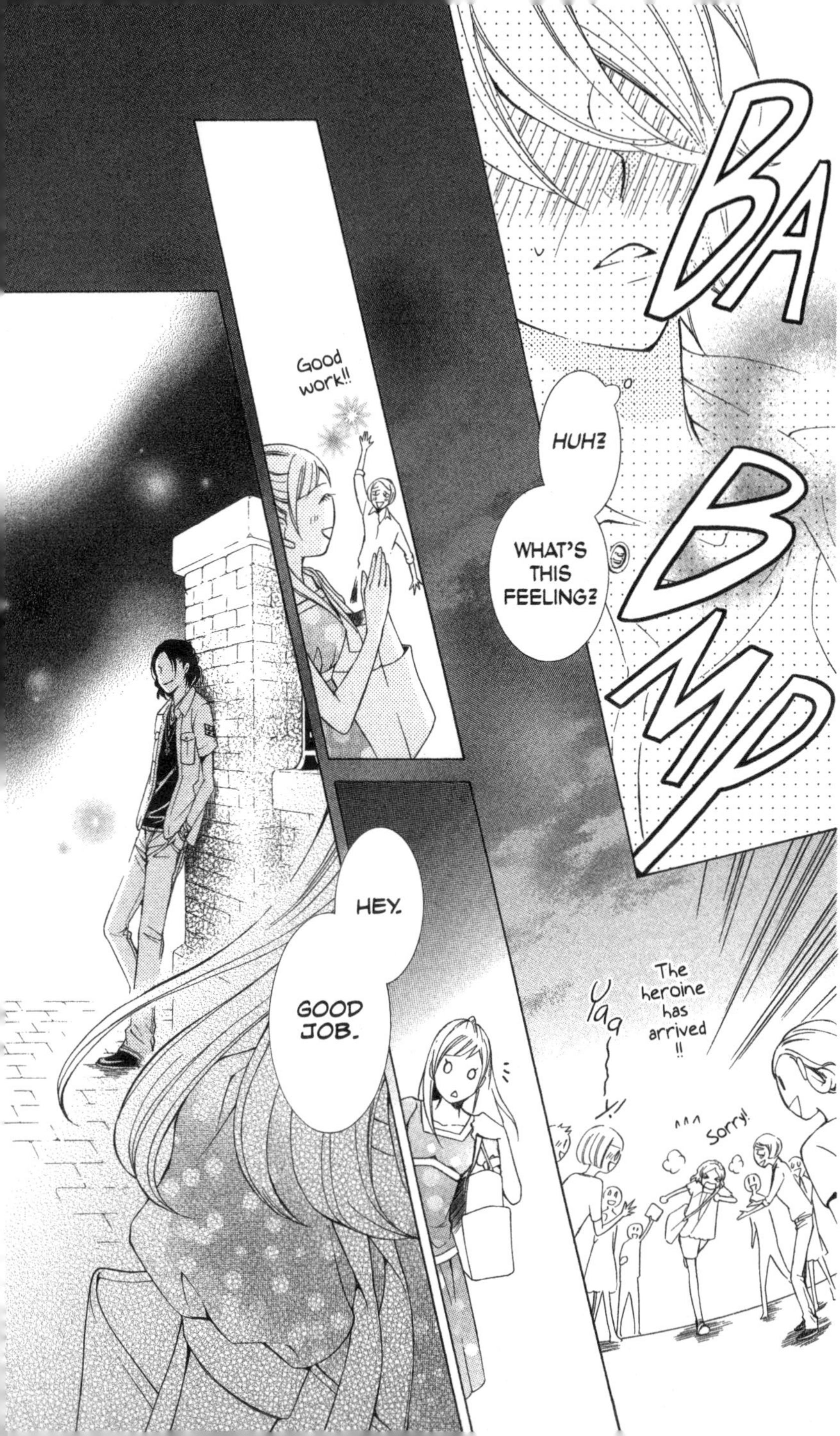
BA
BUMP
HUH?
WHAT'S THIS FEELING?
Yaa~y!
The heroine has arrived!!
^^^
Sorry!
Good work!!
HEY.
GOOD JOB.

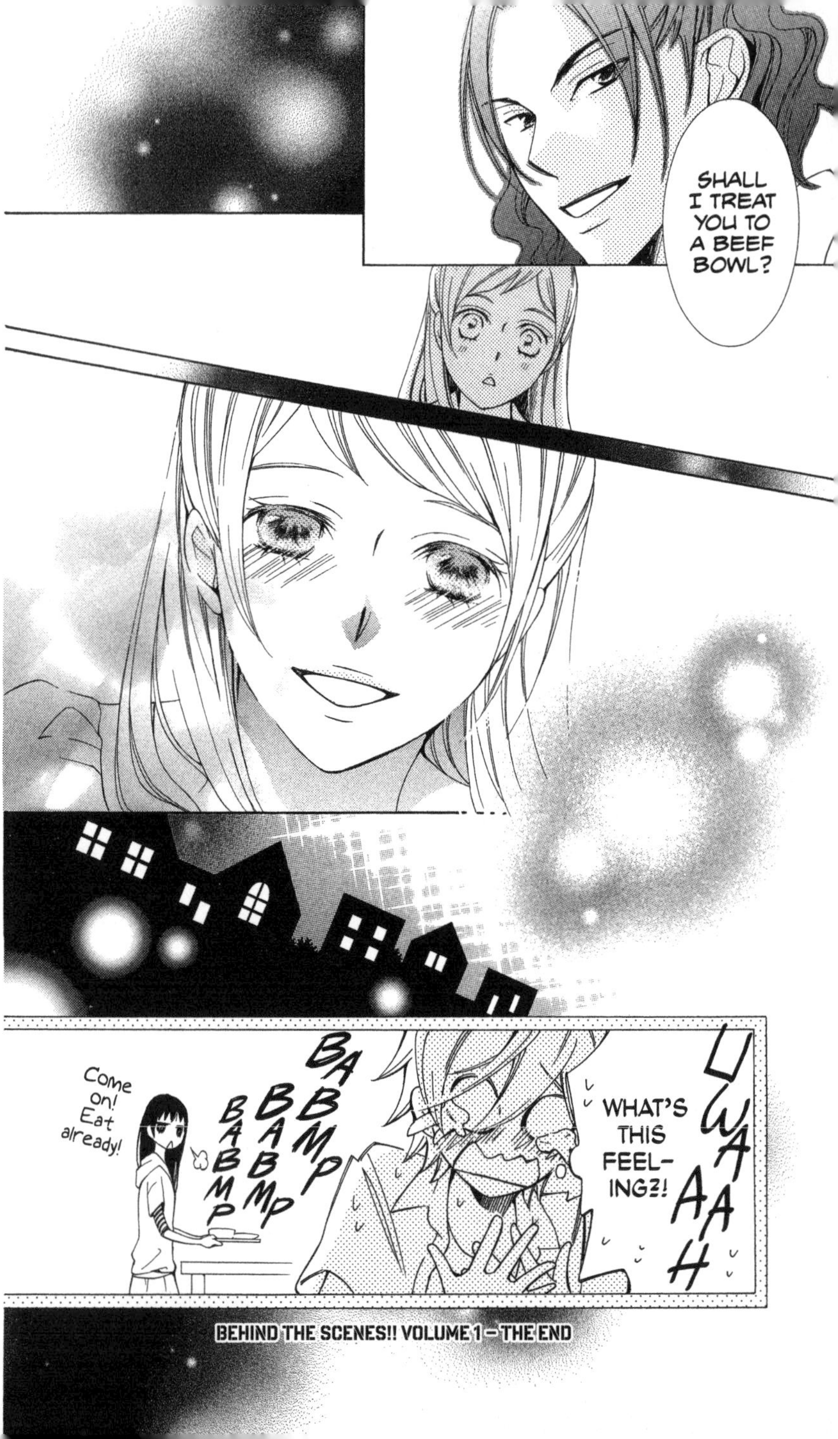
SHALL I TREAT YOU TO A BEEF BOWL?
UWAAAH
WHAT'S THIS FEELING?!
BABMP
BABMP
BABMP
Come on! Eat already!
BEHIND THE SCENES!! VOLUME 1 — THE END

GLOSSARY

Page 6, sidebar: Chiritotechin
An NHK drama about a girl studying to become a teller of *rakugo* stories, a type of traditional Japanese comedic storytelling.

Page 24, panel 1: Cranes
Folding 1,000 origami cranes is believed to bestow one wish, or long life or good luck. It has become a traditional thing to do for people who are ill.

Page 27, panel 2: Athletic clubs
Japanese schools have athletic clubs rather than teams.

Page 69, panel 2: Famous bully
The character Takeshi "Gian" Goda from *Doraemon* is a huge bully.

Page 80, panel 1: Yukata
A lightweight, casual kimono. It literally means "bathing clothes," and *yukata* are often provided at traditional inns and hot springs.

Page 92, panel 2: Nihon Shoki
The second-oldest book of Japanese history, finished in 720 CE.

Page 122, sidebar: Snufkin
A character from the Finnish series *Moomin*.

Page 129, panel 4: Box lunch
A packed meal that usually contains rice and an assortment of side dishes. Box lunches, or *bento*, can be made at home or purchased from stores and restaurants.

Page 133, panel 1: Taisho
The name of the Japanese historical era that spanned 1912–1926.

Page 142, panel 4: Singles party
Gokon in Japanese. These are group blind dates where singles can mingle and potentially make a match with any of the other attendees.

AUTHOR BIO

I've started doing radio calisthenics. I read that if you do them seriously, it can be quite a workout. Especially the jumping! As adults, we don't usually jump in our daily lives, and I can really feel it. It surprises my guts!

—Bisco Hatori

Bisco Hatori made her manga debut with *Isshun kan no Romance* (A Moment of Romance) in *LaLa DX* magazine. The comedy *Ouran High School Host Club* was her breakout hit and was published in English by VIZ Media. Her other works include *Detarame Mousouryoku Opera* (Sloppy Vaporous Opera), *Petite Pêche!* and the vampire romance *Millennium Snow*, which was also published in English by VIZ Media.

Behind the Scenes!!

VOLUME 1

Shojo Beat Edition

STORY AND ART BY **Bisco Hatori**

English Translation & Adaptation/John Werry
Touch-Up Art & Lettering/Sabrina Heep
Design/ Izumi Evers
Editor/Pancha Diaz

Urakata!! by Bisco Hatori
© Bisco Hatori 2015
All rights reserved.
First published in Japan in 2015 by HAKUSENSHA, Inc., Tokyo.
English language translation rights arranged with HAKUSENSHA, Inc.,
Tokyo.

Printed in the U.S.A.

Published by VIZ Media, LLC
P.O. Box 77010
San Francisco, CA 94107

10 9 8 7 6 5 4 3 2 1
First printing, February 2016

www.viz.com

www.shojobeat.com

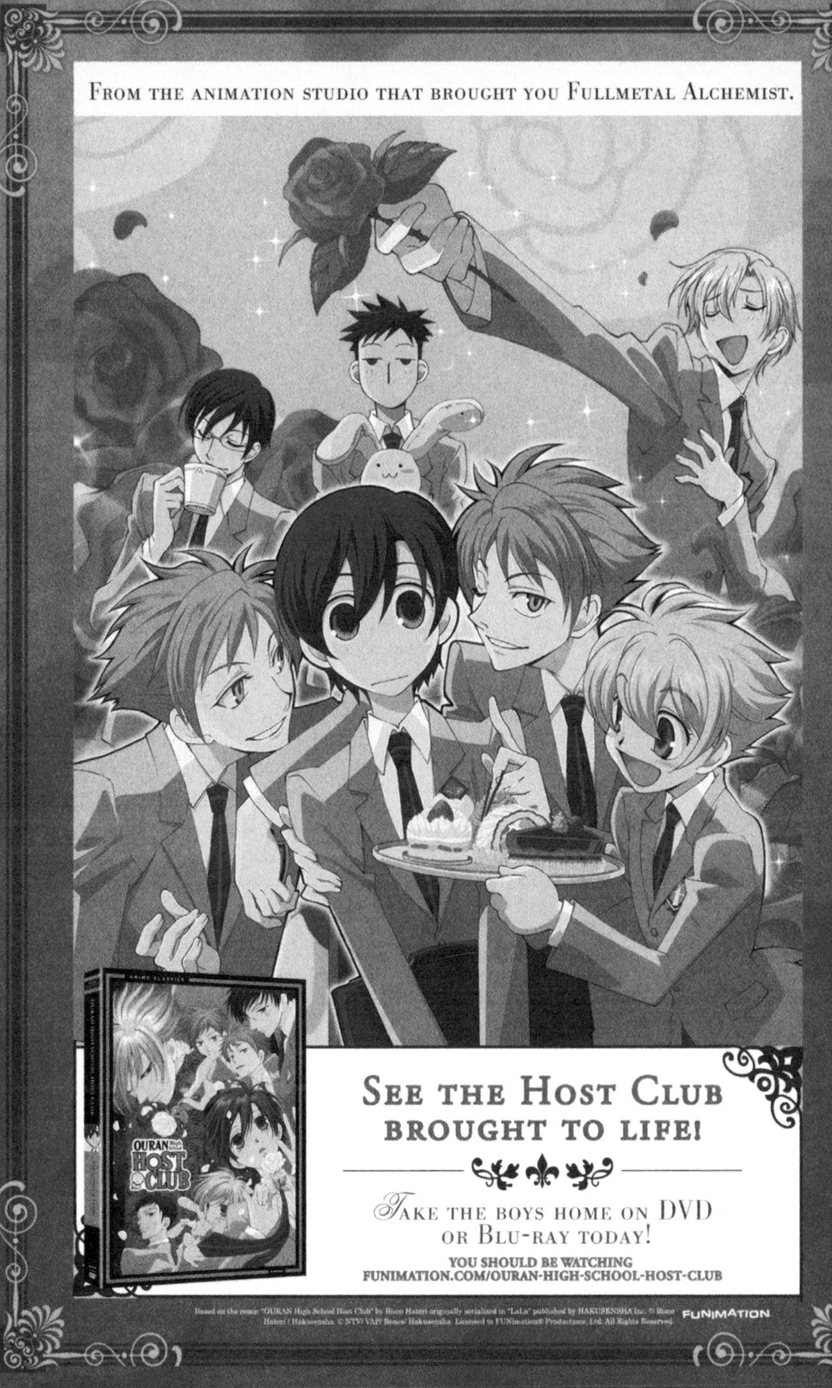
FROM THE ANIMATION STUDIO THAT BROUGHT YOU FULLMETAL ALCHEMIST.
OURAN High School HOST CLUB
SEE THE HOST CLUB BROUGHT TO LIFE!
TAKE THE BOYS HOME ON DVD OR BLU-RAY TODAY!
YOU SHOULD BE WATCHING
FUNIMATION.COM/OURAN-HIGH-SCHOOL-HOST-CLUB
Based on the comic "OURAN High School Host Club" by Bisco Hatori originally serialized in "LaLa" published by HAKUSENSHA Inc. © Bisco Hatori / Hakusensha. © NTV/ VAP/ Bones/ Hakusensha. Licensed to FUNimation® Productions, Ltd. All Rights Reserved.
FUNIMATION

Voice Over!
Seiyu Academy

Story and Art by
Maki Minami

She's ready to shine, and nothing is going to stand in her way!

A new series by the author of the best-selling S·A!

Hime Kino's dream is to one day do voice acting like her hero Sakura Aoyama from the Lovely ♥ Blazers anime, and getting accepted to the prestigious Holly Academy's voice actor department is the first step in the right direction! But Hime's gruff voice has earned her the scorn of teachers and students alike. Hime will not let that stand unchallenged. She'll show everyone that she is too a voice acting princess, whether they like it or not!!

Voice Over!
Seiyu Academy
Story and art by
Maki Minami
Vol. 1

Available now!

YOU MAY BE READING THE WRONG WAY!

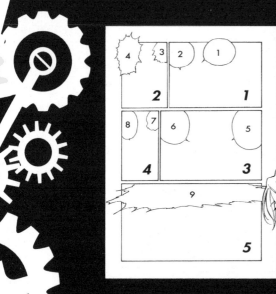

This book reads from right to left to maintain the original presentation and art of the Japanese edition, so action, sound effects and word balloons are reversed. This diagram shows how to follow the panels. Turn to the other side of the book to begin.